CREEPY™

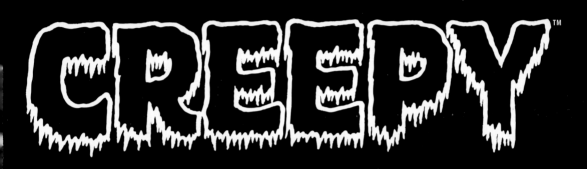

Publisher **Mike Richardson**
Editor **Shawna Gore**
Contributing Editors **Dan Braun** and **Craig Haffner**
Collection Designer **Aimee Danielson-Germany**
Cover Illustration by **Eric Powell**
Colored by **Dan Jackson**
Story Lettering by **Nate Piekos for BLAMBOT**

Published by
Dark Horse Books
A division of
Dark Horse Comics, Inc.
10956 SE Main Street
Milwaukie, OR 97222

First edition: July 2011

ISBN 978-1-59582-750-0

1 3 5 7 9 10 8 6 4 2
Printed by Midas Printing International, Ltd., Huizhou, China.

This book collects issues #1–#4 of the quarterly *Creepy* comic-book series
published by Dark Horse Comics.

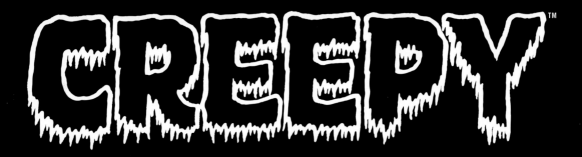

COMICS
2008–2010

DARK HORSE BOOKS

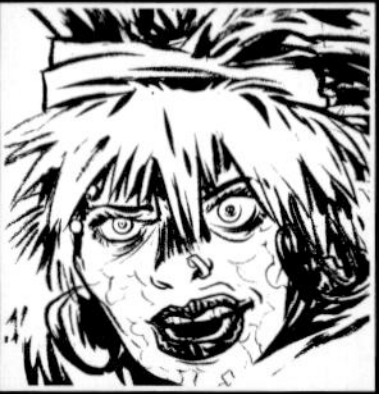

CREEPY #2

Writers: Dan Braun, Mike Baron, Joe R. Lansdale, Joe Harris
Artists: Greg Ruth, Nathan Fox, Rahsan Ekedal,
Jason Shawn Alexander, Angelo Torres
Cover art: Eric Powell
Frontispiece: Rahsan Ekedal

CREEPY #3

Writers: Joe Harris, Dan Braun, Craig Haffner,
Doug Moench, Cody Goodfellow
Artists: Angelo Torres, Jason Shawn Alexander,
Kevin Ferrara, Dennis Calero
Cover: Chuck Pyle
Frontispiece: Gene Colan

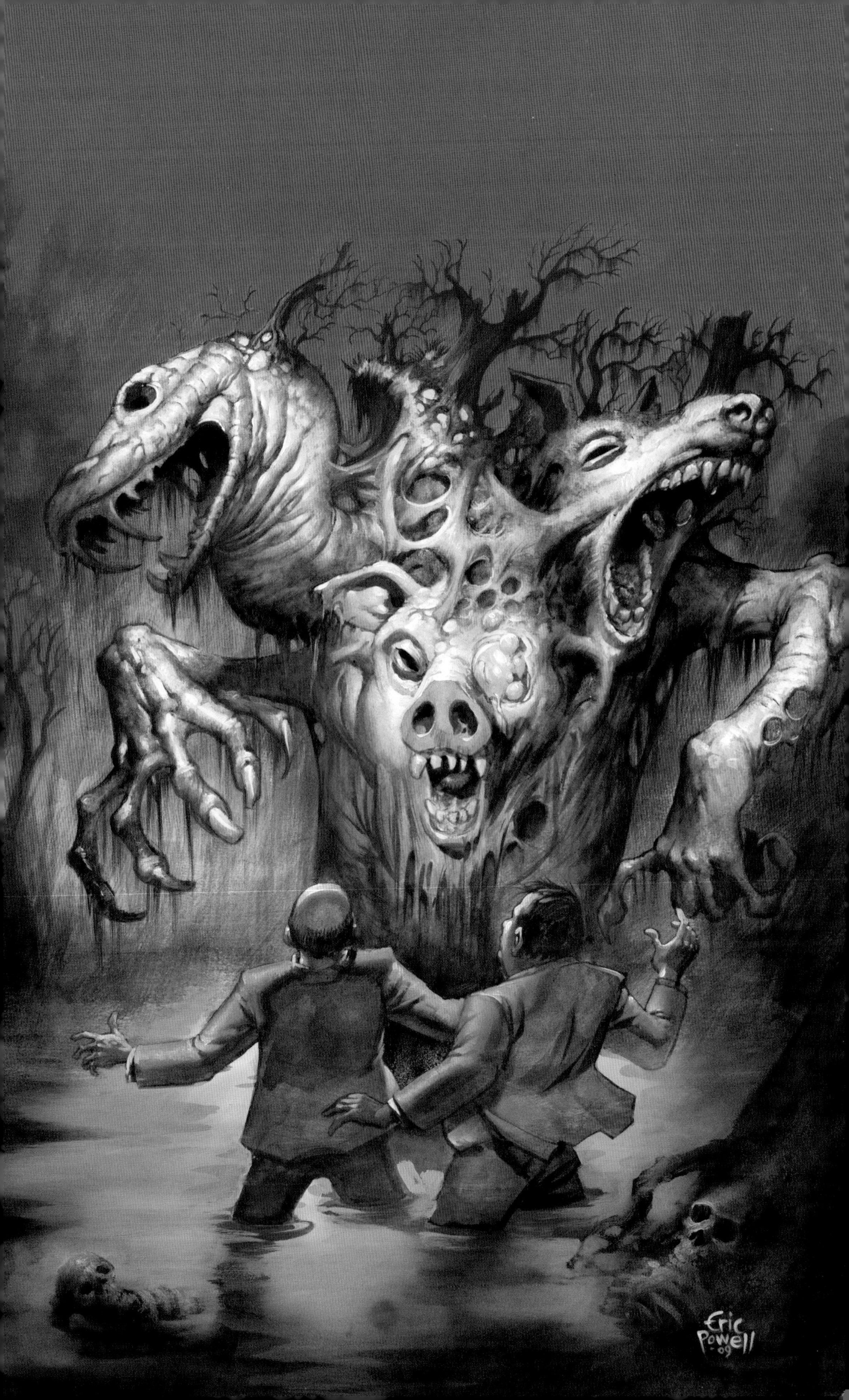
Eric
Powell
'09

DON'T MIND US!

WE'RE JUST ***NAILING*** DOWN A FEW FINISHING TOUCHES ON OUR ***PREMIERE*** ISSUE OF NEW ***CREEPY.*** GO ON, TURN THE PAGE, AND SEE WHAT HAPPENS WHEN YOU INJECT ***NEW BLOOD*** AND ***FRESH BRAINS*** INTO THE BODY OF A FAMILIAR OLD ***FIEND!*** BUT DON'T GET HUNG UP ON THE NEW FACES YOU'LL MEET. JUST ASK ***UNCLE CREEPY***– LIKE THE ***SLIMIEST*** OF MOLDS, WE'LL REALLY GROW ON YOU!

–SISTER CREEPY

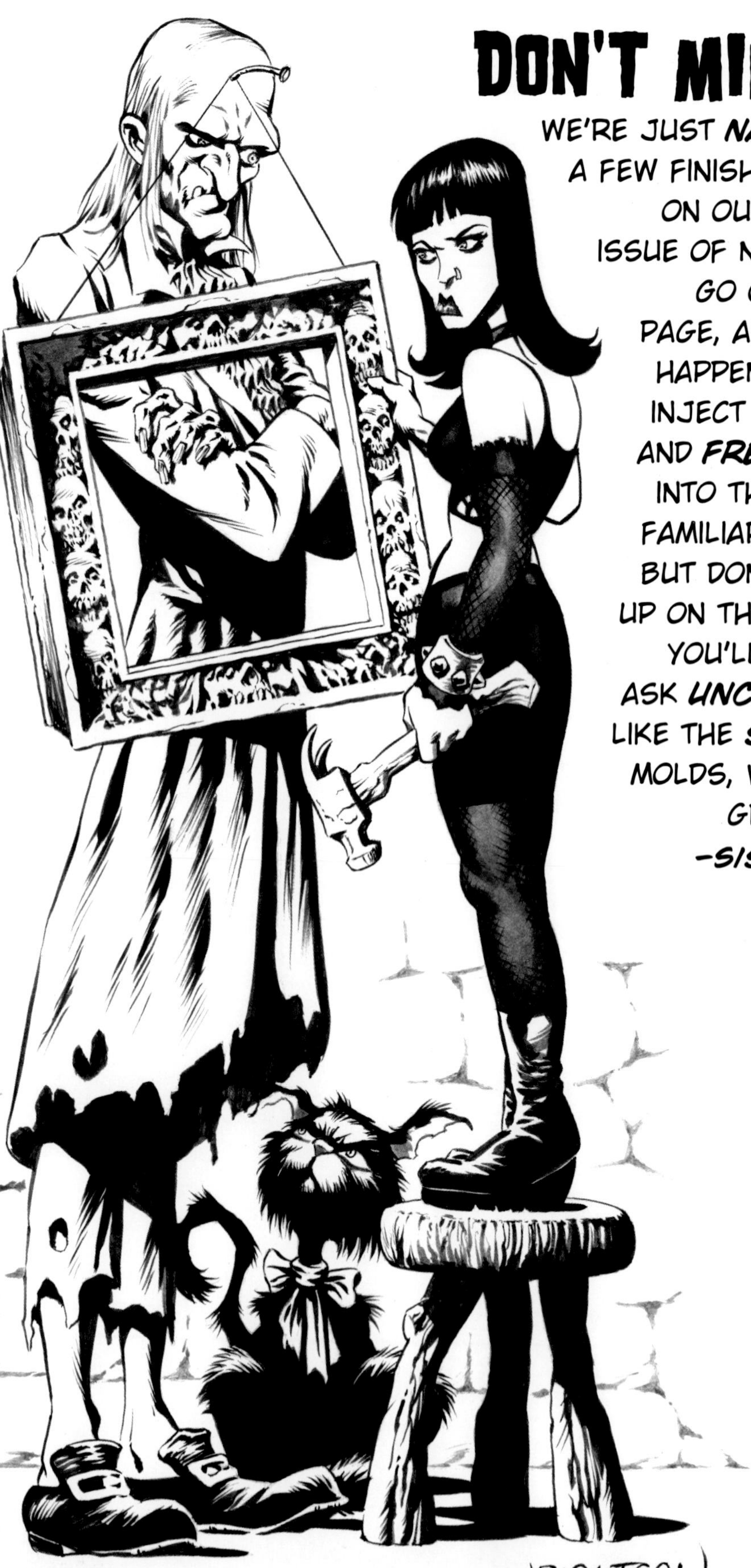
WRIGHTSON

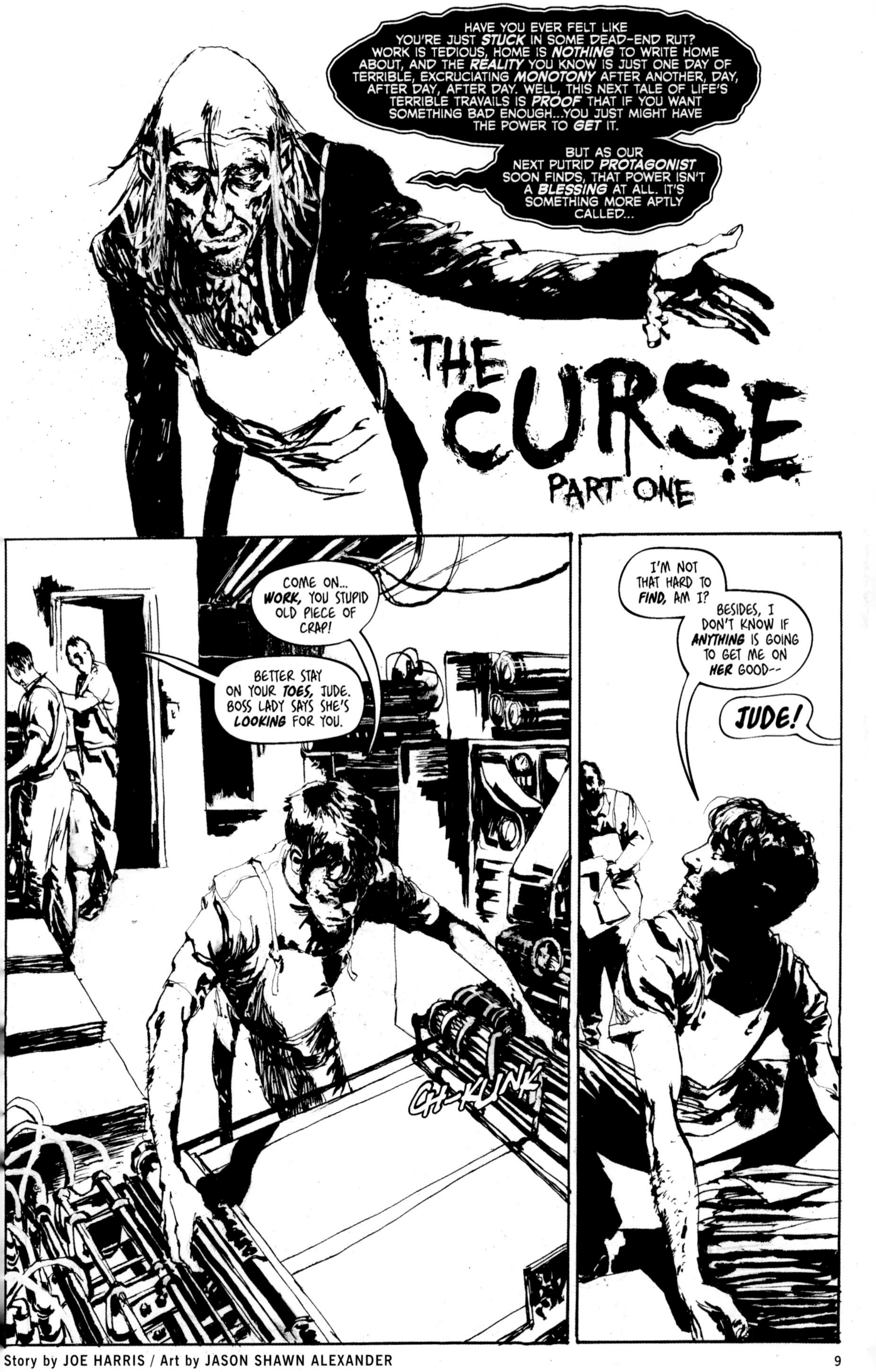
HAVE YOU EVER FELT LIKE YOU'RE JUST STUCK IN SOME DEAD-END RUT? WORK IS TEDIOUS, HOME IS NOTHING TO WRITE HOME ABOUT, AND THE REALITY YOU KNOW IS JUST ONE DAY OF TERRIBLE, EXCRUCIATING MONOTONY AFTER ANOTHER, DAY, AFTER DAY, AFTER DAY. WELL, THIS NEXT TALE OF LIFE'S TERRIBLE TRAVAILS IS PROOF THAT IF YOU WANT SOMETHING BAD ENOUGH...YOU JUST MIGHT HAVE THE POWER TO GET IT.
BUT AS OUR NEXT PUTRID PROTAGONIST SOON FINDS, THAT POWER ISN'T A BLESSING AT ALL. IT'S SOMETHING MORE APTLY CALLED...
THE CURSE
PART ONE
COME ON... WORK, YOU STUPID OLD PIECE OF CRAP!
BETTER STAY ON YOUR TOES, JUDE. BOSS LADY SAYS SHE'S LOOKING FOR YOU.
CH-KUNK
I'M NOT THAT HARD TO FIND, AM I?
BESIDES, I DON'T KNOW IF ANYTHING IS GOING TO GET ME ON HER GOOD--
JUDE!

Story by JOE HARRIS / Art by JASON SHAWN ALEXANDER

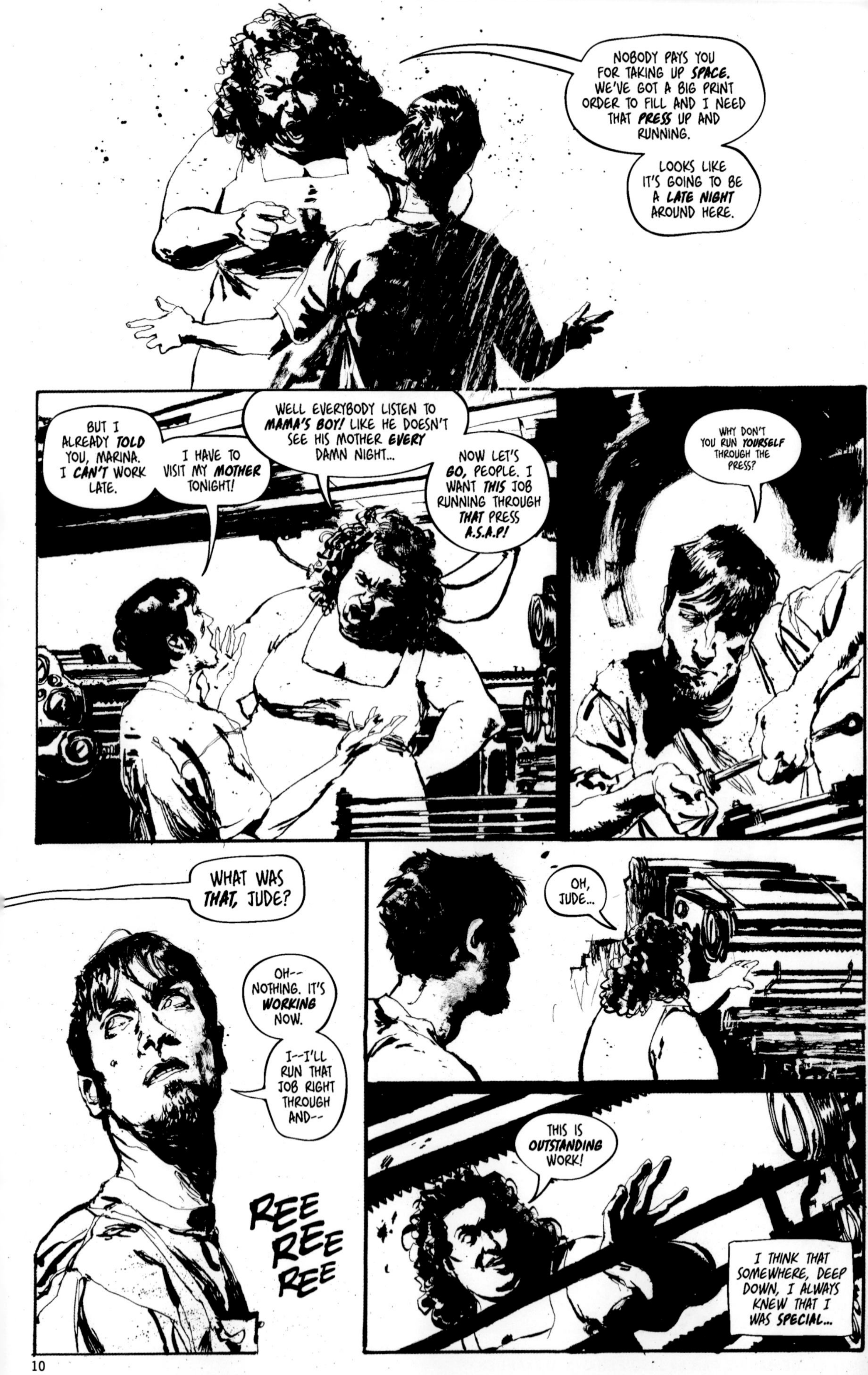

NOBODY PAYS YOU FOR TAKING UP **SPACE.** WE'VE GOT A BIG PRINT ORDER TO FILL AND I NEED THAT **PRESS** UP AND RUNNING.
LOOKS LIKE IT'S GOING TO BE A **LATE NIGHT** AROUND HERE.
BUT I ALREADY **TOLD** YOU, MARINA. I **CAN'T** WORK LATE.
I HAVE TO VISIT MY **MOTHER** TONIGHT!
WELL EVERYBODY LISTEN TO **MAMA'S BOY!** LIKE HE DOESN'T SEE HIS MOTHER **EVERY** DAMN NIGHT...
NOW LET'S **GO,** PEOPLE. I WANT **THIS** JOB RUNNING THROUGH **THAT** PRESS **A.S.A.P!**
WHY DON'T YOU RUN **YOURSELF** THROUGH THE PRESS?
WHAT WAS **THAT,** JUDE?
OH-- NOTHING. IT'S **WORKING** NOW.
I--I'LL RUN THAT JOB RIGHT THROUGH AND--
REE REE REE
OH, JUDE...
THIS IS **OUTSTANDING** WORK!
I THINK THAT SOMEWHERE, DEEP DOWN, I ALWAYS KNEW THAT I WAS **SPECIAL...**

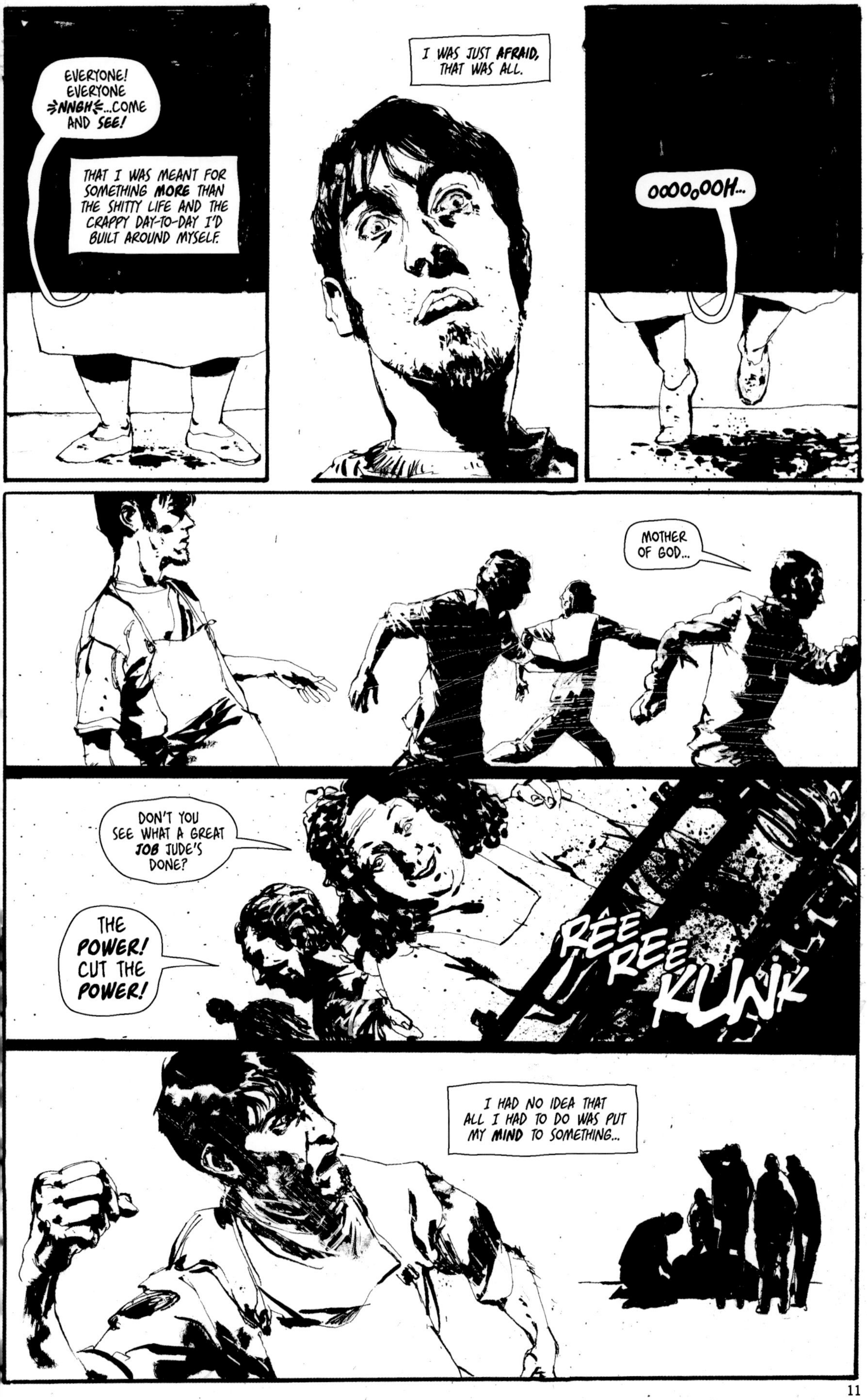
EVERYONE! EVERYONE ≶NNGH≶...COME AND SEE!
THAT I WAS MEANT FOR SOMETHING MORE THAN THE SHITTY LIFE AND THE CRAPPY DAY-TO-DAY I'D BUILT AROUND MYSELF.
I WAS JUST AFRAID, THAT WAS ALL.
OOOOoOOH...
MOTHER OF GOD...
DON'T YOU SEE WHAT A GREAT JOB JUDE'S DONE?
THE POWER! CUT THE POWER!
REE REE KUNK
I HAD NO IDEA THAT ALL I HAD TO DO WAS PUT MY MIND TO SOMETHING...

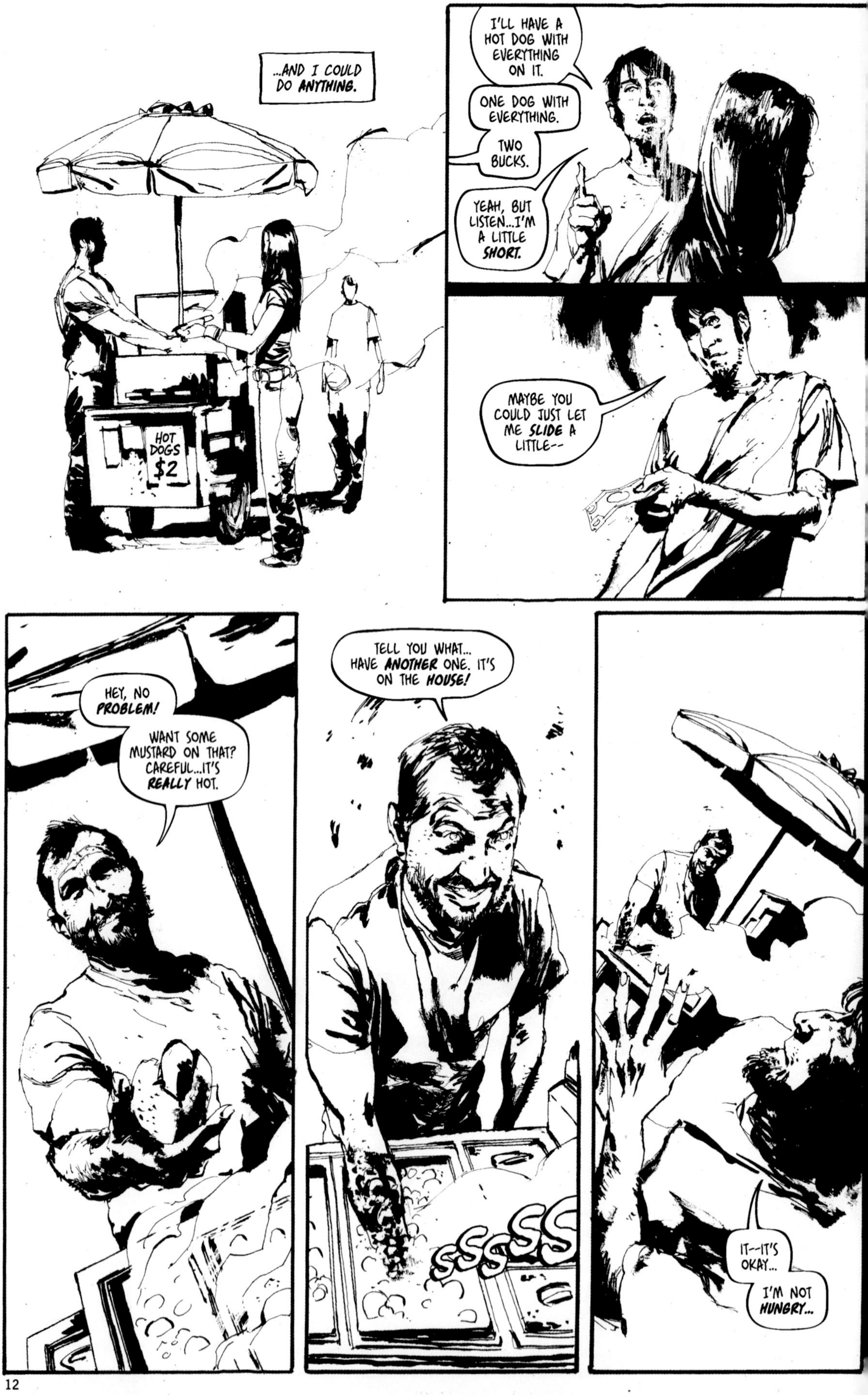
...AND I COULD DO ANYTHING.
I'LL HAVE A HOT DOG WITH EVERYTHING ON IT.
ONE DOG WITH EVERYTHING.
TWO BUCKS.
YEAH, BUT LISTEN...I'M A LITTLE SHORT.
HOT DOGS $2
MAYBE YOU COULD JUST LET ME SLIDE A LITTLE--
HEY, NO PROBLEM!
WANT SOME MUSTARD ON THAT? CAREFUL...IT'S REALLY HOT.
TELL YOU WHAT... HAVE ANOTHER ONE. IT'S ON THE HOUSE!
SSSSSS
IT--IT'S OKAY...
I'M NOT HUNGRY...

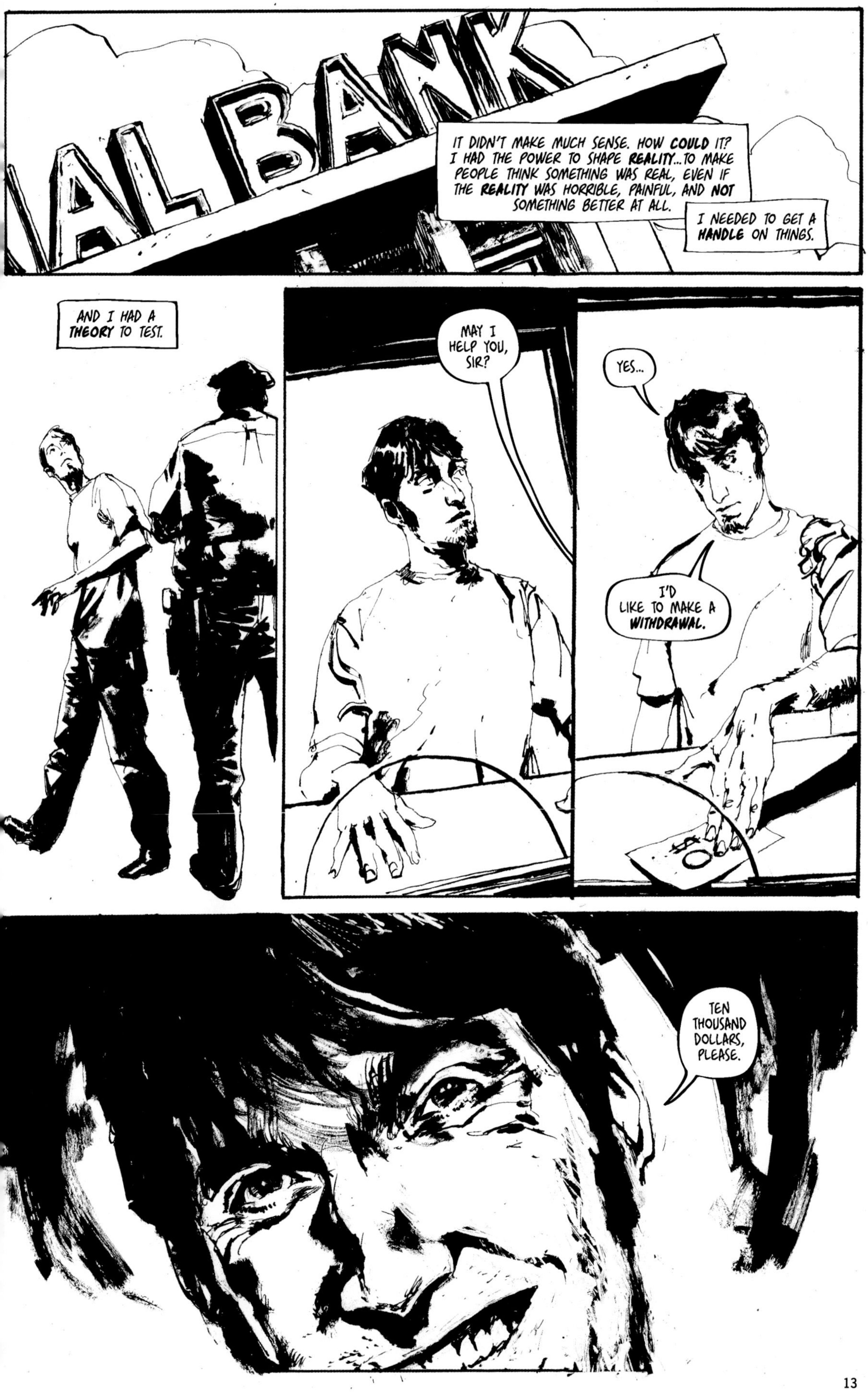
AL BANK
IT DIDN'T MAKE MUCH SENSE. HOW COULD IT? I HAD THE POWER TO SHAPE REALITY...TO MAKE PEOPLE THINK SOMETHING WAS REAL, EVEN IF THE REALITY WAS HORRIBLE, PAINFUL, AND NOT SOMETHING BETTER AT ALL.
I NEEDED TO GET A HANDLE ON THINGS.
AND I HAD A THEORY TO TEST.
MAY I HELP YOU, SIR?
YES...
I'D LIKE TO MAKE A WITHDRAWAL.
TEN THOUSAND DOLLARS, PLEASE.

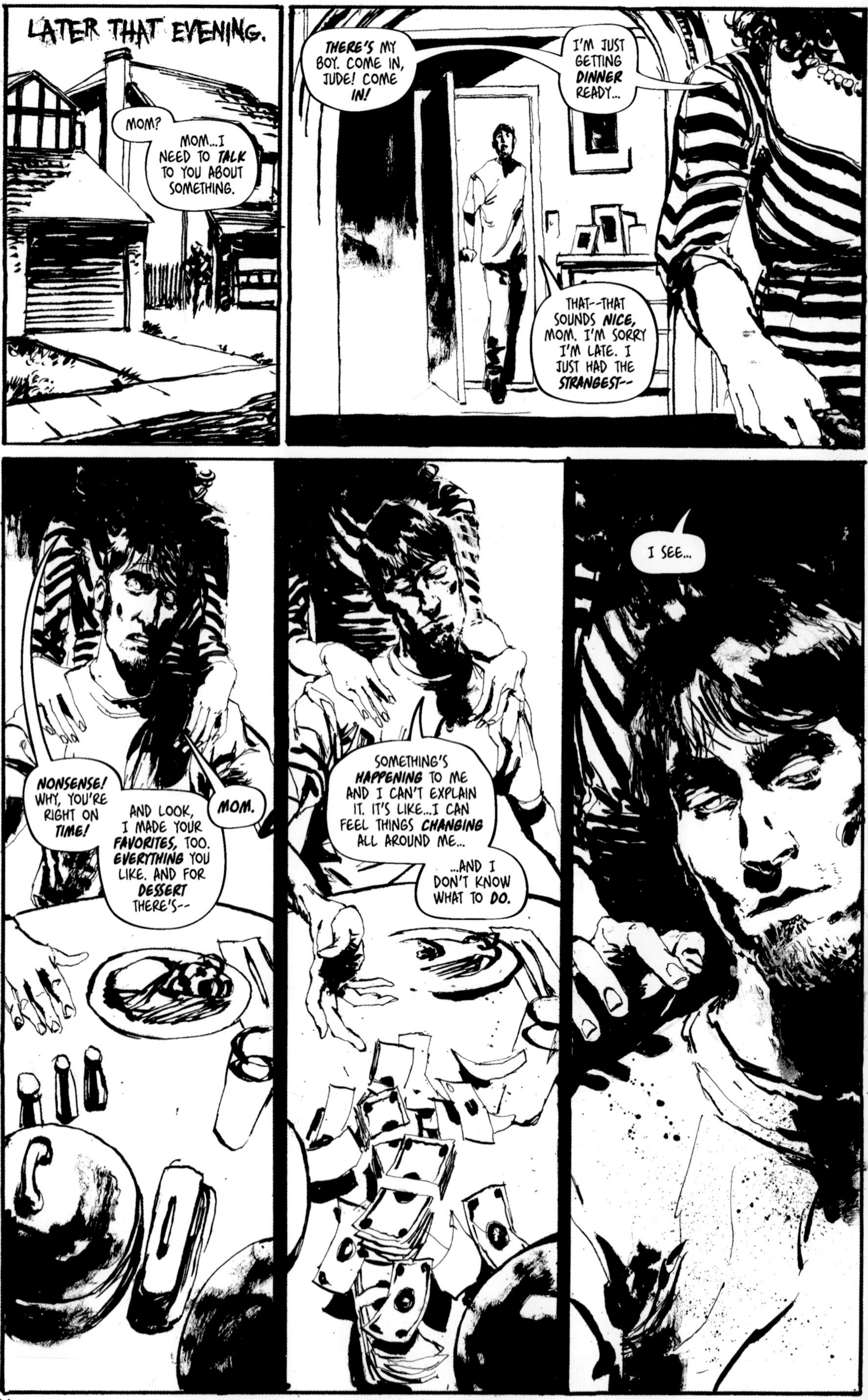
LATER THAT EVENING.
MOM?
MOM...I NEED TO TALK TO YOU ABOUT SOMETHING.
THERE'S MY BOY. COME IN, JUDE! COME IN!
I'M JUST GETTING DINNER READY...
THAT--THAT SOUNDS NICE, MOM. I'M SORRY I'M LATE. I JUST HAD THE STRANGEST--
NONSENSE! WHY, YOU'RE RIGHT ON TIME!
AND LOOK, I MADE YOUR FAVORITES, TOO. EVERYTHING YOU LIKE. AND FOR DESSERT THERE'S--
MOM.
SOMETHING'S HAPPENING TO ME AND I CAN'T EXPLAIN IT. IT'S LIKE...I CAN FEEL THINGS CHANGING ALL AROUND ME...
...AND I DON'T KNOW WHAT TO DO.
I SEE...

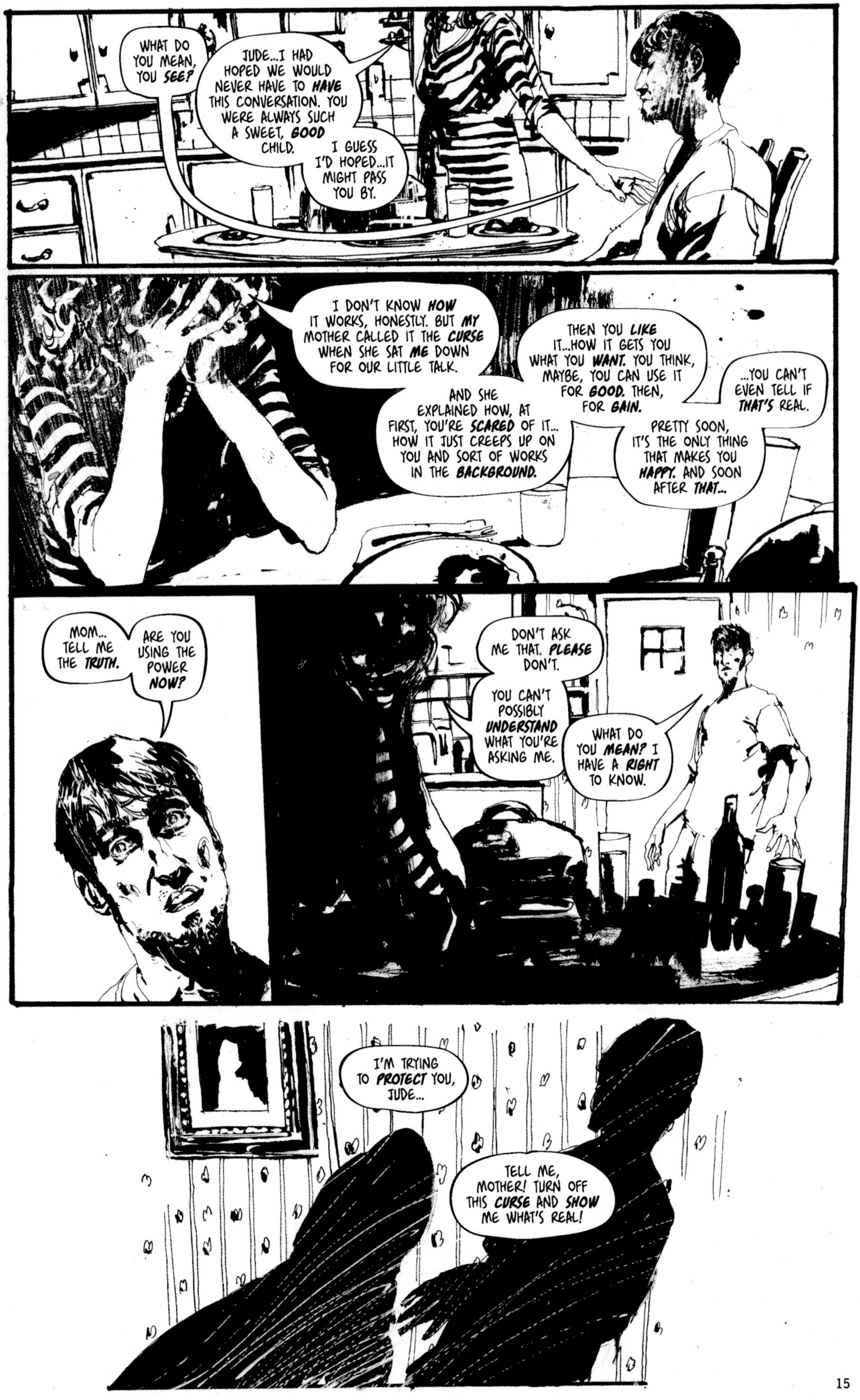
WHAT DO YOU MEAN, YOU SEE?
JUDE...I HAD HOPED WE WOULD NEVER HAVE TO HAVE THIS CONVERSATION. YOU WERE ALWAYS SUCH A SWEET, GOOD CHILD.
I GUESS I'D HOPED...IT MIGHT PASS YOU BY.
I DON'T KNOW HOW IT WORKS, HONESTLY. BUT MY MOTHER CALLED IT THE CURSE WHEN SHE SAT ME DOWN FOR OUR LITTLE TALK.
AND SHE EXPLAINED HOW, AT FIRST, YOU'RE SCARED OF IT... HOW IT JUST CREEPS UP ON YOU AND SORT OF WORKS IN THE BACKGROUND.
THEN YOU LIKE IT...HOW IT GETS YOU WHAT YOU WANT. YOU THINK, MAYBE, YOU CAN USE IT FOR GOOD. THEN, FOR GAIN.
PRETTY SOON, IT'S THE ONLY THING THAT MAKES YOU HAPPY. AND SOON AFTER THAT...
...YOU CAN'T EVEN TELL IF THAT'S REAL.
MOM... TELL ME THE TRUTH.
ARE YOU USING THE POWER NOW?
DON'T ASK ME THAT. PLEASE DON'T.
YOU CAN'T POSSIBLY UNDERSTAND WHAT YOU'RE ASKING ME.
WHAT DO YOU MEAN? I HAVE A RIGHT TO KNOW.
I'M TRYING TO PROTECT YOU, JUDE...
TELL ME, MOTHER! TURN OFF THIS CURSE AND SHOW ME WHAT'S REAL!

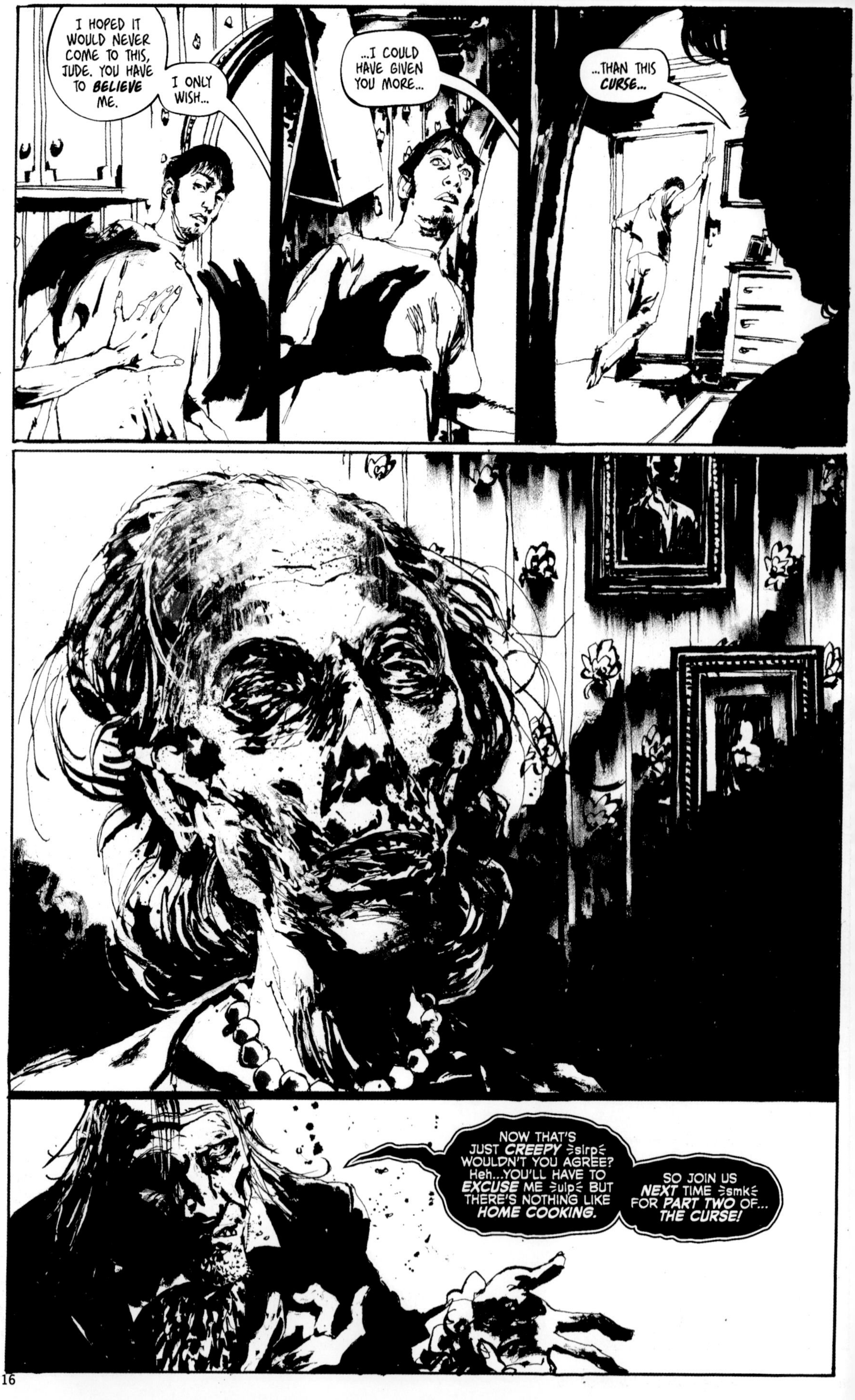
I HOPED IT WOULD NEVER COME TO THIS, JUDE. YOU HAVE TO BELIEVE ME.
I ONLY WISH...
...I COULD HAVE GIVEN YOU MORE...
...THAN THIS CURSE...
NOW THAT'S JUST CREEPY ≶slrp≷ WOULDN'T YOU AGREE? Heh...YOU'LL HAVE TO EXCUSE ME ≶ulp≷ BUT THERE'S NOTHING LIKE HOME COOKING.
SO JOIN US NEXT TIME ≶smk≷ FOR PART TWO OF... THE CURSE!

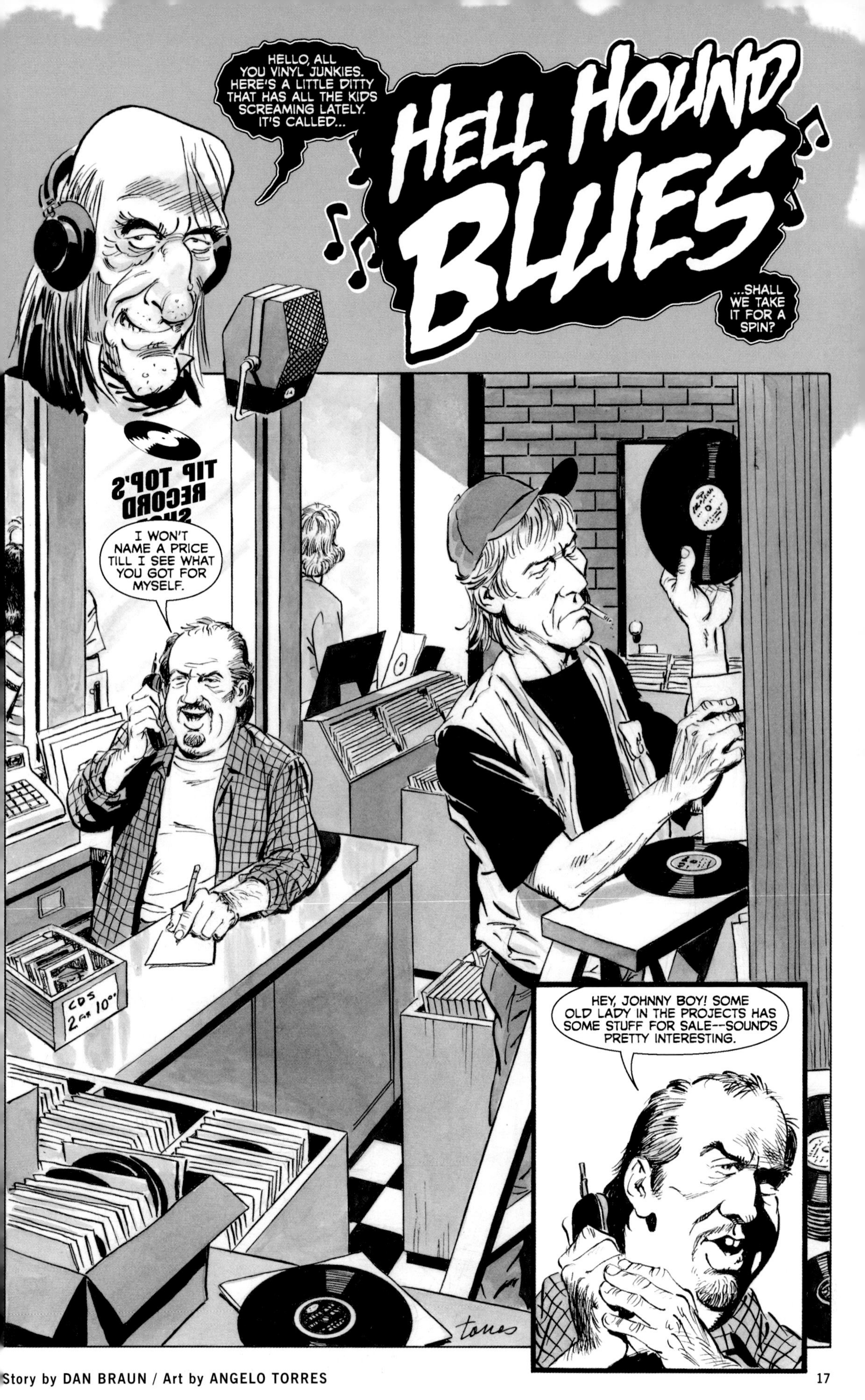
HELLO, ALL YOU VINYL JUNKIES. HERE'S A LITTLE DITTY THAT HAS ALL THE KIDS SCREAMING LATELY. IT'S CALLED...
HELL HOUND BLUES
...SHALL WE TAKE IT FOR A SPIN?
I WON'T NAME A PRICE TILL I SEE WHAT YOU GOT FOR MYSELF.
CDS 2 for 10.00
HEY, JOHNNY BOY! SOME OLD LADY IN THE PROJECTS HAS SOME STUFF FOR SALE--SOUNDS PRETTY INTERESTING.
torres

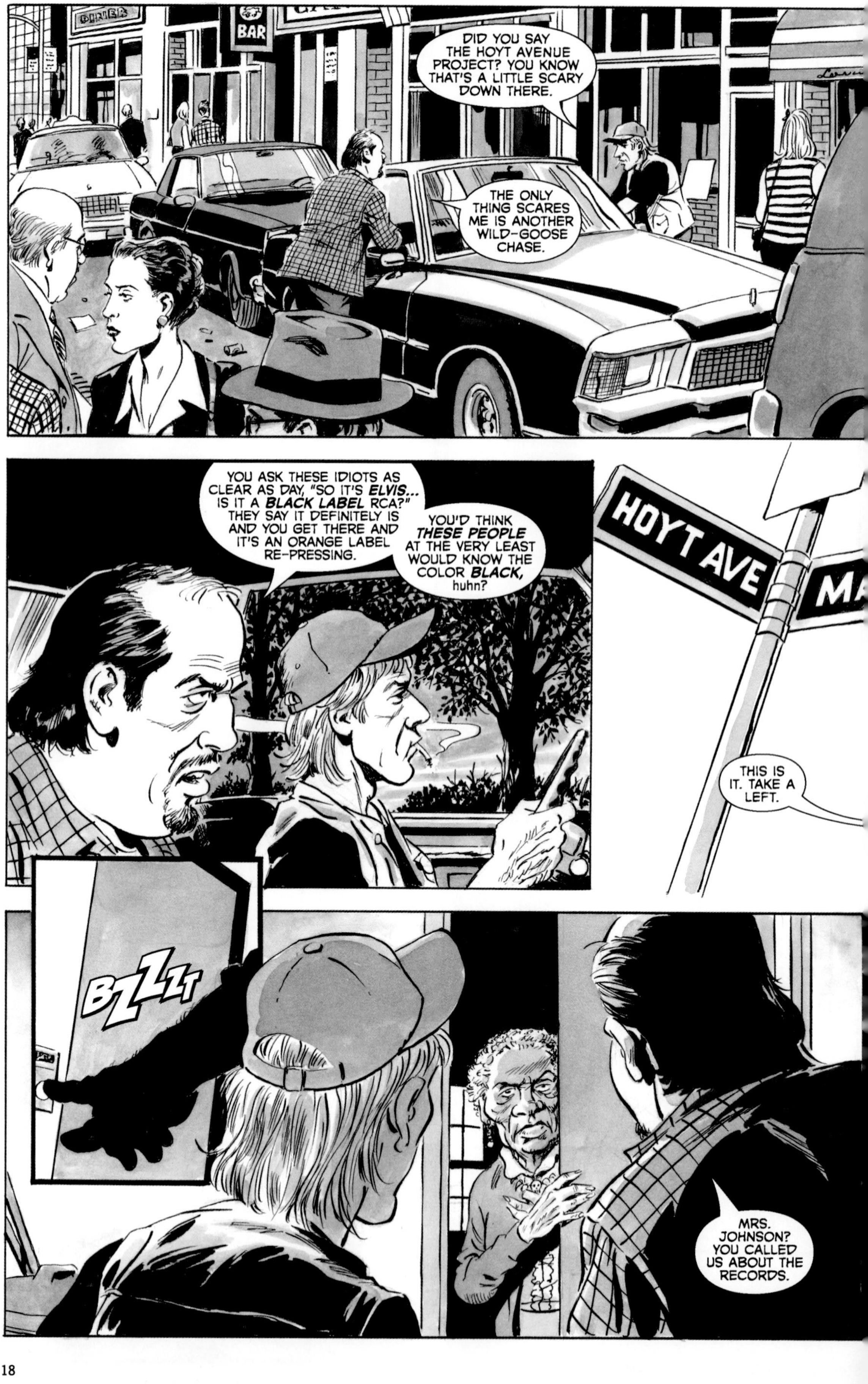
DINER
BAR
DID YOU SAY THE HOYT AVENUE PROJECT? YOU KNOW THAT'S A LITTLE SCARY DOWN THERE.
THE ONLY THING SCARES ME IS ANOTHER WILD-GOOSE CHASE.
YOU ASK THESE IDIOTS AS CLEAR AS DAY, "SO IT'S ELVIS... IS IT A BLACK LABEL RCA?" THEY SAY IT DEFINITELY IS AND YOU GET THERE AND IT'S AN ORANGE LABEL RE-PRESSING.
YOU'D THINK THESE PEOPLE AT THE VERY LEAST WOULD KNOW THE COLOR BLACK, huhn?
HOYT AVE
THIS IS IT. TAKE A LEFT.
BZZZZT
MRS. JOHNSON? YOU CALLED US ABOUT THE RECORDS.

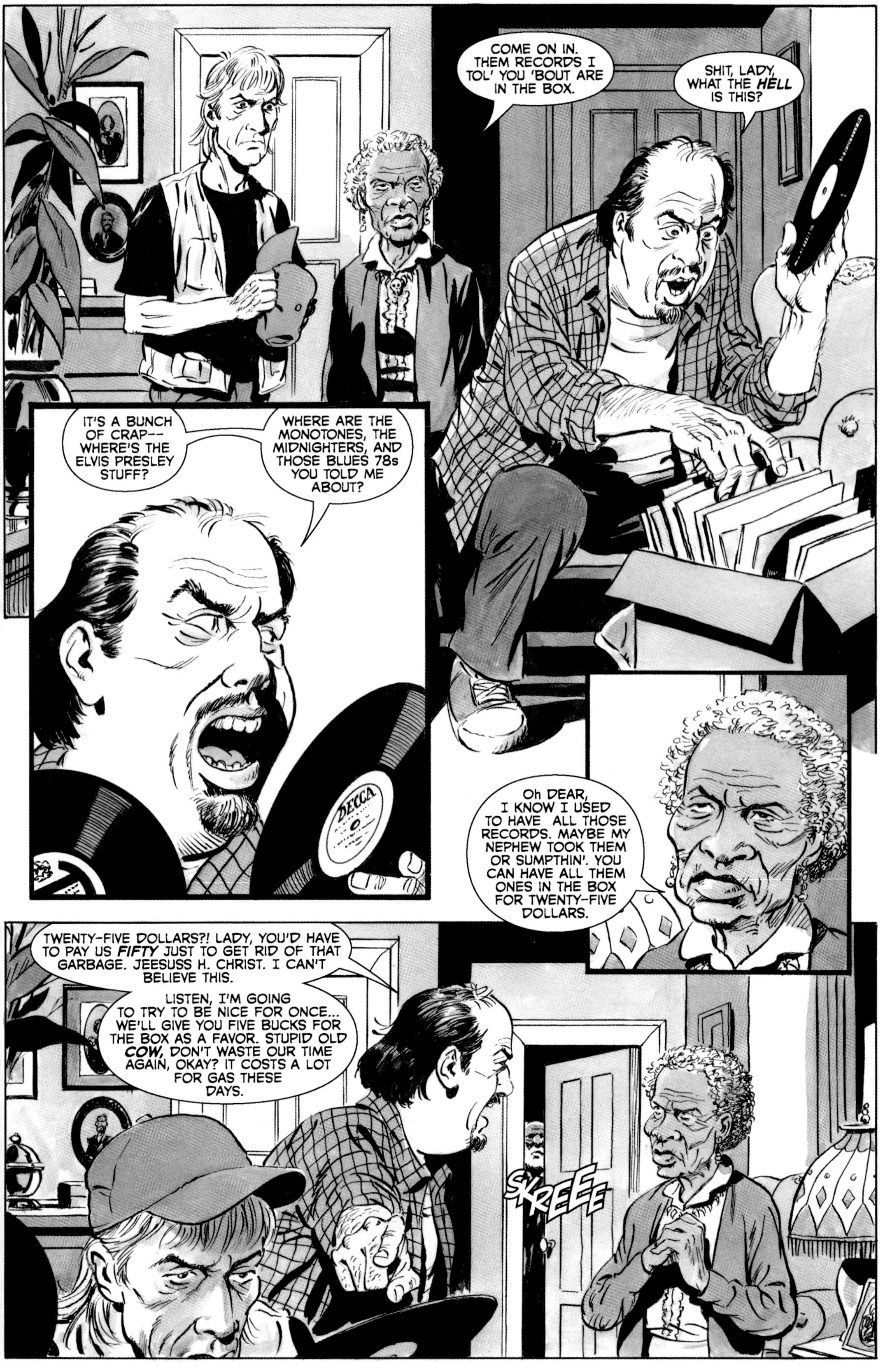
COME ON IN. THEM RECORDS I TOL' YOU 'BOUT ARE IN THE BOX.
SHIT, LADY, WHAT THE HELL IS THIS?
IT'S A BUNCH OF CRAP-- WHERE'S THE ELVIS PRESLEY STUFF?
WHERE ARE THE MONOTONES, THE MIDNIGHTERS, AND THOSE BLUES 78s YOU TOLD ME ABOUT?
DECCA
Oh DEAR, I KNOW I USED TO HAVE ALL THOSE RECORDS. MAYBE MY NEPHEW TOOK THEM OR SUMPTHIN'. YOU CAN HAVE ALL THEM ONES IN THE BOX FOR TWENTY-FIVE DOLLARS.
TWENTY-FIVE DOLLARS?! LADY, YOU'D HAVE TO PAY US FIFTY JUST TO GET RID OF THAT GARBAGE. JEESUSS H. CHRIST. I CAN'T BELIEVE THIS.
LISTEN, I'M GOING TO TRY TO BE NICE FOR ONCE... WE'LL GIVE YOU FIVE BUCKS FOR THE BOX AS A FAVOR. STUPID OLD COW, DON'T WASTE OUR TIME AGAIN, OKAY? IT COSTS A LOT FOR GAS THESE DAYS.
SKREEEE

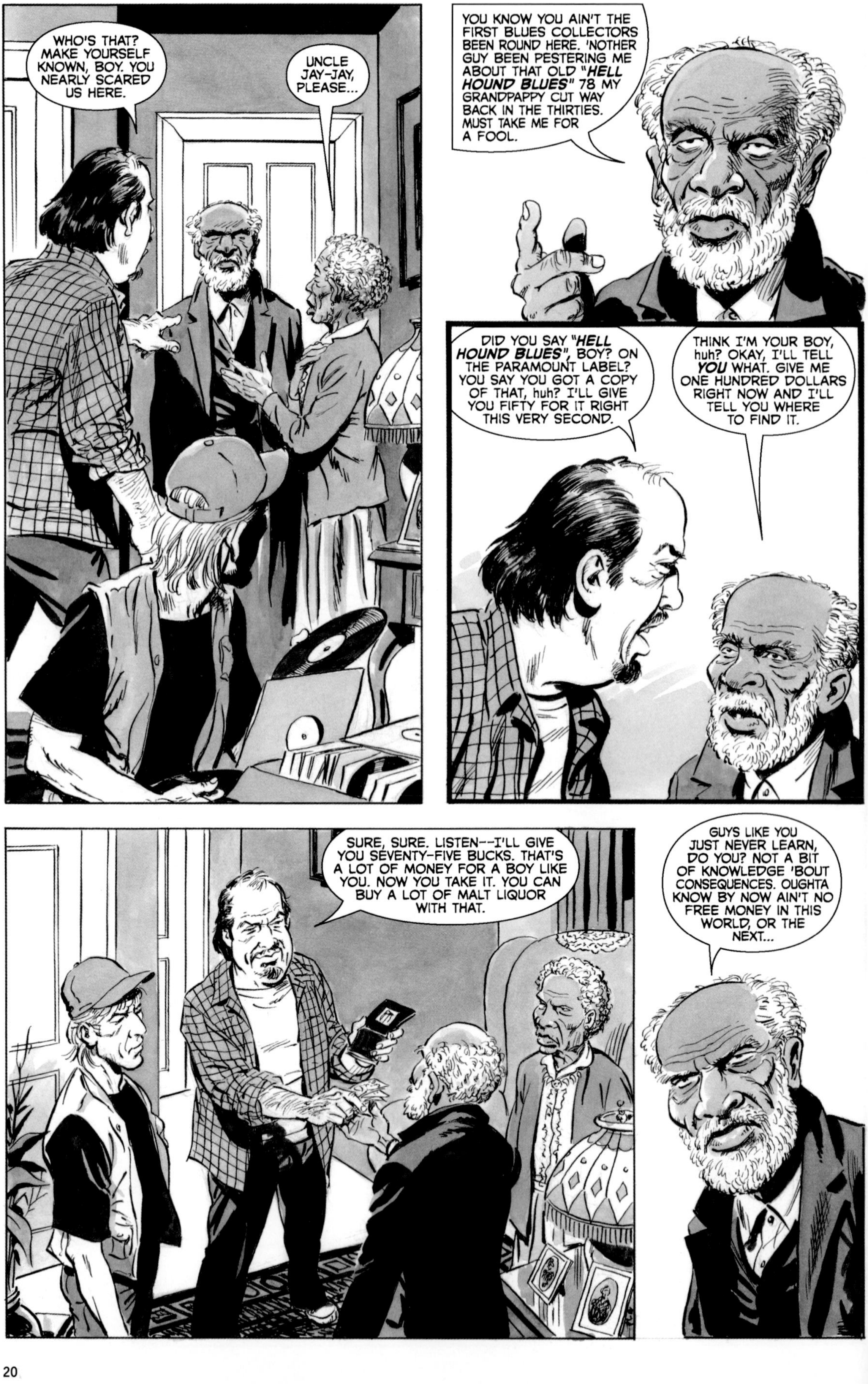
WHO'S THAT? MAKE YOURSELF KNOWN, BOY. YOU NEARLY SCARED US HERE.
UNCLE JAY-JAY, PLEASE...
YOU KNOW YOU AIN'T THE FIRST BLUES COLLECTORS BEEN ROUND HERE. 'NOTHER GUY BEEN PESTERING ME ABOUT THAT OLD "HELL HOUND BLUES" 78 MY GRANDPAPPY CUT WAY BACK IN THE THIRTIES. MUST TAKE ME FOR A FOOL.
DID YOU SAY "HELL HOUND BLUES", BOY? ON THE PARAMOUNT LABEL? YOU SAY YOU GOT A COPY OF THAT, huh? I'LL GIVE YOU FIFTY FOR IT RIGHT THIS VERY SECOND.
THINK I'M YOUR BOY, huh? OKAY, I'LL TELL YOU WHAT. GIVE ME ONE HUNDRED DOLLARS RIGHT NOW AND I'LL TELL YOU WHERE TO FIND IT.
SURE, SURE. LISTEN--I'LL GIVE YOU SEVENTY-FIVE BUCKS. THAT'S A LOT OF MONEY FOR A BOY LIKE YOU. NOW YOU TAKE IT. YOU CAN BUY A LOT OF MALT LIQUOR WITH THAT.
GUYS LIKE YOU JUST NEVER LEARN, DO YOU? NOT A BIT OF KNOWLEDGE 'BOUT CONSEQUENCES. OUGHTA KNOW BY NOW AIN'T NO FREE MONEY IN THIS WORLD, OR THE NEXT...

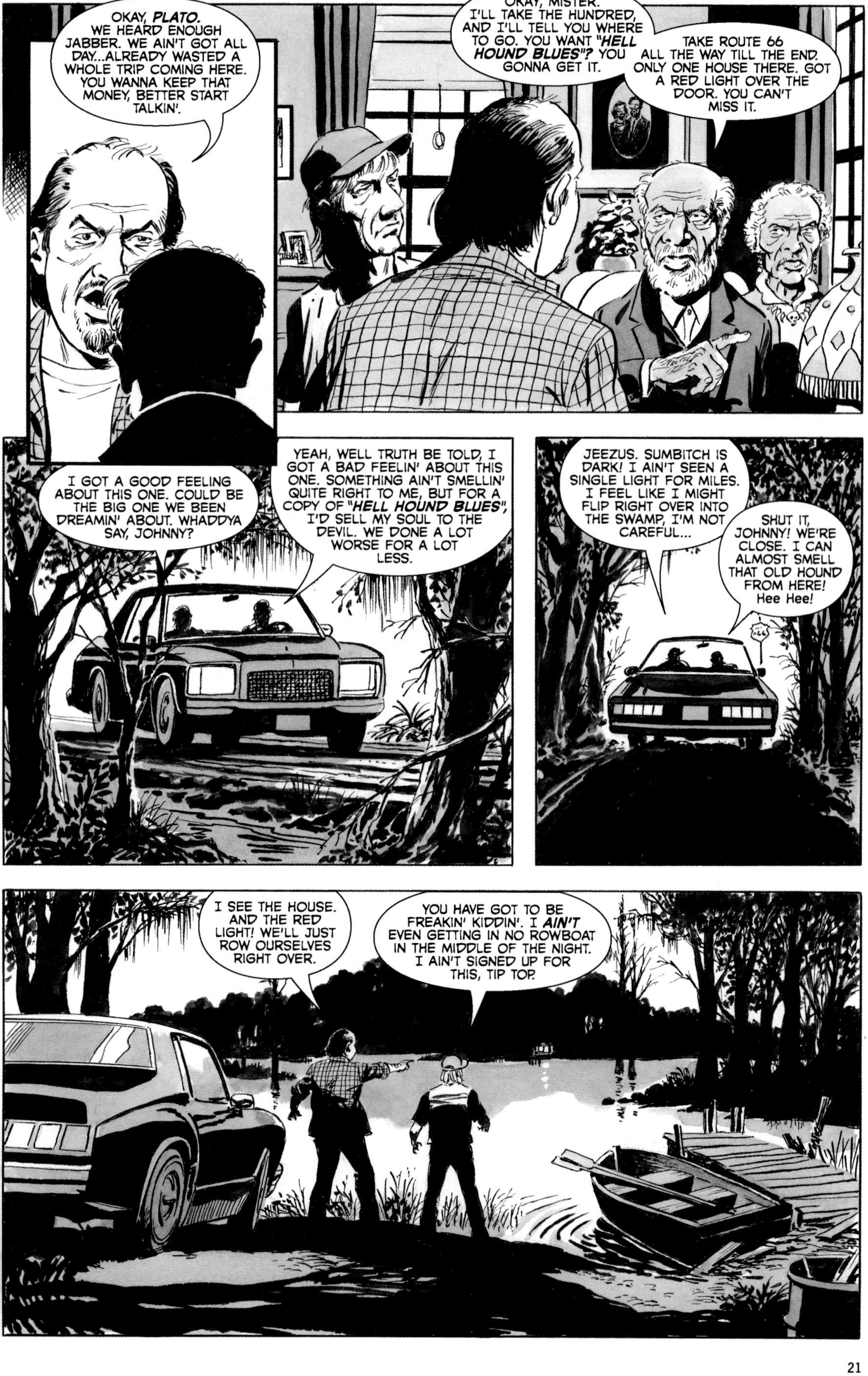
OKAY, *PLATO.* WE HEARD ENOUGH JABBER. WE AIN'T GOT ALL DAY...ALREADY WASTED A WHOLE TRIP COMING HERE. YOU WANNA KEEP THAT MONEY, BETTER START TALKIN'.
OKAY, MISTER. I'LL TAKE THE HUNDRED, AND I'LL TELL YOU WHERE TO GO. YOU WANT "*HELL HOUND BLUES*"? YOU GONNA GET IT.
TAKE ROUTE 66 ALL THE WAY TILL THE END. ONLY ONE HOUSE THERE. GOT A RED LIGHT OVER THE DOOR. YOU CAN'T MISS IT.
I GOT A GOOD FEELING ABOUT THIS ONE. COULD BE THE BIG ONE WE BEEN DREAMIN' ABOUT. WHADDYA SAY, JOHNNY?
YEAH, WELL TRUTH BE TOLD, I GOT A BAD FEELIN' ABOUT THIS ONE. SOMETHING AIN'T SMELLIN' QUITE RIGHT TO ME, BUT FOR A COPY OF "*HELL HOUND BLUES*", I'D SELL MY SOUL TO THE DEVIL. WE DONE A LOT WORSE FOR A LOT LESS.
JEEZUS. SUMBITCH IS DARK! I AIN'T SEEN A SINGLE LIGHT FOR MILES. I FEEL LIKE I MIGHT FLIP RIGHT OVER INTO THE SWAMP, I'M NOT CAREFUL...
SHUT IT, JOHNNY! WE'RE CLOSE. I CAN ALMOST SMELL THAT OLD HOUND FROM HERE! Hee Hee!
I SEE THE HOUSE. AND THE RED LIGHT! WE'LL JUST ROW OURSELVES RIGHT OVER.
YOU HAVE GOT TO BE FREAKIN' KIDDIN'. I *AIN'T* EVEN GETTING IN NO ROWBOAT IN THE MIDDLE OF THE NIGHT. I AIN'T SIGNED UP FOR THIS, TIP TOP.

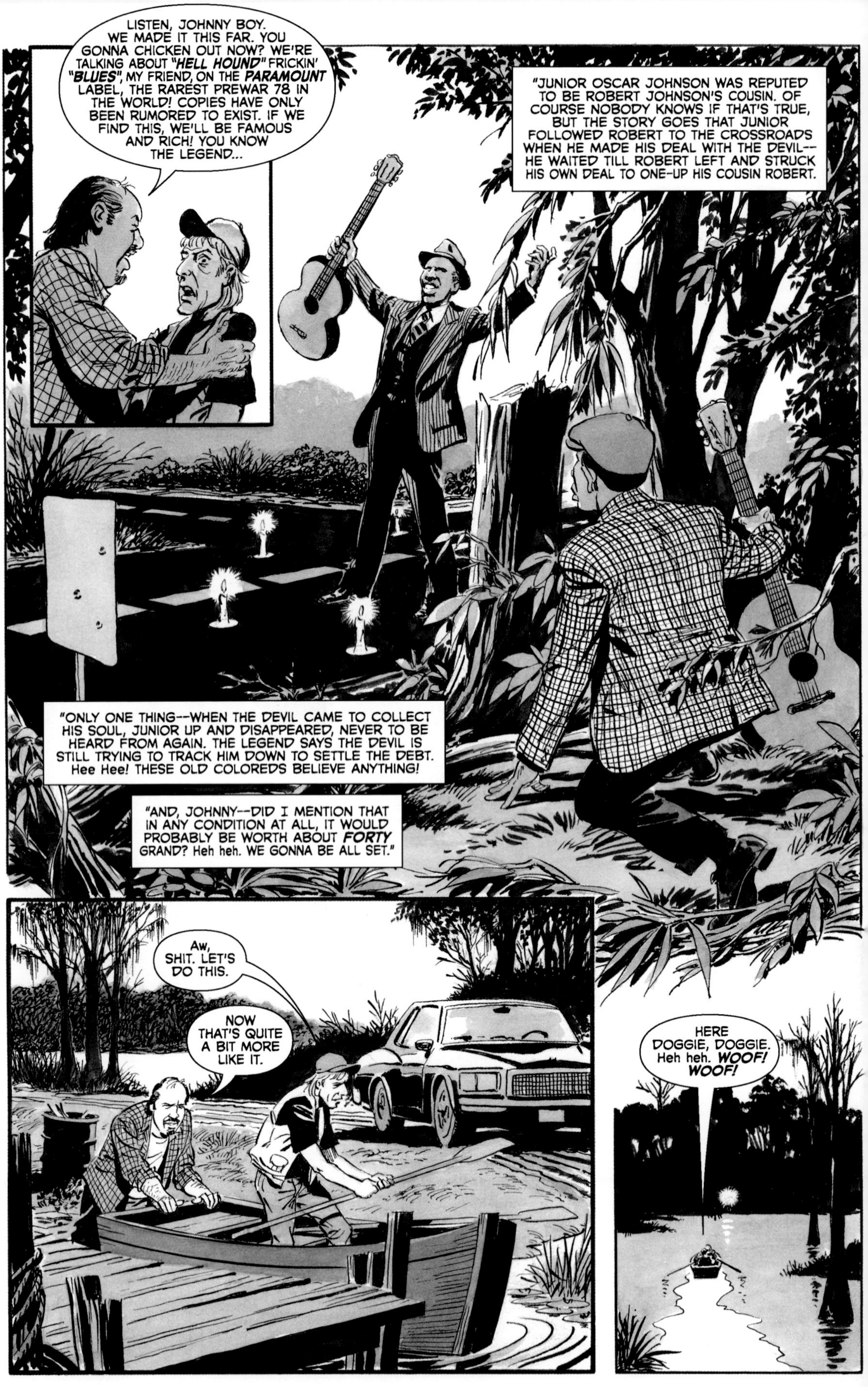
LISTEN, JOHNNY BOY. WE MADE IT THIS FAR. YOU GONNA CHICKEN OUT NOW? WE'RE TALKING ABOUT "HELL HOUND" FRICKIN' "BLUES", MY FRIEND, ON THE PARAMOUNT LABEL, THE RAREST PREWAR 78 IN THE WORLD! COPIES HAVE ONLY BEEN RUMORED TO EXIST. IF WE FIND THIS, WE'LL BE FAMOUS AND RICH! YOU KNOW THE LEGEND...
"JUNIOR OSCAR JOHNSON WAS REPUTED TO BE ROBERT JOHNSON'S COUSIN. OF COURSE NOBODY KNOWS IF THAT'S TRUE, BUT THE STORY GOES THAT JUNIOR FOLLOWED ROBERT TO THE CROSSROADS WHEN HE MADE HIS DEAL WITH THE DEVIL-- HE WAITED TILL ROBERT LEFT AND STRUCK HIS OWN DEAL TO ONE-UP HIS COUSIN ROBERT.
"ONLY ONE THING--WHEN THE DEVIL CAME TO COLLECT HIS SOUL, JUNIOR UP AND DISAPPEARED, NEVER TO BE HEARD FROM AGAIN. THE LEGEND SAYS THE DEVIL IS STILL TRYING TO TRACK HIM DOWN TO SETTLE THE DEBT. Hee Hee! THESE OLD COLOREDS BELIEVE ANYTHING!
"AND, JOHNNY--DID I MENTION THAT IN ANY CONDITION AT ALL, IT WOULD PROBABLY BE WORTH ABOUT FORTY GRAND? Heh heh. WE GONNA BE ALL SET."
Aw, SHIT. LET'S DO THIS.
NOW THAT'S QUITE A BIT MORE LIKE IT.
HERE DOGGIE, DOGGIE. Heh heh. WOOF! WOOF!

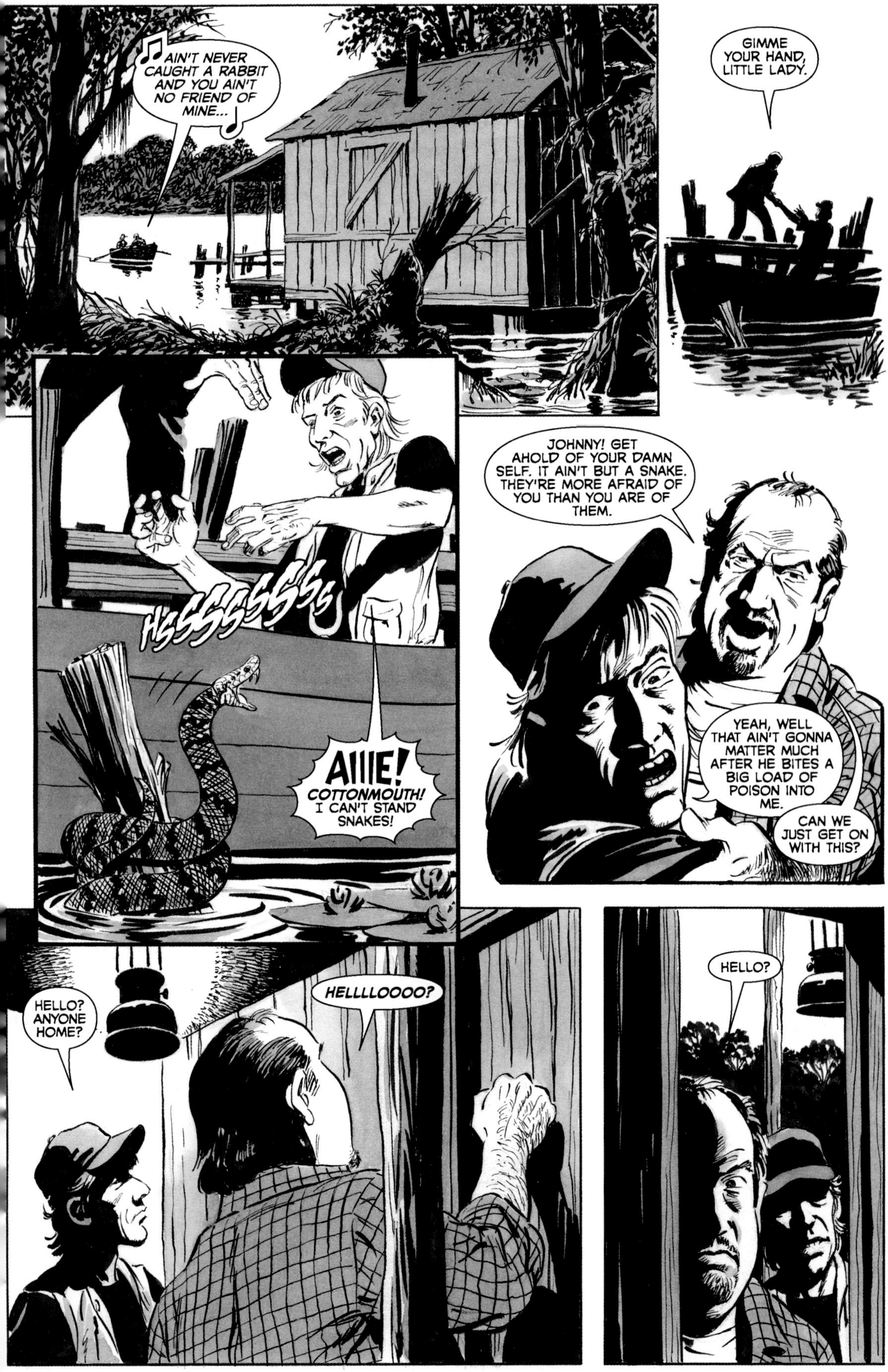
AIN'T NEVER CAUGHT A RABBIT AND YOU AIN'T NO FRIEND OF MINE...
GIMME YOUR HAND, LITTLE LADY.
HSSSSSSSSS
AIIIE! COTTONMOUTH! I CAN'T STAND SNAKES!
JOHNNY! GET AHOLD OF YOUR DAMN SELF. IT AIN'T BUT A SNAKE. THEY'RE MORE AFRAID OF YOU THAN YOU ARE OF THEM.
YEAH, WELL THAT AIN'T GONNA MATTER MUCH AFTER HE BITES A BIG LOAD OF POISON INTO ME.
CAN WE JUST GET ON WITH THIS?
HELLO? ANYONE HOME?
HELLLLOOOO?
HELLO?

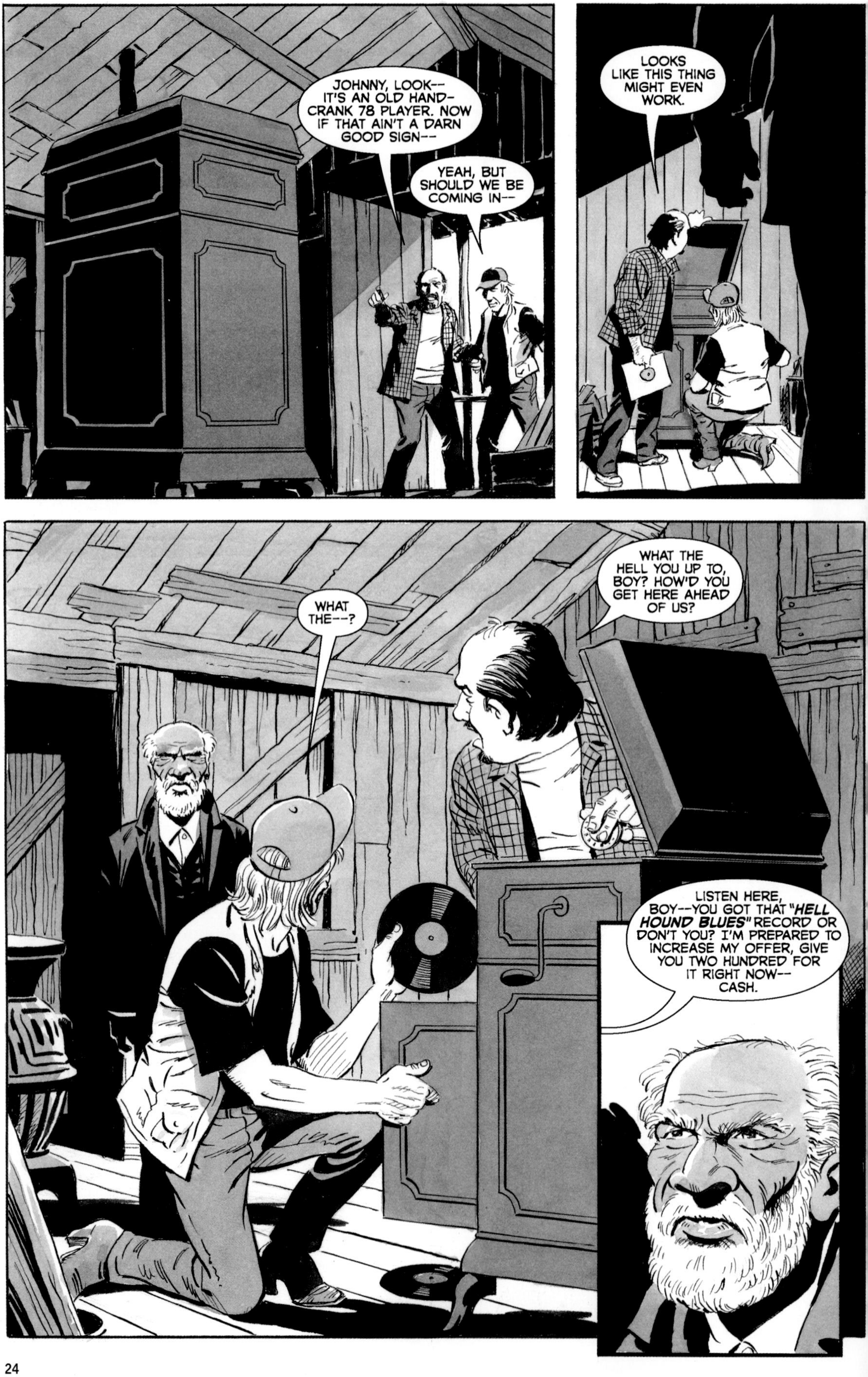
JOHNNY, LOOK-- IT'S AN OLD HAND-CRANK 78 PLAYER. NOW IF THAT AIN'T A DARN GOOD SIGN--
YEAH, BUT SHOULD WE BE COMING IN--
LOOKS LIKE THIS THING MIGHT EVEN WORK.
WHAT THE--?
WHAT THE HELL YOU UP TO, BOY? HOW'D YOU GET HERE AHEAD OF US?
LISTEN HERE, BOY--YOU GOT THAT "***HELL HOUND BLUES***" RECORD OR DON'T YOU? I'M PREPARED TO INCREASE MY OFFER, GIVE YOU TWO HUNDRED FOR IT RIGHT NOW-- CASH.

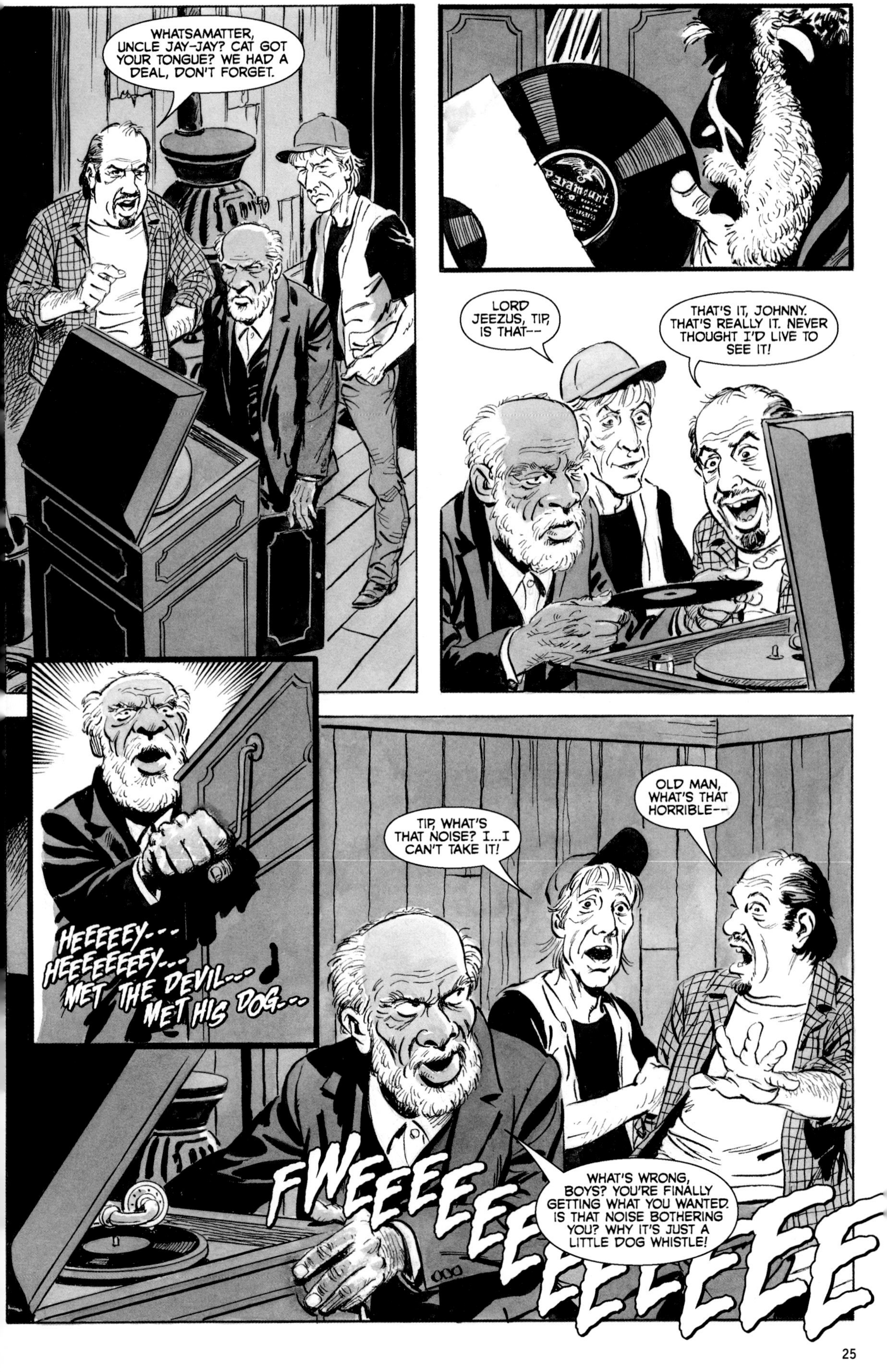
WHATSAMATTER, UNCLE JAY-JAY? CAT GOT YOUR TONGUE? WE HAD A DEAL, DON'T FORGET.
Paramount
LORD JEEZUS, TIP, IS THAT--
THAT'S IT, JOHNNY. THAT'S REALLY IT. NEVER THOUGHT I'D LIVE TO SEE IT!
HEEEEEY... HEEEEEEEEY... MET THE DEVIL... MET HIS DOG...
TIP, WHAT'S THAT NOISE? I...I CAN'T TAKE IT!
OLD MAN, WHAT'S THAT HORRIBLE--
WHAT'S WRONG, BOYS? YOU'RE FINALLY GETTING WHAT YOU WANTED. IS THAT NOISE BOTHERING YOU? WHY IT'S JUST A LITTLE DOG WHISTLE!
FWEEEEEEEEEEEEEEE

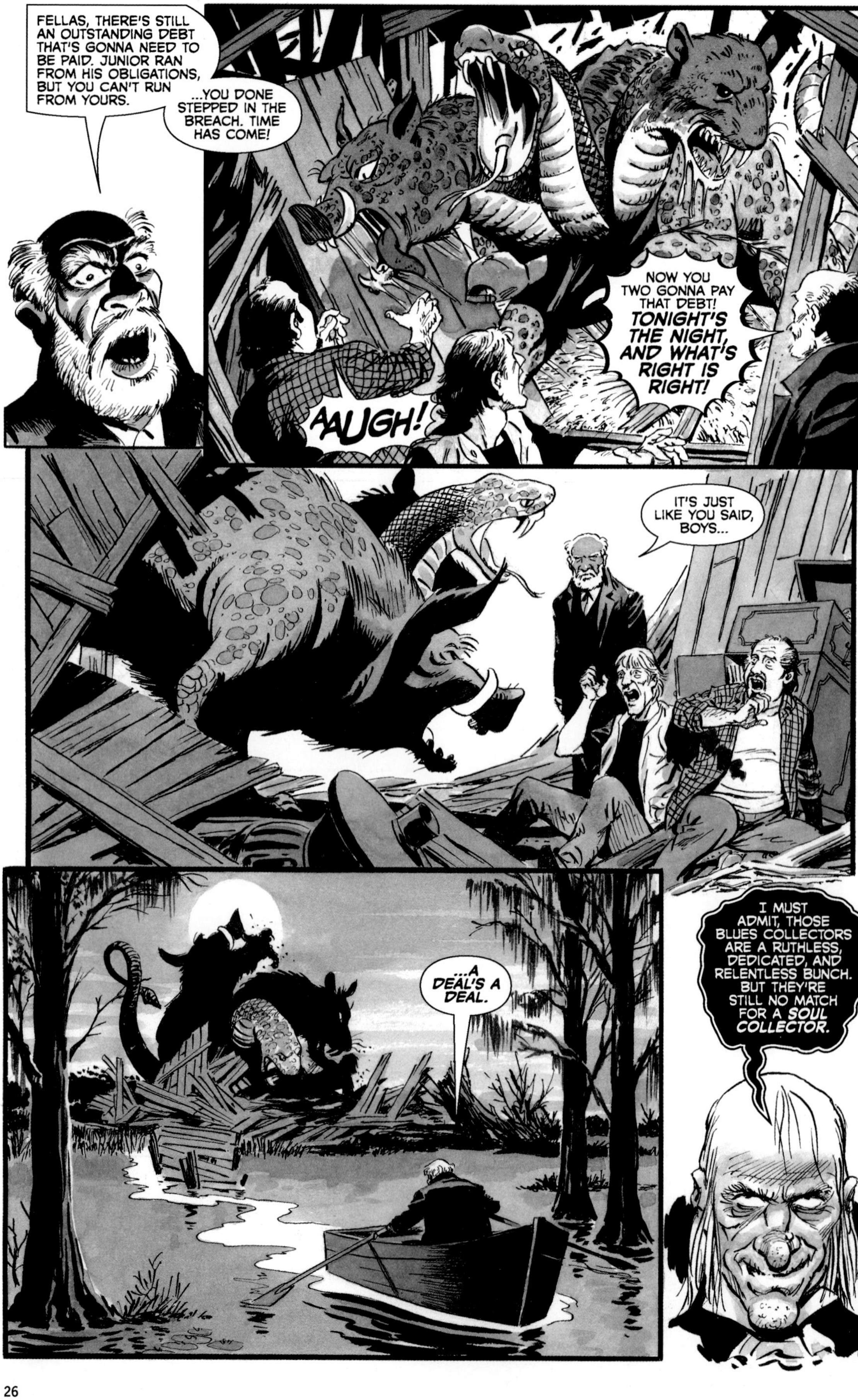
FELLAS, THERE'S STILL AN OUTSTANDING DEBT THAT'S GONNA NEED TO BE PAID. JUNIOR RAN FROM HIS OBLIGATIONS, BUT YOU CAN'T RUN FROM YOURS.
...YOU DONE STEPPED IN THE BREACH. TIME HAS COME!
NOW YOU TWO GONNA PAY THAT DEBT! TONIGHT'S THE NIGHT, AND WHAT'S RIGHT IS RIGHT!
AAUGH!
IT'S JUST LIKE YOU SAID, BOYS...
...A DEAL'S A DEAL.
I MUST ADMIT, THOSE BLUES COLLECTORS ARE A RUTHLESS, DEDICATED, AND RELENTLESS BUNCH. BUT THEY'RE STILL NO MATCH FOR A SOUL COLLECTOR.

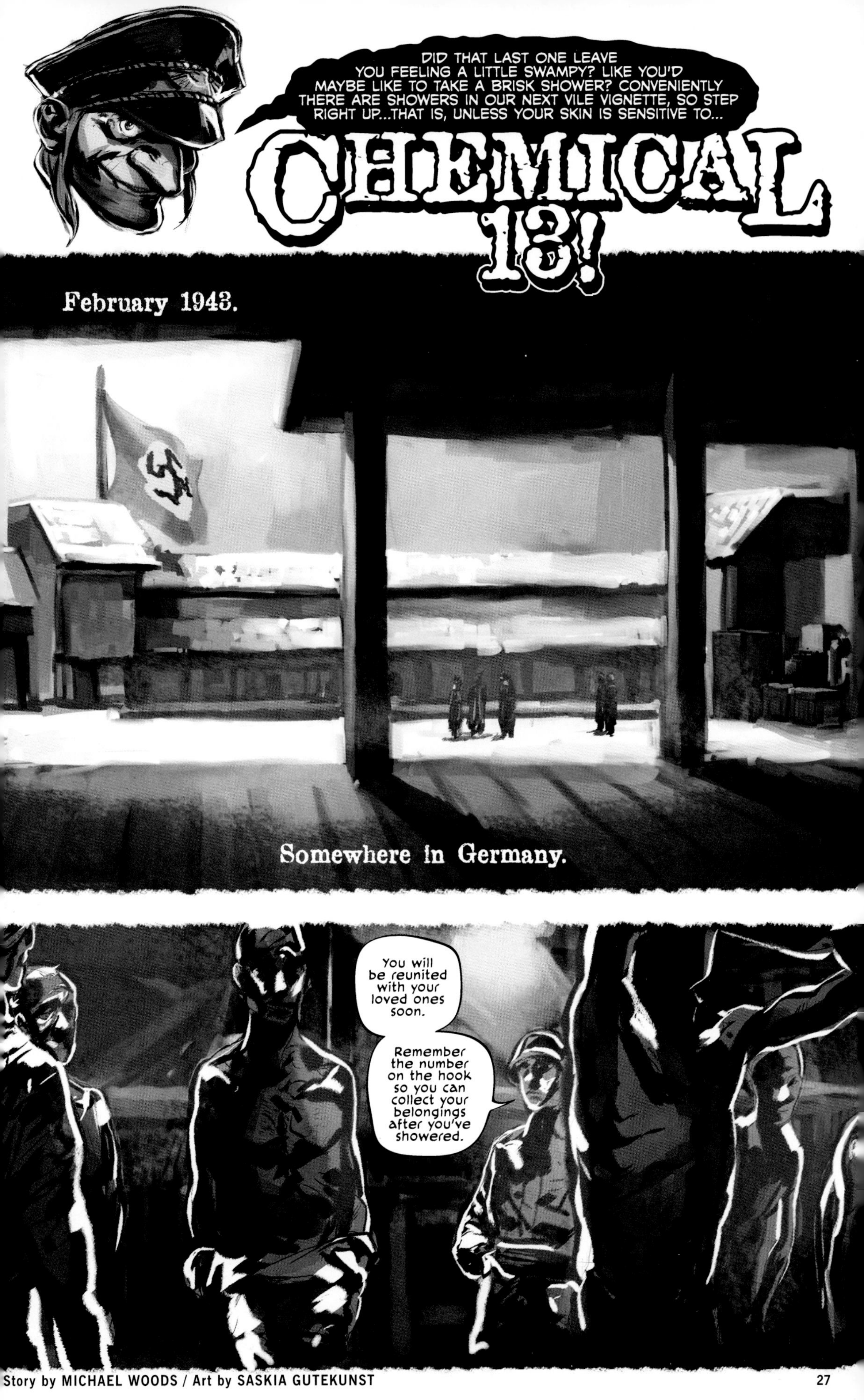
DID THAT LAST ONE LEAVE YOU FEELING A LITTLE SWAMPY? LIKE YOU'D MAYBE LIKE TO TAKE A BRISK SHOWER? CONVENIENTLY THERE ARE SHOWERS IN OUR NEXT VILE VIGNETTE, SO STEP RIGHT UP...THAT IS, UNLESS YOUR SKIN IS SENSITIVE TO...
CHEMICAL 13!
February 1943.
Somewhere in Germany.
You will be reunited with your loved ones soon.
Remember the number on the hook so you can collect your belongings after you've showered.

Story by MICHAEL WOODS / Art by SASKIA GUTEKUNST

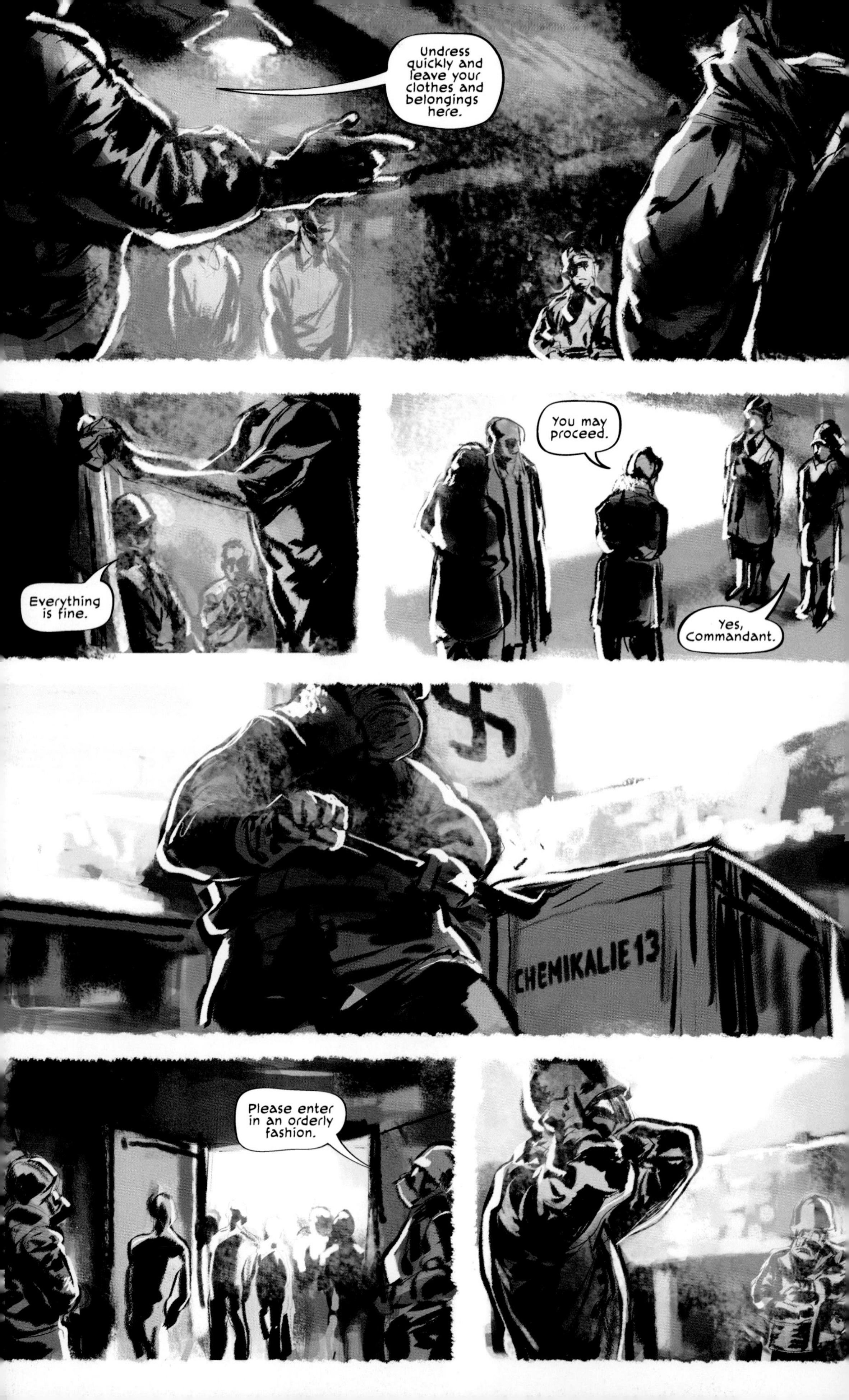
Undress quickly and leave your clothes and belongings here.
Everything is fine.
You may proceed.
Yes, Commandant.
CHEMIKALIE 13
Please enter in an orderly fashion.

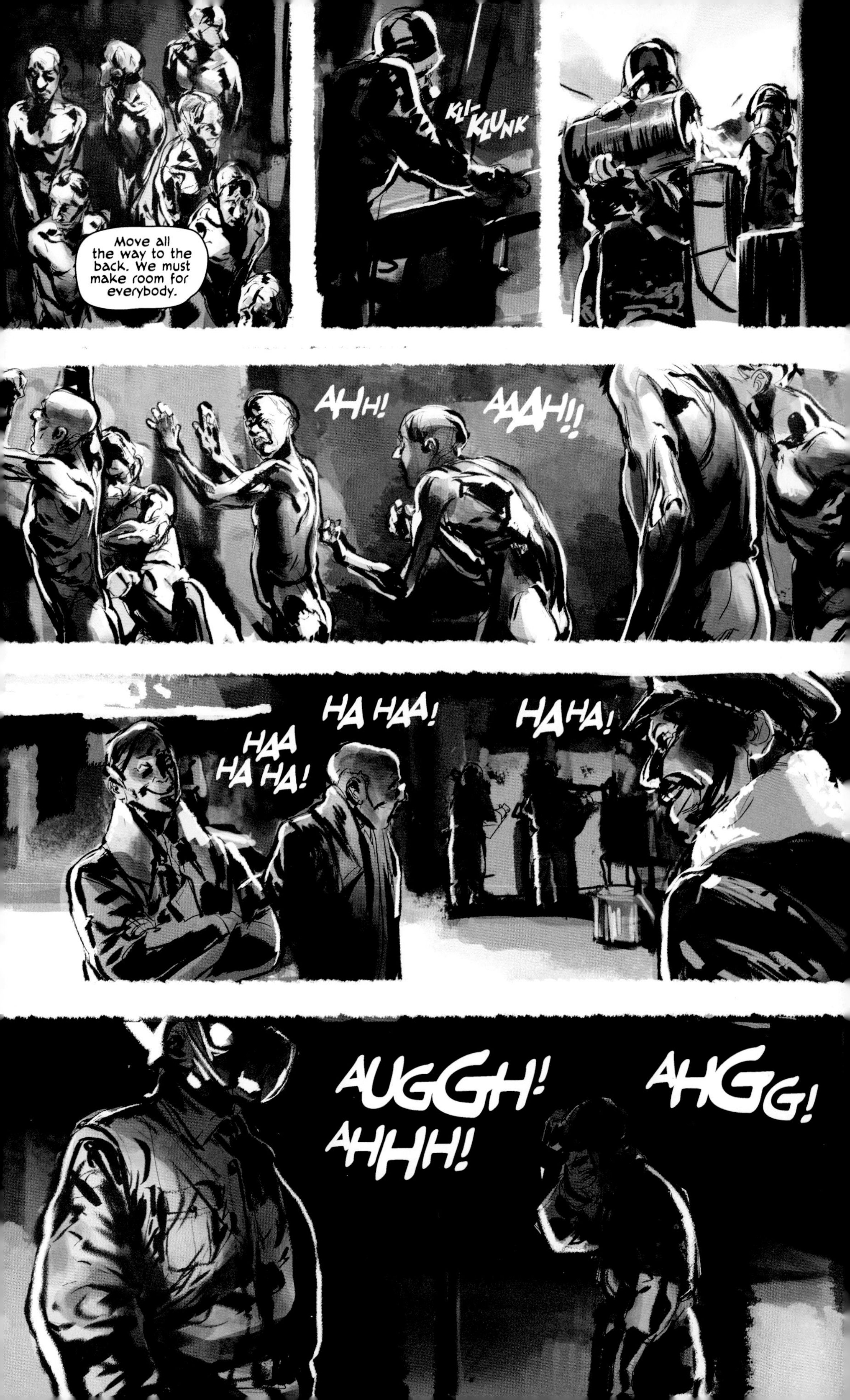
Move all the way to the back. We must make room for everybody.
KLI-KLUNK
AHH!
AAAH!!
HA HAA!
HAA HA HA!
HAHA!
AUGGH!
AHHH!
AHGG!

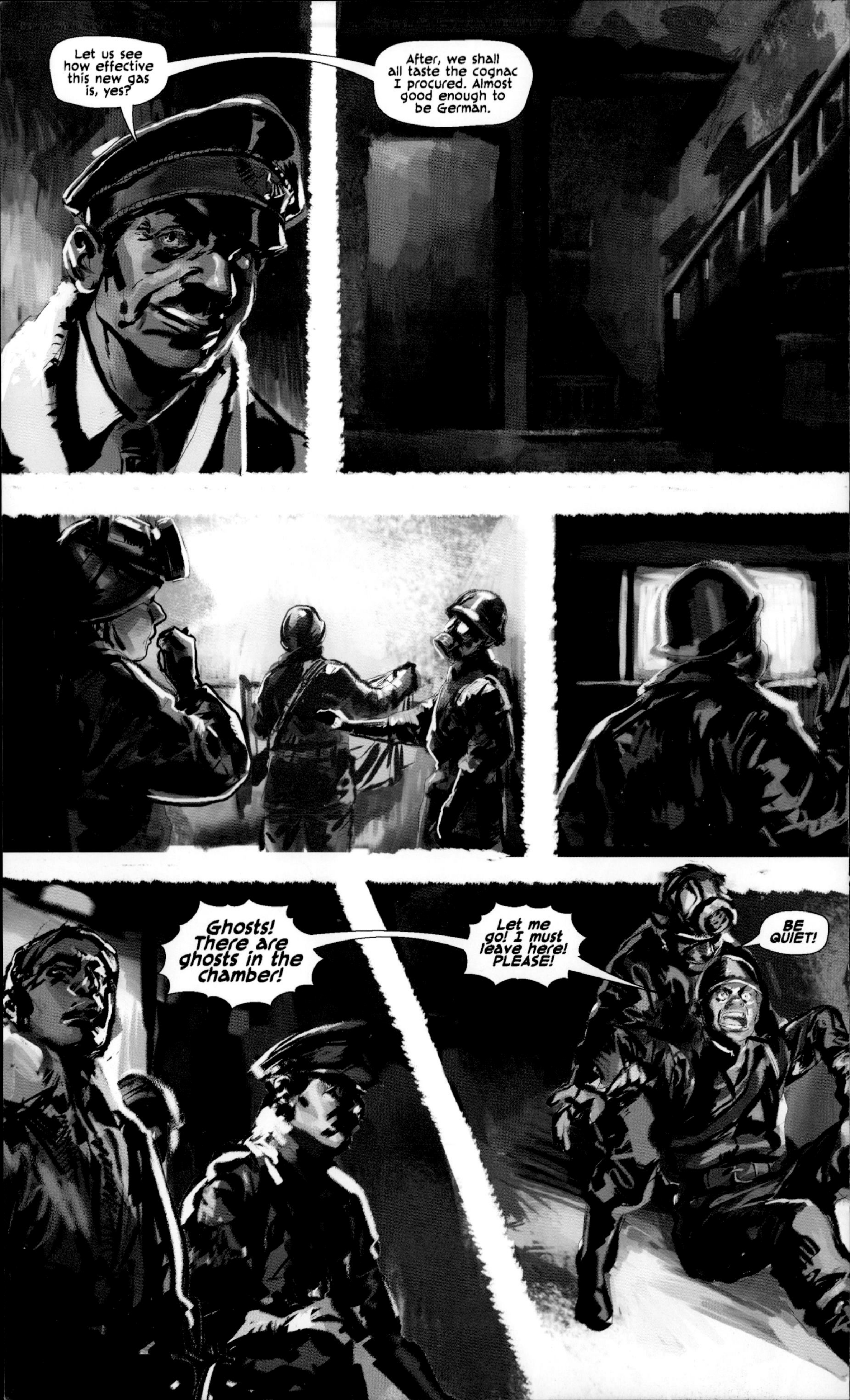
Let us see how effective this new gas is, yes?
After, we shall all taste the cognac I procured. Almost good enough to be German.
Ghosts! There are ghosts in the chamber!
Let me go! I must leave here! PLEASE!
BE QUIET!

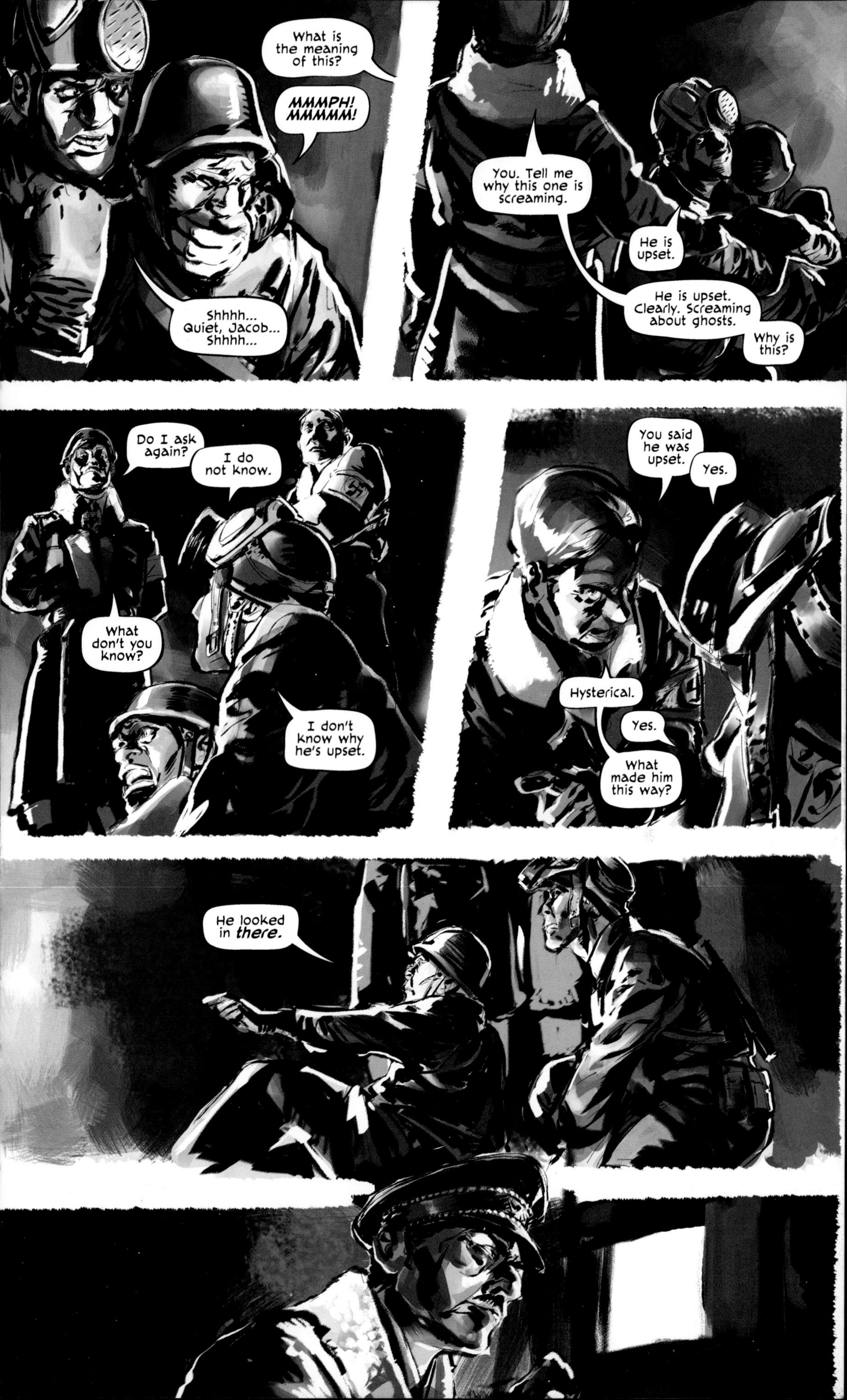
What is the meaning of this?
MMMPH! MMMMM!
Shhhh... Quiet, Jacob... Shhhh...
You. Tell me why this one is screaming.
He is upset.
He is upset. Clearly. Screaming about ghosts.
Why is this?
Do I ask again?
I do not know.
What don't you know?
I don't know why he's upset.
You said he was upset.
Yes.
Hysterical.
Yes.
What made him this way?
He looked in *there.*

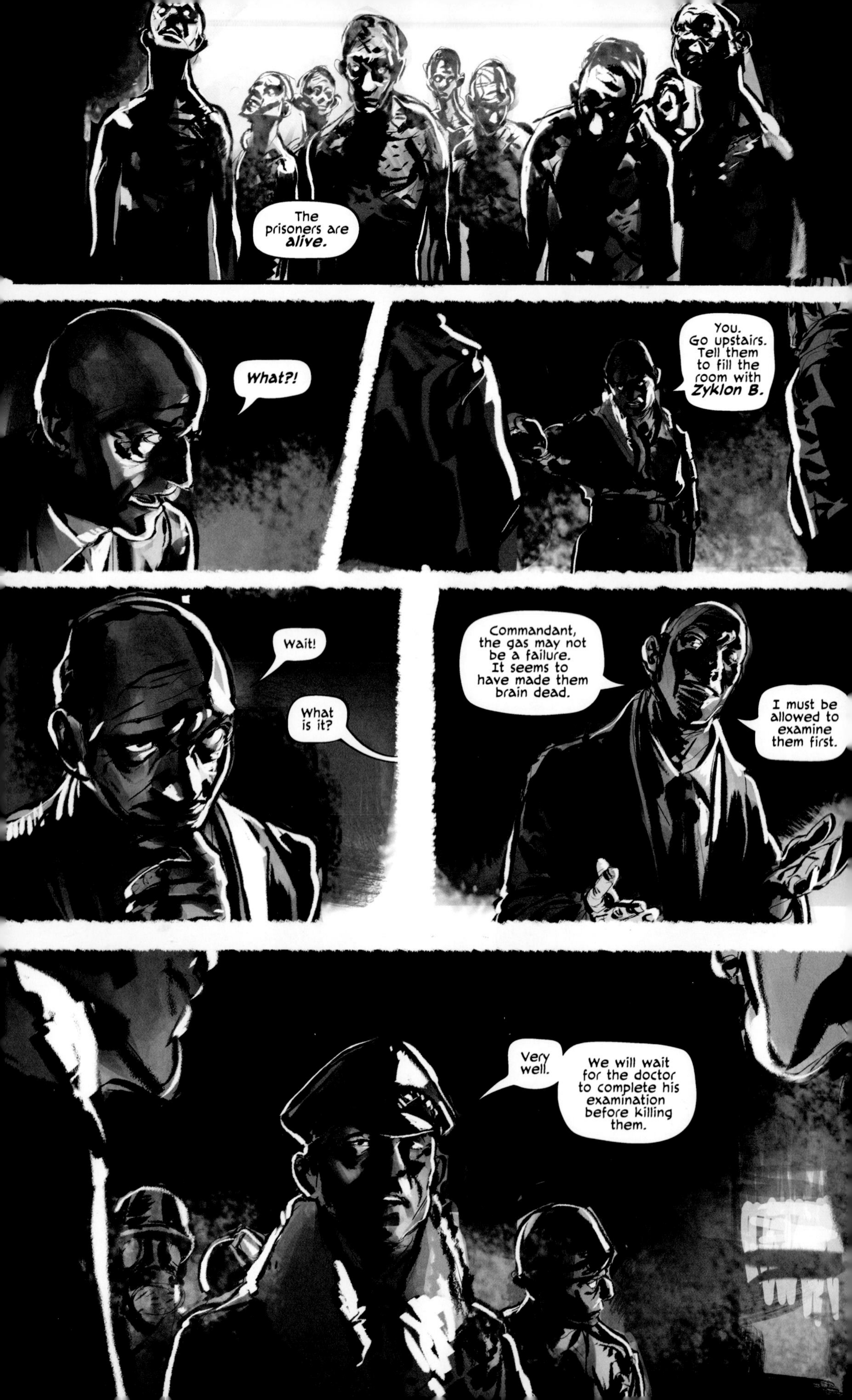
The prisoners are alive.
What?!
You. Go upstairs. Tell them to fill the room with Zyklon B.
Wait!
What is it?
Commandant, the gas may not be a failure. It seems to have made them brain dead.
I must be allowed to examine them first.
Very well.
We will wait for the doctor to complete his examination before killing them.

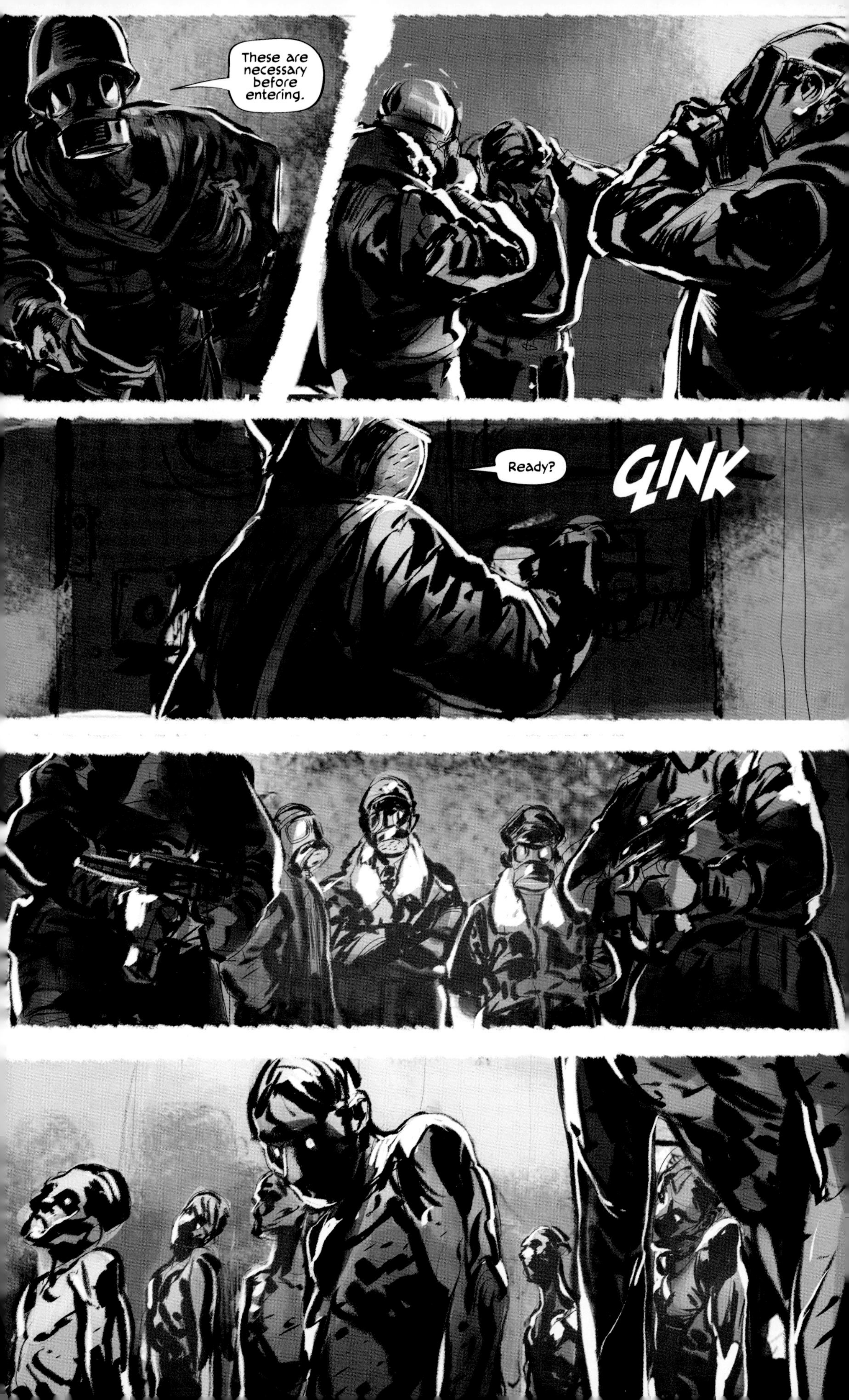
These are necessary before entering.
Ready?
CLINK

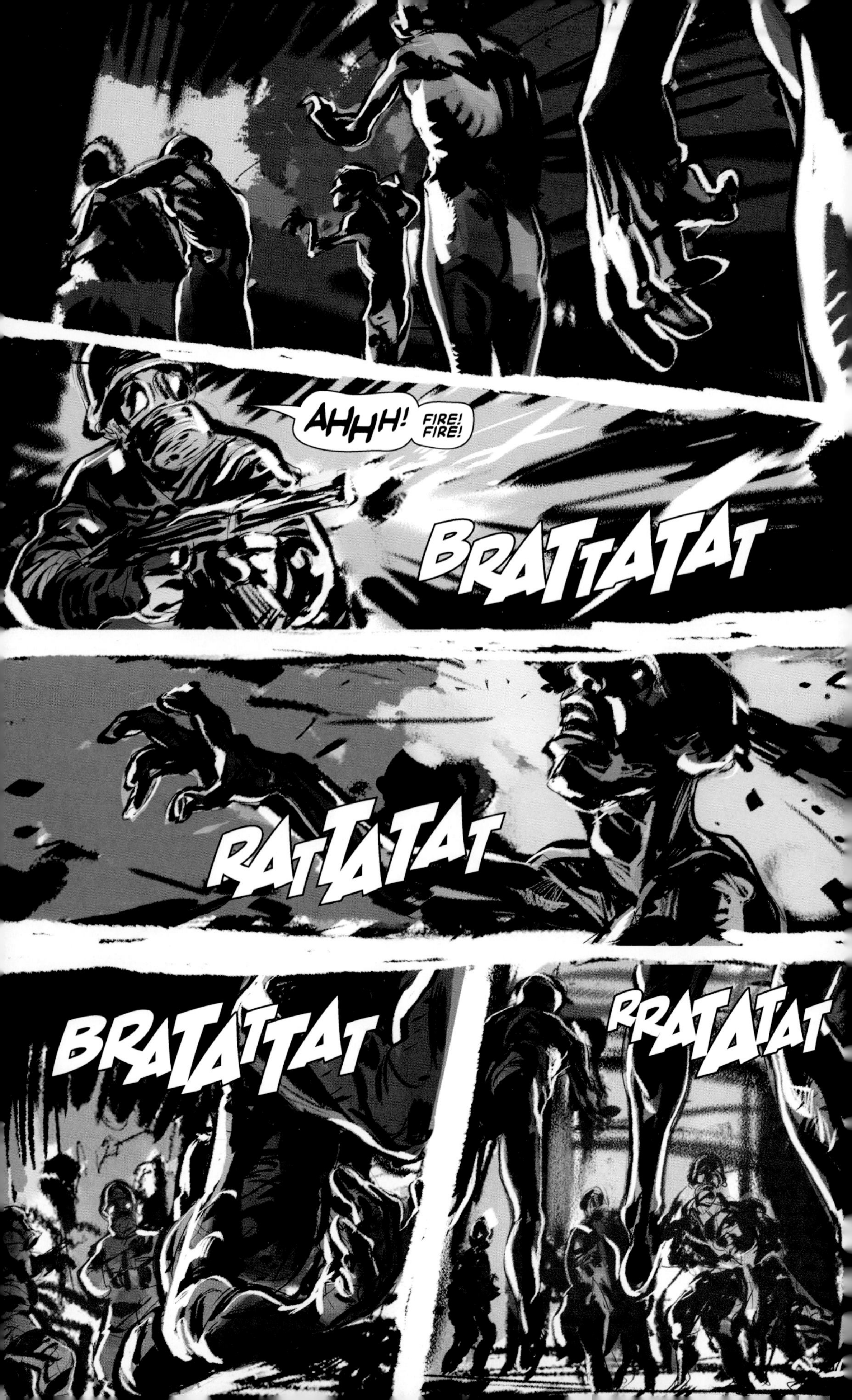
AHHH!
FIRE! FIRE!
BRATTATAT
RATTATAT
BRATATTAT
RRATATAT

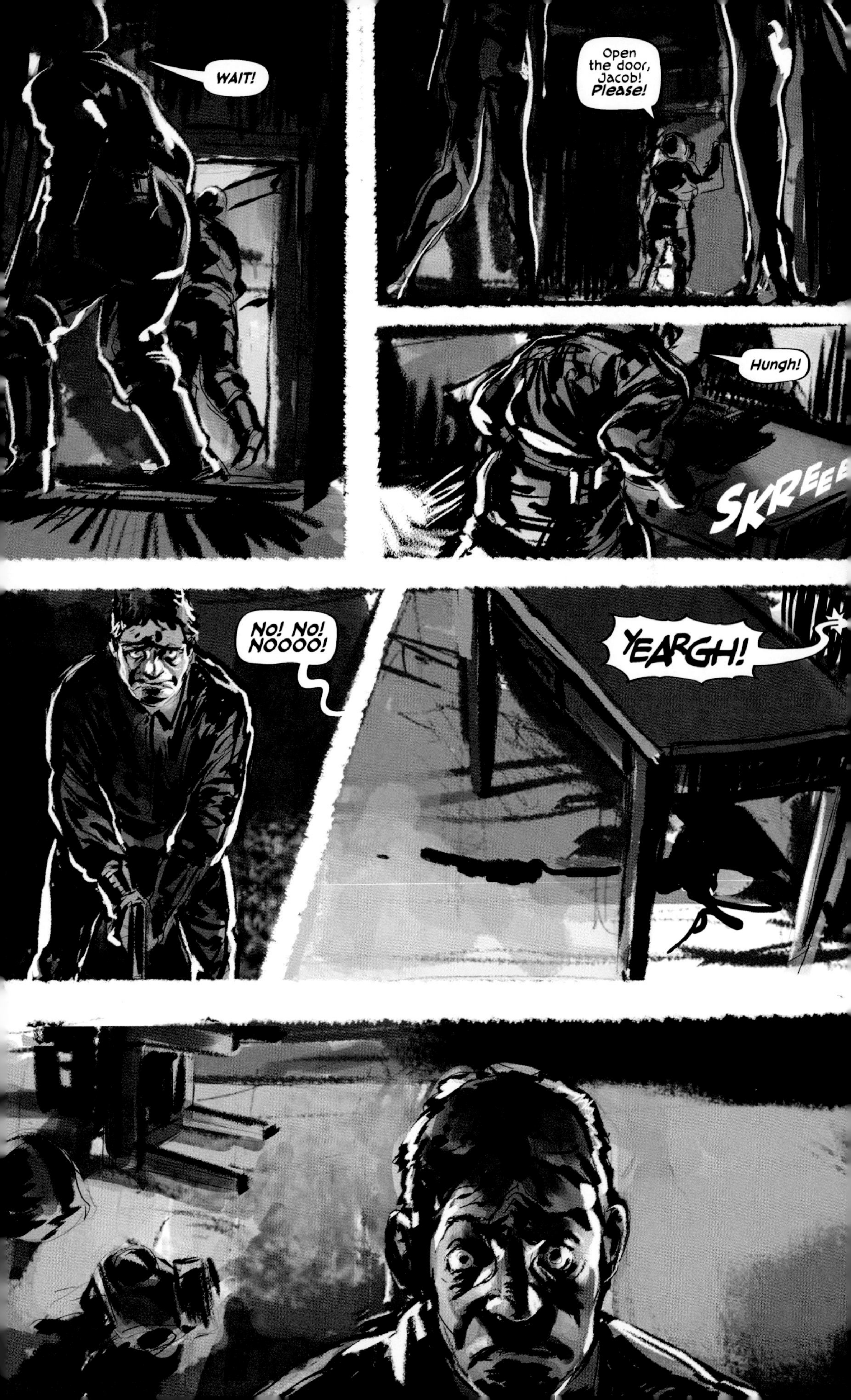
WAIT!
Open the door, Jacob! Please!
Hungh!
SKREEE
NO! NO! NOOOO!
YEARGH!

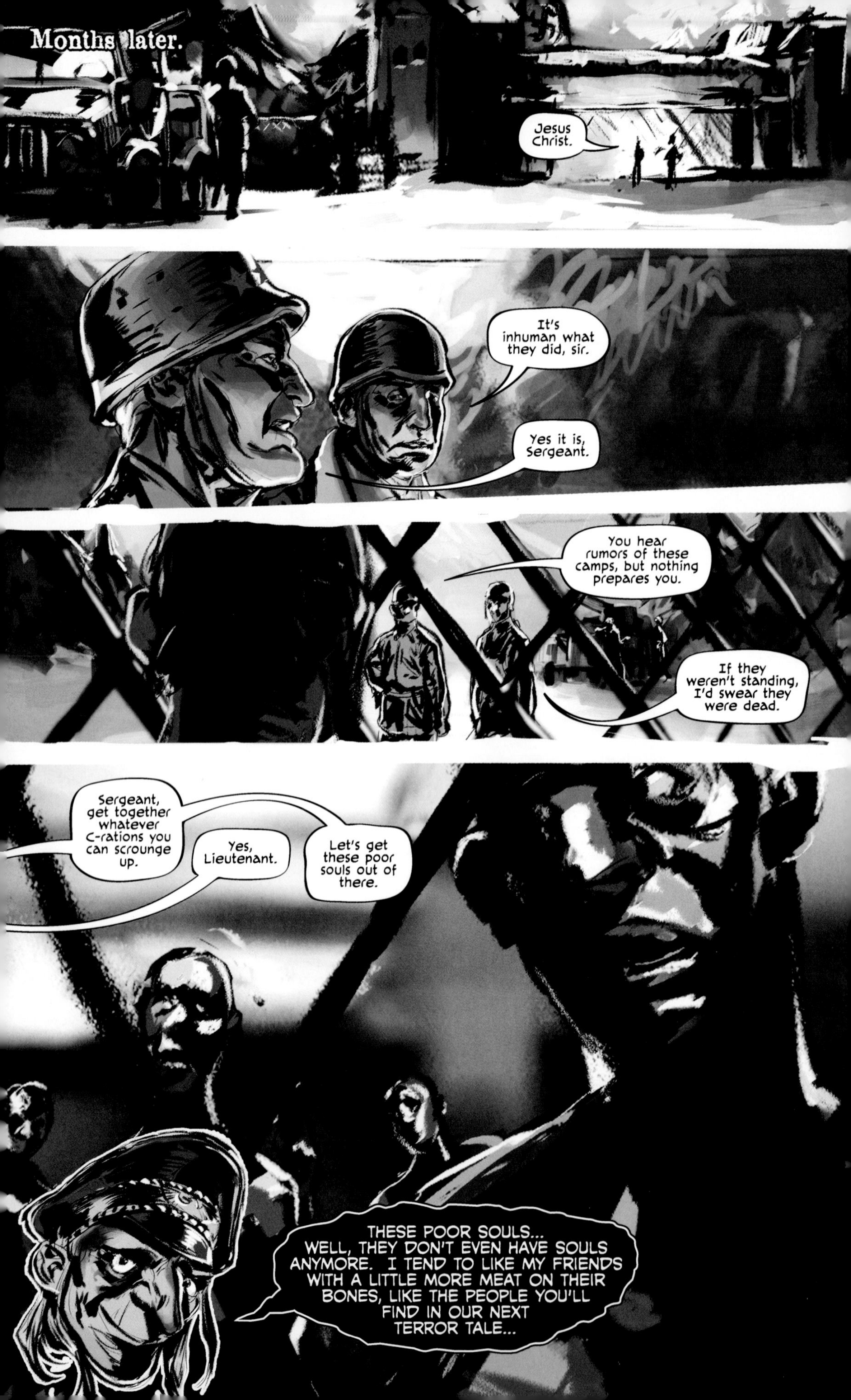
Months later.
Jesus Christ.
It's inhuman what they did, sir.
Yes it is, Sergeant.
You hear rumors of these camps, but nothing prepares you.
If they weren't standing, I'd swear they were dead.
Sergeant, get together whatever C-rations you can scrounge up.
Let's get these poor souls out of there.
Yes, Lieutenant.
THESE POOR SOULS... WELL, THEY DON'T EVEN HAVE SOULS ANYMORE. I TEND TO LIKE MY FRIENDS WITH A LITTLE MORE MEAT ON THEIR BONES, LIKE THE PEOPLE YOU'LL FIND IN OUR NEXT TERROR TALE...

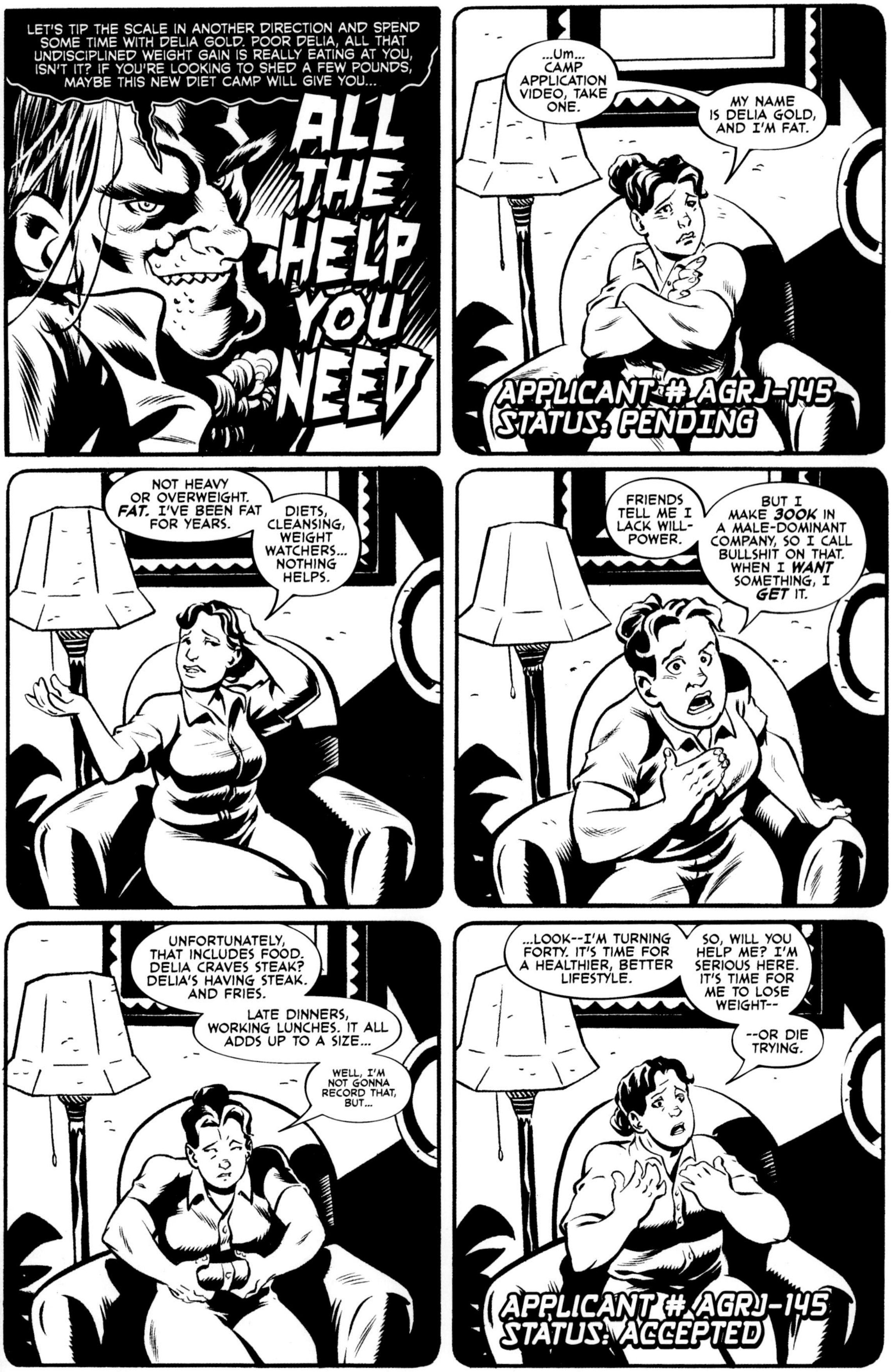
LET'S TIP THE SCALE IN ANOTHER DIRECTION AND SPEND SOME TIME WITH DELIA GOLD. POOR DELIA, ALL THAT UNDISCIPLINED WEIGHT GAIN IS REALLY EATING AT YOU, ISN'T IT? IF YOU'RE LOOKING TO SHED A FEW POUNDS, MAYBE THIS NEW DIET CAMP WILL GIVE YOU...
ALL THE HELP YOU NEED
...Um... CAMP APPLICATION VIDEO, TAKE ONE.
MY NAME IS DELIA GOLD, AND I'M FAT.
APPLICANT # AGRJ-145
STATUS: PENDING
NOT HEAVY OR OVERWEIGHT. FAT. I'VE BEEN FAT FOR YEARS.
DIETS, CLEANSING, WEIGHT WATCHERS... NOTHING HELPS.
FRIENDS TELL ME I LACK WILL-POWER.
BUT I MAKE 300K IN A MALE-DOMINANT COMPANY, SO I CALL BULLSHIT ON THAT. WHEN I WANT SOMETHING, I GET IT.
UNFORTUNATELY, THAT INCLUDES FOOD. DELIA CRAVES STEAK? DELIA'S HAVING STEAK. AND FRIES.
LATE DINNERS, WORKING LUNCHES. IT ALL ADDS UP TO A SIZE...
WELL, I'M NOT GONNA RECORD THAT, BUT...
...LOOK--I'M TURNING FORTY. IT'S TIME FOR A HEALTHIER, BETTER LIFESTYLE.
SO, WILL YOU HELP ME? I'M SERIOUS HERE. IT'S TIME FOR ME TO LOSE WEIGHT--
--OR DIE TRYING.
APPLICANT # AGRJ-145
STATUS: ACCEPTED

Story by NEIL KLEID / Art by BRIAN CHURILLA

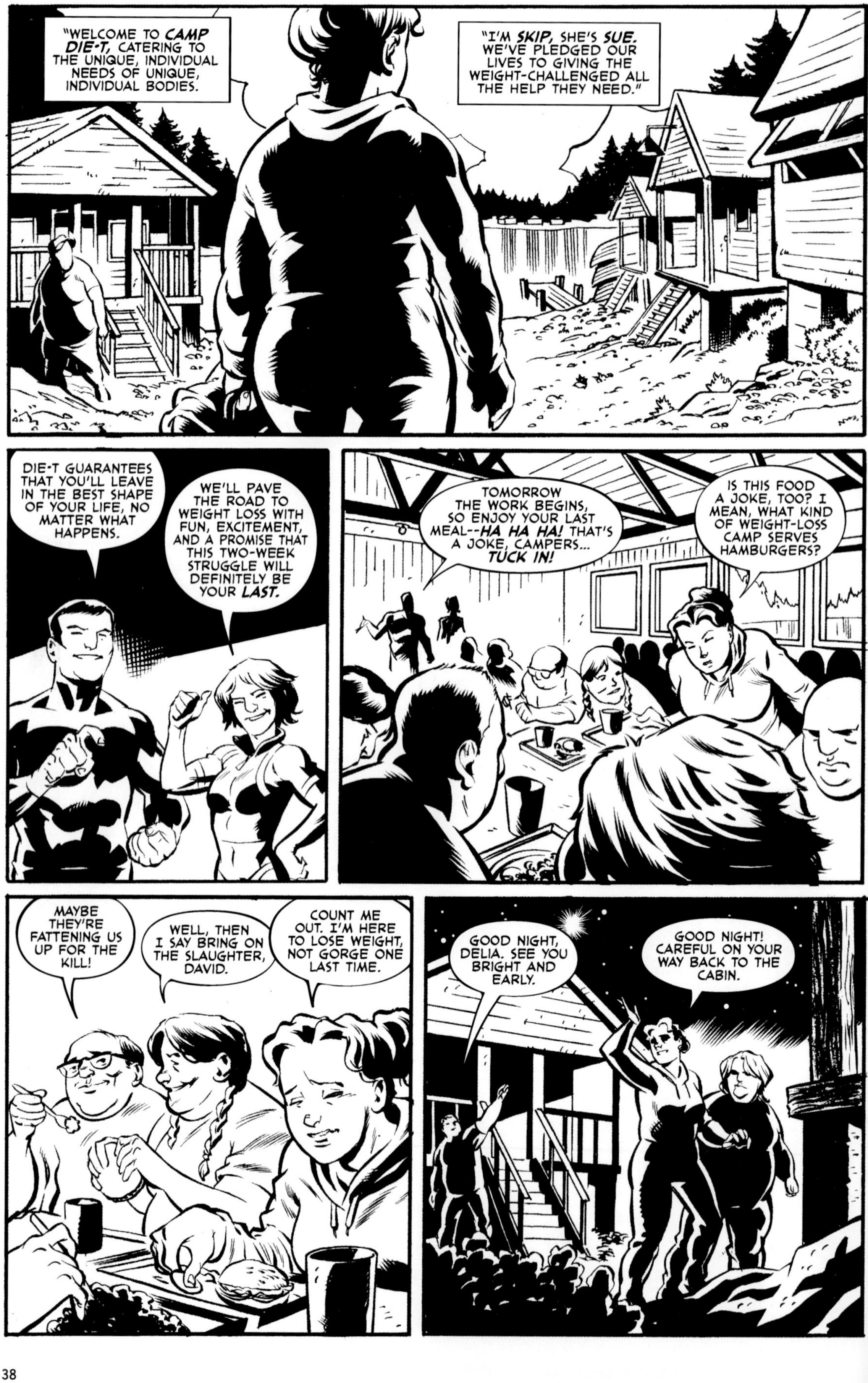
"WELCOME TO CAMP DIE-T, CATERING TO THE UNIQUE, INDIVIDUAL NEEDS OF UNIQUE, INDIVIDUAL BODIES.
"I'M SKIP, SHE'S SUE. WE'VE PLEDGED OUR LIVES TO GIVING THE WEIGHT-CHALLENGED ALL THE HELP THEY NEED."
DIE-T GUARANTEES THAT YOU'LL LEAVE IN THE BEST SHAPE OF YOUR LIFE, NO MATTER WHAT HAPPENS.
WE'LL PAVE THE ROAD TO WEIGHT LOSS WITH FUN, EXCITEMENT, AND A PROMISE THAT THIS TWO-WEEK STRUGGLE WILL DEFINITELY BE YOUR LAST.
TOMORROW THE WORK BEGINS, SO ENJOY YOUR LAST MEAL--HA HA HA! THAT'S A JOKE, CAMPERS... TUCK IN!
IS THIS FOOD A JOKE, TOO? I MEAN, WHAT KIND OF WEIGHT-LOSS CAMP SERVES HAMBURGERS?
MAYBE THEY'RE FATTENING US UP FOR THE KILL!
WELL, THEN I SAY BRING ON THE SLAUGHTER, DAVID.
COUNT ME OUT. I'M HERE TO LOSE WEIGHT, NOT GORGE ONE LAST TIME.
GOOD NIGHT, DELIA. SEE YOU BRIGHT AND EARLY.
GOOD NIGHT! CAREFUL ON YOUR WAY BACK TO THE CABIN.

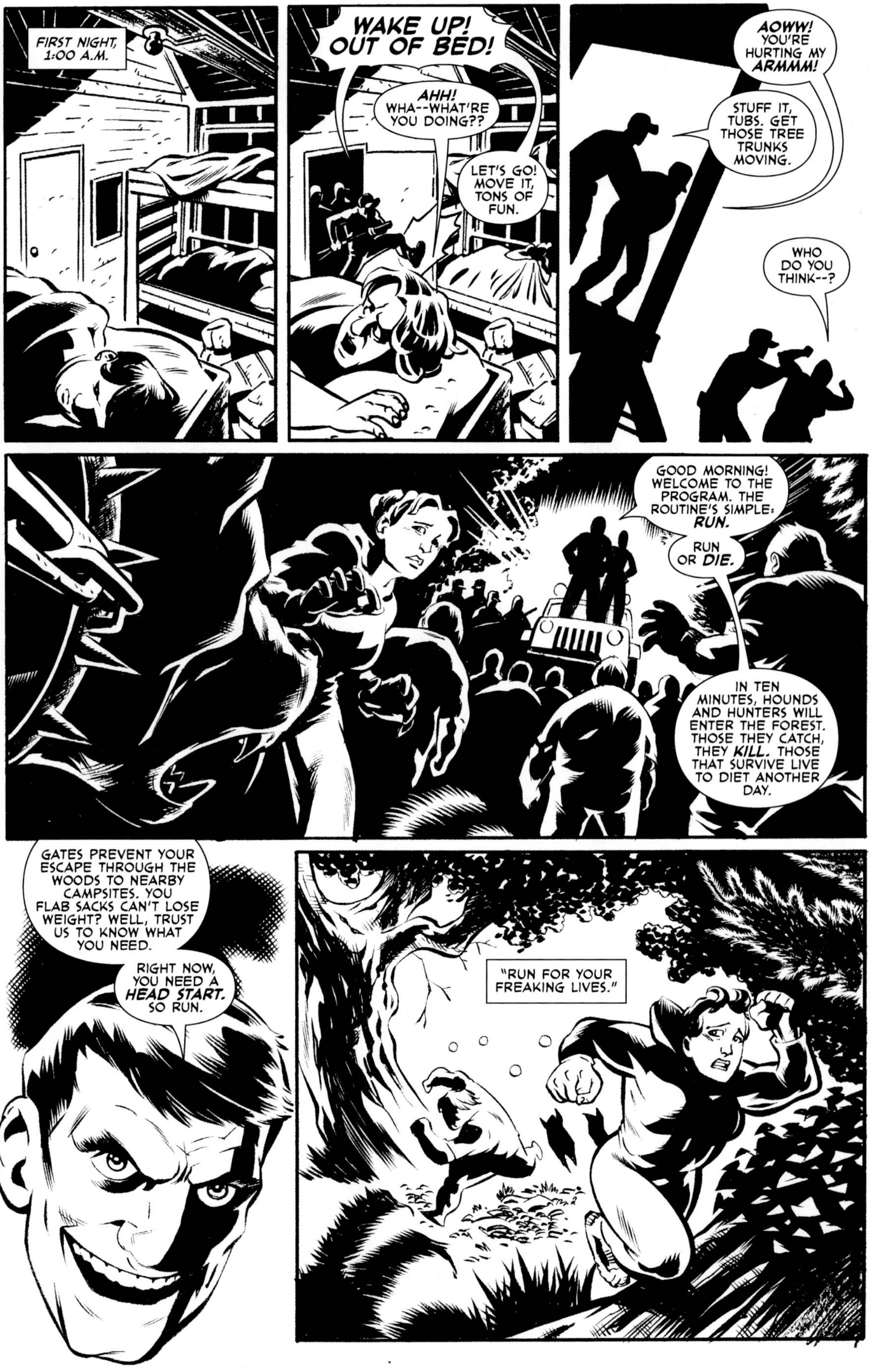
FIRST NIGHT, 1:00 A.M.
WAKE UP! OUT OF BED!
AHH! WHA--WHAT'RE YOU DOING??
LET'S GO! MOVE IT, TONS OF FUN.
AOWW! YOU'RE HURTING MY ARMMM!
STUFF IT, TUBS. GET THOSE TREE TRUNKS MOVING.
WHO DO YOU THINK--?
GOOD MORNING! WELCOME TO THE PROGRAM. THE ROUTINE'S SIMPLE: RUN.
RUN OR DIE.
IN TEN MINUTES, HOUNDS AND HUNTERS WILL ENTER THE FOREST. THOSE THEY CATCH, THEY KILL. THOSE THAT SURVIVE LIVE TO DIET ANOTHER DAY.
GATES PREVENT YOUR ESCAPE THROUGH THE WOODS TO NEARBY CAMPSITES. YOU FLAB SACKS CAN'T LOSE WEIGHT? WELL, TRUST US TO KNOW WHAT YOU NEED.
RIGHT NOW, YOU NEED A HEAD START. SO RUN.
"RUN FOR YOUR FREAKING LIVES."

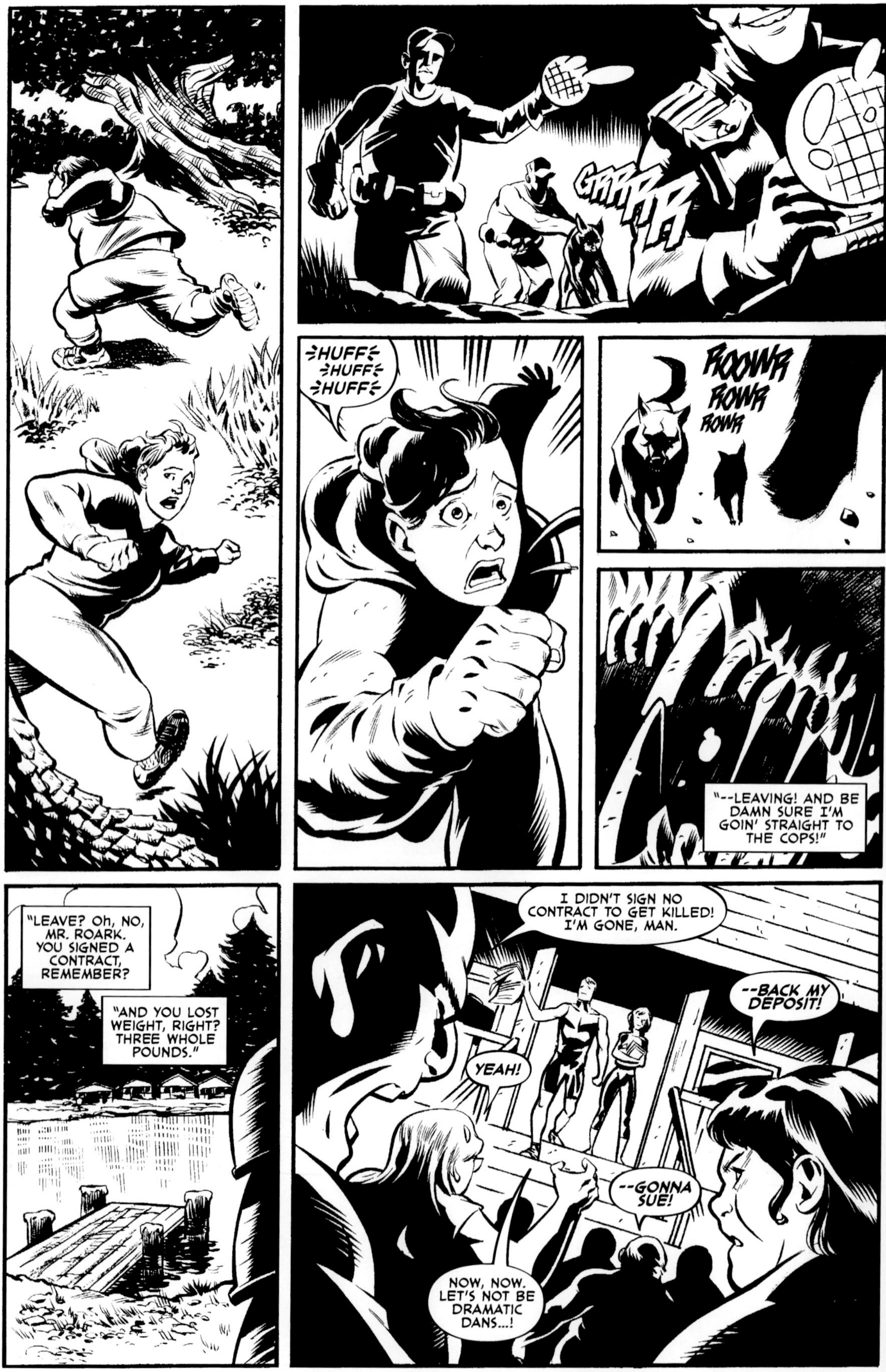
GRRRR
-HUFF- -HUFF- -HUFF-
ROOWR ROWR ROWR
"--LEAVING! AND BE DAMN SURE I'M GOIN' STRAIGHT TO THE COPS!"
"LEAVE? Oh, NO, MR. ROARK. YOU SIGNED A CONTRACT, REMEMBER?
"AND YOU LOST WEIGHT, RIGHT? THREE WHOLE POUNDS."
I DIDN'T SIGN NO CONTRACT TO GET KILLED! I'M GONE, MAN.
--BACK MY DEPOSIT!
YEAH!
--GONNA SUE!
NOW, NOW. LET'S NOT BE DRAMATIC DANS...!

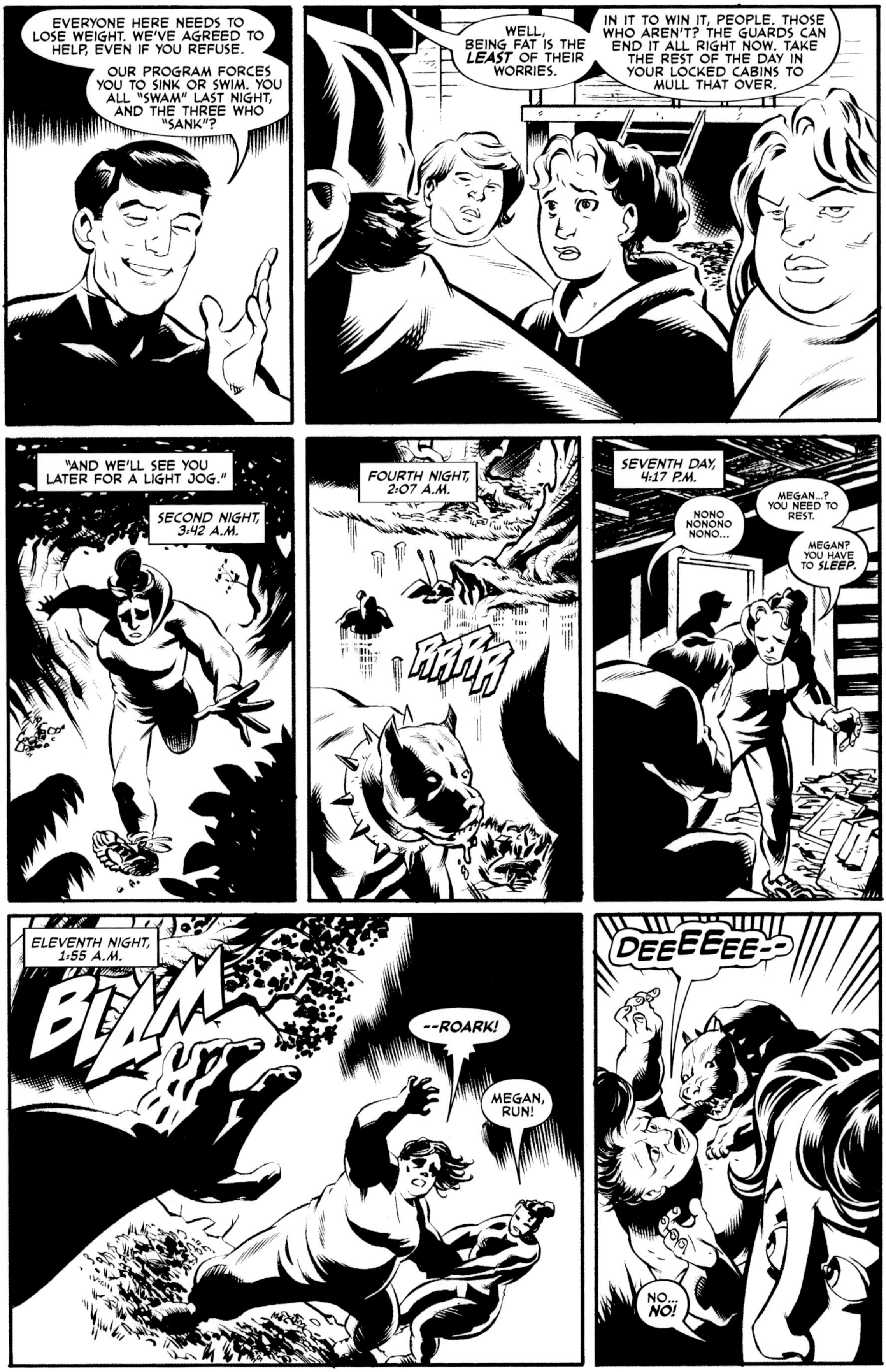
EVERYONE HERE NEEDS TO LOSE WEIGHT. WE'VE AGREED TO HELP, EVEN IF YOU REFUSE.
OUR PROGRAM FORCES YOU TO SINK OR SWIM. YOU ALL "SWAM" LAST NIGHT, AND THE THREE WHO "SANK"?
WELL, BEING FAT IS THE LEAST OF THEIR WORRIES.
IN IT TO WIN IT, PEOPLE. THOSE WHO AREN'T? THE GUARDS CAN END IT ALL RIGHT NOW. TAKE THE REST OF THE DAY IN YOUR LOCKED CABINS TO MULL THAT OVER.
"AND WE'LL SEE YOU LATER FOR A LIGHT JOG."
SECOND NIGHT, 3:42 A.M.
FOURTH NIGHT, 2:07 A.M.
RRRR
SEVENTH DAY, 4:17 P.M.
NONO NONONO NONO...
MEGAN...? YOU NEED TO REST.
MEGAN? YOU HAVE TO SLEEP.
ELEVENTH NIGHT, 1:55 A.M.
BLAM
--ROARK!
MEGAN, RUN!
DEEEEEEE--
NO... NO!

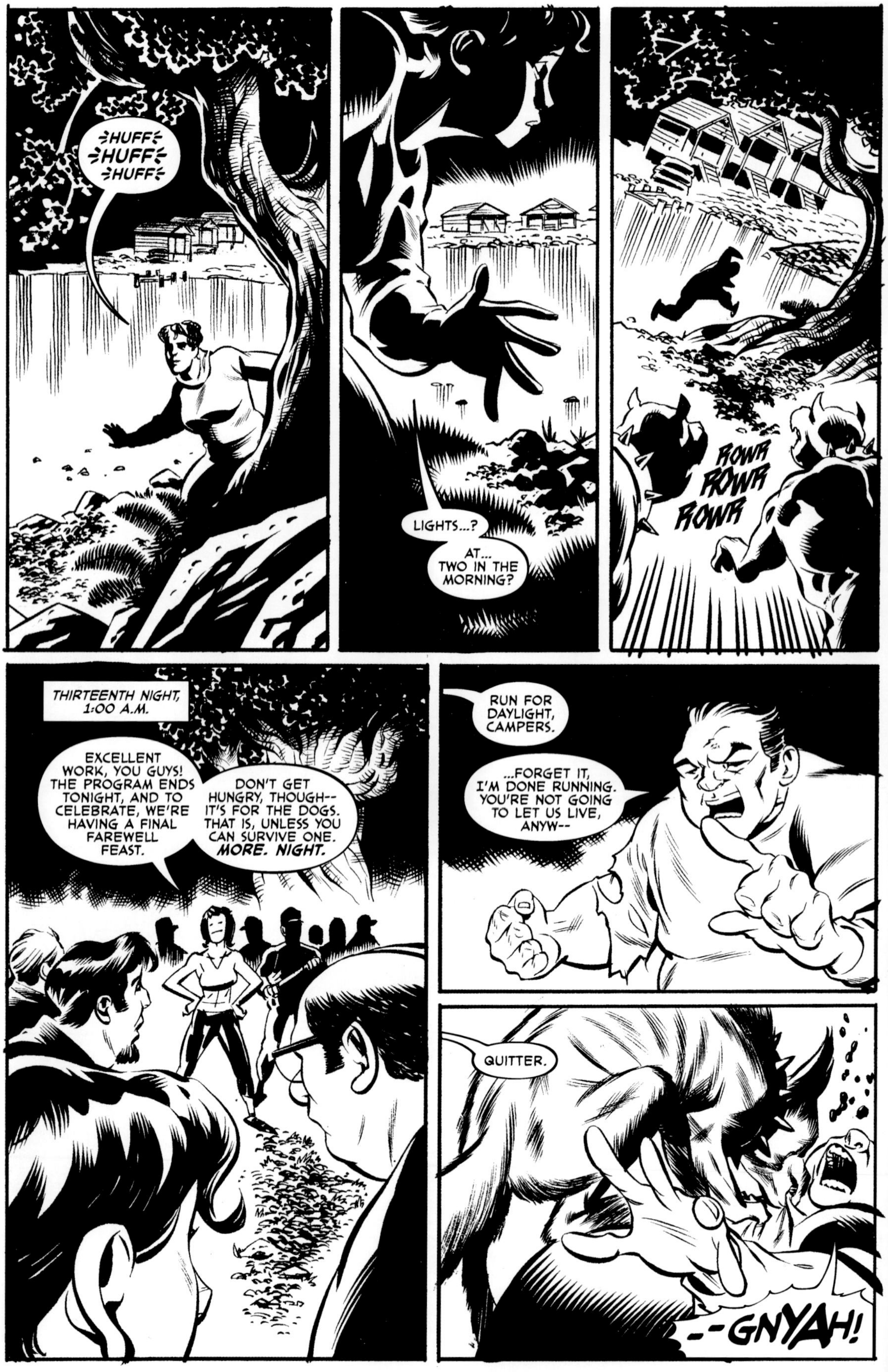
HUFF
HUFF
HUFF
LIGHTS...?
AT... TWO IN THE MORNING?
ROWR ROWR ROWR
THIRTEENTH NIGHT, 1:00 A.M.
EXCELLENT WORK, YOU GUYS! THE PROGRAM ENDS TONIGHT, AND TO CELEBRATE, WE'RE HAVING A FINAL FAREWELL FEAST.
DON'T GET HUNGRY, THOUGH-- IT'S FOR THE DOGS. THAT IS, UNLESS YOU CAN SURVIVE ONE. MORE. NIGHT.
RUN FOR DAYLIGHT, CAMPERS.
...FORGET IT, I'M DONE RUNNING. YOU'RE NOT GOING TO LET US LIVE, ANYW--
QUITTER.
--GNYAH!

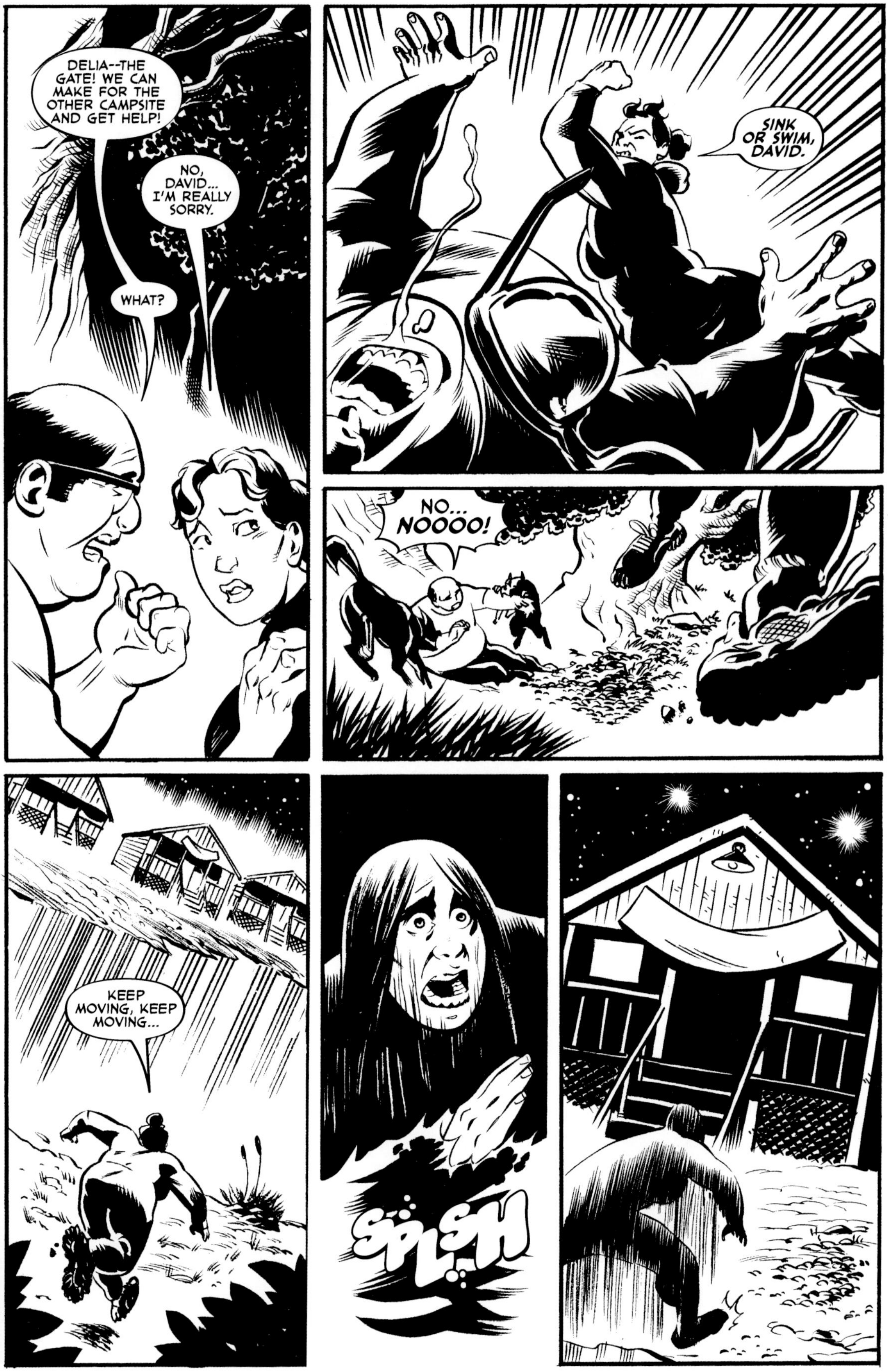
DELIA--THE GATE! WE CAN MAKE FOR THE OTHER CAMPSITE AND GET HELP!
NO, DAVID... I'M REALLY SORRY.
WHAT?
SINK OR SWIM, DAVID.
NO... NOOOO!
KEEP MOVING, KEEP MOVING...
SPLSH

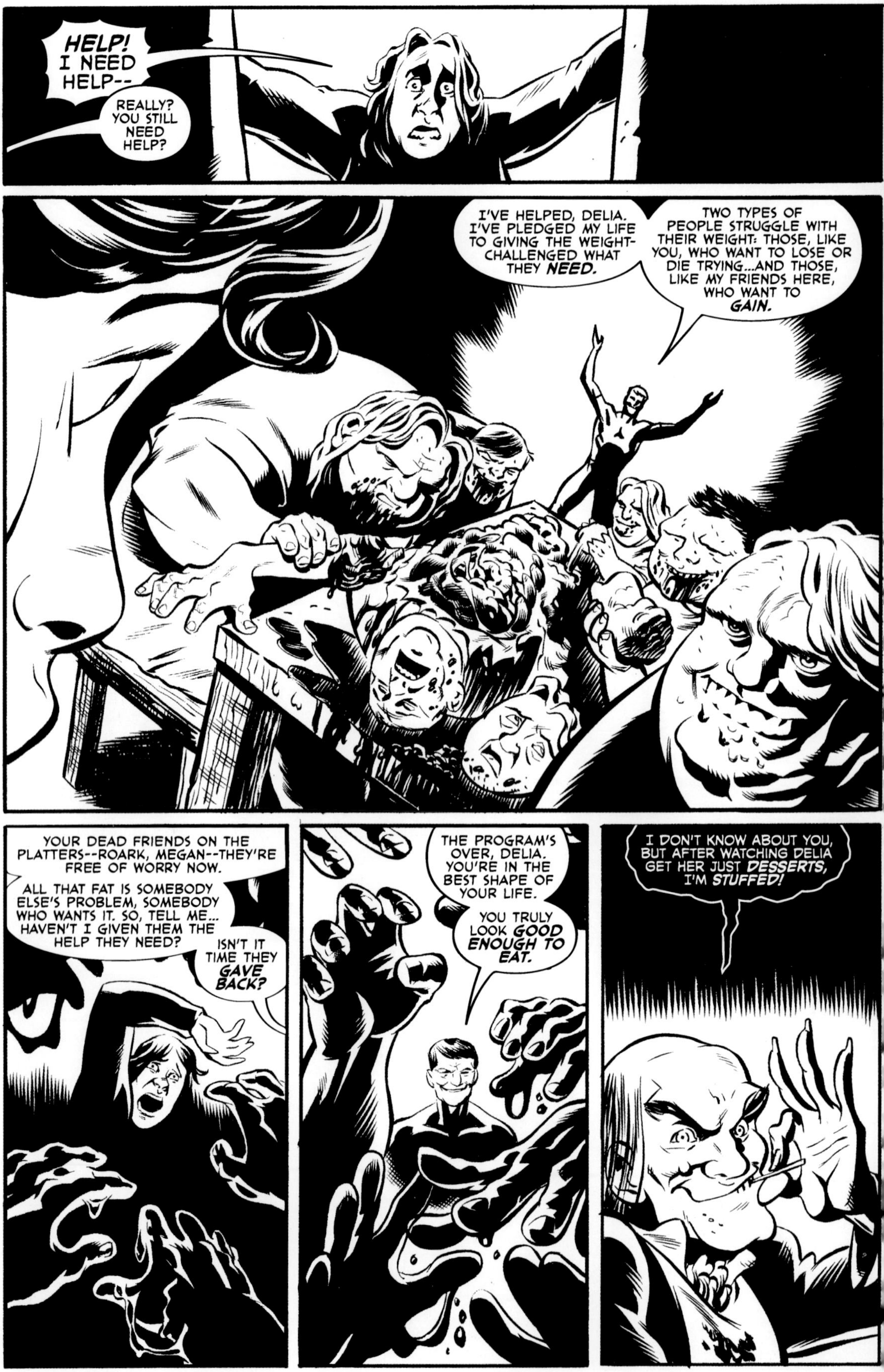
HELP! I NEED HELP--
REALLY? YOU STILL NEED HELP?
I'VE HELPED, DELIA. I'VE PLEDGED MY LIFE TO GIVING THE WEIGHT-CHALLENGED WHAT THEY NEED.
TWO TYPES OF PEOPLE STRUGGLE WITH THEIR WEIGHT: THOSE, LIKE YOU, WHO WANT TO LOSE OR DIE TRYING...AND THOSE, LIKE MY FRIENDS HERE, WHO WANT TO GAIN.
YOUR DEAD FRIENDS ON THE PLATTERS--ROARK, MEGAN--THEY'RE FREE OF WORRY NOW.
ALL THAT FAT IS SOMEBODY ELSE'S PROBLEM, SOMEBODY WHO WANTS IT. SO, TELL ME... HAVEN'T I GIVEN THEM THE HELP THEY NEED?
ISN'T IT TIME THEY GAVE BACK?
THE PROGRAM'S OVER, DELIA. YOU'RE IN THE BEST SHAPE OF YOUR LIFE.
YOU TRULY LOOK GOOD ENOUGH TO EAT.
I DON'T KNOW ABOUT YOU, BUT AFTER WATCHING DELIA GET HER JUST DESSERTS, I'M STUFFED!

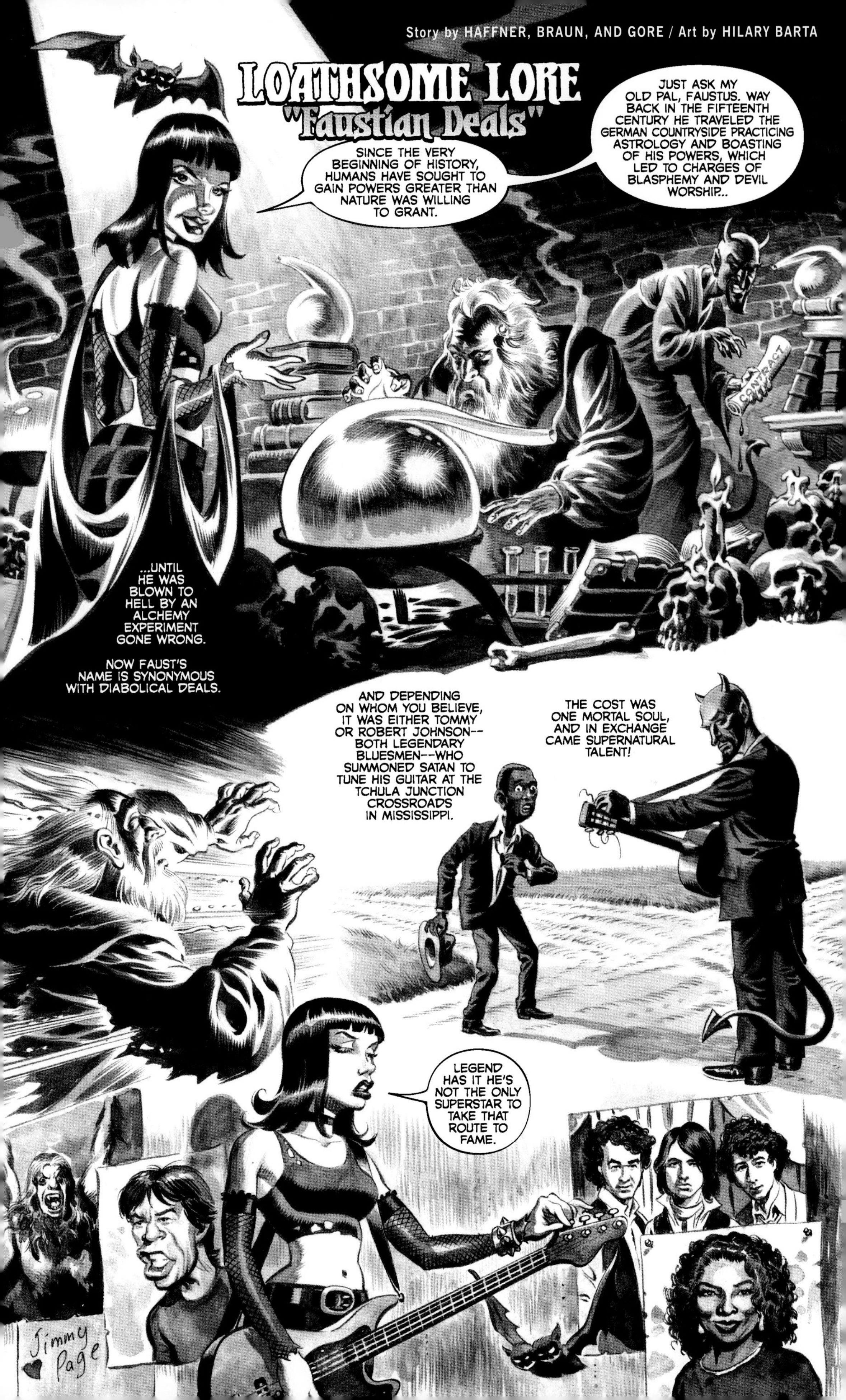
Story by HAFFNER, BRAUN, AND GORE / Art by HILARY BARTA
LOATHSOME LORE
"Faustian Deals"
SINCE THE VERY BEGINNING OF HISTORY, HUMANS HAVE SOUGHT TO GAIN POWERS GREATER THAN NATURE WAS WILLING TO GRANT.
JUST ASK MY OLD PAL, FAUSTUS. WAY BACK IN THE FIFTEENTH CENTURY HE TRAVELED THE GERMAN COUNTRYSIDE PRACTICING ASTROLOGY AND BOASTING OF HIS POWERS, WHICH LED TO CHARGES OF BLASPHEMY AND DEVIL WORSHIP...
CONTRACT
...UNTIL HE WAS BLOWN TO HELL BY AN ALCHEMY EXPERIMENT GONE WRONG.
NOW FAUST'S NAME IS SYNONYMOUS WITH DIABOLICAL DEALS.
AND DEPENDING ON WHOM YOU BELIEVE, IT WAS EITHER TOMMY OR ROBERT JOHNSON--BOTH LEGENDARY BLUESMEN--WHO SUMMONED SATAN TO TUNE HIS GUITAR AT THE TCHULA JUNCTION CROSSROADS IN MISSISSIPPI.
THE COST WAS ONE MORTAL SOUL, AND IN EXCHANGE CAME SUPERNATURAL TALENT!
LEGEND HAS IT HE'S NOT THE ONLY SUPERSTAR TO TAKE THAT ROUTE TO FAME.
Jimmy Page

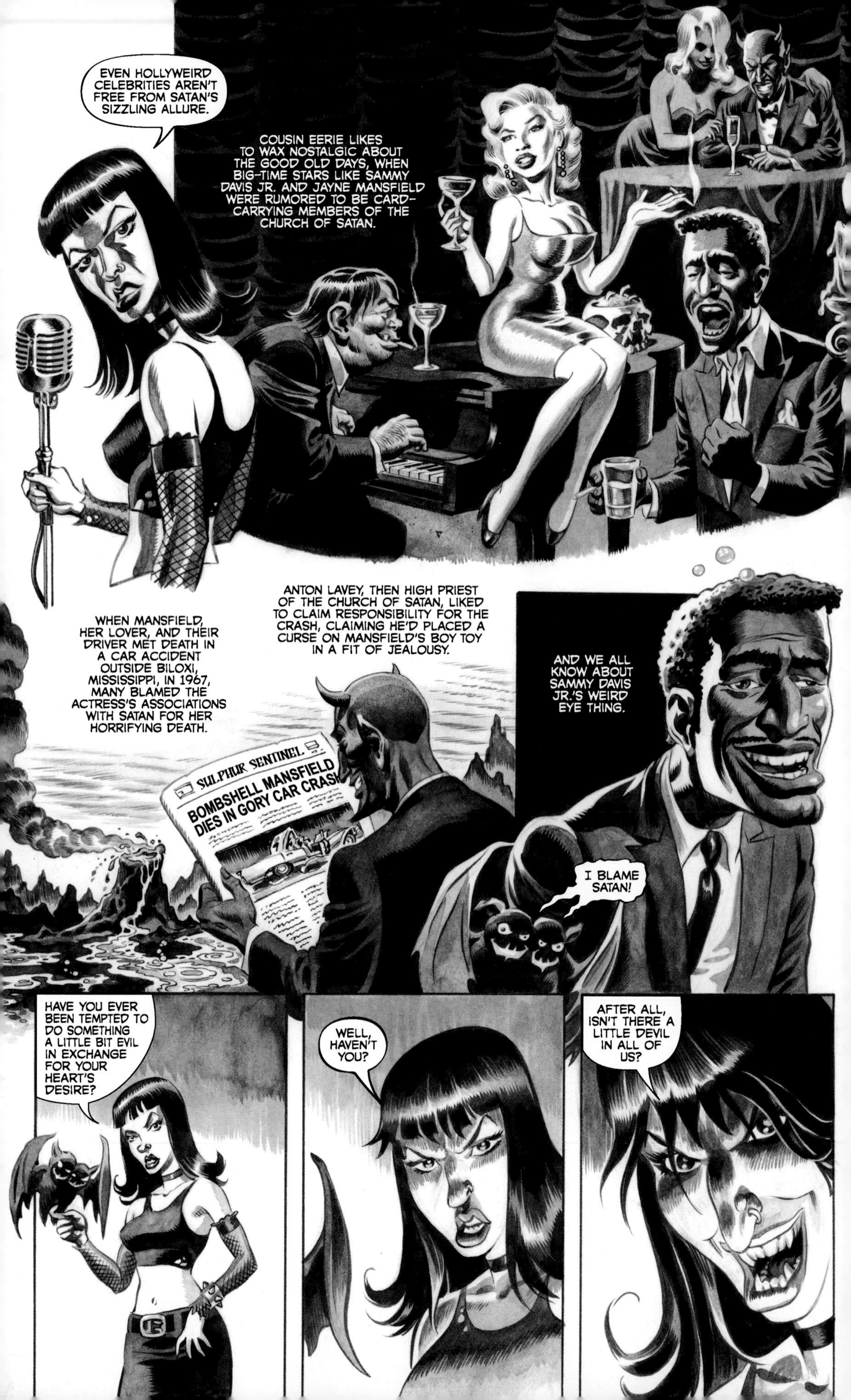
EVEN HOLLYWEIRD CELEBRITIES AREN'T FREE FROM SATAN'S SIZZLING ALLURE.
COUSIN EERIE LIKES TO WAX NOSTALGIC ABOUT THE GOOD OLD DAYS, WHEN BIG-TIME STARS LIKE SAMMY DAVIS JR. AND JAYNE MANSFIELD WERE RUMORED TO BE CARD-CARRYING MEMBERS OF THE CHURCH OF SATAN.
WHEN MANSFIELD, HER LOVER, AND THEIR DRIVER MET DEATH IN A CAR ACCIDENT OUTSIDE BILOXI, MISSISSIPPI, IN 1967, MANY BLAMED THE ACTRESS'S ASSOCIATIONS WITH SATAN FOR HER HORRIFYING DEATH.
ANTON LAVEY, THEN HIGH PRIEST OF THE CHURCH OF SATAN, LIKED TO CLAIM RESPONSIBILITY FOR THE CRASH, CLAIMING HE'D PLACED A CURSE ON MANSFIELD'S BOY TOY IN A FIT OF JEALOUSY.
SULPHUR SENTINEL
BOMBSHELL MANSFIELD DIES IN GORY CAR CRASH
AND WE ALL KNOW ABOUT SAMMY DAVIS JR.'S WEIRD EYE THING.
I BLAME SATAN!
HAVE YOU EVER BEEN TEMPTED TO DO SOMETHING A LITTLE BIT EVIL IN EXCHANGE FOR YOUR HEART'S DESIRE?
WELL, HAVEN'T YOU?
AFTER ALL, ISN'T THERE A LITTLE DEVIL IN ALL OF US?

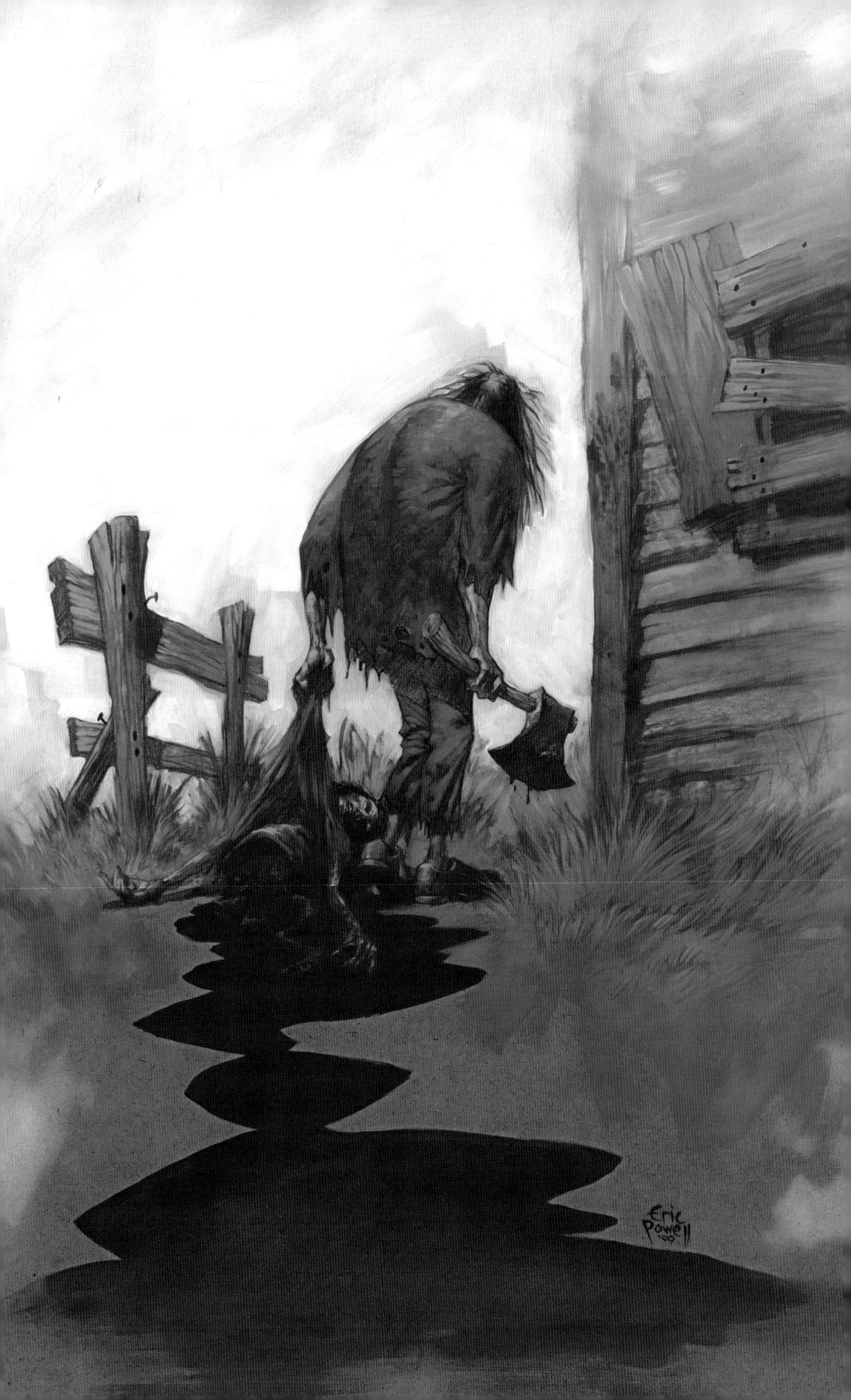
Eric Powell '09

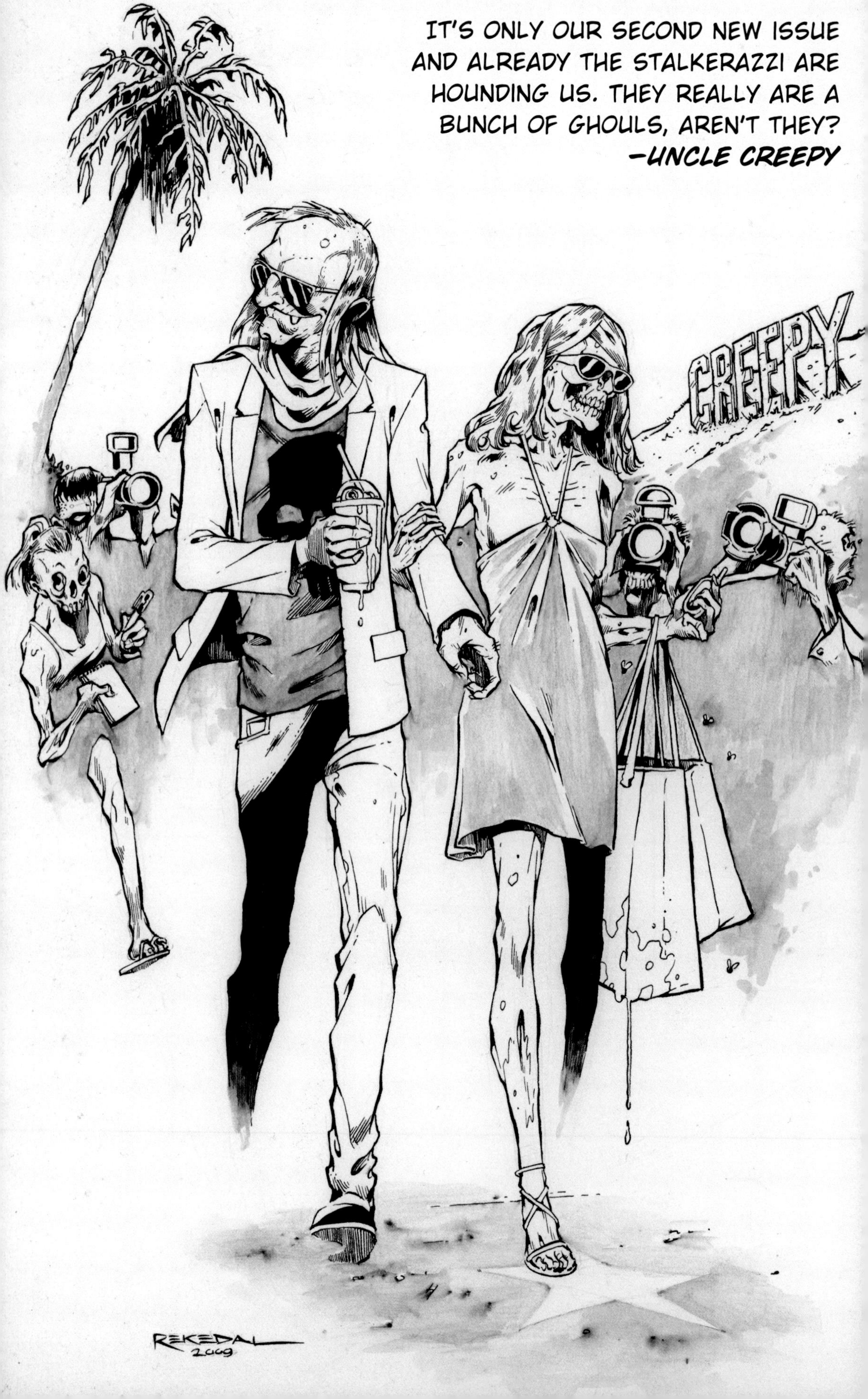
IT'S ONLY OUR SECOND NEW ISSUE AND ALREADY THE STALKERAZZI ARE HOUNDING US. THEY REALLY ARE A BUNCH OF GHOULS, AREN'T THEY?
—UNCLE CREEPY
CREEPY
REKEDAL 2009

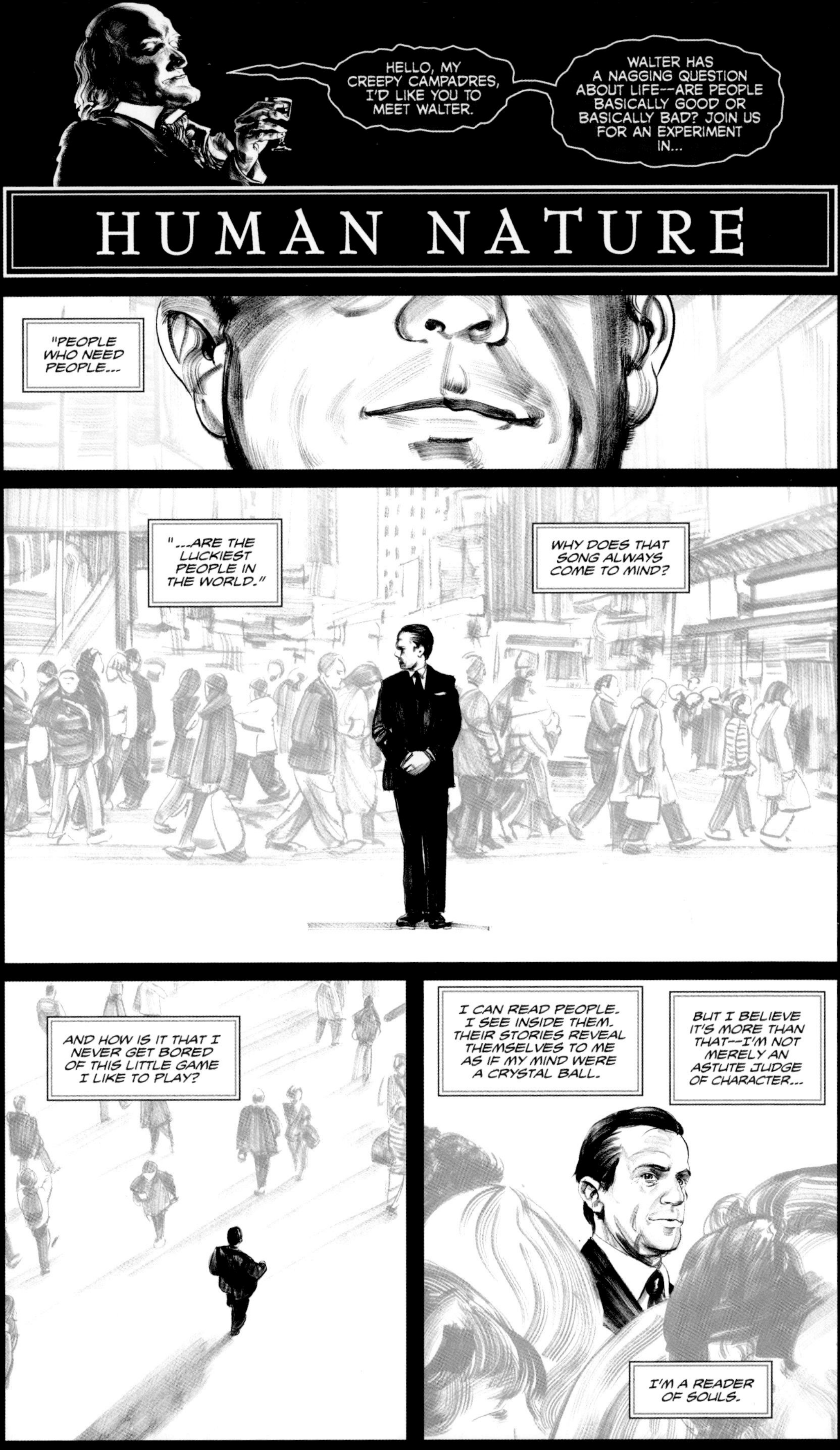
HELLO, MY CREEPY CAMPADRES, I'D LIKE YOU TO MEET WALTER.
WALTER HAS A NAGGING QUESTION ABOUT LIFE--ARE PEOPLE BASICALLY GOOD OR BASICALLY BAD? JOIN US FOR AN EXPERIMENT IN...
HUMAN NATURE
"PEOPLE WHO NEED PEOPLE...
"...ARE THE LUCKIEST PEOPLE IN THE WORLD."
WHY DOES THAT SONG ALWAYS COME TO MIND?
AND HOW IS IT THAT I NEVER GET BORED OF THIS LITTLE GAME I LIKE TO PLAY?
I CAN READ PEOPLE. I SEE INSIDE THEM. THEIR STORIES REVEAL THEMSELVES TO ME AS IF MY MIND WERE A CRYSTAL BALL.
BUT I BELIEVE IT'S MORE THAN THAT--I'M NOT MERELY AN ASTUTE JUDGE OF CHARACTER...
I'M A READER OF SOULS.

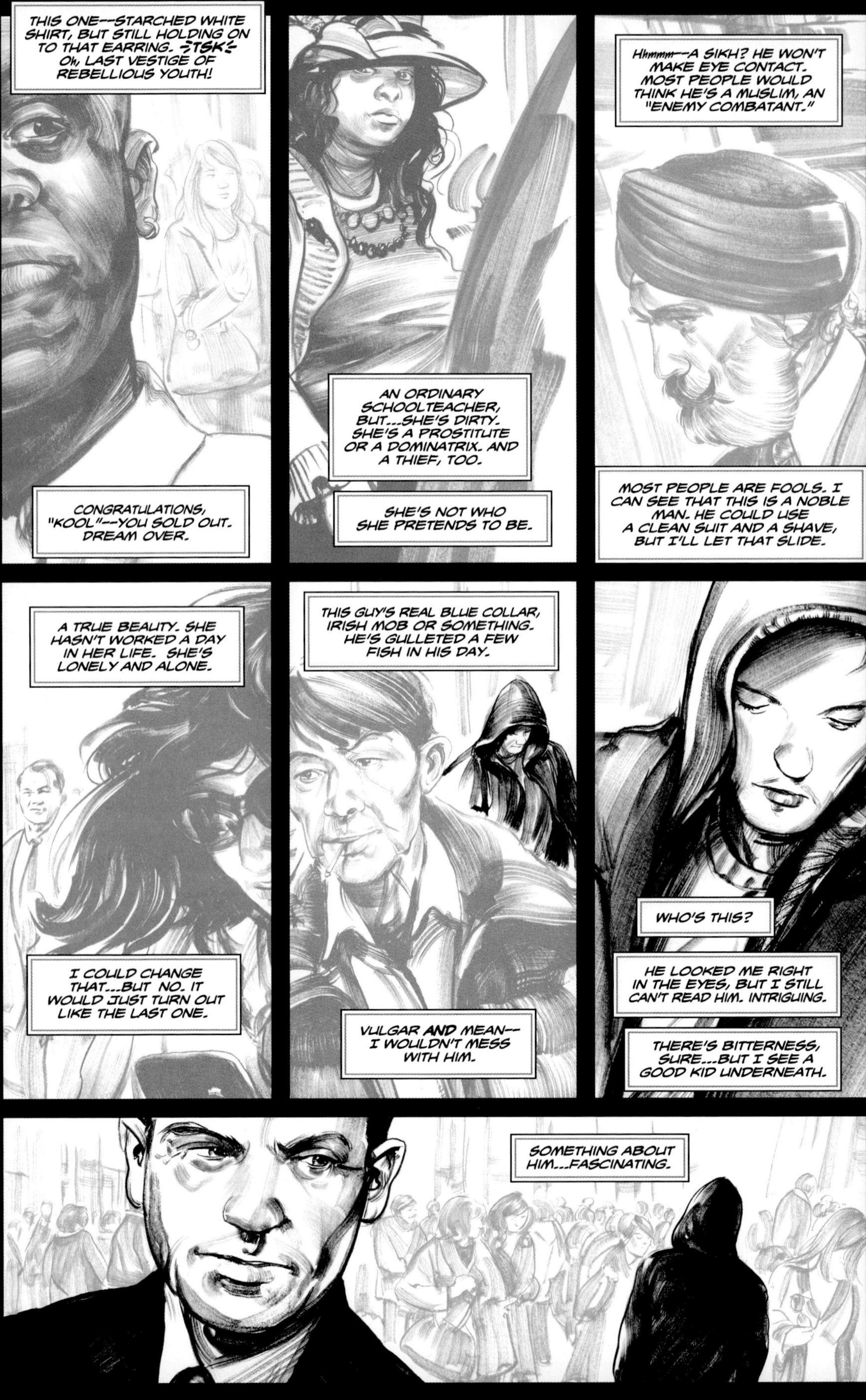
THIS ONE--STARCHED WHITE SHIRT, BUT STILL HOLDING ON TO THAT EARRING. -TSK- Oh, LAST VESTIGE OF REBELLIOUS YOUTH!
CONGRATULATIONS, "KOOL"--YOU SOLD OUT. DREAM OVER.
AN ORDINARY SCHOOLTEACHER, BUT...SHE'S DIRTY. SHE'S A PROSTITUTE OR A DOMINATRIX. AND A THIEF, TOO.
SHE'S NOT WHO SHE PRETENDS TO BE.
Hhmmm--A SIKH? HE WON'T MAKE EYE CONTACT. MOST PEOPLE WOULD THINK HE'S A MUSLIM, AN "ENEMY COMBATANT."
MOST PEOPLE ARE FOOLS. I CAN SEE THAT THIS IS A NOBLE MAN. HE COULD USE A CLEAN SUIT AND A SHAVE, BUT I'LL LET THAT SLIDE.
A TRUE BEAUTY. SHE HASN'T WORKED A DAY IN HER LIFE. SHE'S LONELY AND ALONE.
I COULD CHANGE THAT...BUT NO. IT WOULD JUST TURN OUT LIKE THE LAST ONE.
THIS GUY'S REAL BLUE COLLAR, IRISH MOB OR SOMETHING. HE'S GULLETED A FEW FISH IN HIS DAY.
VULGAR AND MEAN--I WOULDN'T MESS WITH HIM.
WHO'S THIS?
HE LOOKED ME RIGHT IN THE EYES, BUT I STILL CAN'T READ HIM. INTRIGUING.
THERE'S BITTERNESS, SURE...BUT I SEE A GOOD KID UNDERNEATH.
SOMETHING ABOUT HIM...FASCINATING.

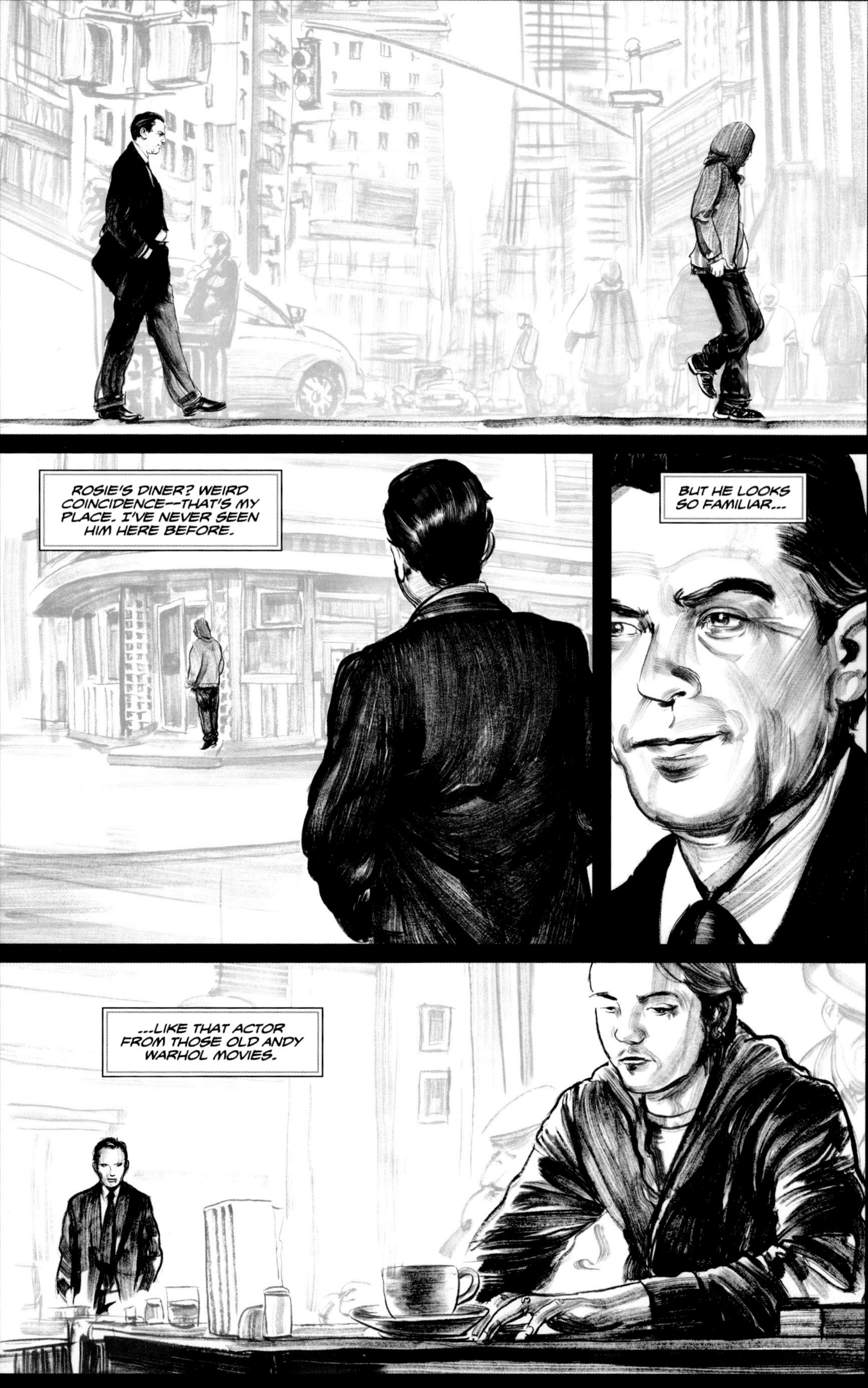
ROSIE'S DINER? WEIRD COINCIDENCE--THAT'S MY PLACE. I'VE NEVER SEEN HIM HERE BEFORE.
BUT HE LOOKS SO FAMILIAR...
...LIKE THAT ACTOR FROM THOSE OLD ANDY WARHOL MOVIES.

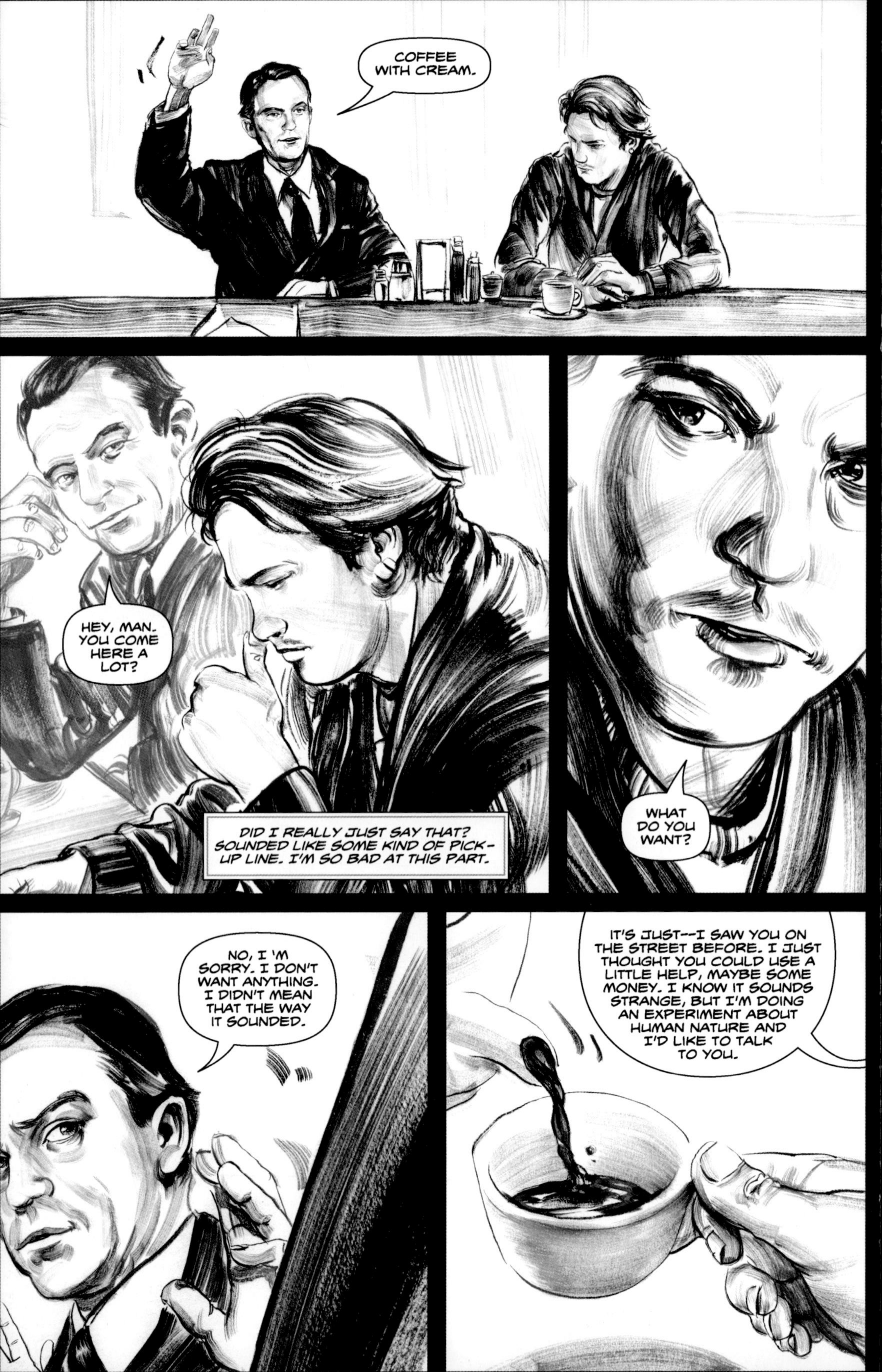
COFFEE WITH CREAM.
HEY, MAN. YOU COME HERE A LOT?
DID I REALLY JUST SAY THAT? SOUNDED LIKE SOME KIND OF PICK-UP LINE. I'M SO BAD AT THIS PART.
WHAT DO YOU WANT?
NO, I'M SORRY. I DON'T WANT ANYTHING. I DIDN'T MEAN THAT THE WAY IT SOUNDED.
IT'S JUST--I SAW YOU ON THE STREET BEFORE. I JUST THOUGHT YOU COULD USE A LITTLE HELP, MAYBE SOME MONEY. I KNOW IT SOUNDS STRANGE, BUT I'M DOING AN EXPERIMENT ABOUT HUMAN NATURE AND I'D LIKE TO TALK TO YOU.

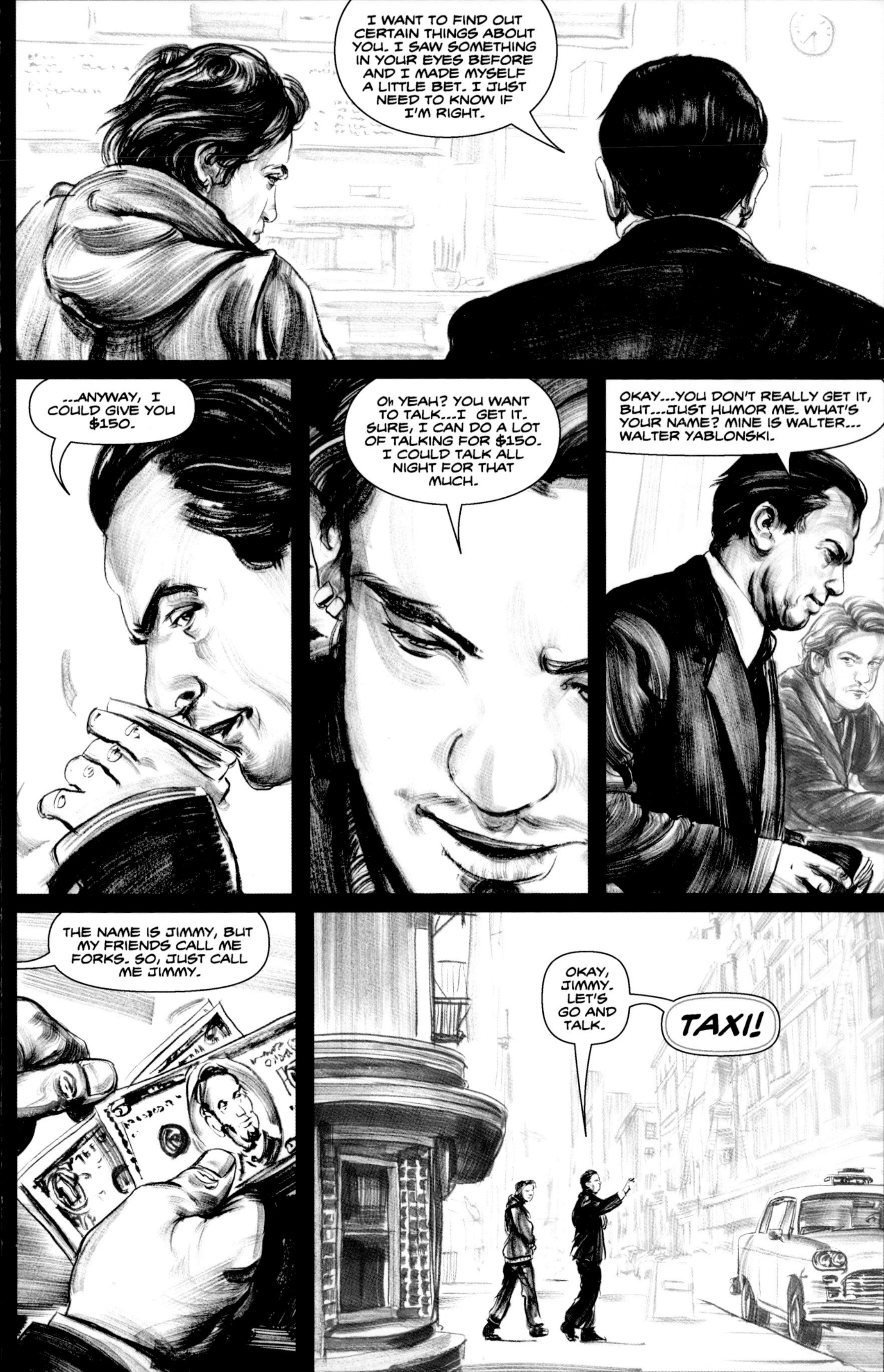
I WANT TO FIND OUT CERTAIN THINGS ABOUT YOU. I SAW SOMETHING IN YOUR EYES BEFORE AND I MADE MYSELF A LITTLE BET. I JUST NEED TO KNOW IF I'M RIGHT.
...ANYWAY, I COULD GIVE YOU $150.
Oh YEAH? YOU WANT TO TALK...I GET IT. SURE, I CAN DO A LOT OF TALKING FOR $150. I COULD TALK ALL NIGHT FOR THAT MUCH.
OKAY...YOU DON'T REALLY GET IT, BUT...JUST HUMOR ME. WHAT'S YOUR NAME? MINE IS WALTER... WALTER YABLONSKI.
THE NAME IS JIMMY, BUT MY FRIENDS CALL ME FORKS. SO, JUST CALL ME JIMMY.
OKAY, JIMMY. LET'S GO AND TALK.
TAXI!

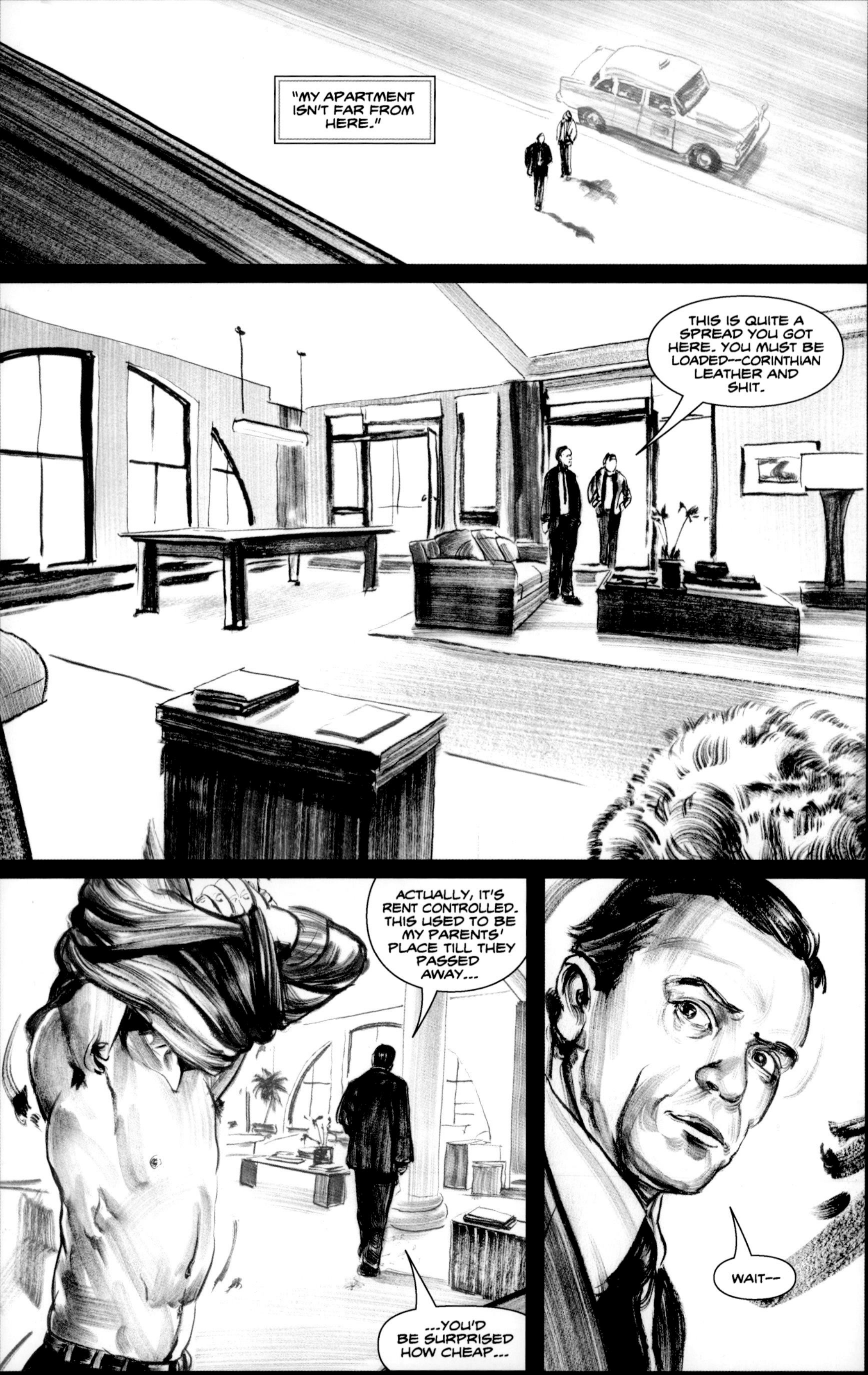
"MY APARTMENT ISN'T FAR FROM HERE."
THIS IS QUITE A SPREAD YOU GOT HERE. YOU MUST BE LOADED--CORINTHIAN LEATHER AND SHIT.
ACTUALLY, IT'S RENT CONTROLLED. THIS USED TO BE MY PARENTS' PLACE TILL THEY PASSED AWAY...
...YOU'D BE SURPRISED HOW CHEAP...
WAIT--

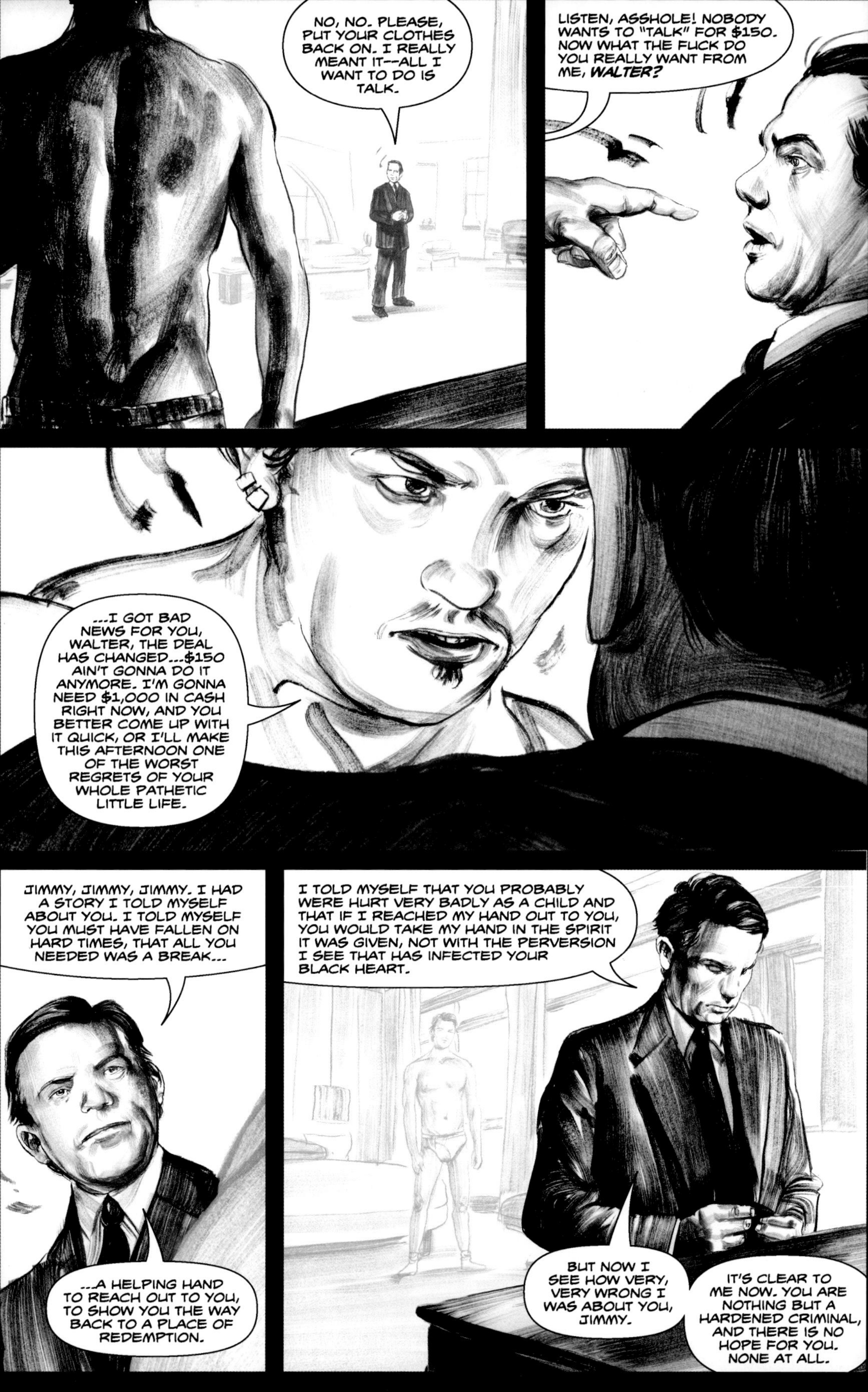
NO, NO. PLEASE, PUT YOUR CLOTHES BACK ON. I REALLY MEANT IT--ALL I WANT TO DO IS TALK.
LISTEN, ASSHOLE! NOBODY WANTS TO "TALK" FOR $150. NOW WHAT THE FUCK DO YOU REALLY WANT FROM ME, WALTER?
...I GOT BAD NEWS FOR YOU, WALTER, THE DEAL HAS CHANGED...$150 AIN'T GONNA DO IT ANYMORE. I'M GONNA NEED $1,000 IN CASH RIGHT NOW, AND YOU BETTER COME UP WITH IT QUICK, OR I'LL MAKE THIS AFTERNOON ONE OF THE WORST REGRETS OF YOUR WHOLE PATHETIC LITTLE LIFE.
JIMMY, JIMMY, JIMMY. I HAD A STORY I TOLD MYSELF ABOUT YOU. I TOLD MYSELF YOU MUST HAVE FALLEN ON HARD TIMES, THAT ALL YOU NEEDED WAS A BREAK...
...A HELPING HAND TO REACH OUT TO YOU, TO SHOW YOU THE WAY BACK TO A PLACE OF REDEMPTION.
I TOLD MYSELF THAT YOU PROBABLY WERE HURT VERY BADLY AS A CHILD AND THAT IF I REACHED MY HAND OUT TO YOU, YOU WOULD TAKE MY HAND IN THE SPIRIT IT WAS GIVEN, NOT WITH THE PERVERSION I SEE THAT HAS INFECTED YOUR BLACK HEART.
BUT NOW I SEE HOW VERY, VERY WRONG I WAS ABOUT YOU, JIMMY.
IT'S CLEAR TO ME NOW. YOU ARE NOTHING BUT A HARDENED CRIMINAL, AND THERE IS NO HOPE FOR YOU. NONE AT ALL.

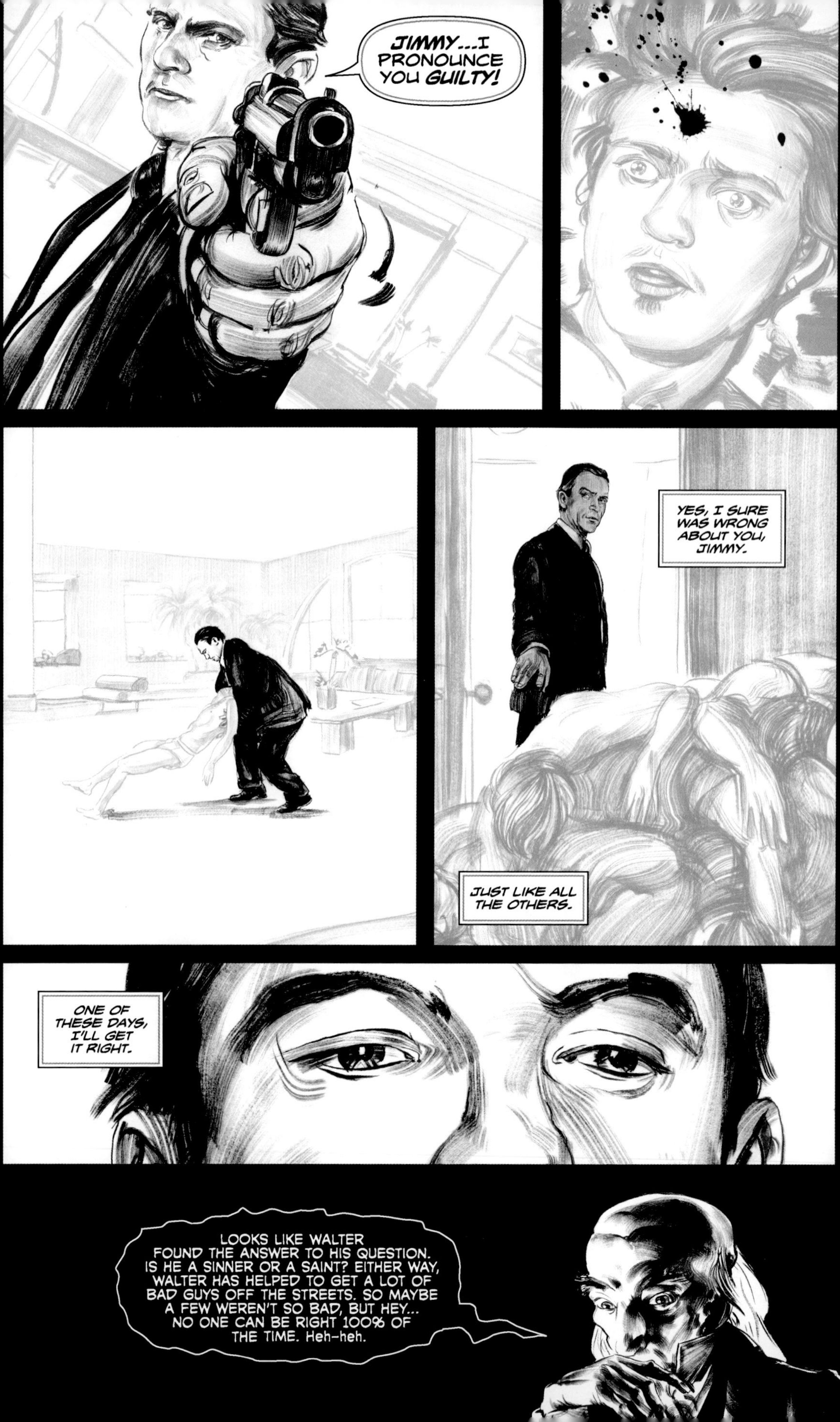

JIMMY...I PRONOUNCE YOU GUILTY!
YES, I SURE WAS WRONG ABOUT YOU, JIMMY.
JUST LIKE ALL THE OTHERS.
ONE OF THESE DAYS, I'LL GET IT RIGHT.
LOOKS LIKE WALTER FOUND THE ANSWER TO HIS QUESTION. IS HE A SINNER OR A SAINT? EITHER WAY, WALTER HAS HELPED TO GET A LOT OF BAD GUYS OFF THE STREETS. SO MAYBE A FEW WEREN'T SO BAD, BUT HEY... NO ONE CAN BE RIGHT 100% OF THE TIME. Heh-heh.

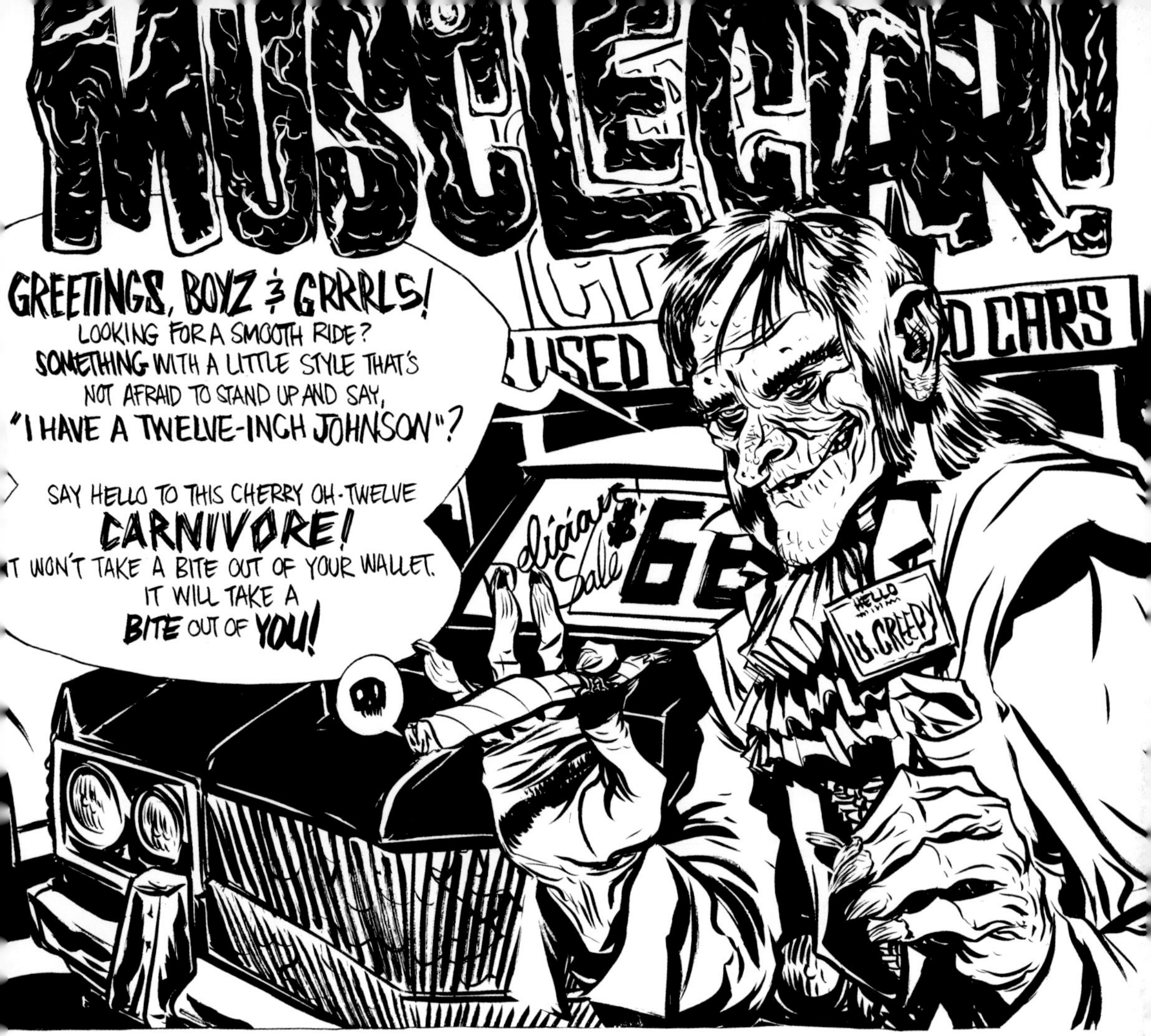
MUSCLECAR!
GREETINGS, BOYZ & GRRRLS! LOOKING FOR A SMOOTH RIDE? SOMETHING WITH A LITTLE STYLE THAT'S NOT AFRAID TO STAND UP AND SAY, "I HAVE A TWELVE-INCH JOHNSON"?
SAY HELLO TO THIS CHERRY OH-TWELVE CARNIVORE! IT WON'T TAKE A BITE OUT OF YOUR WALLET. IT WILL TAKE A BITE OUT OF YOU!
USED
D CARS
Sale
$66
HELLO
U. CREEPY

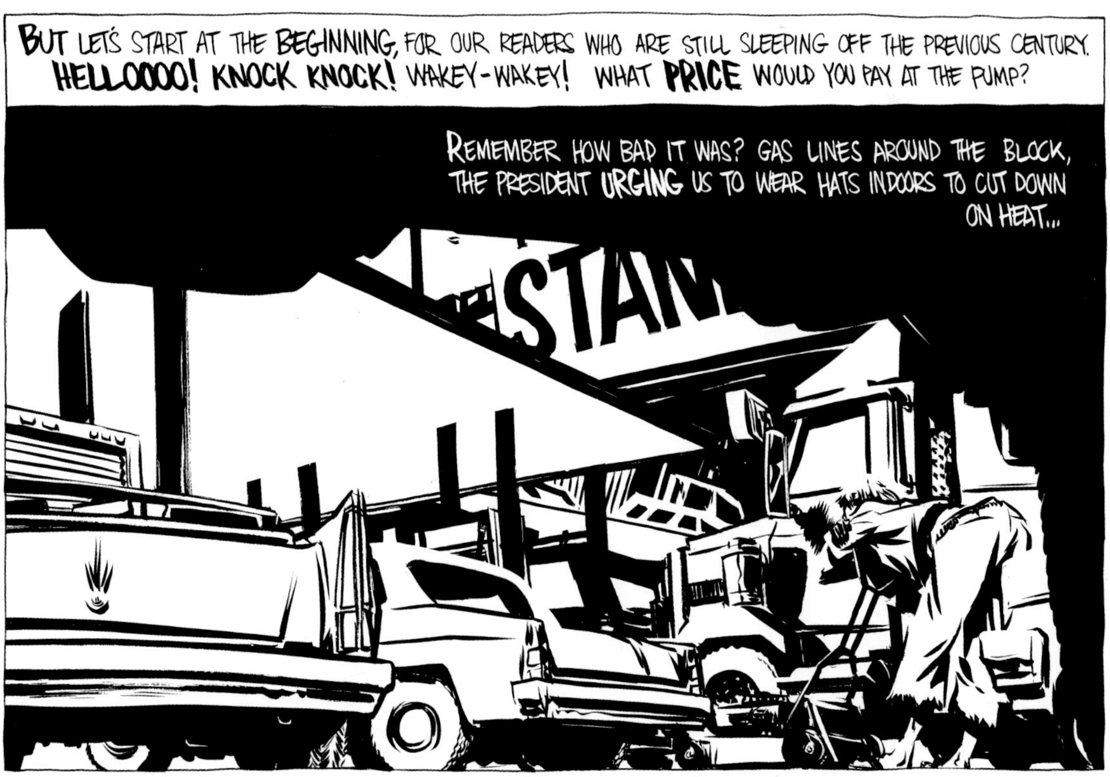
BUT LET'S START AT THE BEGINNING, FOR OUR READERS WHO ARE STILL SLEEPING OFF THE PREVIOUS CENTURY. HELLOOOO! KNOCK KNOCK! WAKEY-WAKEY! WHAT PRICE WOULD YOU PAY AT THE PUMP?
REMEMBER HOW BAD IT WAS? GAS LINES AROUND THE BLOCK, THE PRESIDENT URGING US TO WEAR HATS INDOORS TO CUT DOWN ON HEAT...
STAN

Story by MIKE BARON / Art by NATHAN FOX

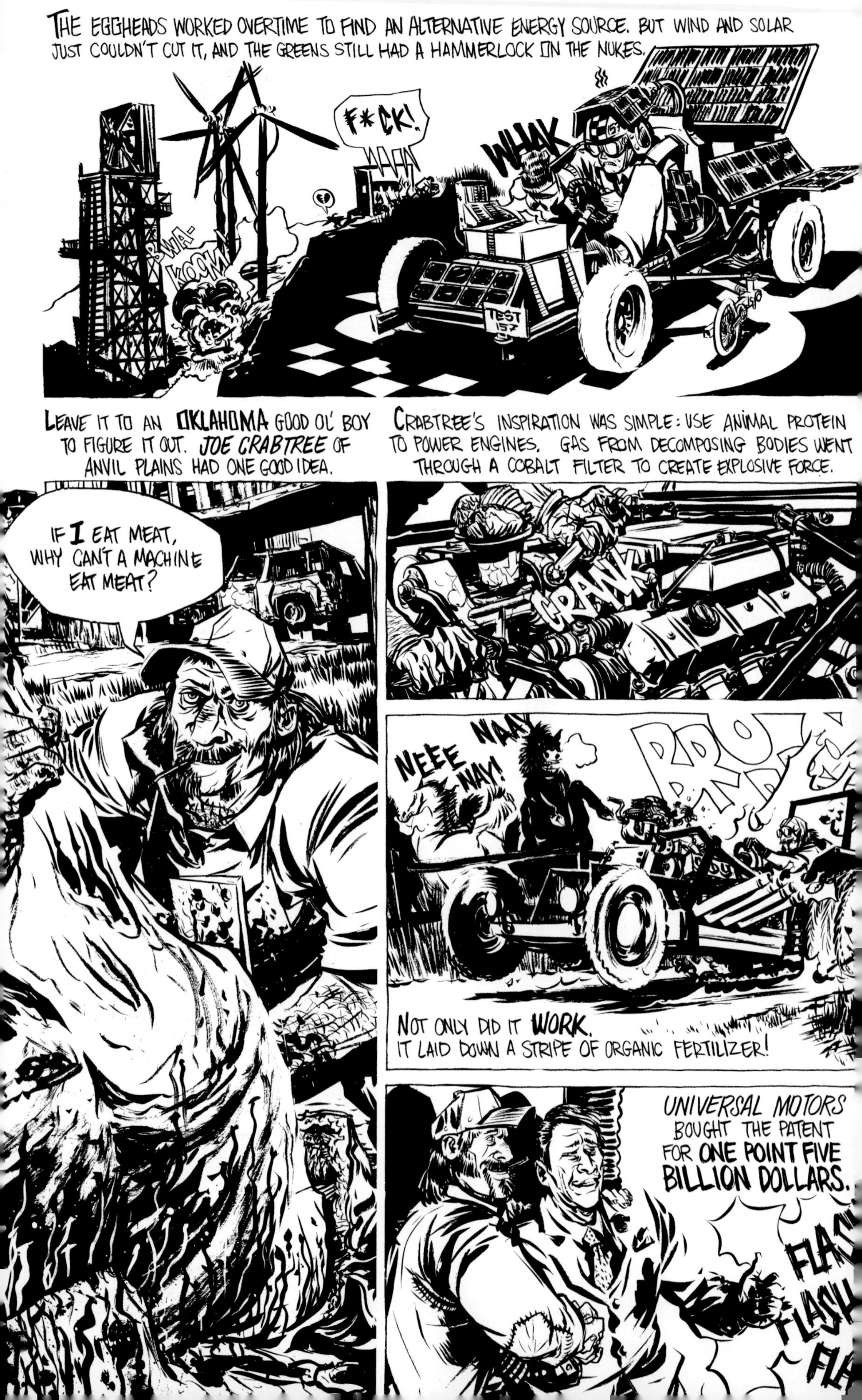
THE EGGHEADS WORKED OVERTIME TO FIND AN ALTERNATIVE ENERGY SOURCE. BUT WIND AND SOLAR JUST COULDN'T CUT IT, AND THE GREENS STILL HAD A HAMMERLOCK ON THE NUKES.
F*CK!
WHAK
BWA-KOOM
TEST 157
LEAVE IT TO AN OKLAHOMA GOOD OL' BOY TO FIGURE IT OUT. JOE CRABTREE OF ANVIL PLAINS HAD ONE GOOD IDEA.
CRABTREE'S INSPIRATION WAS SIMPLE: USE ANIMAL PROTEIN TO POWER ENGINES. GAS FROM DECOMPOSING BODIES WENT THROUGH A COBALT FILTER TO CREATE EXPLOSIVE FORCE.
IF I EAT MEAT, WHY CAN'T A MACHINE EAT MEAT?
CRANK
NEEE NAA NAY!
NOT ONLY DID IT WORK. IT LAID DOWN A STRIPE OF ORGANIC FERTILIZER!
UNIVERSAL MOTORS BOUGHT THE PATENT FOR ONE POINT FIVE BILLION DOLLARS.
FLASH

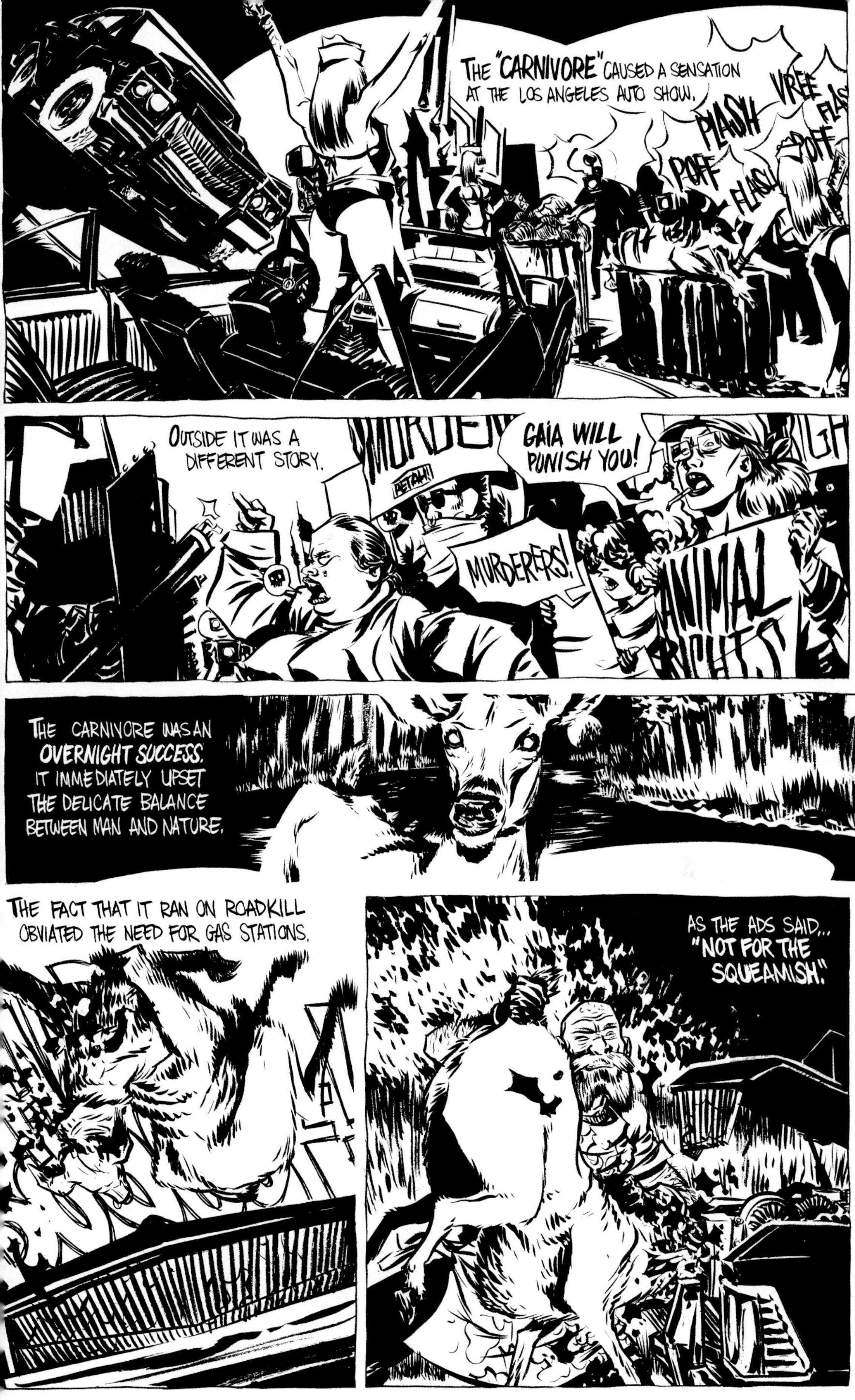
THE "CARNIVORE" CAUSED A SENSATION AT THE LOS ANGELES AUTO SHOW.
PLASH
VREE
POFF
POFF
OUTSIDE IT WAS A DIFFERENT STORY.
GAIA WILL PUNISH YOU!
MURDERERS!
ANIMAL
THE CARNIVORE WAS AN OVERNIGHT SUCCESS. IT IMMEDIATELY UPSET THE DELICATE BALANCE BETWEEN MAN AND NATURE.
THE FACT THAT IT RAN ON ROADKILL OBVIATED THE NEED FOR GAS STATIONS.
AS THE ADS SAID... "NOT FOR THE SQUEAMISH."

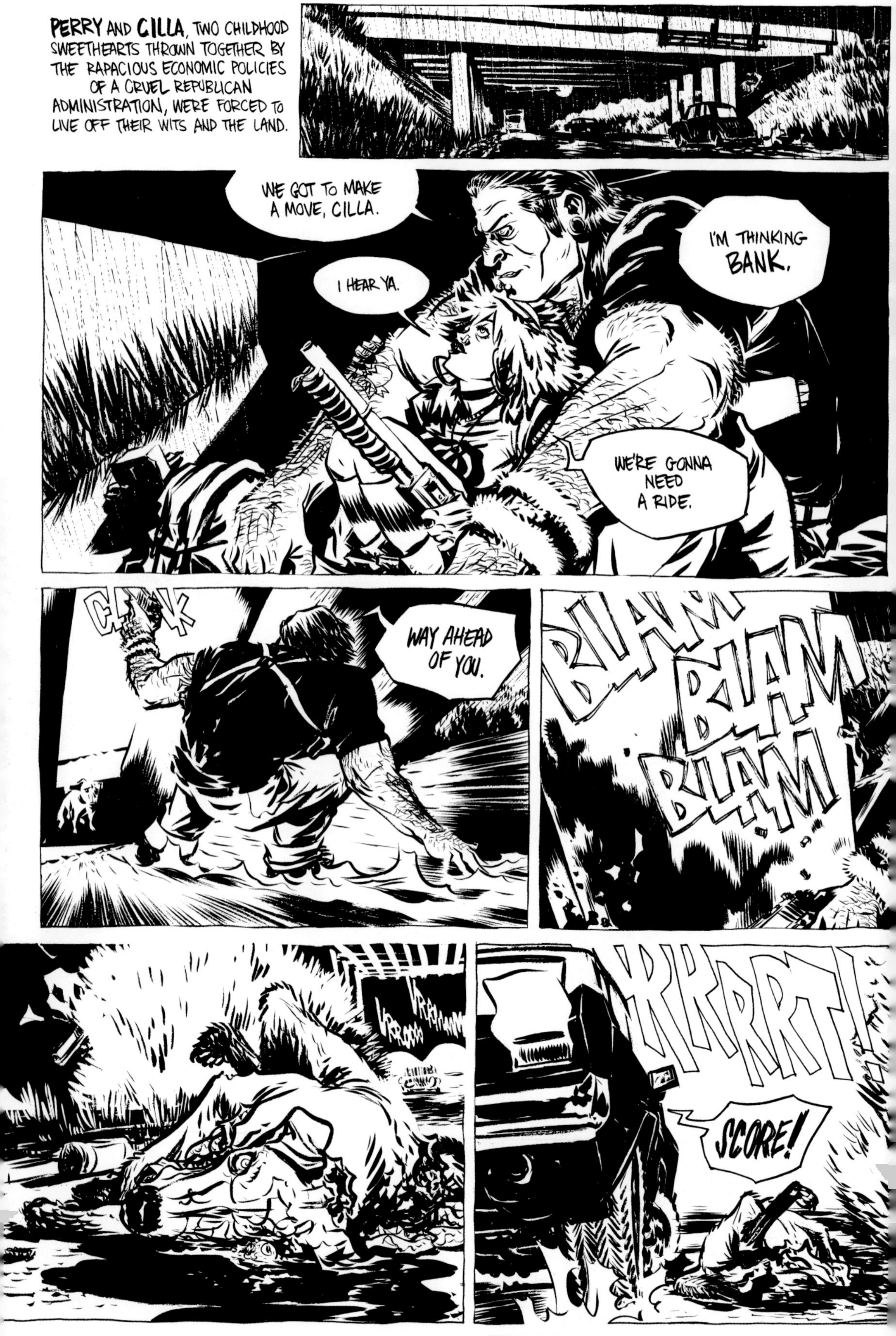
PERRY AND CILLA, TWO CHILDHOOD SWEETHEARTS THROWN TOGETHER BY THE RAPACIOUS ECONOMIC POLICIES OF A CRUEL REPUBLICAN ADMINISTRATION, WERE FORCED TO LIVE OFF THEIR WITS AND THE LAND.
WE GOT TO MAKE A MOVE, CILLA.
I HEAR YA.
I'M THINKING BANK.
WE'RE GONNA NEED A RIDE.
WAY AHEAD OF YOU.
BLAM BLAM BLAM
SCORE!

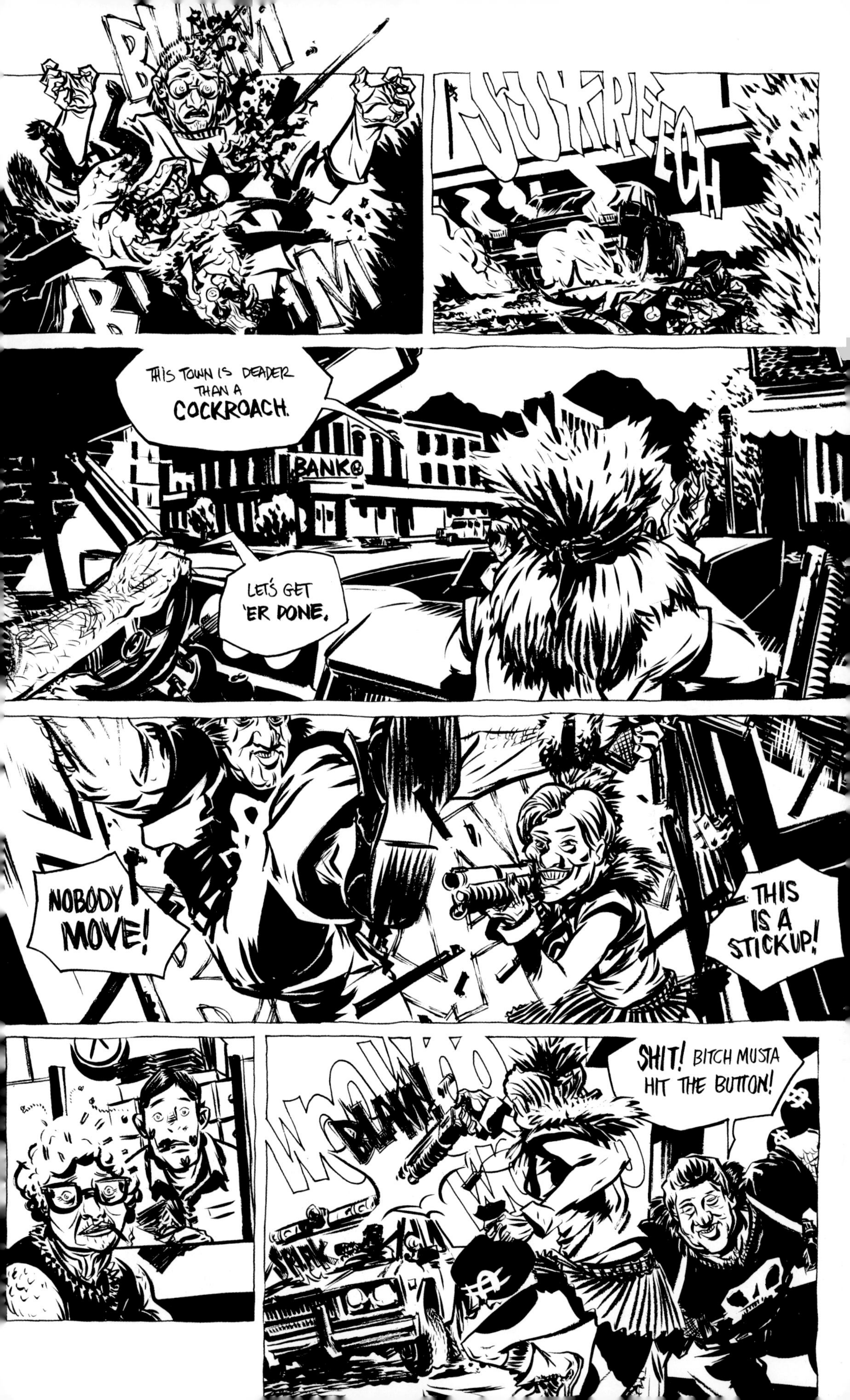
BLAM
BLAM
THIS TOWN IS DEADER THAN A COCKROACH.
BANK
LET'S GET 'ER DONE.
NOBODY MOVE!
THIS IS A STICKUP!
BLAM!
SHIT! BITCH MUSTA HIT THE BUTTON!

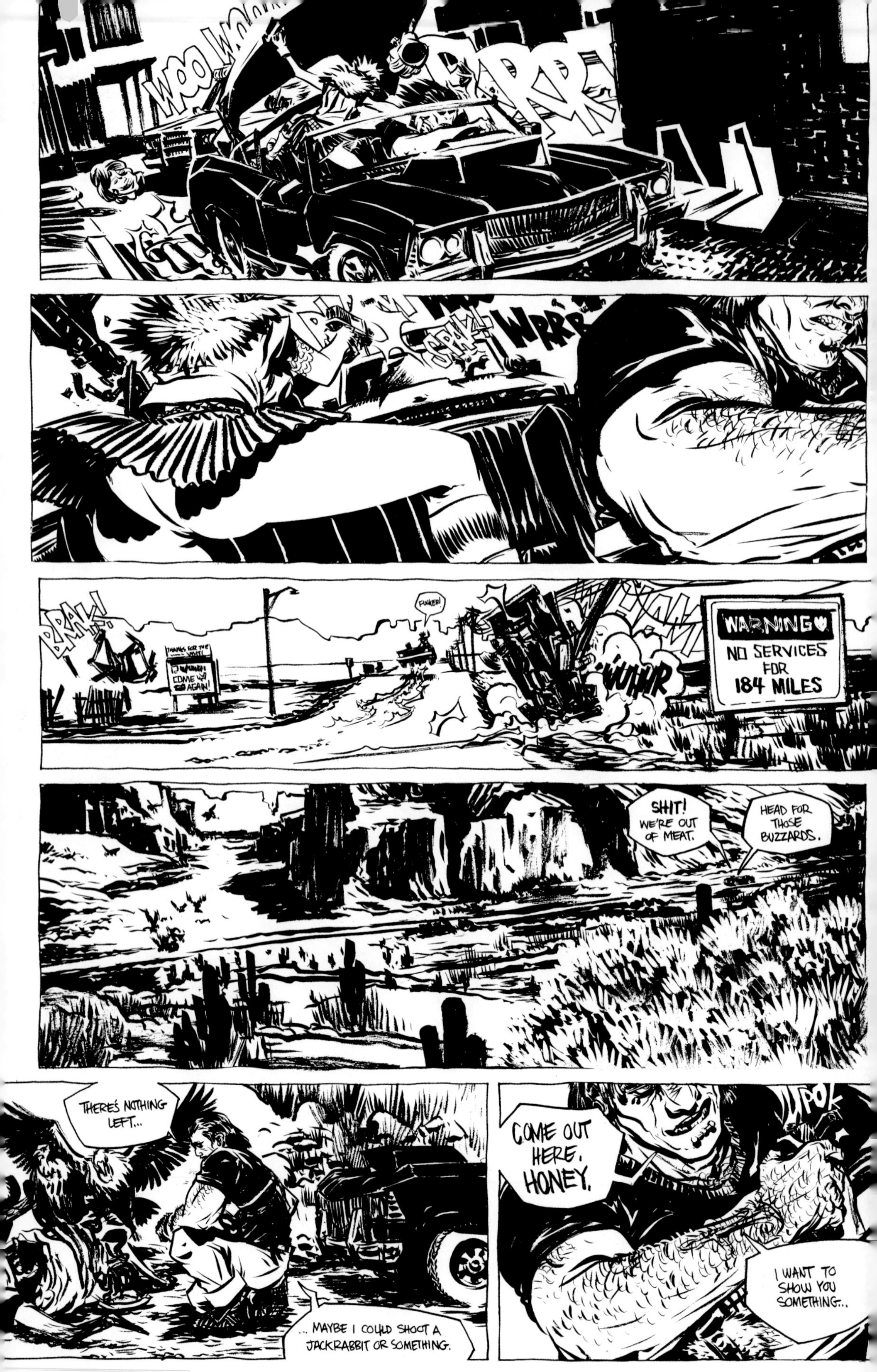
FUCKER!
WUHR
WARNING
NO SERVICES FOR 184 MILES
SHIT! WE'RE OUT OF MEAT.
HEAD FOR THOSE BUZZARDS.
THERE'S NOTHING LEFT...
... MAYBE I COULD SHOOT A JACKRABBIT OR SOMETHING.
COME OUT HERE, HONEY.
POK
I WANT TO SHOW YOU SOMETHING...

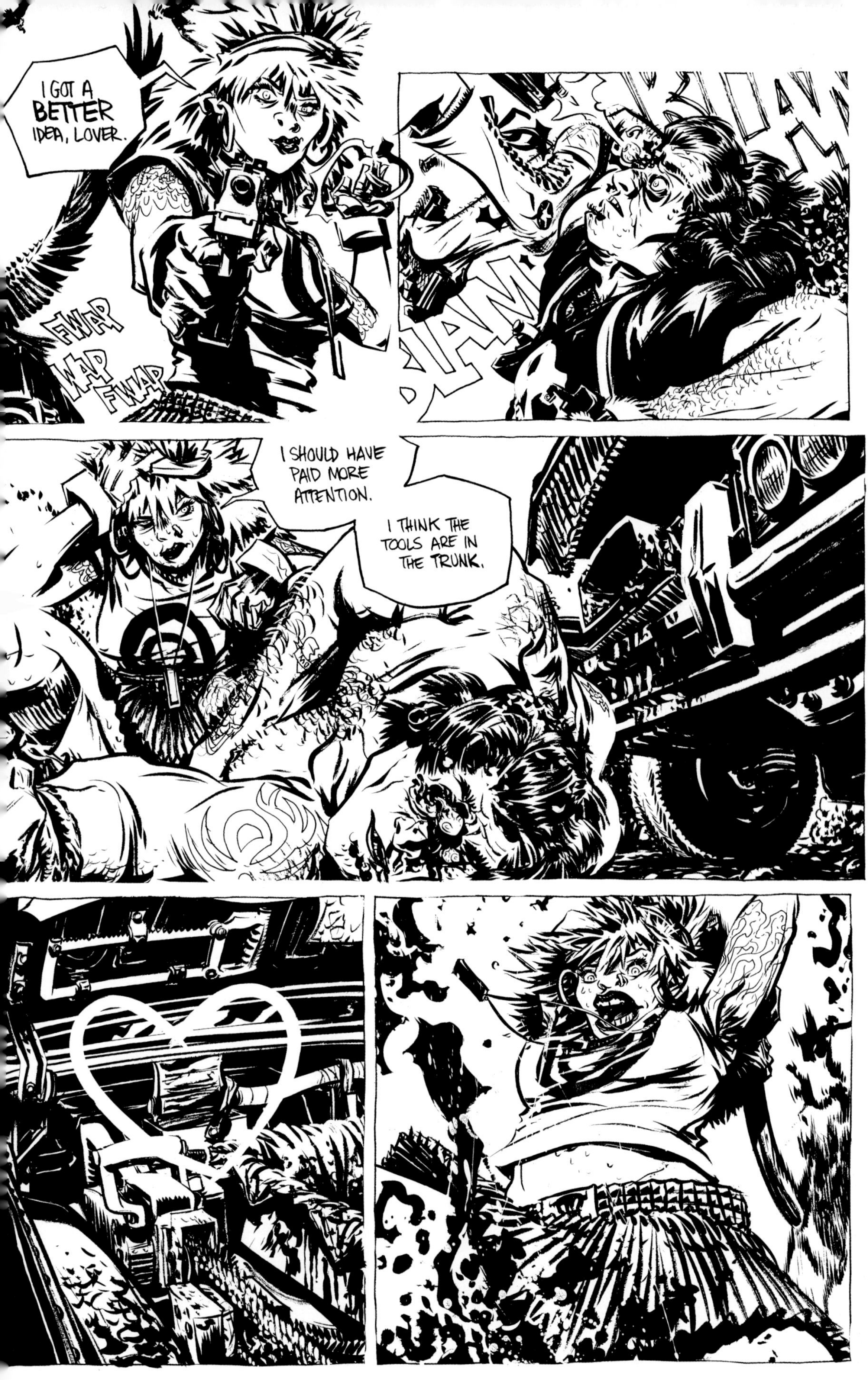
I GOT A BETTER IDEA, LOVER.
FWAP
WAP
FWAP
I SHOULD HAVE PAID MORE ATTENTION.
I THINK THE TOOLS ARE IN THE TRUNK.

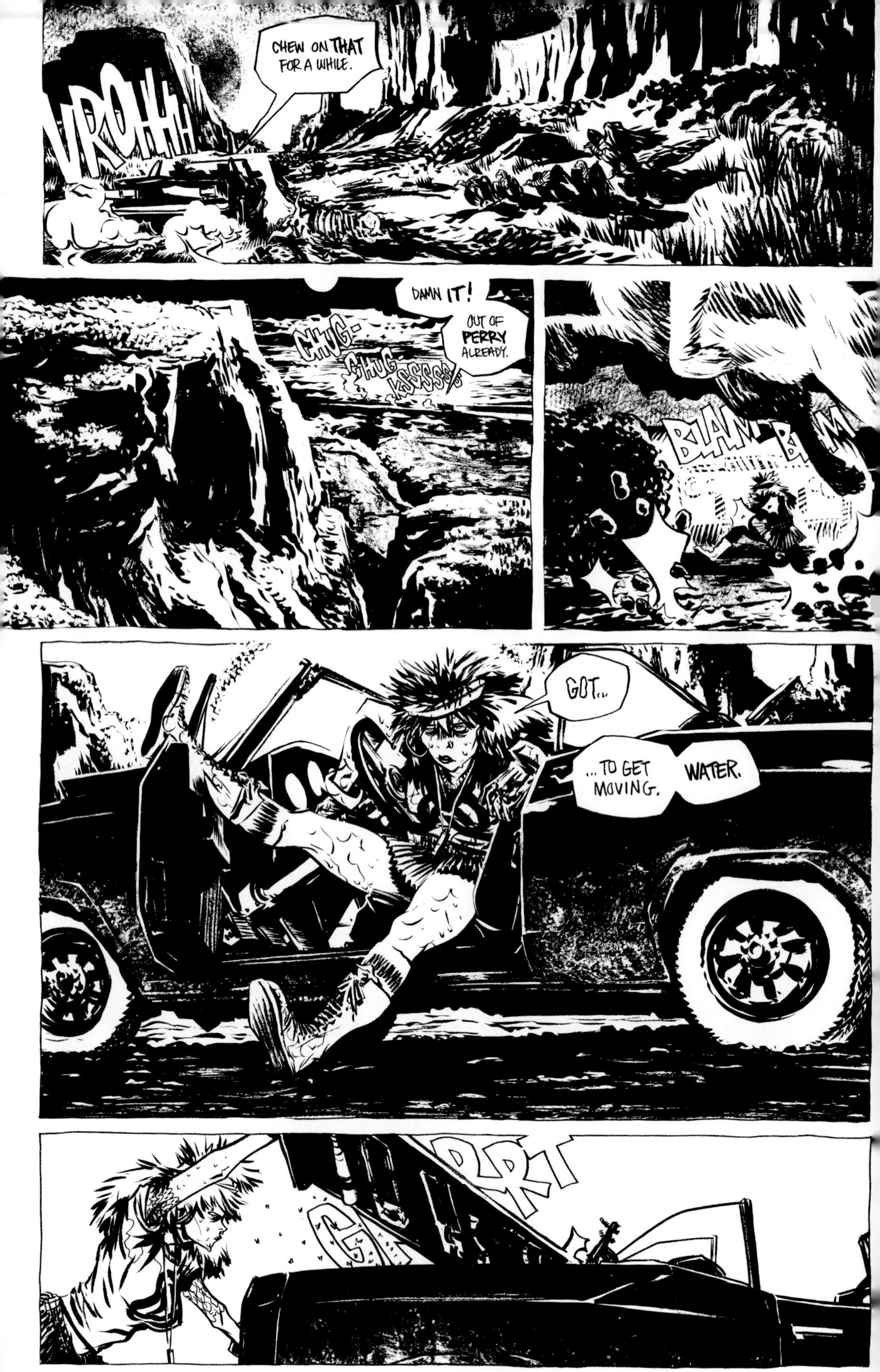
CHEW ON THAT FOR A WHILE.
VROOHH
DAMN IT!
CHUG-
CHUG-
KSSSSS
OUT OF PERRY ALREADY.
BLAM BLAM
GOT...
...TO GET MOVING.
WATER.
PLRT

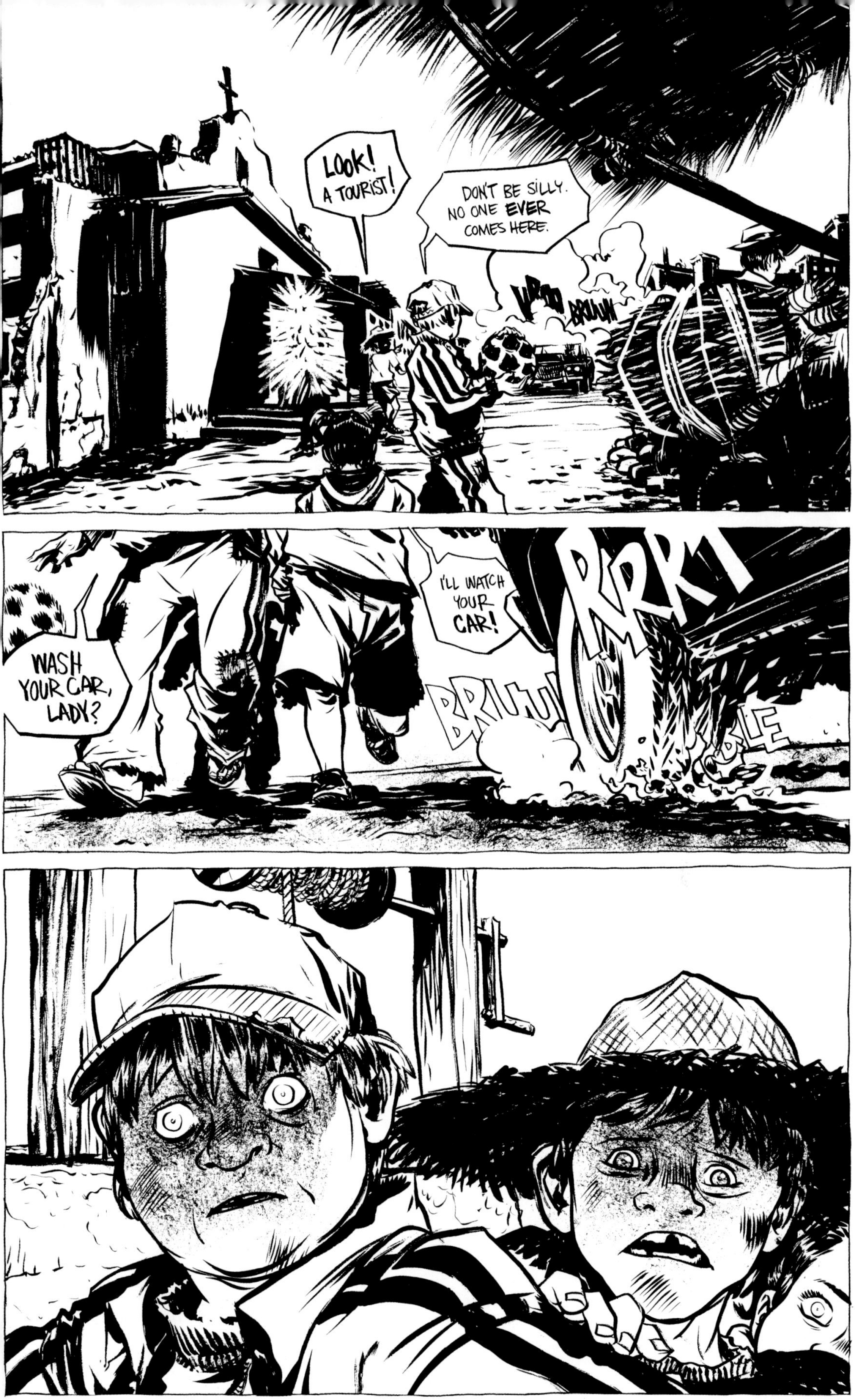
LOOK! A TOURIST!
DON'T BE SILLY. NO ONE EVER COMES HERE.
VROO
BRUUM
WASH YOUR CAR, LADY?
I'LL WATCH YOUR CAR!
RRRT
BRUUU

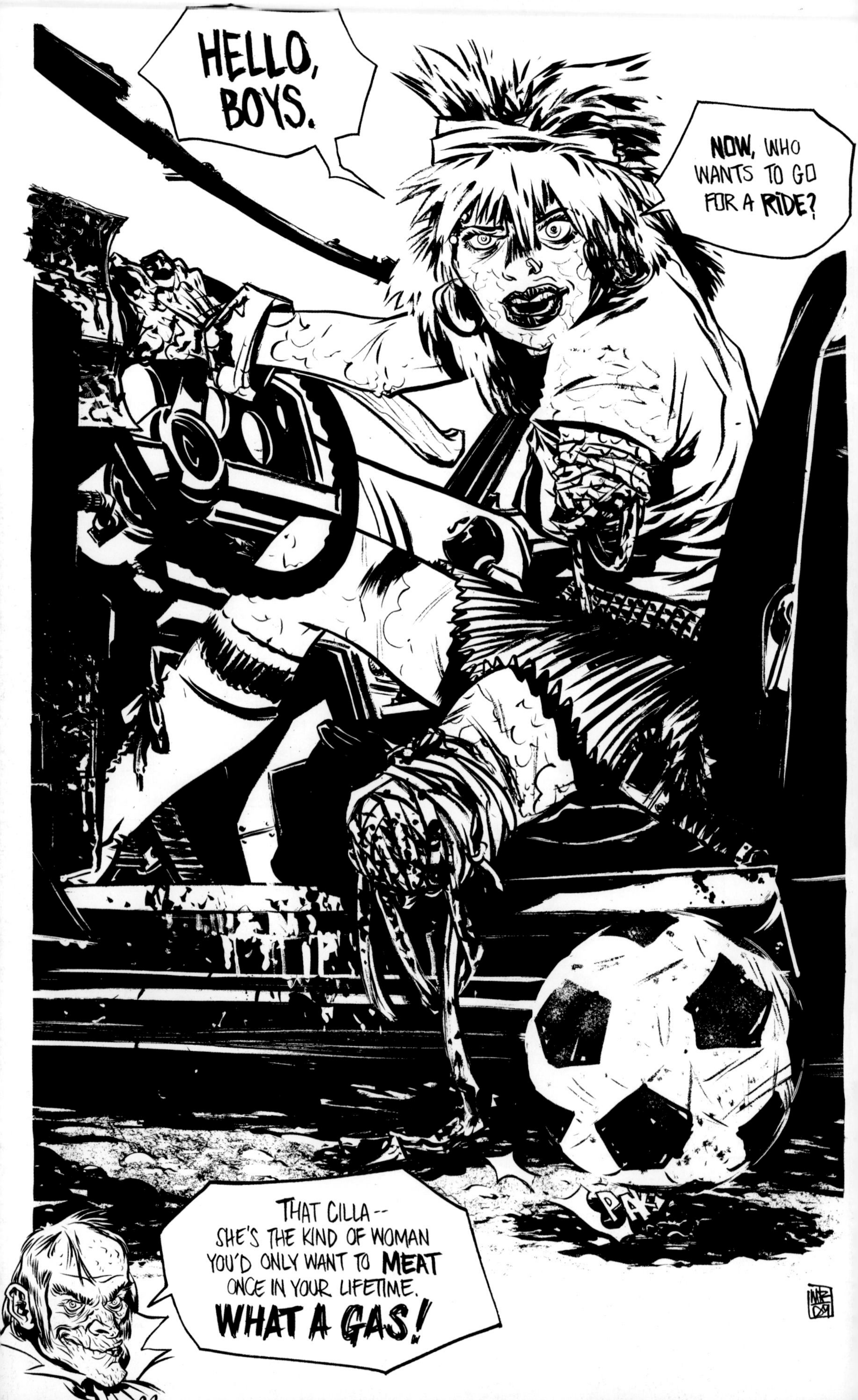

HELLO, BOYS.
NOW, WHO WANTS TO GO FOR A RIDE?
THAT CILLA-- SHE'S THE KIND OF WOMAN YOU'D ONLY WANT TO MEAT ONCE IN YOUR LIFETIME. WHAT A GAS!

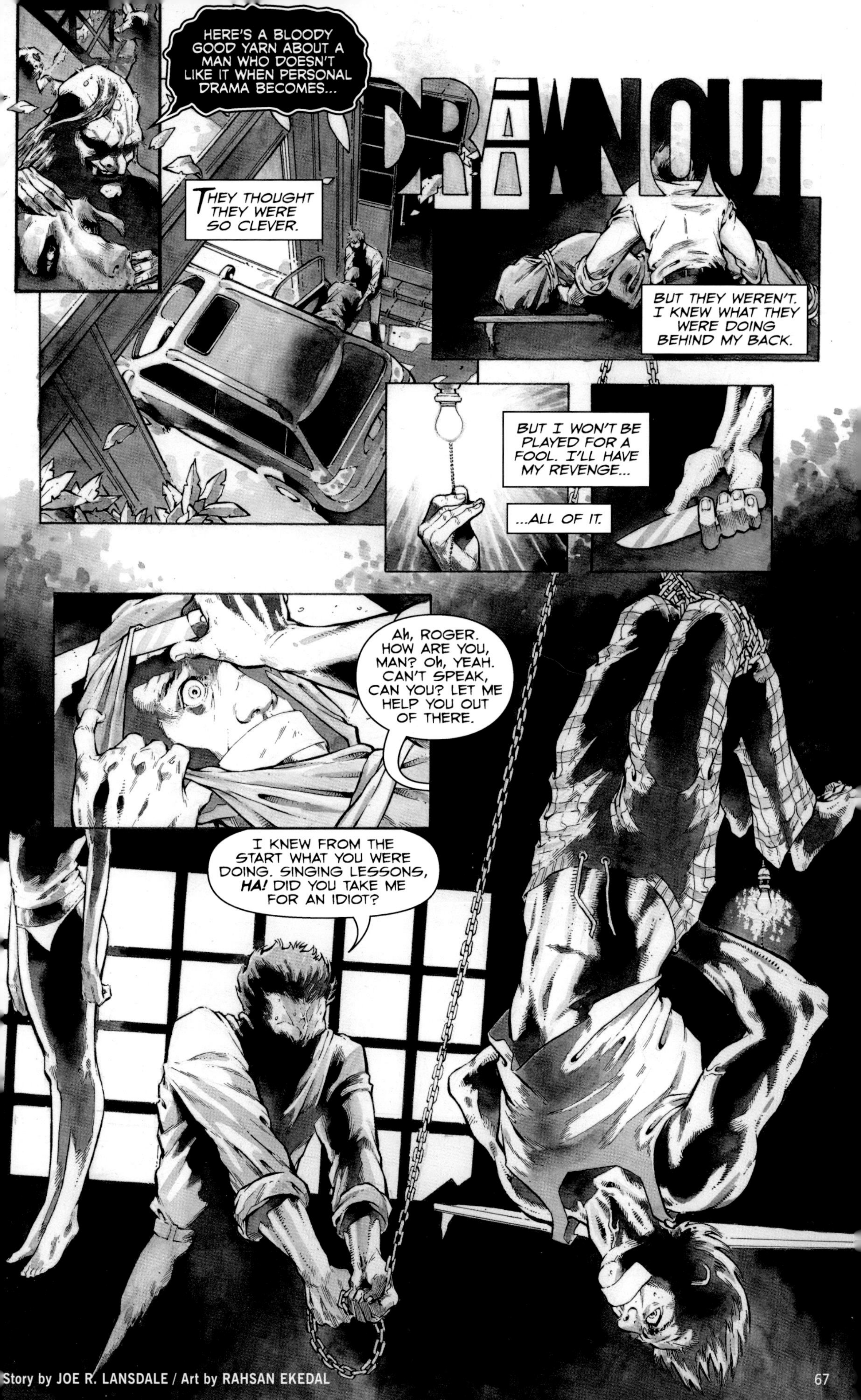
HERE'S A BLOODY GOOD YARN ABOUT A MAN WHO DOESN'T LIKE IT WHEN PERSONAL DRAMA BECOMES...
DRAWN OUT
THEY THOUGHT THEY WERE SO CLEVER.
BUT THEY WEREN'T. I KNEW WHAT THEY WERE DOING BEHIND MY BACK.
BUT I WON'T BE PLAYED FOR A FOOL. I'LL HAVE MY REVENGE...
...ALL OF IT.
Ah, ROGER. HOW ARE YOU, MAN? Oh, YEAH. CAN'T SPEAK, CAN YOU? LET ME HELP YOU OUT OF THERE.
I KNEW FROM THE START WHAT YOU WERE DOING. SINGING LESSONS, HA! DID YOU TAKE ME FOR AN IDIOT?

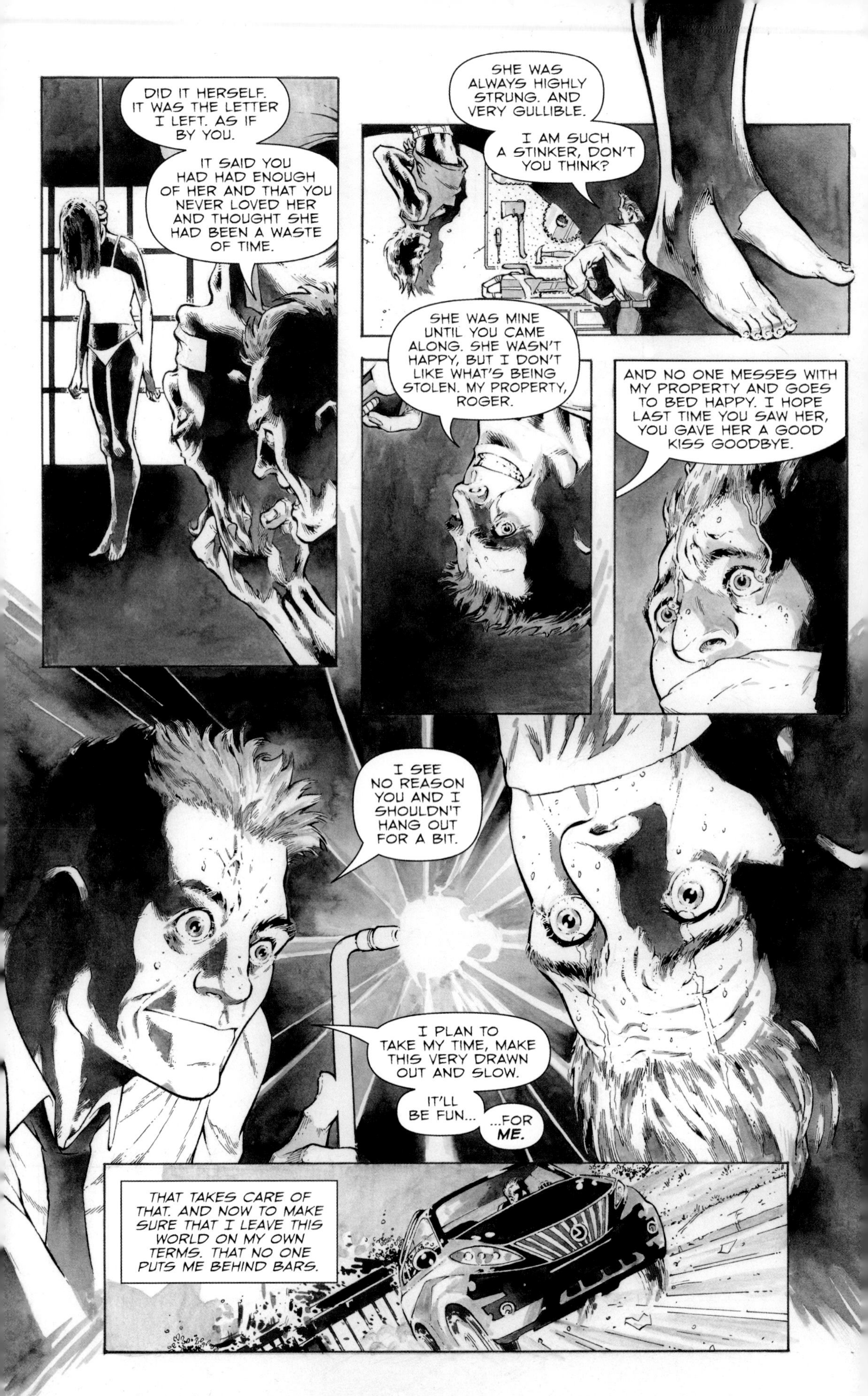
DID IT HERSELF. IT WAS THE LETTER I LEFT. AS IF BY YOU.
IT SAID YOU HAD HAD ENOUGH OF HER AND THAT YOU NEVER LOVED HER AND THOUGHT SHE HAD BEEN A WASTE OF TIME.
SHE WAS ALWAYS HIGHLY STRUNG. AND VERY GULLIBLE.
I AM SUCH A STINKER, DON'T YOU THINK?
SHE WAS MINE UNTIL YOU CAME ALONG. SHE WASN'T HAPPY, BUT I DON'T LIKE WHAT'S BEING STOLEN. MY PROPERTY, ROGER.
AND NO ONE MESSES WITH MY PROPERTY AND GOES TO BED HAPPY. I HOPE LAST TIME YOU SAW HER, YOU GAVE HER A GOOD KISS GOODBYE.
I SEE NO REASON YOU AND I SHOULDN'T HANG OUT FOR A BIT.
I PLAN TO TAKE MY TIME, MAKE THIS VERY DRAWN OUT AND SLOW.
IT'LL BE FUN...
...FOR ME.
THAT TAKES CARE OF THAT. AND NOW TO MAKE SURE THAT I LEAVE THIS WORLD ON MY OWN TERMS. THAT NO ONE PUTS ME BEHIND BARS.

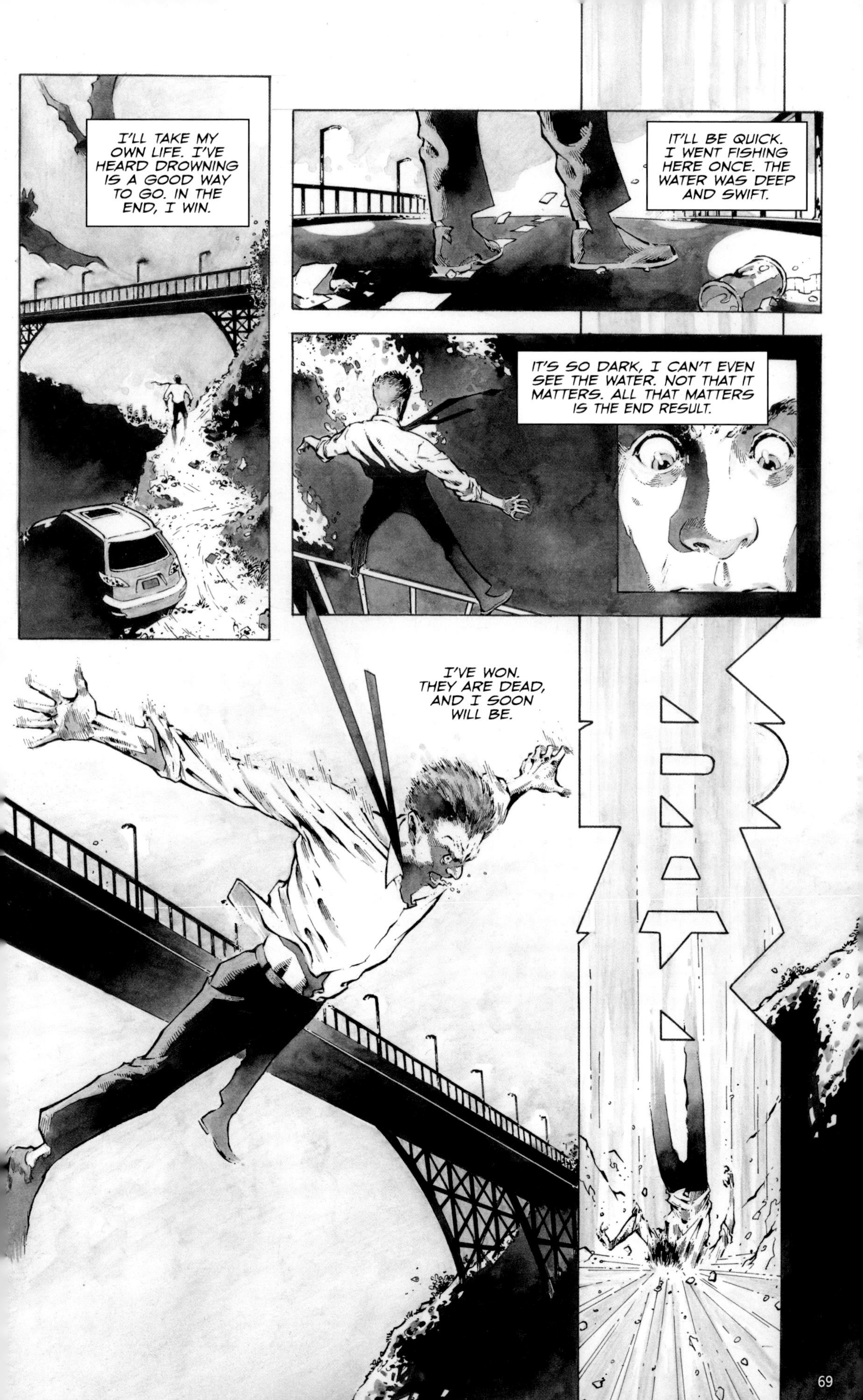
I'LL TAKE MY OWN LIFE. I'VE HEARD DROWNING IS A GOOD WAY TO GO. IN THE END, I WIN.
IT'LL BE QUICK. I WENT FISHING HERE ONCE. THE WATER WAS DEEP AND SWIFT.
IT'S SO DARK, I CAN'T EVEN SEE THE WATER. NOT THAT IT MATTERS. ALL THAT MATTERS IS THE END RESULT.
I'VE WON. THEY ARE DEAD, AND I SOON WILL BE.

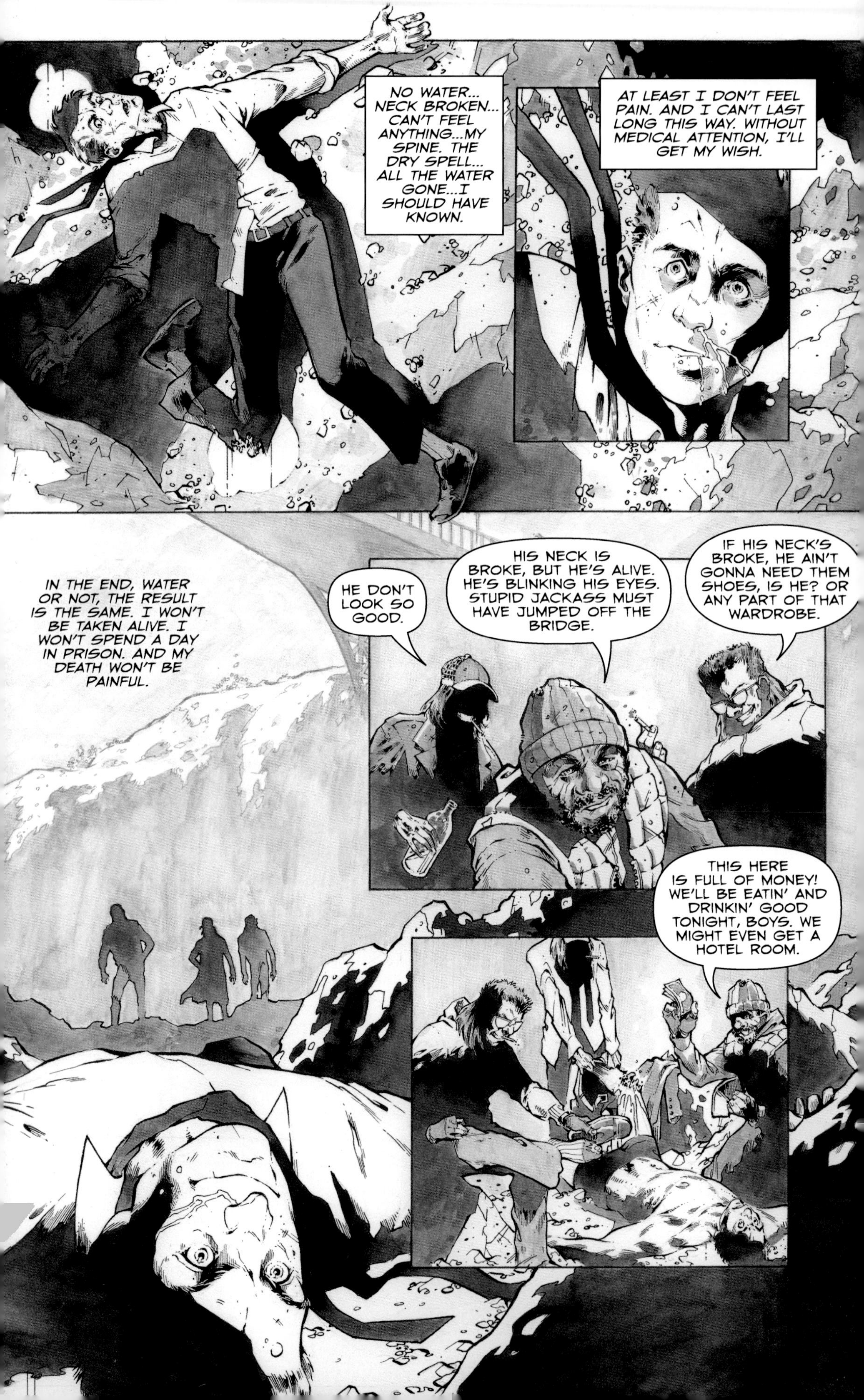
NO WATER... NECK BROKEN... CAN'T FEEL ANYTHING...MY SPINE. THE DRY SPELL... ALL THE WATER GONE...I SHOULD HAVE KNOWN.
AT LEAST I DON'T FEEL PAIN. AND I CAN'T LAST LONG THIS WAY. WITHOUT MEDICAL ATTENTION, I'LL GET MY WISH.
IN THE END, WATER OR NOT, THE RESULT IS THE SAME. I WON'T BE TAKEN ALIVE. I WON'T SPEND A DAY IN PRISON. AND MY DEATH WON'T BE PAINFUL.
HE DON'T LOOK SO GOOD.
HIS NECK IS BROKE, BUT HE'S ALIVE. HE'S BLINKING HIS EYES. STUPID JACKASS MUST HAVE JUMPED OFF THE BRIDGE.
IF HIS NECK'S BROKE, HE AIN'T GONNA NEED THEM SHOES, IS HE? OR ANY PART OF THAT WARDROBE.
THIS HERE IS FULL OF MONEY! WE'LL BE EATIN' AND DRINKIN' GOOD TONIGHT, BOYS. WE MIGHT EVEN GET A HOTEL ROOM.

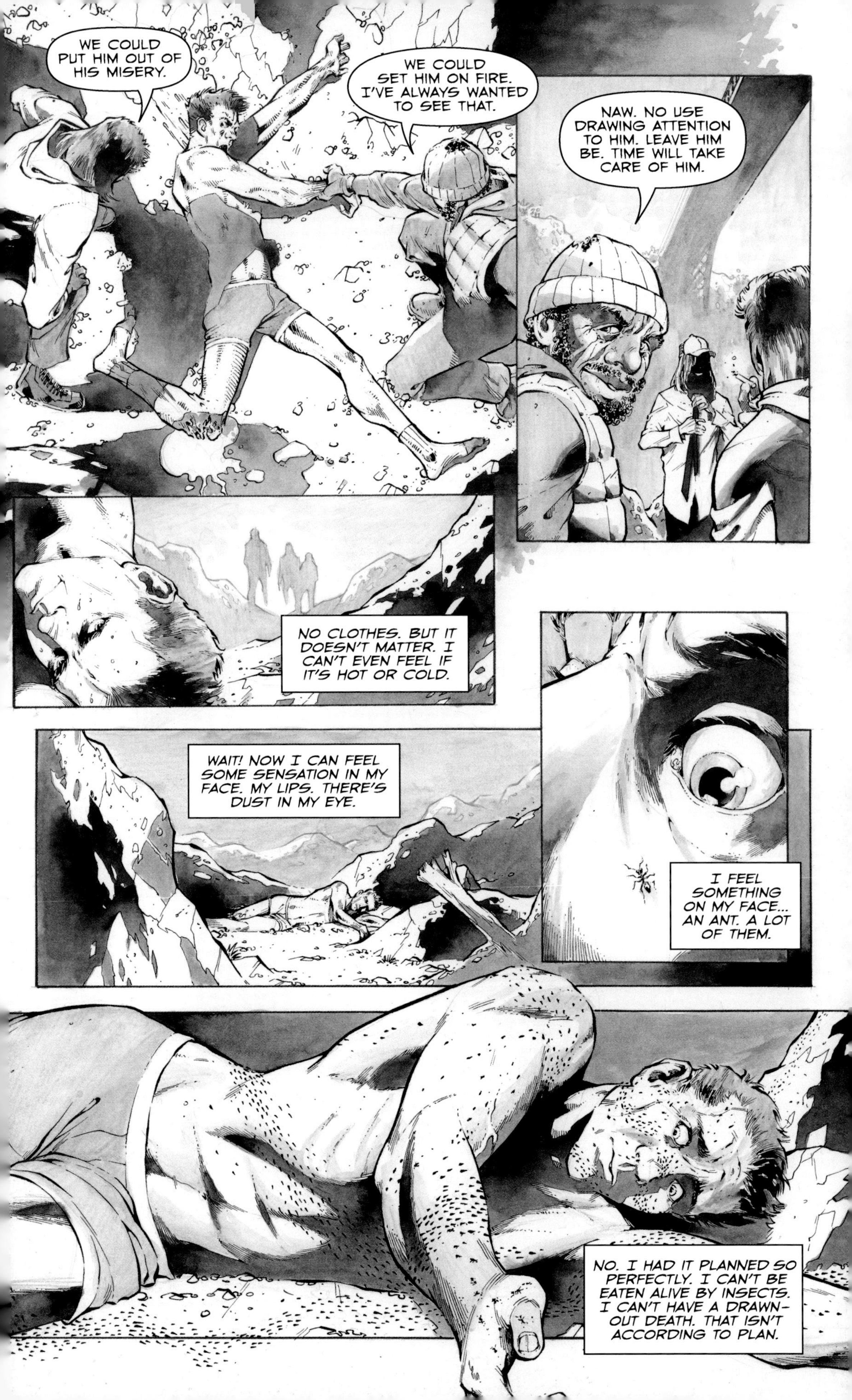
WE COULD PUT HIM OUT OF HIS MISERY.
WE COULD SET HIM ON FIRE. I'VE ALWAYS WANTED TO SEE THAT.
NAW. NO USE DRAWING ATTENTION TO HIM. LEAVE HIM BE. TIME WILL TAKE CARE OF HIM.
NO CLOTHES. BUT IT DOESN'T MATTER. I CAN'T EVEN FEEL IF IT'S HOT OR COLD.
WAIT! NOW I CAN FEEL SOME SENSATION IN MY FACE. MY LIPS. THERE'S DUST IN MY EYE.
I FEEL SOMETHING ON MY FACE... AN ANT. A LOT OF THEM.
NO. I HAD IT PLANNED SO PERFECTLY. I CAN'T BE EATEN ALIVE BY INSECTS. I CAN'T HAVE A DRAWN-OUT DEATH. THAT ISN'T ACCORDING TO PLAN.

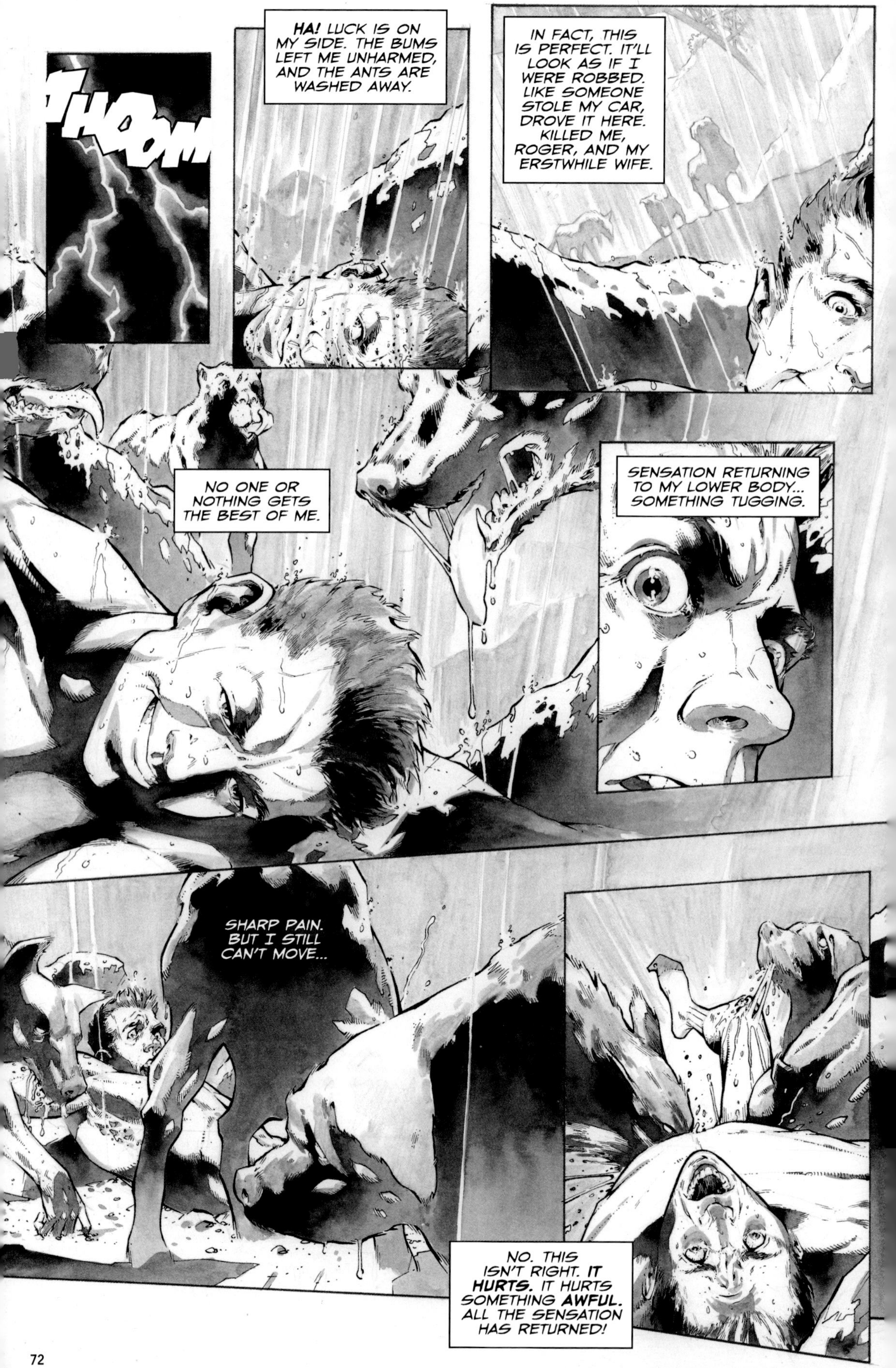
THOOM
HA! LUCK IS ON MY SIDE. THE BUMS LEFT ME UNHARMED, AND THE ANTS ARE WASHED AWAY.
IN FACT, THIS IS PERFECT. IT'LL LOOK AS IF I WERE ROBBED. LIKE SOMEONE STOLE MY CAR, DROVE IT HERE. KILLED ME, ROGER, AND MY ERSTWHILE WIFE.
NO ONE OR NOTHING GETS THE BEST OF ME.
SENSATION RETURNING TO MY LOWER BODY... SOMETHING TUGGING.
SHARP PAIN. BUT I STILL CAN'T MOVE...
NO. THIS ISN'T RIGHT. **IT HURTS.** IT HURTS SOMETHING **AWFUL.** ALL THE SENSATION HAS RETURNED!

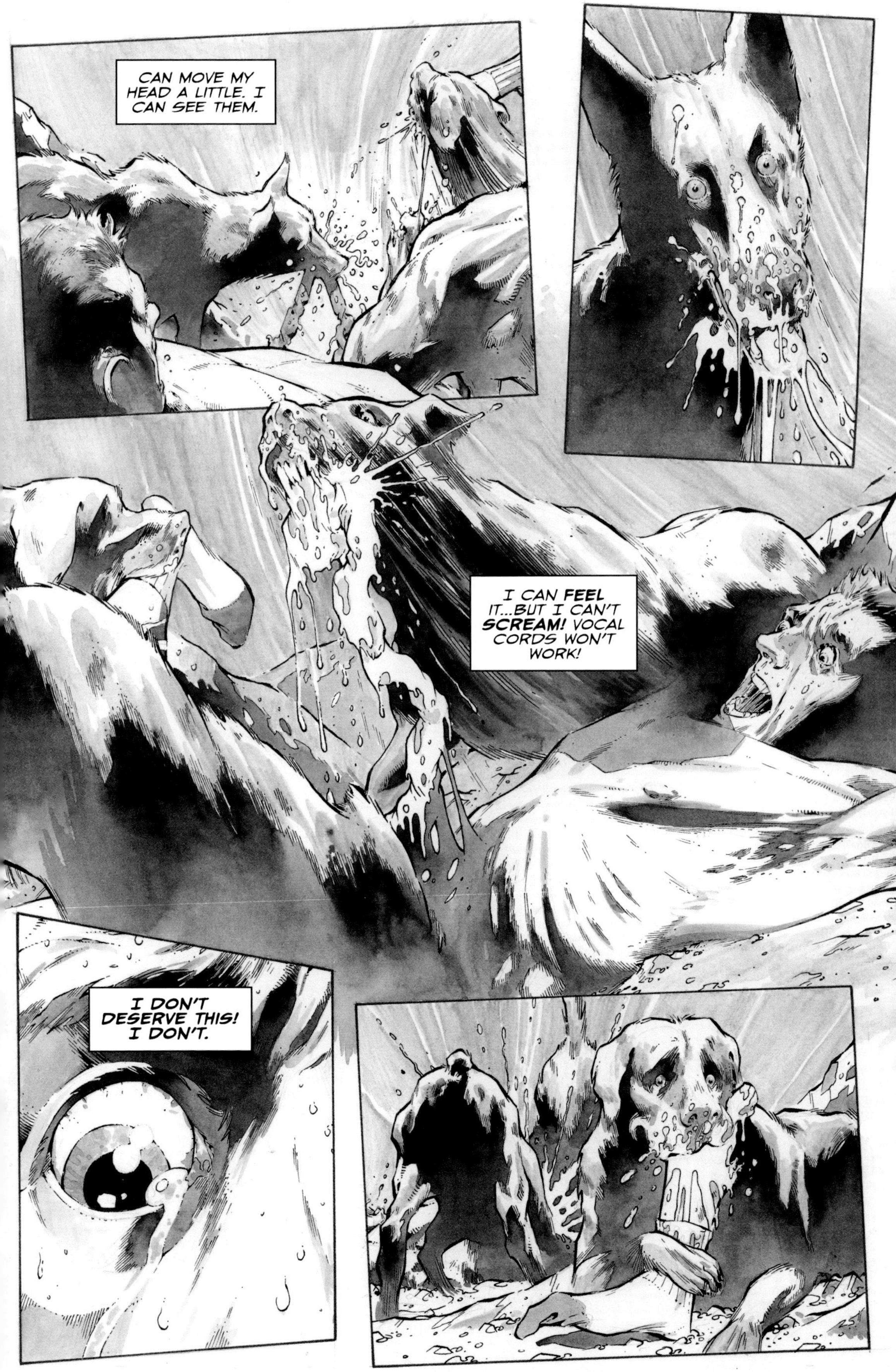
CAN MOVE MY HEAD A LITTLE. I CAN SEE THEM.
I CAN FEEL IT...BUT I CAN'T SCREAM! VOCAL CORDS WON'T WORK!
I DON'T DESERVE THIS! I DON'T.

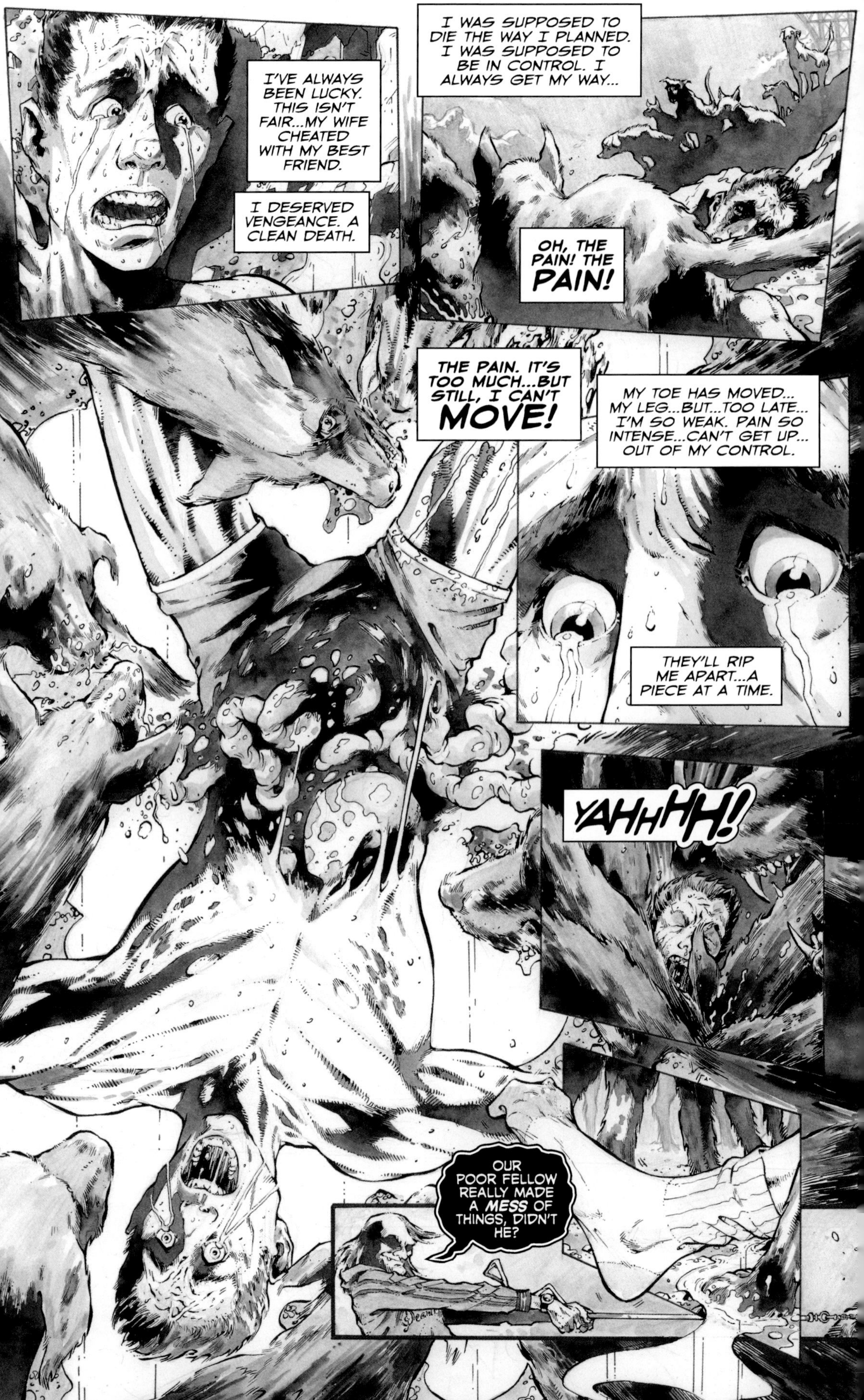
I'VE ALWAYS BEEN LUCKY. THIS ISN'T FAIR...MY WIFE CHEATED WITH MY BEST FRIEND.
I DESERVED VENGEANCE. A CLEAN DEATH.
I WAS SUPPOSED TO DIE THE WAY I PLANNED. I WAS SUPPOSED TO BE IN CONTROL. I ALWAYS GET MY WAY...
OH, THE PAIN! THE PAIN!
THE PAIN. IT'S TOO MUCH...BUT STILL, I CAN'T MOVE!
MY TOE HAS MOVED... MY LEG...BUT...TOO LATE... I'M SO WEAK. PAIN SO INTENSE...CAN'T GET UP... OUT OF MY CONTROL.
THEY'LL RIP ME APART...A PIECE AT A TIME.
YAHHHH!
OUR POOR FELLOW REALLY MADE A MESS OF THINGS, DIDN'T HE?

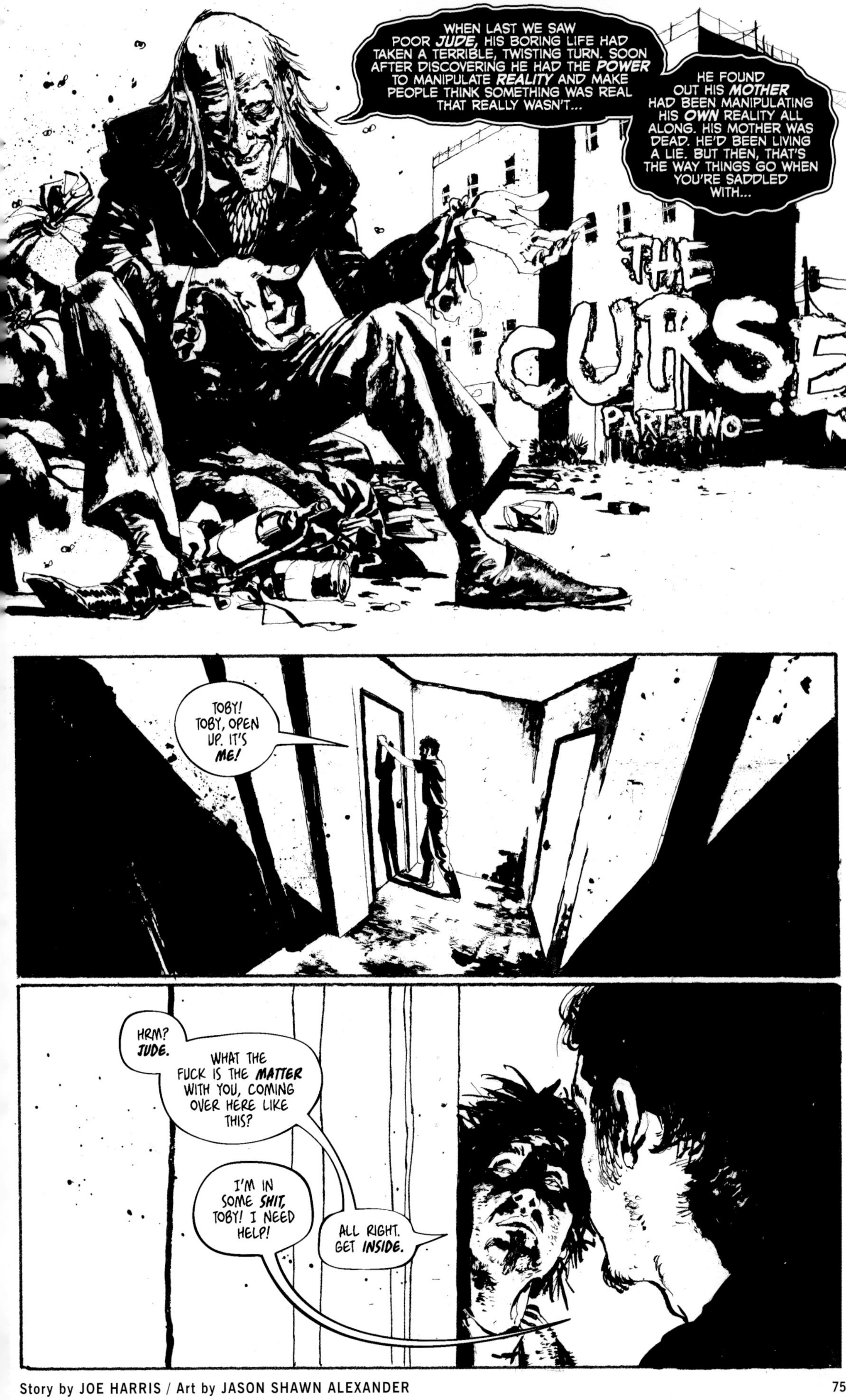
WHEN LAST WE SAW POOR JUDE, HIS BORING LIFE HAD TAKEN A TERRIBLE, TWISTING TURN. SOON AFTER DISCOVERING HE HAD THE POWER TO MANIPULATE REALITY AND MAKE PEOPLE THINK SOMETHING WAS REAL THAT REALLY WASN'T...
HE FOUND OUT HIS MOTHER HAD BEEN MANIPULATING HIS OWN REALITY ALL ALONG. HIS MOTHER WAS DEAD. HE'D BEEN LIVING A LIE. BUT THEN, THAT'S THE WAY THINGS GO WHEN YOU'RE SADDLED WITH...
THE CURSE
PART TWO
TOBY! TOBY, OPEN UP. IT'S ME!
HRM? JUDE.
WHAT THE FUCK IS THE MATTER WITH YOU, COMING OVER HERE LIKE THIS?
I'M IN SOME SHIT, TOBY! I NEED HELP!
ALL RIGHT. GET INSIDE.

Story by JOE HARRIS / Art by JASON SHAWN ALEXANDER

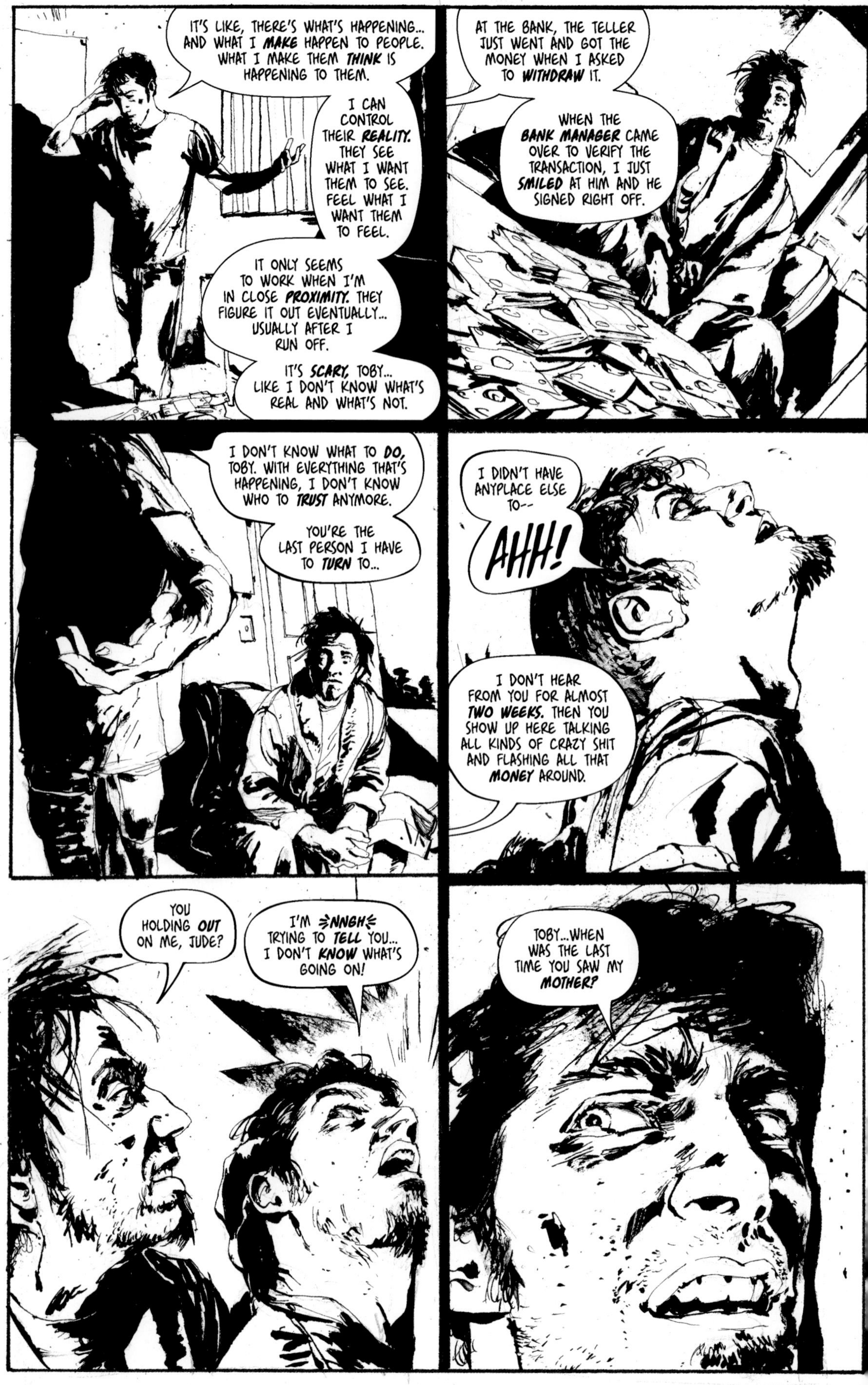

IT'S LIKE, THERE'S WHAT'S HAPPENING... AND WHAT I MAKE HAPPEN TO PEOPLE. WHAT I MAKE THEM THINK IS HAPPENING TO THEM.
I CAN CONTROL THEIR REALITY. THEY SEE WHAT I WANT THEM TO SEE. FEEL WHAT I WANT THEM TO FEEL.
IT ONLY SEEMS TO WORK WHEN I'M IN CLOSE PROXIMITY. THEY FIGURE IT OUT EVENTUALLY... USUALLY AFTER I RUN OFF.
IT'S SCARY, TOBY... LIKE I DON'T KNOW WHAT'S REAL AND WHAT'S NOT.
AT THE BANK, THE TELLER JUST WENT AND GOT THE MONEY WHEN I ASKED TO WITHDRAW IT.
WHEN THE BANK MANAGER CAME OVER TO VERIFY THE TRANSACTION, I JUST SMILED AT HIM AND HE SIGNED RIGHT OFF.
I DON'T KNOW WHAT TO DO, TOBY. WITH EVERYTHING THAT'S HAPPENING, I DON'T KNOW WHO TO TRUST ANYMORE.
YOU'RE THE LAST PERSON I HAVE TO TURN TO...
I DIDN'T HAVE ANYPLACE ELSE TO--
AHH!
I DON'T HEAR FROM YOU FOR ALMOST TWO WEEKS. THEN YOU SHOW UP HERE TALKING ALL KINDS OF CRAZY SHIT AND FLASHING ALL THAT MONEY AROUND.
YOU HOLDING OUT ON ME, JUDE?
I'M NNGH TRYING TO TELL YOU... I DON'T KNOW WHAT'S GOING ON!
TOBY...WHEN WAS THE LAST TIME YOU SAW MY MOTHER?

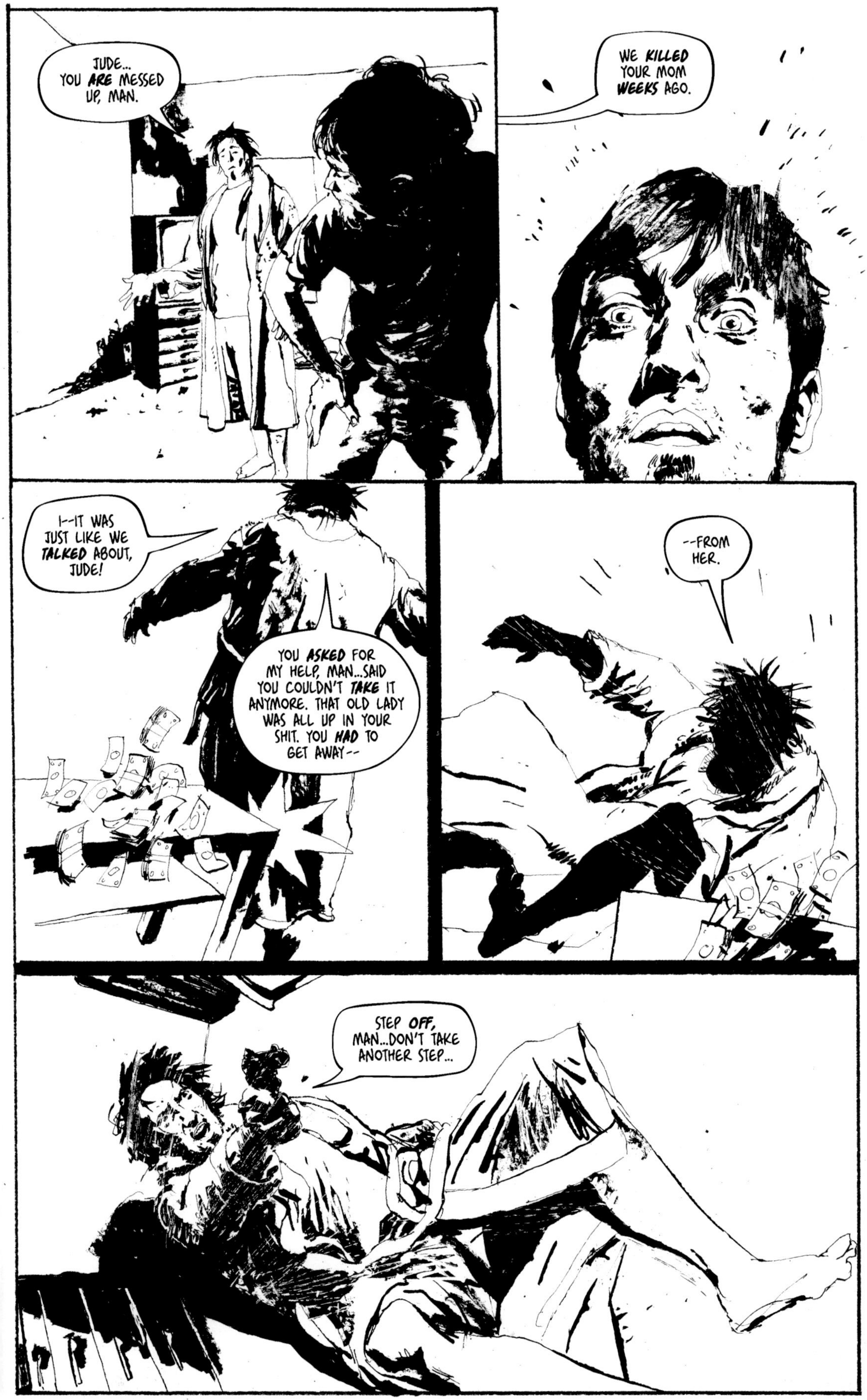
JUDE... YOU **ARE** MESSED UP, MAN.
WE **KILLED** YOUR MOM **WEEKS** AGO.
I--IT WAS JUST LIKE WE **TALKED** ABOUT, JUDE!
YOU **ASKED** FOR MY HELP, MAN...SAID YOU COULDN'T **TAKE** IT ANYMORE. THAT OLD LADY WAS ALL UP IN YOUR SHIT. YOU **HAD** TO GET AWAY--
--FROM HER.
STEP **OFF**, MAN...DON'T TAKE ANOTHER STEP...

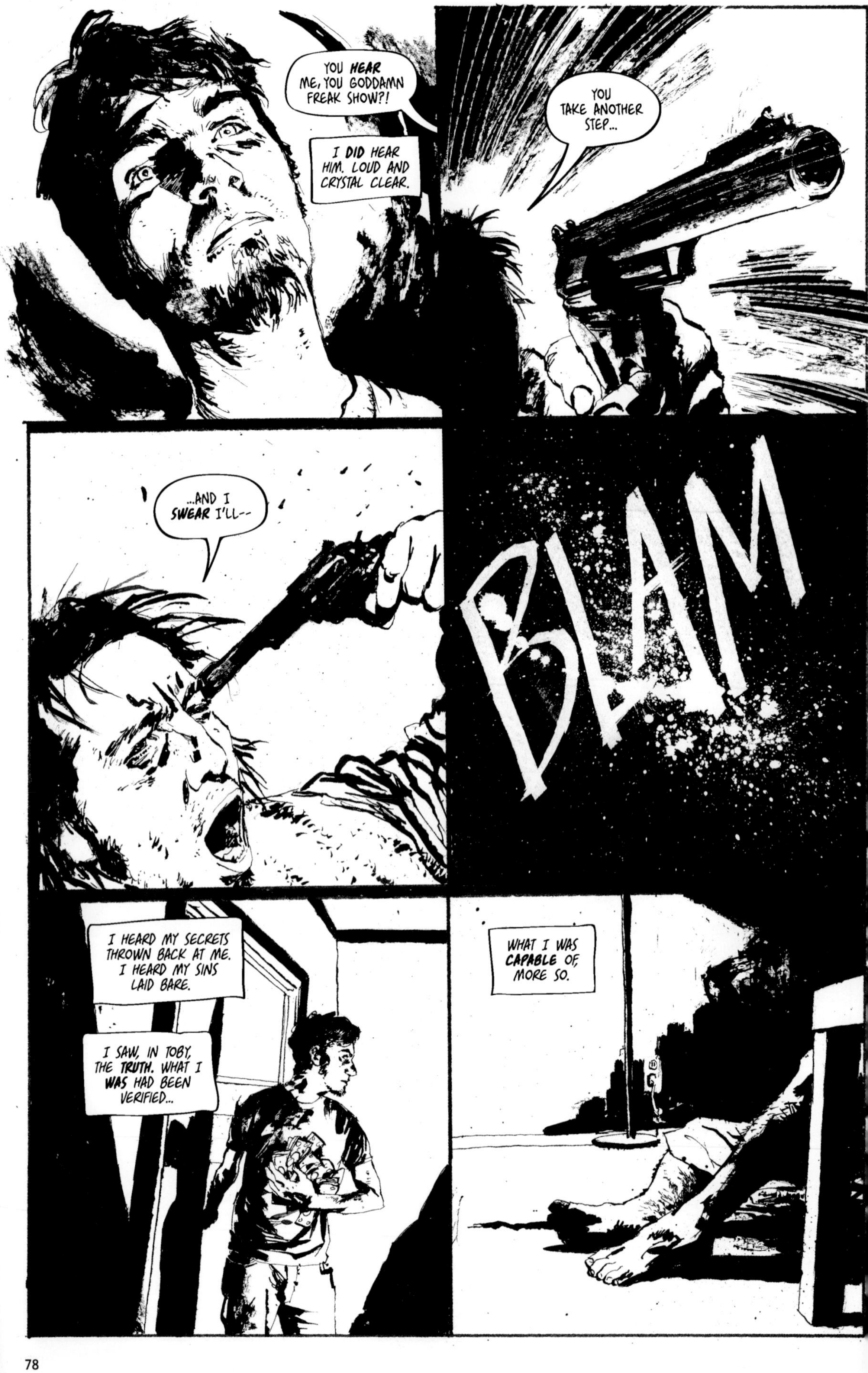
YOU HEAR ME, YOU GODDAMN FREAK SHOW?!
I DID HEAR HIM. LOUD AND CRYSTAL CLEAR.
YOU TAKE ANOTHER STEP...
...AND I SWEAR I'LL--
BLAM
I HEARD MY SECRETS THROWN BACK AT ME. I HEARD MY SINS LAID BARE.
I SAW, IN TOBY, THE TRUTH. WHAT I WAS HAD BEEN VERIFIED...
WHAT I WAS CAPABLE OF, MORE SO.

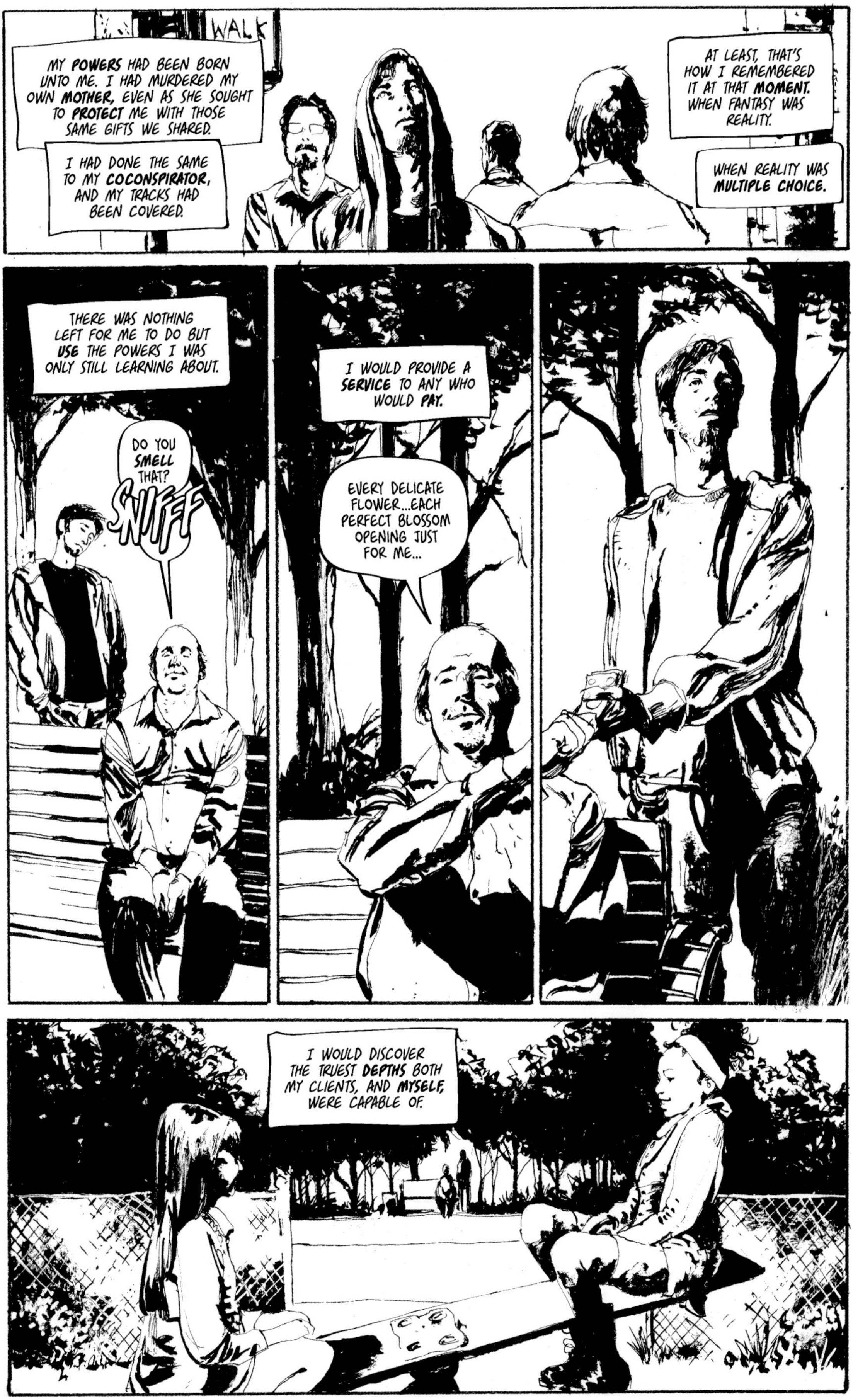
WALK
MY POWERS HAD BEEN BORN UNTO ME. I HAD MURDERED MY OWN MOTHER, EVEN AS SHE SOUGHT TO PROTECT ME WITH THOSE SAME GIFTS WE SHARED.
I HAD DONE THE SAME TO MY COCONSPIRATOR, AND MY TRACKS HAD BEEN COVERED.
AT LEAST, THAT'S HOW I REMEMBERED IT AT THAT MOMENT. WHEN FANTASY WAS REALITY.
WHEN REALITY WAS MULTIPLE CHOICE.
THERE WAS NOTHING LEFT FOR ME TO DO BUT USE THE POWERS I WAS ONLY STILL LEARNING ABOUT.
DO YOU SMELL THAT?
SNIFFF
I WOULD PROVIDE A SERVICE TO ANY WHO WOULD PAY.
EVERY DELICATE FLOWER...EACH PERFECT BLOSSOM OPENING JUST FOR ME...
I WOULD DISCOVER THE TRUEST DEPTHS BOTH MY CLIENTS, AND MYSELF, WERE CAPABLE OF.

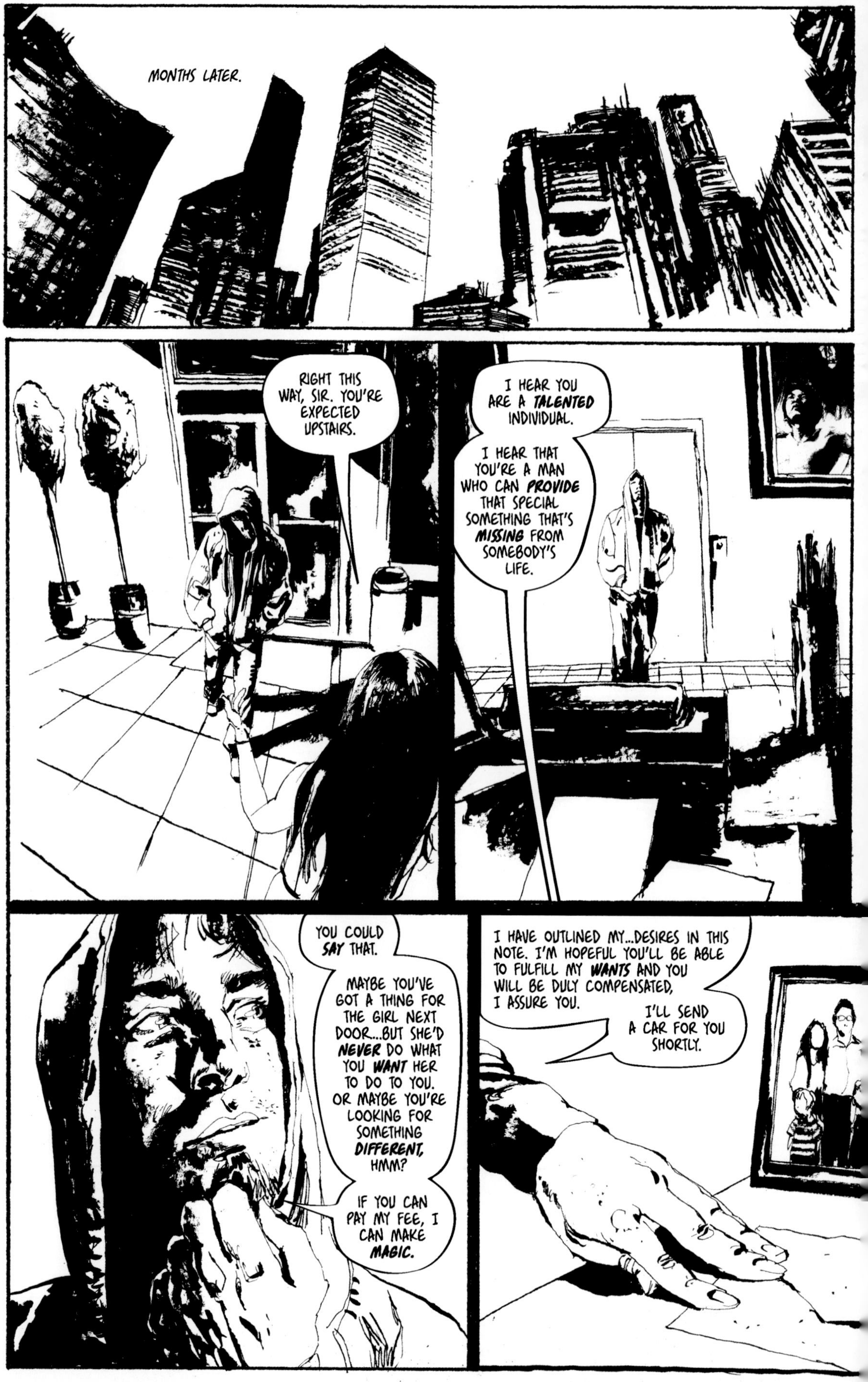
MONTHS LATER.
RIGHT THIS WAY, SIR. YOU'RE EXPECTED UPSTAIRS.
I HEAR YOU ARE A TALENTED INDIVIDUAL.
I HEAR THAT YOU'RE A MAN WHO CAN PROVIDE THAT SPECIAL SOMETHING THAT'S MISSING FROM SOMEBODY'S LIFE.
YOU COULD SAY THAT.
MAYBE YOU'VE GOT A THING FOR THE GIRL NEXT DOOR...BUT SHE'D NEVER DO WHAT YOU WANT HER TO DO TO YOU. OR MAYBE YOU'RE LOOKING FOR SOMETHING DIFFERENT, HMM?
IF YOU CAN PAY MY FEE, I CAN MAKE MAGIC.
I HAVE OUTLINED MY...DESIRES IN THIS NOTE. I'M HOPEFUL YOU'LL BE ABLE TO FULFILL MY WANTS AND YOU WILL BE DULY COMPENSATED, I ASSURE YOU.
I'LL SEND A CAR FOR YOU SHORTLY.

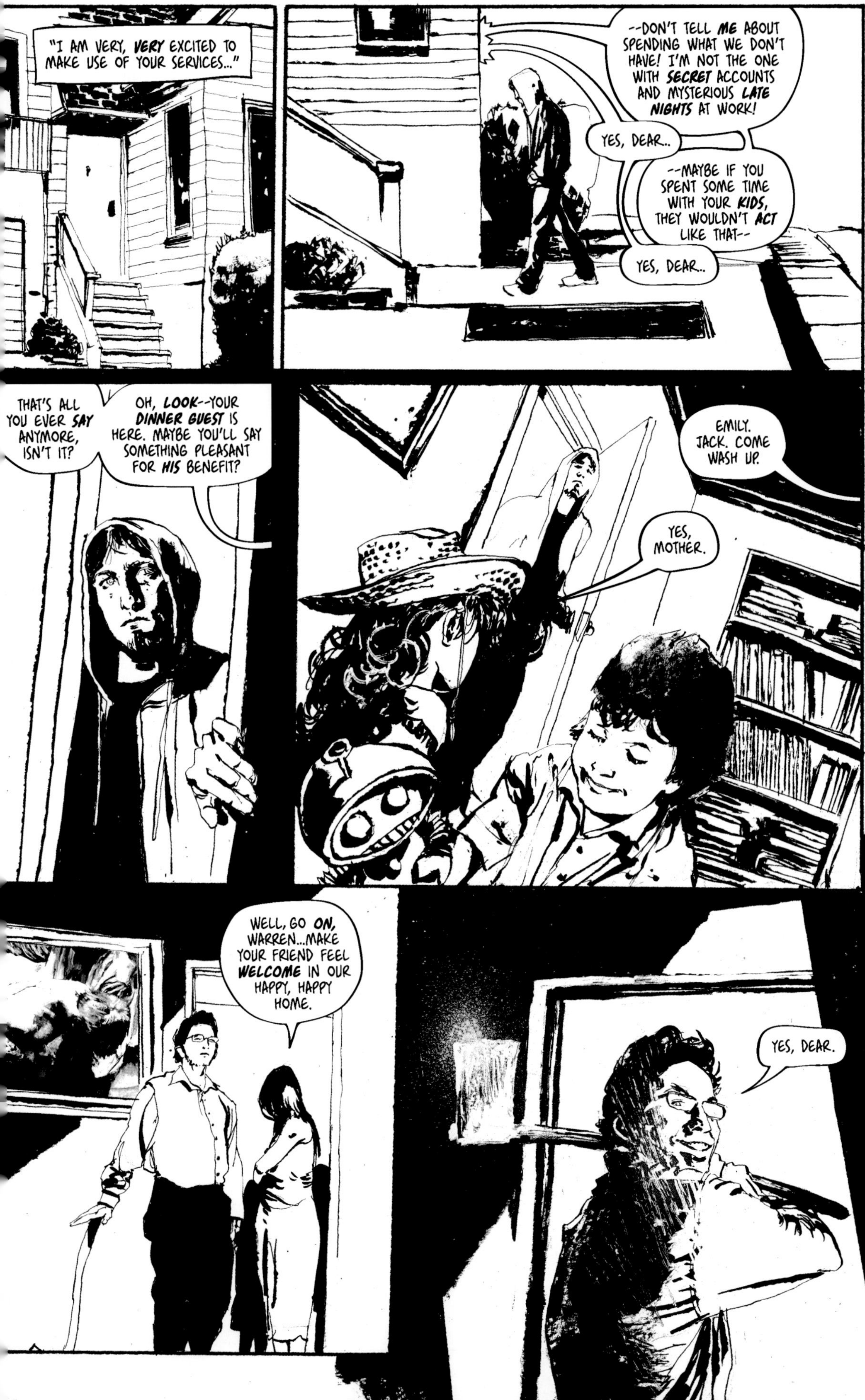
"I AM VERY, VERY EXCITED TO MAKE USE OF YOUR SERVICES..."
--DON'T TELL ME ABOUT SPENDING WHAT WE DON'T HAVE! I'M NOT THE ONE WITH SECRET ACCOUNTS AND MYSTERIOUS LATE NIGHTS AT WORK!
YES, DEAR..
--MAYBE IF YOU SPENT SOME TIME WITH YOUR KIDS, THEY WOULDN'T ACT LIKE THAT--
YES, DEAR..
THAT'S ALL YOU EVER SAY ANYMORE, ISN'T IT?
OH, LOOK--YOUR DINNER GUEST IS HERE. MAYBE YOU'LL SAY SOMETHING PLEASANT FOR HIS BENEFIT?
EMILY. JACK. COME WASH UP.
YES, MOTHER.
WELL, GO ON, WARREN...MAKE YOUR FRIEND FEEL WELCOME IN OUR HAPPY, HAPPY HOME.
YES, DEAR.

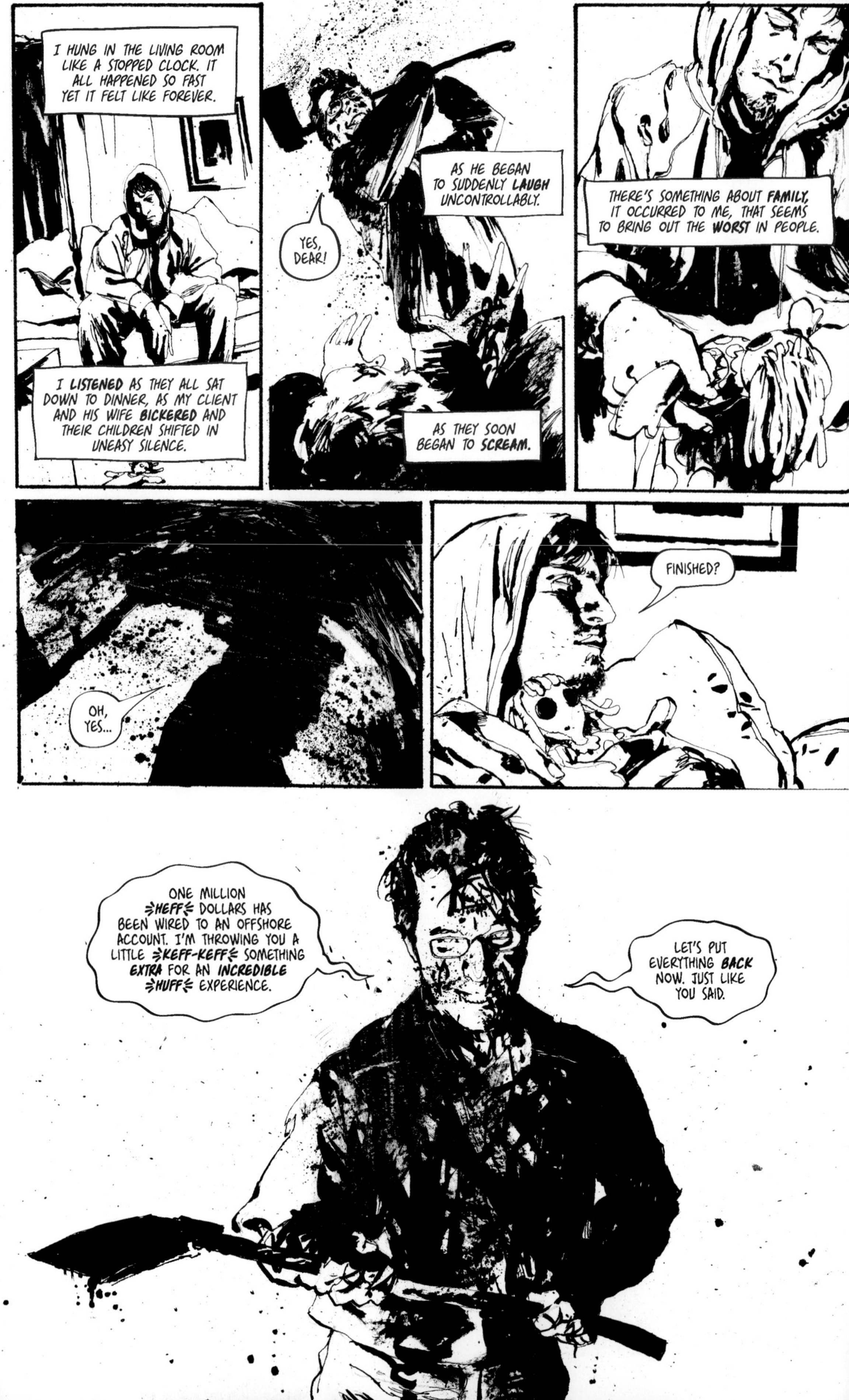
I HUNG IN THE LIVING ROOM LIKE A STOPPED CLOCK. IT ALL HAPPENED SO FAST YET IT FELT LIKE FOREVER.
I LISTENED AS THEY ALL SAT DOWN TO DINNER, AS MY CLIENT AND HIS WIFE BICKERED AND THEIR CHILDREN SHIFTED IN UNEASY SILENCE.
YES, DEAR!
AS HE BEGAN TO SUDDENLY LAUGH UNCONTROLLABLY.
AS THEY SOON BEGAN TO SCREAM.
THERE'S SOMETHING ABOUT FAMILY, IT OCCURRED TO ME, THAT SEEMS TO BRING OUT THE WORST IN PEOPLE.
OH, YES...
FINISHED?
ONE MILLION *HEFF* DOLLARS HAS BEEN WIRED TO AN OFFSHORE ACCOUNT. I'M THROWING YOU A LITTLE *KEFF-KEFF* SOMETHING EXTRA FOR AN INCREDIBLE *HUFF* EXPERIENCE.
LET'S PUT EVERYTHING BACK NOW. JUST LIKE YOU SAID.

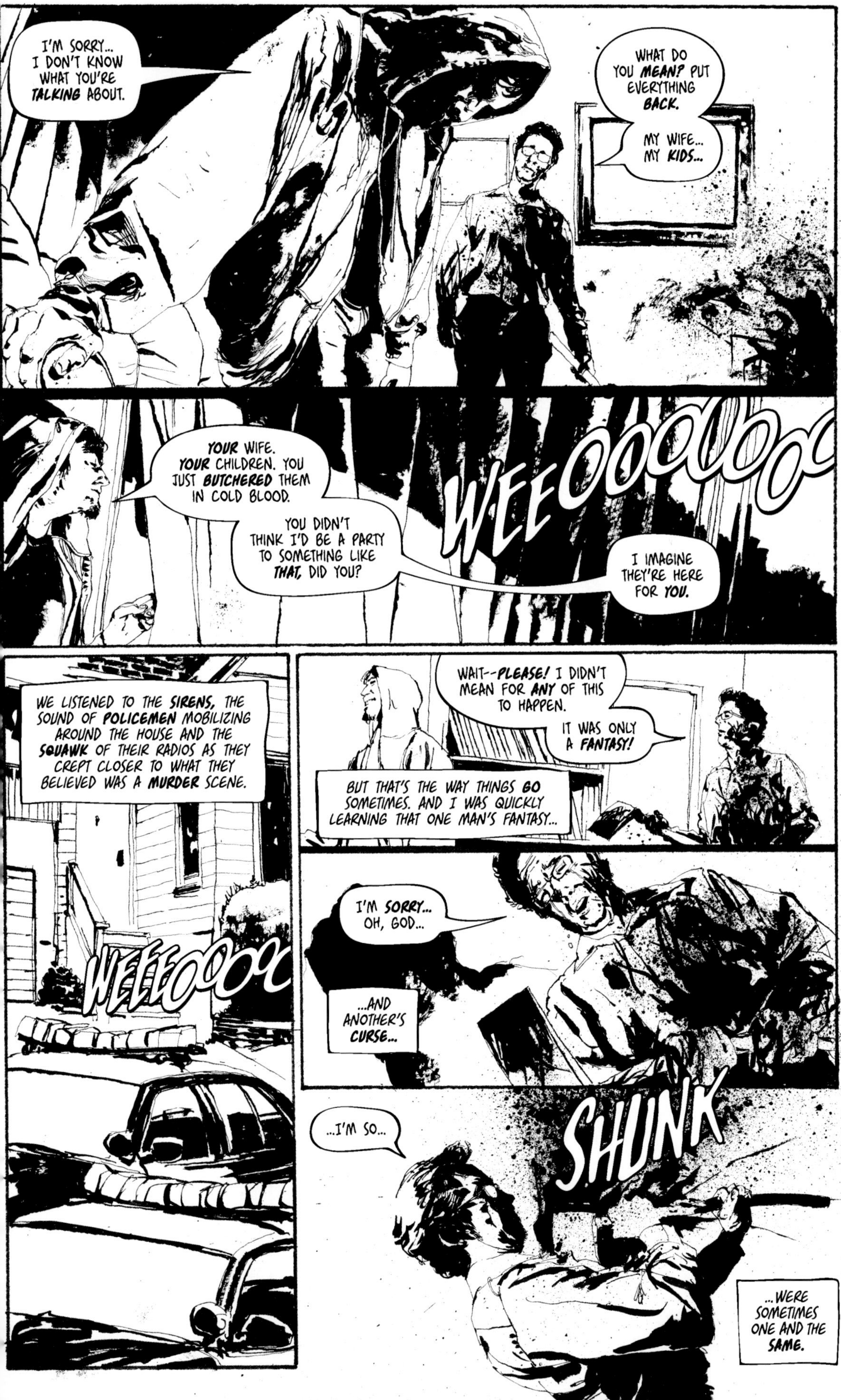

I'M SORRY... I DON'T KNOW WHAT YOU'RE TALKING ABOUT.
WHAT DO YOU MEAN? PUT EVERYTHING BACK.
MY WIFE... MY KIDS...
YOUR WIFE. YOUR CHILDREN. YOU JUST BUTCHERED THEM IN COLD BLOOD.
YOU DIDN'T THINK I'D BE A PARTY TO SOMETHING LIKE THAT, DID YOU?
WEEOOOOOOO
I IMAGINE THEY'RE HERE FOR YOU.
WE LISTENED TO THE SIRENS, THE SOUND OF POLICEMEN MOBILIZING AROUND THE HOUSE AND THE SQUAWK OF THEIR RADIOS AS THEY CREPT CLOSER TO WHAT THEY BELIEVED WAS A MURDER SCENE.
WEEEOOOO
WAIT--PLEASE! I DIDN'T MEAN FOR ANY OF THIS TO HAPPEN.
IT WAS ONLY A FANTASY!
BUT THAT'S THE WAY THINGS GO SOMETIMES. AND I WAS QUICKLY LEARNING THAT ONE MAN'S FANTASY...
I'M SORRY... OH, GOD...
...AND ANOTHER'S CURSE...
...I'M SO...
SHUNK
...WERE SOMETIMES ONE AND THE SAME.

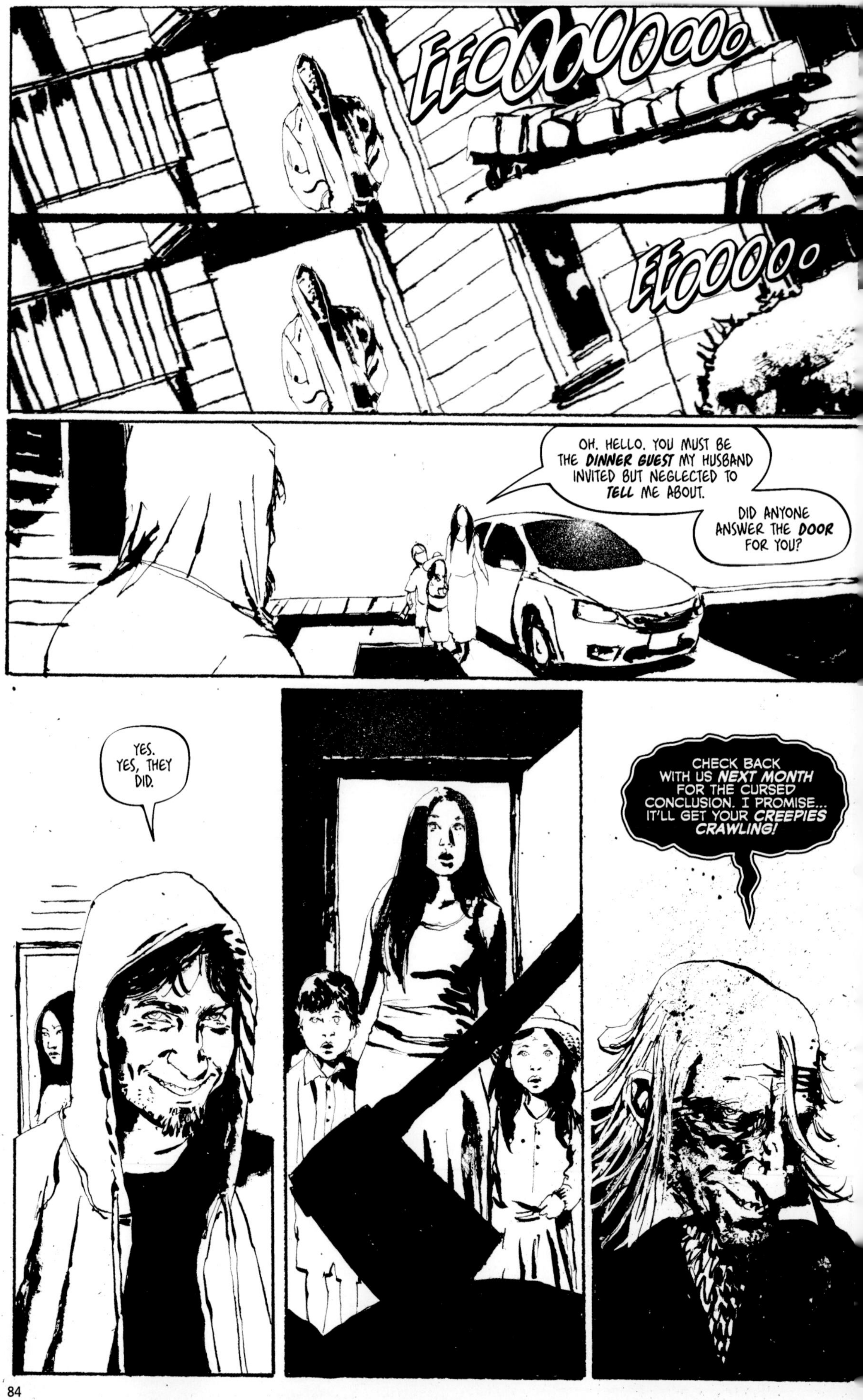
EEOOOOOooo
EEOOOOo
OH. HELLO. YOU MUST BE THE DINNER GUEST MY HUSBAND INVITED BUT NEGLECTED TO TELL ME ABOUT.
DID ANYONE ANSWER THE DOOR FOR YOU?
YES. YES, THEY DID.
CHECK BACK WITH US NEXT MONTH FOR THE CURSED CONCLUSION. I PROMISE... IT'LL GET YOUR CREEPIES CRAWLING!

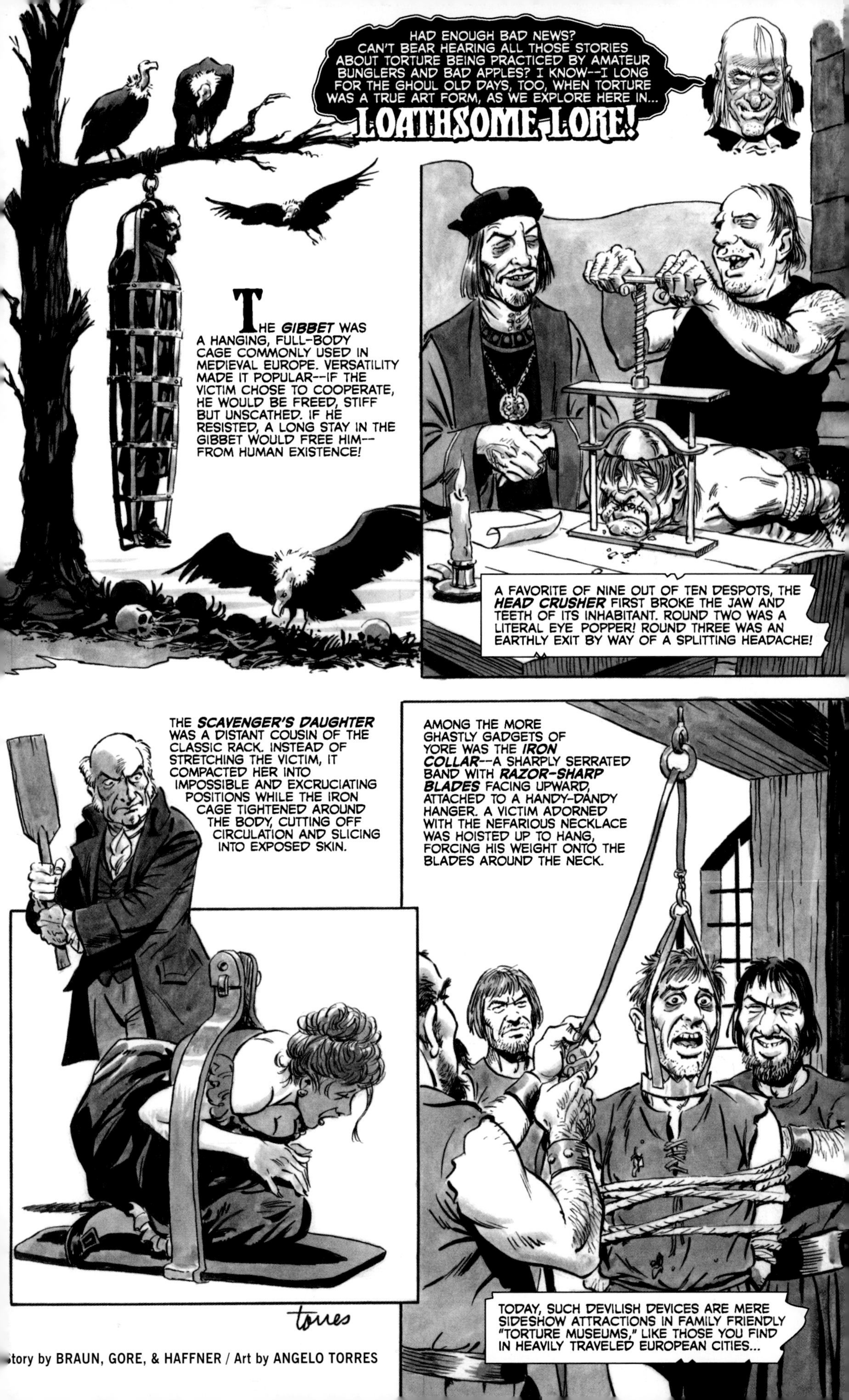
HAD ENOUGH BAD NEWS? CAN'T BEAR HEARING ALL THOSE STORIES ABOUT TORTURE BEING PRACTICED BY AMATEUR BUNGLERS AND BAD APPLES? I KNOW--I LONG FOR THE GHOUL OLD DAYS, TOO, WHEN TORTURE WAS A TRUE ART FORM, AS WE EXPLORE HERE IN...
LOATHSOME LORE!
THE *GIBBET* WAS A HANGING, FULL-BODY CAGE COMMONLY USED IN MEDIEVAL EUROPE. VERSATILITY MADE IT POPULAR--IF THE VICTIM CHOSE TO COOPERATE, HE WOULD BE FREED, STIFF BUT UNSCATHED. IF HE RESISTED, A LONG STAY IN THE GIBBET WOULD FREE HIM--FROM HUMAN EXISTENCE!
A FAVORITE OF NINE OUT OF TEN DESPOTS, THE *HEAD CRUSHER* FIRST BROKE THE JAW AND TEETH OF ITS INHABITANT. ROUND TWO WAS A LITERAL EYE POPPER! ROUND THREE WAS AN EARTHLY EXIT BY WAY OF A SPLITTING HEADACHE!
THE *SCAVENGER'S DAUGHTER* WAS A DISTANT COUSIN OF THE CLASSIC RACK. INSTEAD OF STRETCHING THE VICTIM, IT COMPACTED HER INTO IMPOSSIBLE AND EXCRUCIATING POSITIONS WHILE THE IRON CAGE TIGHTENED AROUND THE BODY, CUTTING OFF CIRCULATION AND SLICING INTO EXPOSED SKIN.
AMONG THE MORE GHASTLY GADGETS OF YORE WAS THE *IRON COLLAR*--A SHARPLY SERRATED BAND WITH *RAZOR-SHARP BLADES* FACING UPWARD, ATTACHED TO A HANDY-DANDY HANGER. A VICTIM ADORNED WITH THE NEFARIOUS NECKLACE WAS HOISTED UP TO HANG, FORCING HIS WEIGHT ONTO THE BLADES AROUND THE NECK.
torres
TODAY, SUCH DEVILISH DEVICES ARE MERE SIDESHOW ATTRACTIONS IN FAMILY FRIENDLY "TORTURE MUSEUMS," LIKE THOSE YOU FIND IN HEAVILY TRAVELED EUROPEAN CITIES...
Story by BRAUN, GORE, & HAFFNER / Art by ANGELO TORRES

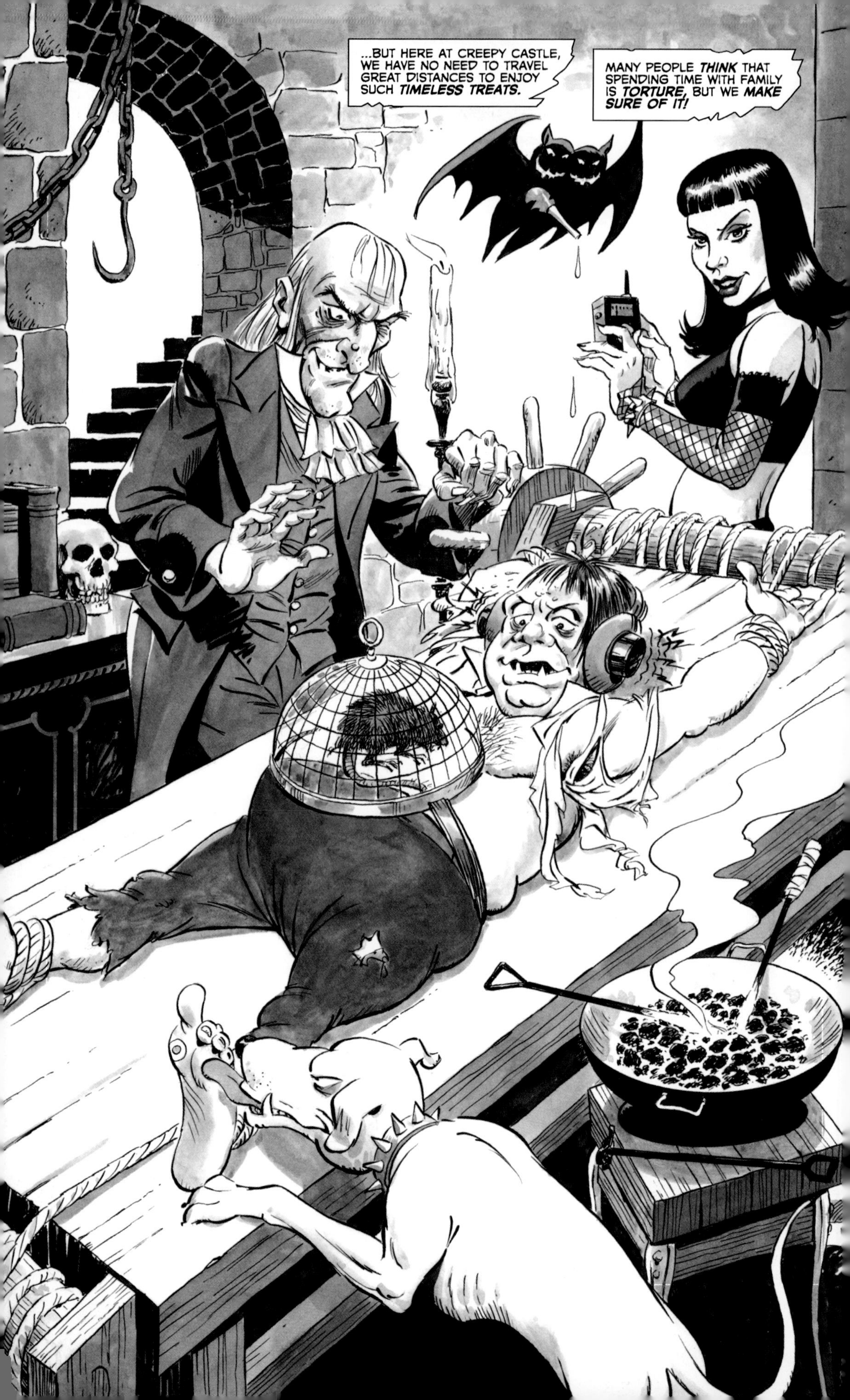
...BUT HERE AT CREEPY CASTLE, WE HAVE NO NEED TO TRAVEL GREAT DISTANCES TO ENJOY SUCH TIMELESS TREATS.
MANY PEOPLE THINK THAT SPENDING TIME WITH FAMILY IS TORTURE, BUT WE MAKE SURE OF IT!

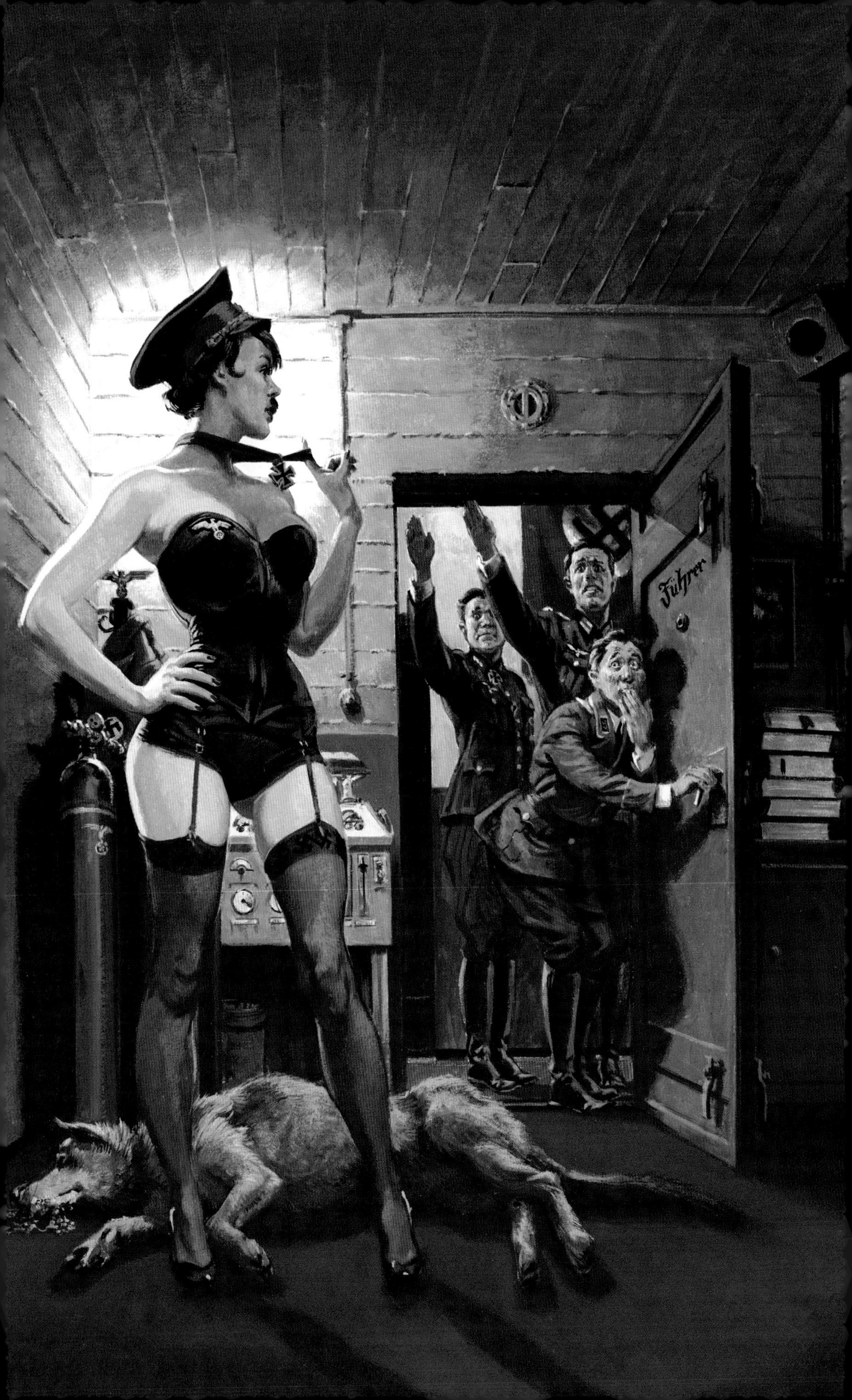
Führer

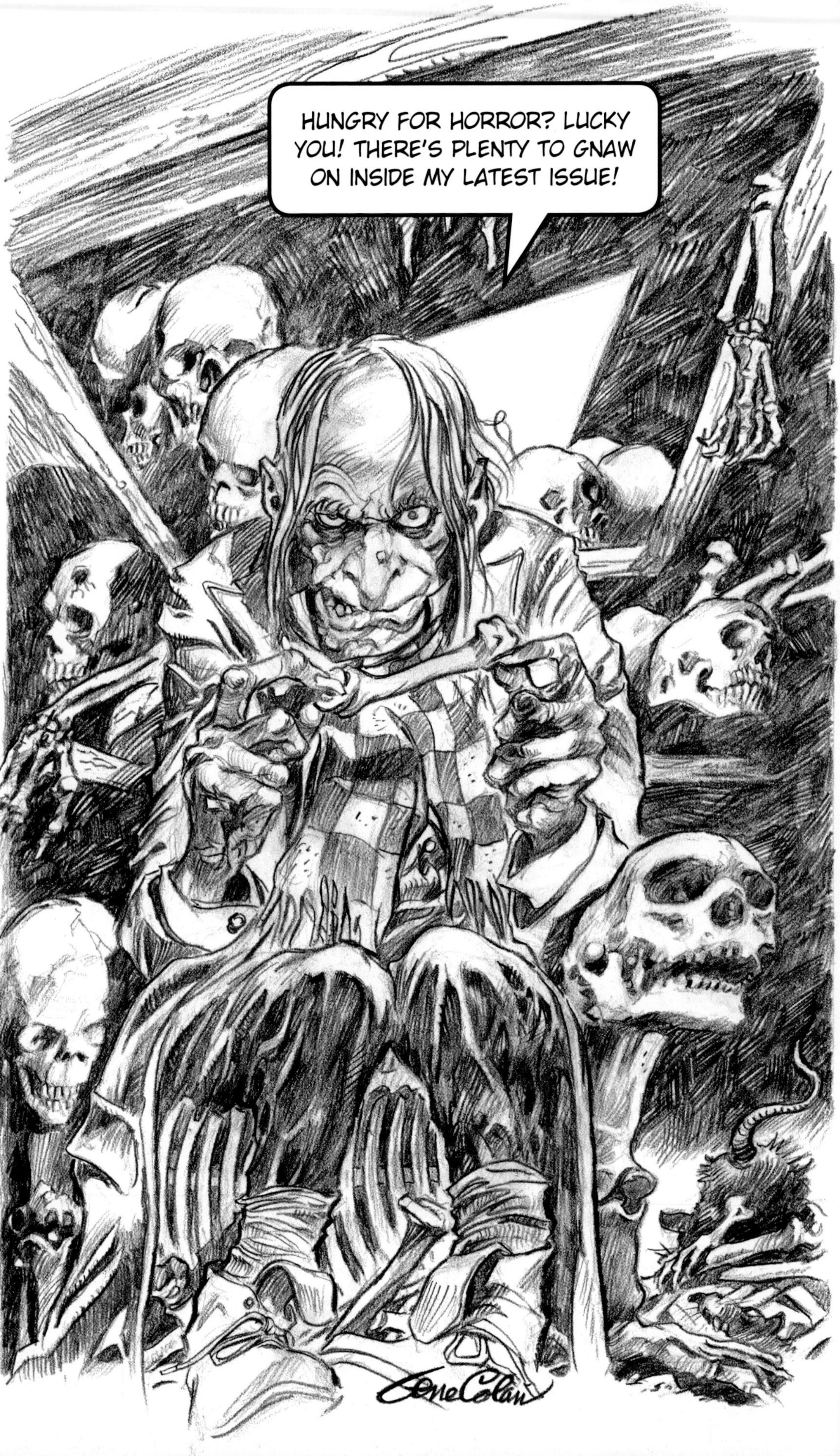
HUNGRY FOR HORROR? LUCKY YOU! THERE'S PLENTY TO GNAW ON INSIDE MY LATEST ISSUE!
Gene Colan

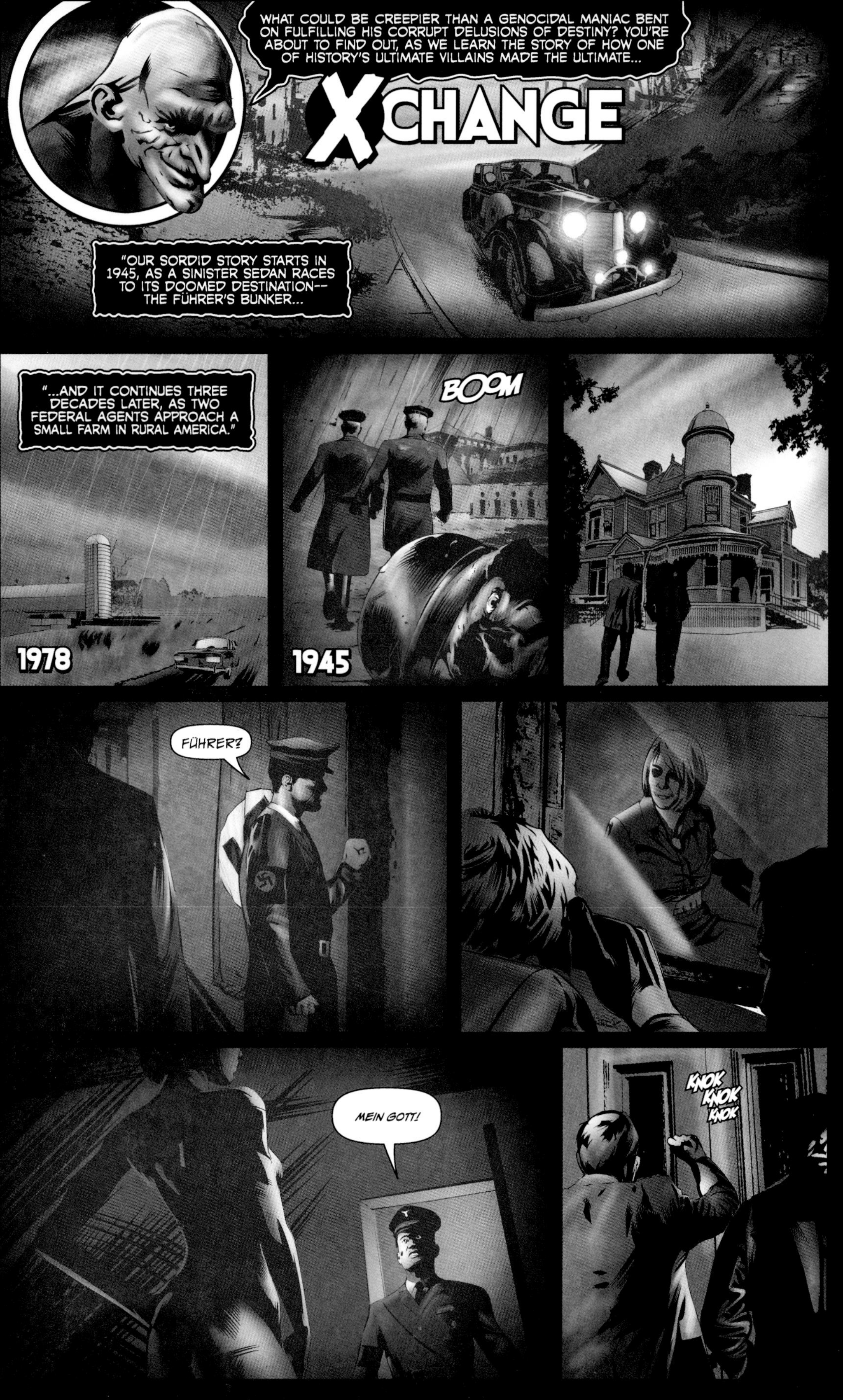
WHAT COULD BE CREEPIER THAN A GENOCIDAL MANIAC BENT ON FULFILLING HIS CORRUPT DELUSIONS OF DESTINY? YOU'RE ABOUT TO FIND OUT, AS WE LEARN THE STORY OF HOW ONE OF HISTORY'S ULTIMATE VILLAINS MADE THE ULTIMATE...
XCHANGE
"OUR SORDID STORY STARTS IN 1945, AS A SINISTER SEDAN RACES TO ITS DOOMED DESTINATION-- THE FÜHRER'S BUNKER...
"...AND IT CONTINUES THREE DECADES LATER, AS TWO FEDERAL AGENTS APPROACH A SMALL FARM IN RURAL AMERICA."
1978
BOOM
1945
FÜHRER?
MEIN GOTT!
KNOK
KNOK
KNOK

Script by DAN BRAUN and CRAIG HAFFNER / Art by DENNIS CALERO

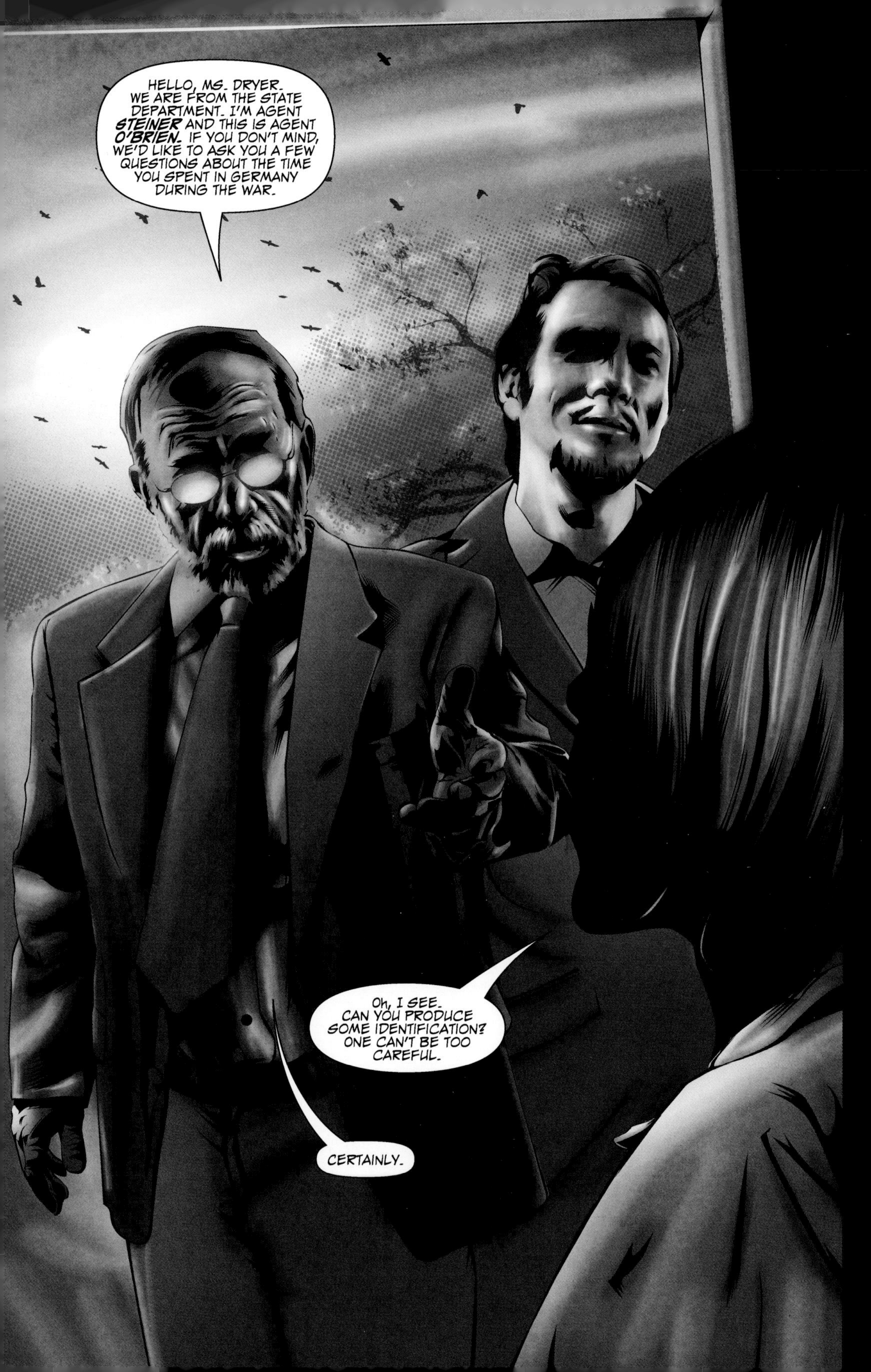
HELLO, MS. DRYER. WE ARE FROM THE STATE DEPARTMENT. I'M AGENT STEINER AND THIS IS AGENT O'BRIEN. IF YOU DON'T MIND, WE'D LIKE TO ASK YOU A FEW QUESTIONS ABOUT THE TIME YOU SPENT IN GERMANY DURING THE WAR.
Oh, I SEE. CAN YOU PRODUCE SOME IDENTIFICATION? ONE CAN'T BE TOO CAREFUL.
CERTAINLY.

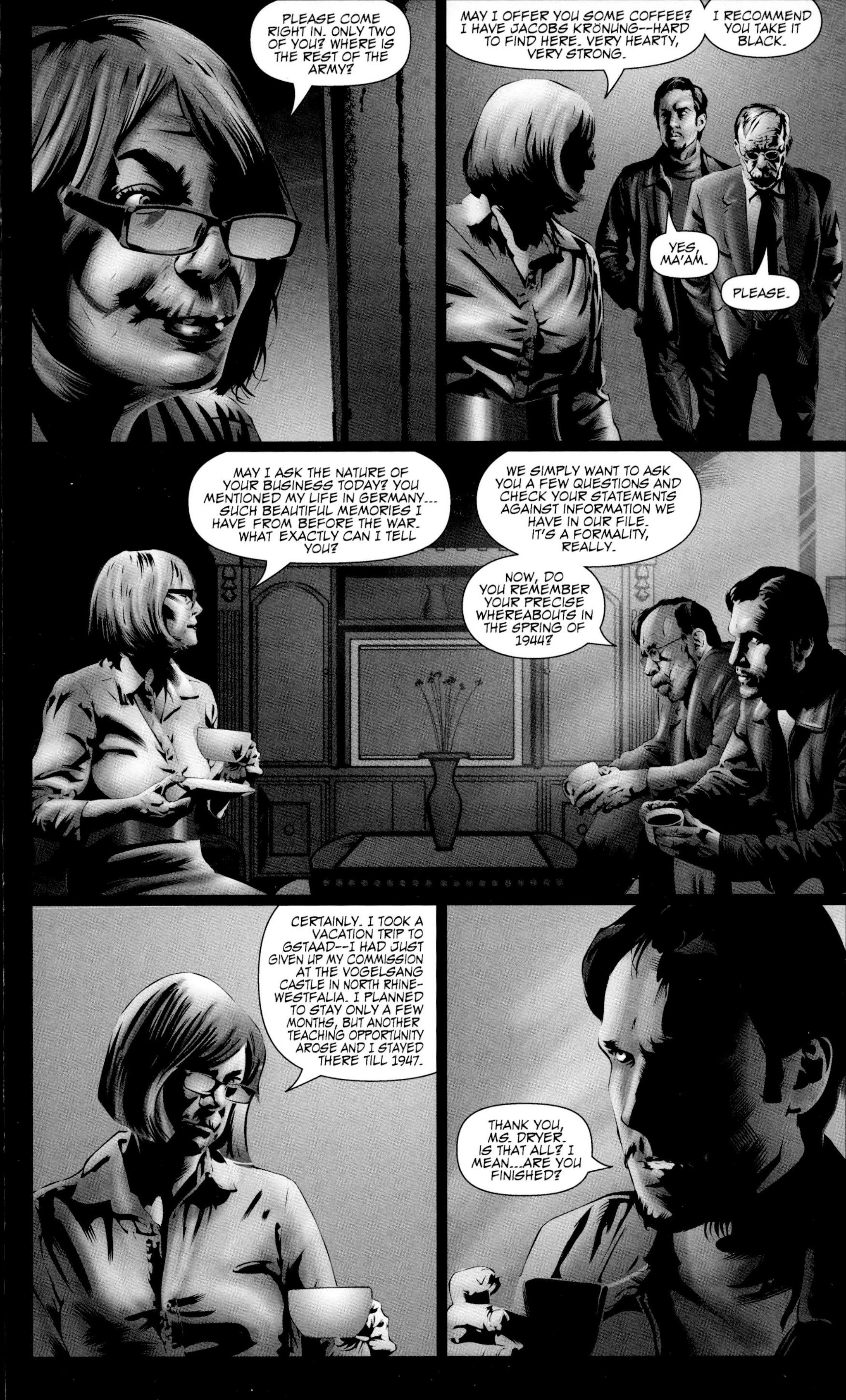
PLEASE COME RIGHT IN. ONLY TWO OF YOU? WHERE IS THE REST OF THE ARMY?
MAY I OFFER YOU SOME COFFEE? I HAVE JACOBS KRÖNUNG--HARD TO FIND HERE. VERY HEARTY, VERY STRONG.
I RECOMMEND YOU TAKE IT BLACK.
YES, MA'AM.
PLEASE.
MAY I ASK THE NATURE OF YOUR BUSINESS TODAY? YOU MENTIONED MY LIFE IN GERMANY... SUCH BEAUTIFUL MEMORIES I HAVE FROM BEFORE THE WAR. WHAT EXACTLY CAN I TELL YOU?
WE SIMPLY WANT TO ASK YOU A FEW QUESTIONS AND CHECK YOUR STATEMENTS AGAINST INFORMATION WE HAVE IN OUR FILE. IT'S A FORMALITY, REALLY.
NOW, DO YOU REMEMBER YOUR PRECISE WHEREABOUTS IN THE SPRING OF 1944?
CERTAINLY. I TOOK A VACATION TRIP TO GSTAAD--I HAD JUST GIVEN UP MY COMMISSION AT THE VOGELSANG CASTLE IN NORTH RHINE-WESTFALIA. I PLANNED TO STAY ONLY A FEW MONTHS, BUT ANOTHER TEACHING OPPORTUNITY AROSE AND I STAYED THERE TILL 1947.
THANK YOU, MS. DRYER. IS THAT ALL? I MEAN...ARE YOU FINISHED?

I'M SORRY?

MY PARTNER HERE MAY HAVE TIME FOR SMALL TALK, BUT I DO NOT. SHALL I BE BLUNT?

FIRST, WE KNOW YOUR NAME IS NOT OLGA DRYER BUT OLGA KINSKI. YOU HAVE, IN FACT, NEVER BEEN TO GSTAAD A SINGLE DAY IN YOUR LIFE. WE HAVE COMPELLING EVIDENCE THAT YOU WERE ACTUALLY IN BERLIN DURING THAT TIME.

WE ALSO HAVE EVIDENCE LINKING YOU DIRECTLY WITH THE HIGHEST LEVELS OF THE GESTAPO AND THE S.S.

YOU WERE IN PRETTY TIGHT WITH THE HARD-LINERS-- HIMMLER, GÖRING, AND GOEBBELS.

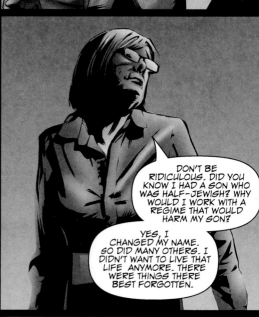

DON'T BE RIDICULOUS. DID YOU KNOW I HAD A SON WHO WAS HALF-JEWISH? WHY WOULD I WORK WITH A REGIME THAT WOULD HARM MY SON?

YES, I CHANGED MY NAME. SO DID MANY OTHERS. I DIDN'T WANT TO LIVE THAT LIFE ANYMORE. THERE WERE THINGS THERE BEST FORGOTTEN.

OLGA, SINCE YOU BROUGHT IT UP...WE KNOW ABOUT YOUR SON AND WE DO KNOW HIS WHEREABOUTS. IF YOU COOPERATE, THERE IS INFORMATION WE CAN SHARE WITH YOU.

MY SON...YOU KNOW WHERE MY SON IS?

I HAVEN'T SEEN HIM SINCE THAT TERRIBLE DAY... WHEN I LET THEM TAKE HIM. I TRIED TO FIND HIM, TO NO AVAIL. I ALWAYS ASSUMED THE WORST.

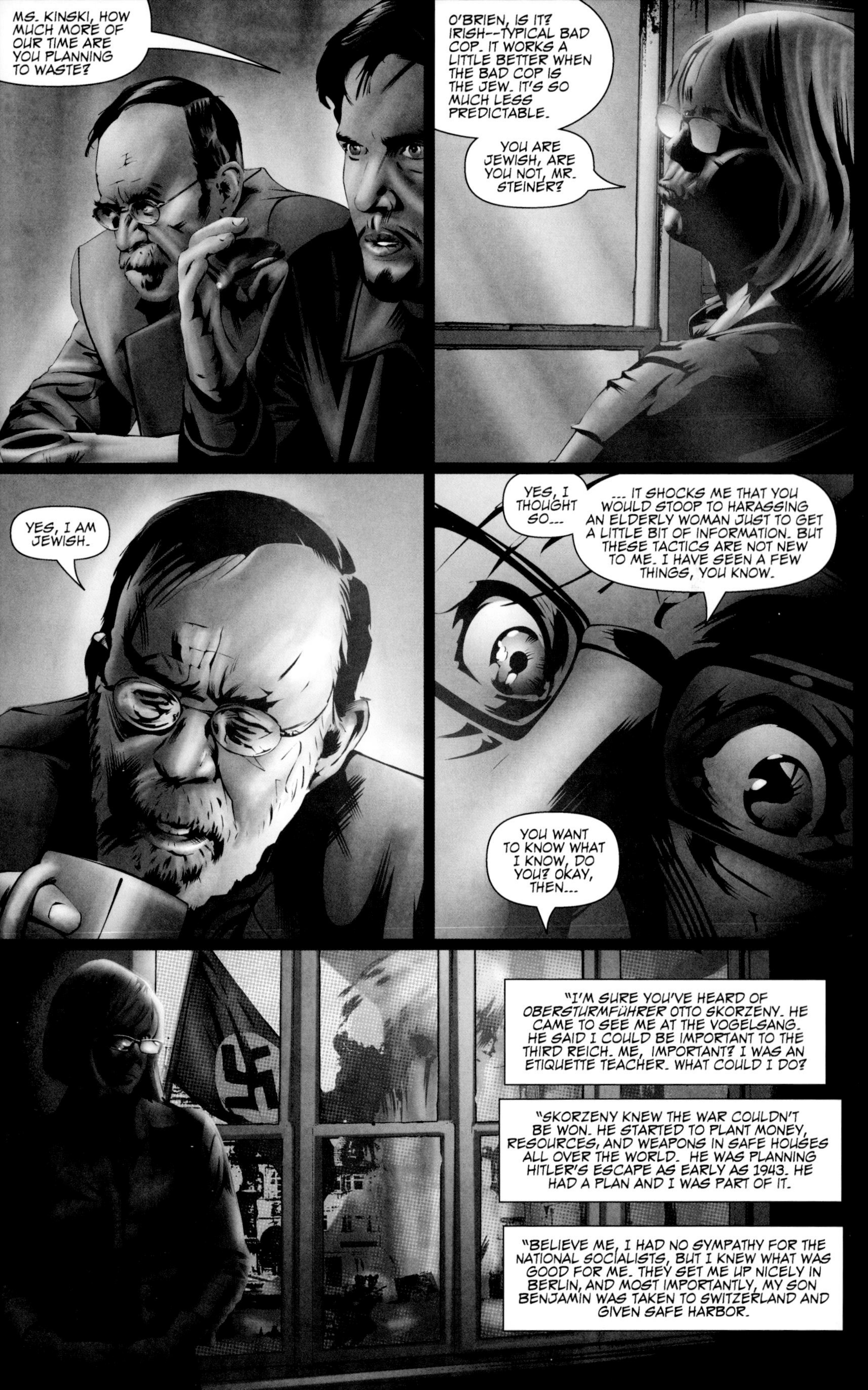
MS. KINSKI, HOW MUCH MORE OF OUR TIME ARE YOU PLANNING TO WASTE?
O'BRIEN, IS IT? IRISH--TYPICAL BAD COP. IT WORKS A LITTLE BETTER WHEN THE BAD COP IS THE JEW. IT'S SO MUCH LESS PREDICTABLE.
YOU ARE JEWISH, ARE YOU NOT, MR. STEINER?
YES, I AM JEWISH.
YES, I THOUGHT SO...
... IT SHOCKS ME THAT YOU WOULD STOOP TO HARASSING AN ELDERLY WOMAN JUST TO GET A LITTLE BIT OF INFORMATION. BUT THESE TACTICS ARE NOT NEW TO ME. I HAVE SEEN A FEW THINGS, YOU KNOW.
YOU WANT TO KNOW WHAT I KNOW, DO YOU? OKAY, THEN...
"I'M SURE YOU'VE HEARD OF *OBERSTURMFÜHRER* OTTO SKORZENY. HE CAME TO SEE ME AT THE VOGELSANG. HE SAID I COULD BE IMPORTANT TO THE THIRD REICH. ME, IMPORTANT? I WAS AN ETIQUETTE TEACHER. WHAT COULD I DO?
"SKORZENY KNEW THE WAR COULDN'T BE WON. HE STARTED TO PLANT MONEY, RESOURCES, AND WEAPONS IN SAFE HOUSES ALL OVER THE WORLD. HE WAS PLANNING HITLER'S ESCAPE AS EARLY AS 1943. HE HAD A PLAN AND I WAS PART OF IT.
"BELIEVE ME, I HAD NO SYMPATHY FOR THE NATIONAL SOCIALISTS, BUT I KNEW WHAT WAS GOOD FOR ME. THEY SET ME UP NICELY IN BERLIN, AND MOST IMPORTANTLY, MY SON BENJAMIN WAS TAKEN TO SWITZERLAND AND GIVEN SAFE HARBOR.

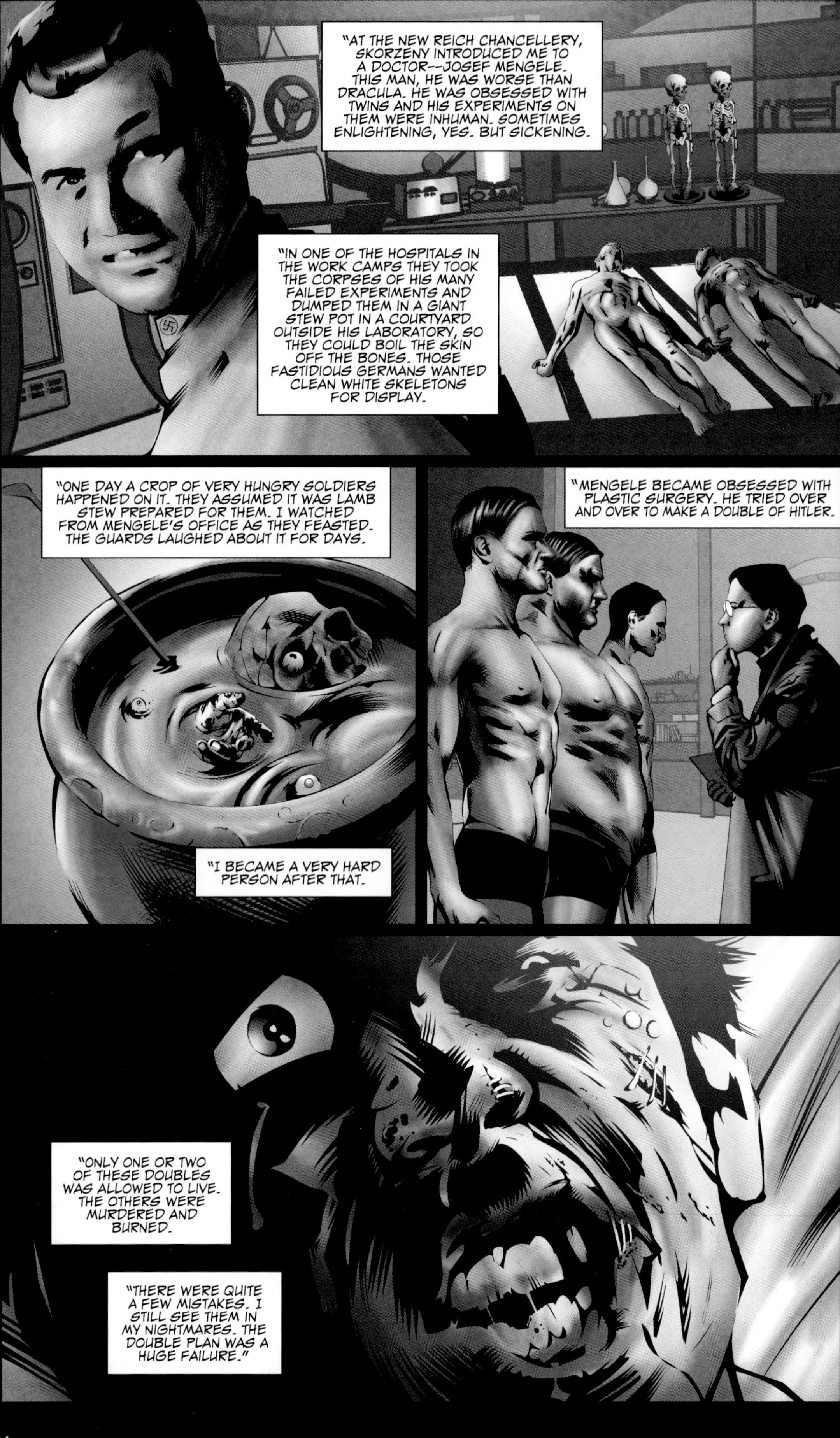
"AT THE NEW REICH CHANCELLERY, SKORZENY INTRODUCED ME TO A DOCTOR--JOSEF MENGELE. THIS MAN, HE WAS WORSE THAN DRACULA. HE WAS OBSESSED WITH TWINS AND HIS EXPERIMENTS ON THEM WERE INHUMAN. SOMETIMES ENLIGHTENING, YES. BUT SICKENING.
"IN ONE OF THE HOSPITALS IN THE WORK CAMPS THEY TOOK THE CORPSES OF HIS MANY FAILED EXPERIMENTS AND DUMPED THEM IN A GIANT STEW POT IN A COURTYARD OUTSIDE HIS LABORATORY, SO THEY COULD BOIL THE SKIN OFF THE BONES. THOSE FASTIDIOUS GERMANS WANTED CLEAN WHITE SKELETONS FOR DISPLAY.
"ONE DAY A CROP OF VERY HUNGRY SOLDIERS HAPPENED ON IT. THEY ASSUMED IT WAS LAMB STEW PREPARED FOR THEM. I WATCHED FROM MENGELE'S OFFICE AS THEY FEASTED. THE GUARDS LAUGHED ABOUT IT FOR DAYS.
"I BECAME A VERY HARD PERSON AFTER THAT.
"MENGELE BECAME OBSESSED WITH PLASTIC SURGERY. HE TRIED OVER AND OVER TO MAKE A DOUBLE OF HITLER.
"ONLY ONE OR TWO OF THESE DOUBLES WAS ALLOWED TO LIVE. THE OTHERS WERE MURDERED AND BURNED.
"THERE WERE QUITE A FEW MISTAKES. I STILL SEE THEM IN MY NIGHTMARES. THE DOUBLE PLAN WAS A HUGE FAILURE."

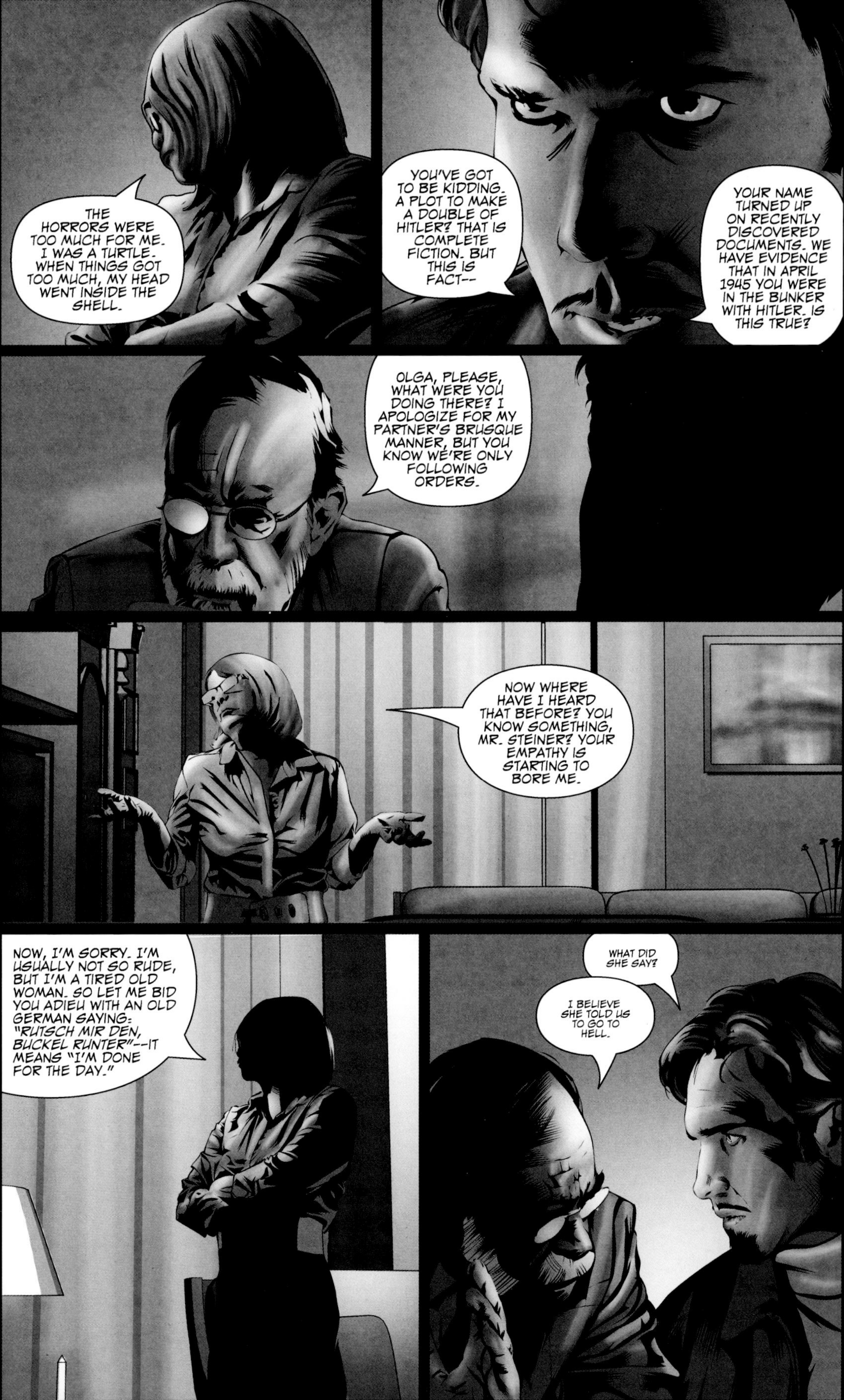
THE HORRORS WERE TOO MUCH FOR ME. I WAS A TURTLE. WHEN THINGS GOT TOO MUCH, MY HEAD WENT INSIDE THE SHELL.
YOU'VE GOT TO BE KIDDING. A PLOT TO MAKE A DOUBLE OF HITLER? THAT IS COMPLETE FICTION. BUT THIS IS FACT--
YOUR NAME TURNED UP ON RECENTLY DISCOVERED DOCUMENTS. WE HAVE EVIDENCE THAT IN APRIL 1945 YOU WERE IN THE BUNKER WITH HITLER. IS THIS TRUE?
OLGA, PLEASE, WHAT WERE YOU DOING THERE? I APOLOGIZE FOR MY PARTNER'S BRUSQUE MANNER, BUT YOU KNOW WE'RE ONLY FOLLOWING ORDERS.
NOW WHERE HAVE I HEARD THAT BEFORE? YOU KNOW SOMETHING, MR. STEINER? YOUR EMPATHY IS STARTING TO BORE ME.
NOW, I'M SORRY. I'M USUALLY NOT SO RUDE, BUT I'M A TIRED OLD WOMAN. SO LET ME BID YOU ADIEU WITH AN OLD GERMAN SAYING: *"RUTSCH MIR DEN, BUCKEL RUNTER"*--IT MEANS "I'M DONE FOR THE DAY."
WHAT DID SHE SAY?
I BELIEVE SHE TOLD US TO GO TO HELL.

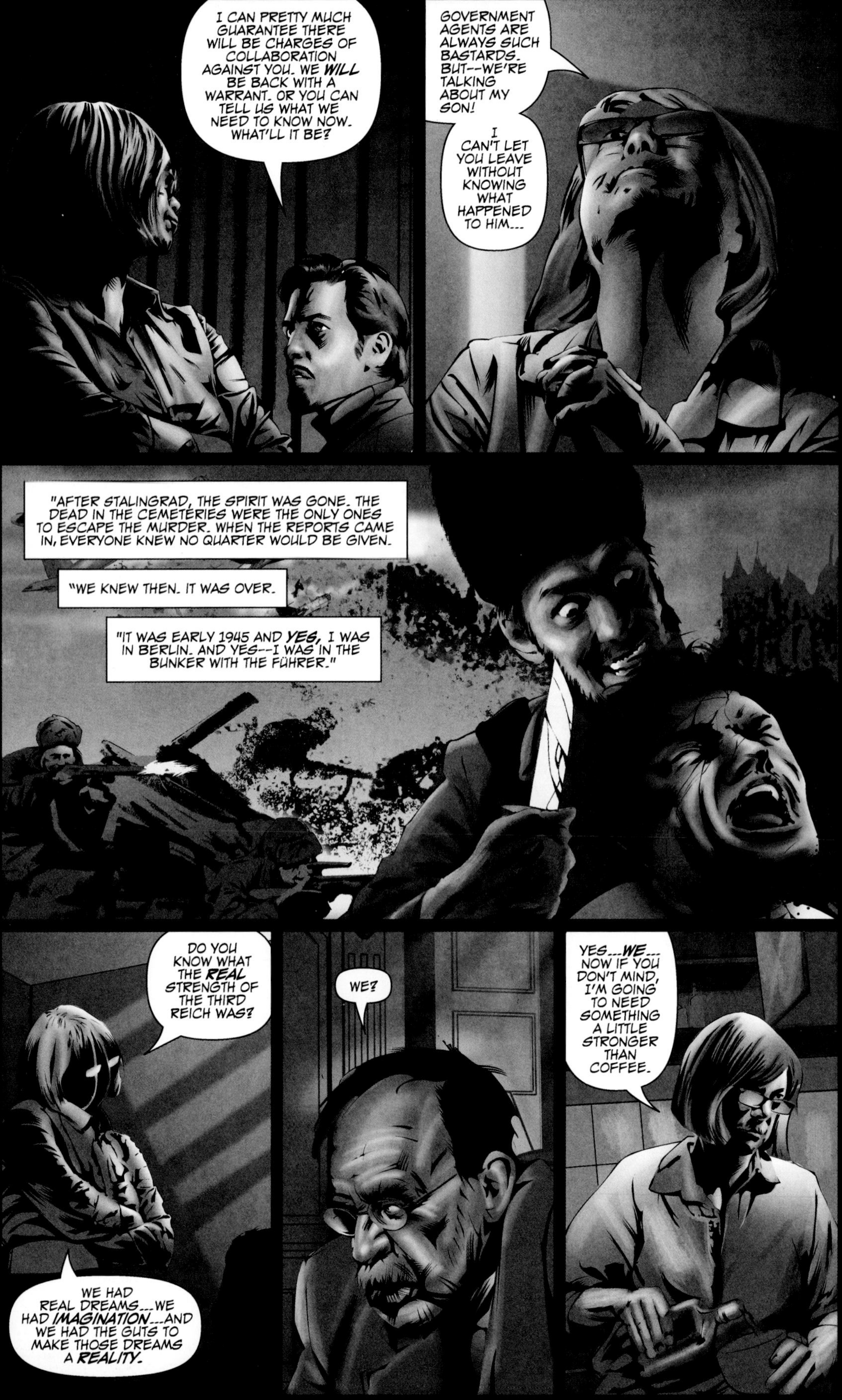
I CAN PRETTY MUCH GUARANTEE THERE WILL BE CHARGES OF COLLABORATION AGAINST YOU. WE WILL BE BACK WITH A WARRANT. OR YOU CAN TELL US WHAT WE NEED TO KNOW NOW. WHAT'LL IT BE?
GOVERNMENT AGENTS ARE ALWAYS SUCH BASTARDS. BUT--WE'RE TALKING ABOUT MY SON!
I CAN'T LET YOU LEAVE WITHOUT KNOWING WHAT HAPPENED TO HIM...
"AFTER STALINGRAD, THE SPIRIT WAS GONE. THE DEAD IN THE CEMETERIES WERE THE ONLY ONES TO ESCAPE THE MURDER. WHEN THE REPORTS CAME IN, EVERYONE KNEW NO QUARTER WOULD BE GIVEN.
"WE KNEW THEN. IT WAS OVER.
"IT WAS EARLY 1945 AND YES, I WAS IN BERLIN. AND YES--I WAS IN THE BUNKER WITH THE FÜHRER."
DO YOU KNOW WHAT THE REAL STRENGTH OF THE THIRD REICH WAS?
WE HAD REAL DREAMS...WE HAD IMAGINATION...AND WE HAD THE GUTS TO MAKE THOSE DREAMS A REALITY.
WE?
YES...WE... NOW IF YOU DON'T MIND, I'M GOING TO NEED SOMETHING A LITTLE STRONGER THAN COFFEE.

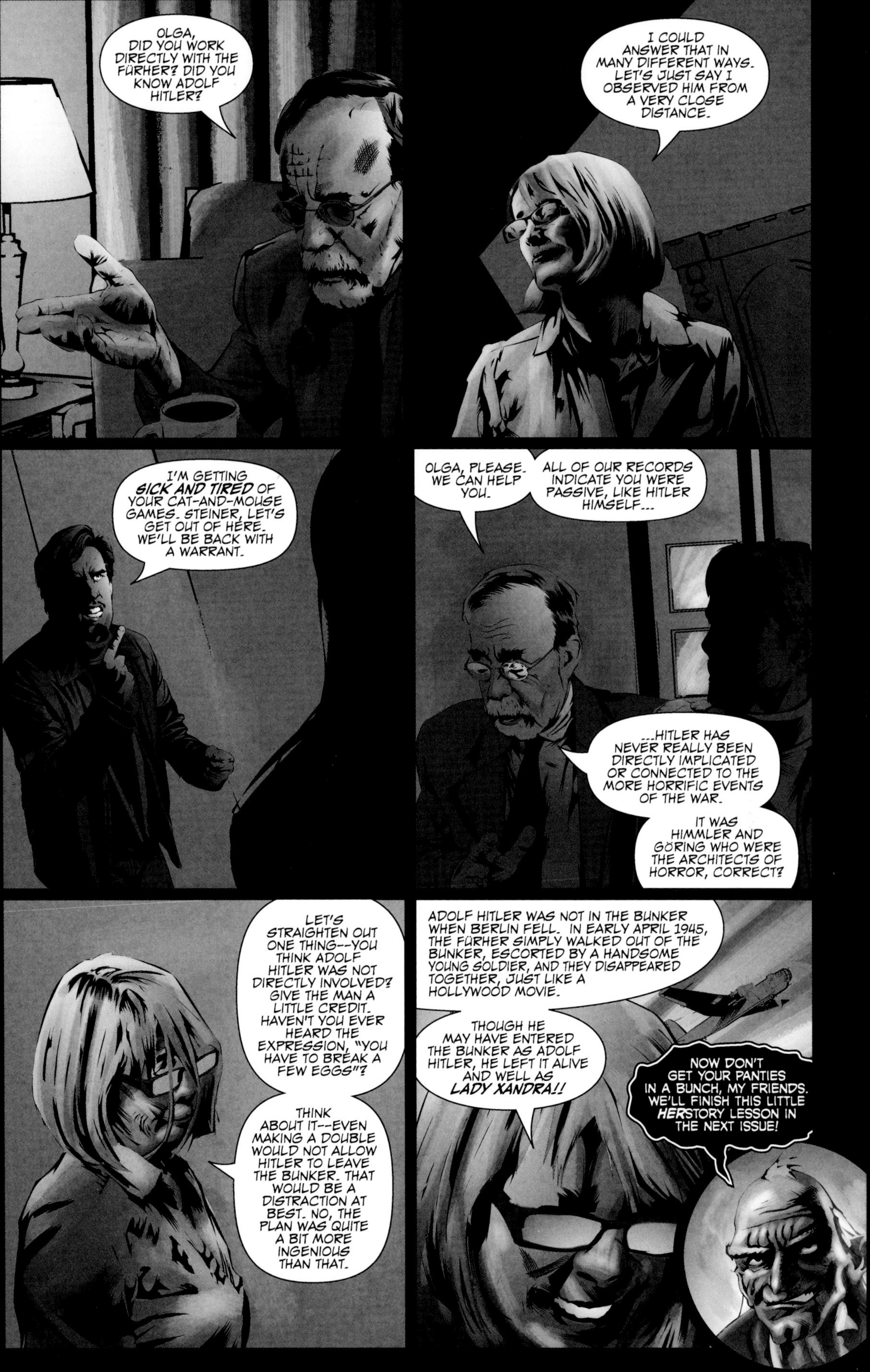
OLGA, DID YOU WORK DIRECTLY WITH THE FÜRHER? DID YOU KNOW ADOLF HITLER?
I COULD ANSWER THAT IN MANY DIFFERENT WAYS. LET'S JUST SAY I OBSERVED HIM FROM A VERY CLOSE DISTANCE.
I'M GETTING SICK AND TIRED OF YOUR CAT-AND-MOUSE GAMES. STEINER, LET'S GET OUT OF HERE. WE'LL BE BACK WITH A WARRANT.
OLGA, PLEASE. WE CAN HELP YOU.
ALL OF OUR RECORDS INDICATE YOU WERE PASSIVE, LIKE HITLER HIMSELF...
...HITLER HAS NEVER REALLY BEEN DIRECTLY IMPLICATED OR CONNECTED TO THE MORE HORRIFIC EVENTS OF THE WAR.
IT WAS HIMMLER AND GÖRING WHO WERE THE ARCHITECTS OF HORROR, CORRECT?
LET'S STRAIGHTEN OUT ONE THING--YOU THINK ADOLF HITLER WAS NOT DIRECTLY INVOLVED? GIVE THE MAN A LITTLE CREDIT. HAVEN'T YOU EVER HEARD THE EXPRESSION, "YOU HAVE TO BREAK A FEW EGGS"?
THINK ABOUT IT--EVEN MAKING A DOUBLE WOULD NOT ALLOW HITLER TO LEAVE THE BUNKER. THAT WOULD BE A DISTRACTION AT BEST. NO, THE PLAN WAS QUITE A BIT MORE INGENIOUS THAN THAT.
ADOLF HITLER WAS NOT IN THE BUNKER WHEN BERLIN FELL. IN EARLY APRIL 1945, THE FÜRHER SIMPLY WALKED OUT OF THE BUNKER, ESCORTED BY A HANDSOME YOUNG SOLDIER, AND THEY DISAPPEARED TOGETHER, JUST LIKE A HOLLYWOOD MOVIE.
THOUGH HE MAY HAVE ENTERED THE BUNKER AS ADOLF HITLER, HE LEFT IT ALIVE AND WELL AS LADY XANDRA!!
NOW DON'T GET YOUR PANTIES IN A BUNCH, MY FRIENDS. WE'LL FINISH THIS LITTLE HERSTORY LESSON IN THE NEXT ISSUE!

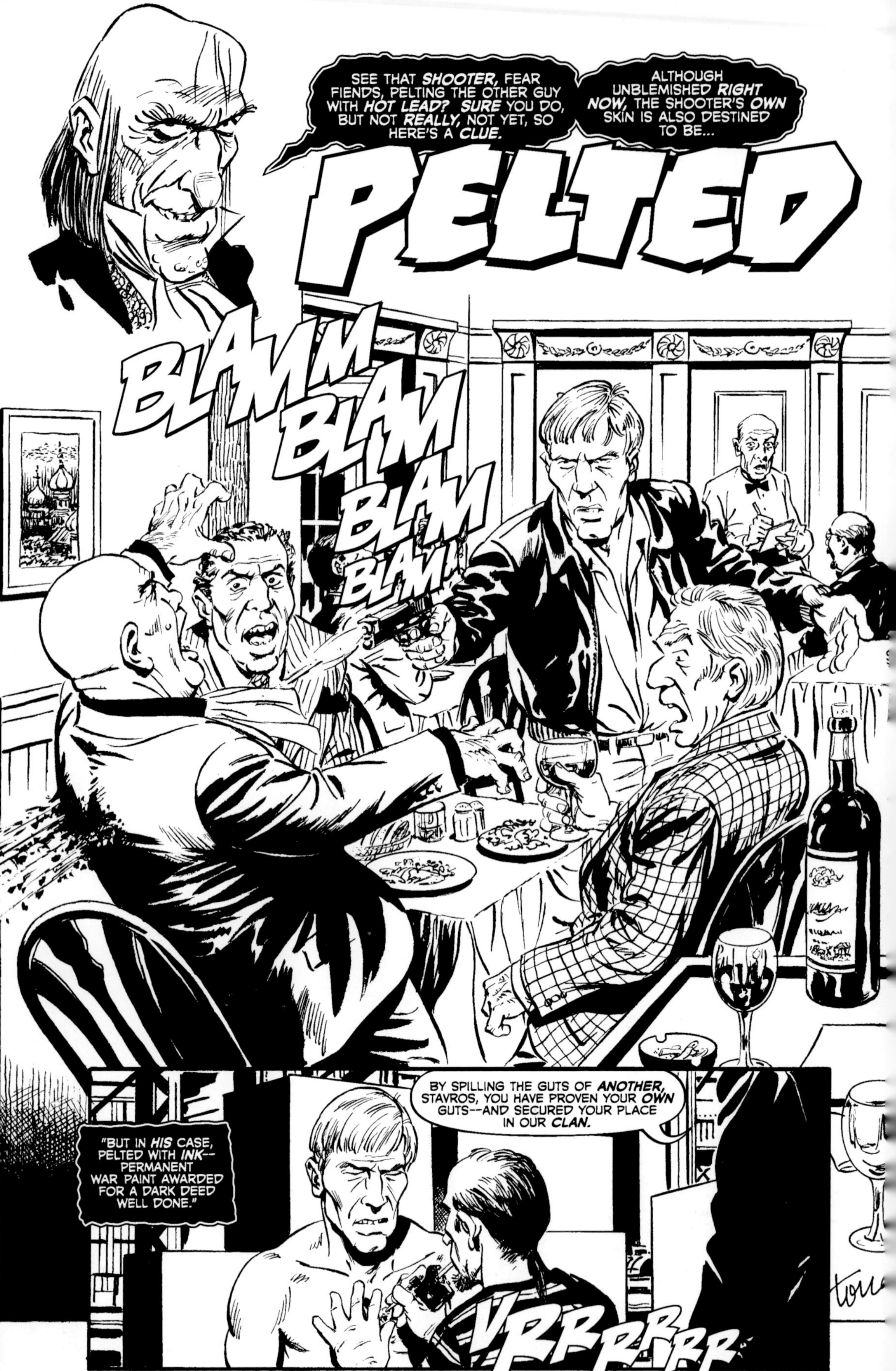
SEE THAT SHOOTER, FEAR FIENDS, PELTING THE OTHER GUY WITH HOT LEAD? SURE YOU DO, BUT NOT REALLY, NOT YET, SO HERE'S A CLUE.
ALTHOUGH UNBLEMISHED RIGHT NOW, THE SHOOTER'S OWN SKIN IS ALSO DESTINED TO BE...
PELTED
BLAMM BLAM BLAM BLAM
"BUT IN HIS CASE, PELTED WITH INK-- PERMANENT WAR PAINT AWARDED FOR A DARK DEED WELL DONE."
BY SPILLING THE GUTS OF ANOTHER, STAVROS, YOU HAVE PROVEN YOUR OWN GUTS--AND SECURED YOUR PLACE IN OUR CLAN.
VRRRRRR

Script by DOUG MOENCH / Art by ANGELO TORRES

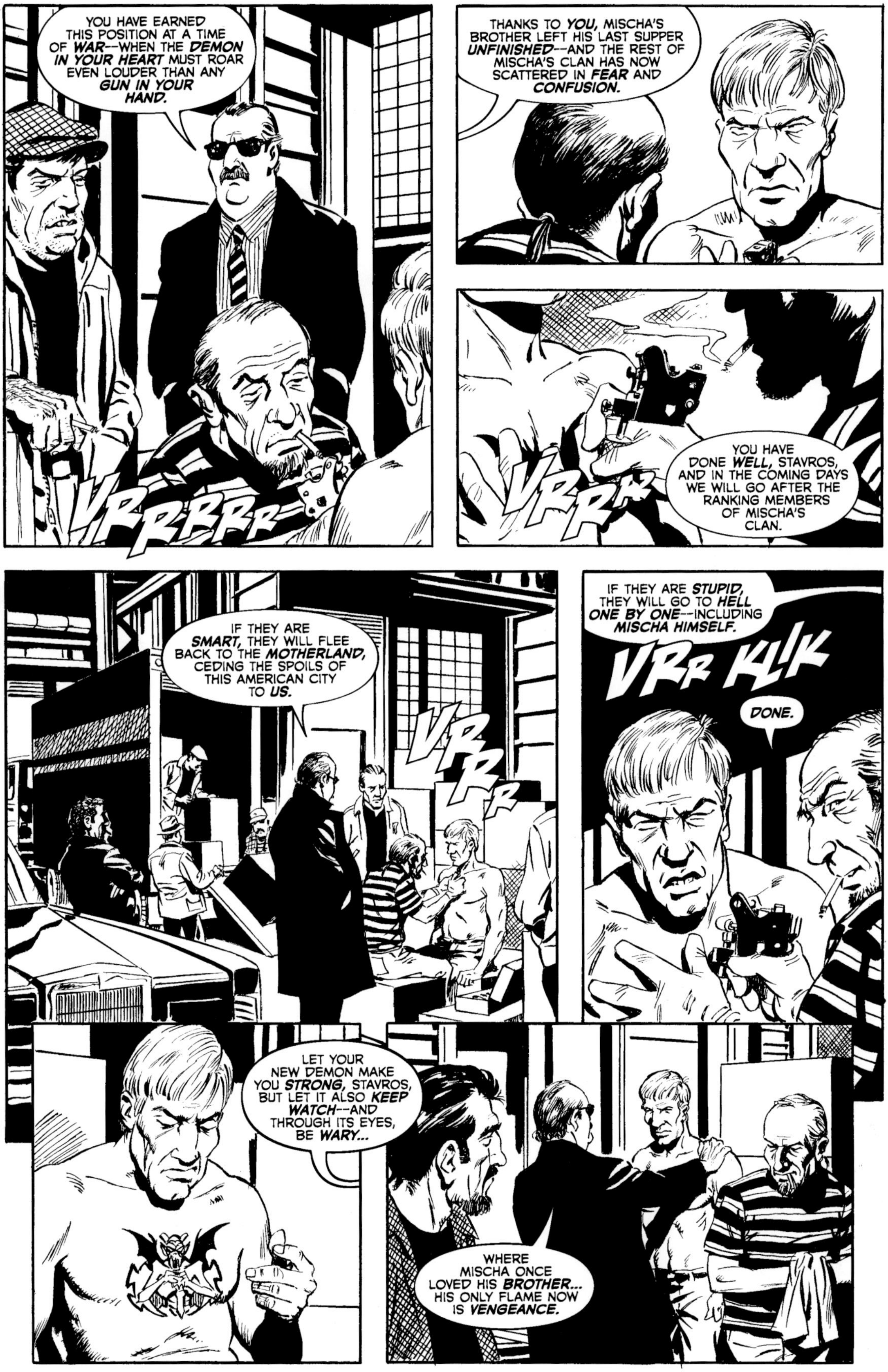
YOU HAVE EARNED THIS POSITION AT A TIME OF WAR--WHEN THE DEMON IN YOUR HEART MUST ROAR EVEN LOUDER THAN ANY GUN IN YOUR HAND.
VRRRRR
THANKS TO YOU, MISCHA'S BROTHER LEFT HIS LAST SUPPER UNFINISHED--AND THE REST OF MISCHA'S CLAN HAS NOW SCATTERED IN FEAR AND CONFUSION.
VRRR
YOU HAVE DONE WELL, STAVROS, AND IN THE COMING DAYS WE WILL GO AFTER THE RANKING MEMBERS OF MISCHA'S CLAN.
IF THEY ARE SMART, THEY WILL FLEE BACK TO THE MOTHERLAND, CEDING THE SPOILS OF THIS AMERICAN CITY TO US.
VRRRR
IF THEY ARE STUPID, THEY WILL GO TO HELL ONE BY ONE--INCLUDING MISCHA HIMSELF.
VRR KLIK
DONE.
LET YOUR NEW DEMON MAKE YOU STRONG, STAVROS, BUT LET IT ALSO KEEP WATCH--AND THROUGH ITS EYES, BE WARY...
WHERE MISCHA ONCE LOVED HIS BROTHER... HIS ONLY FLAME NOW IS VENGEANCE.

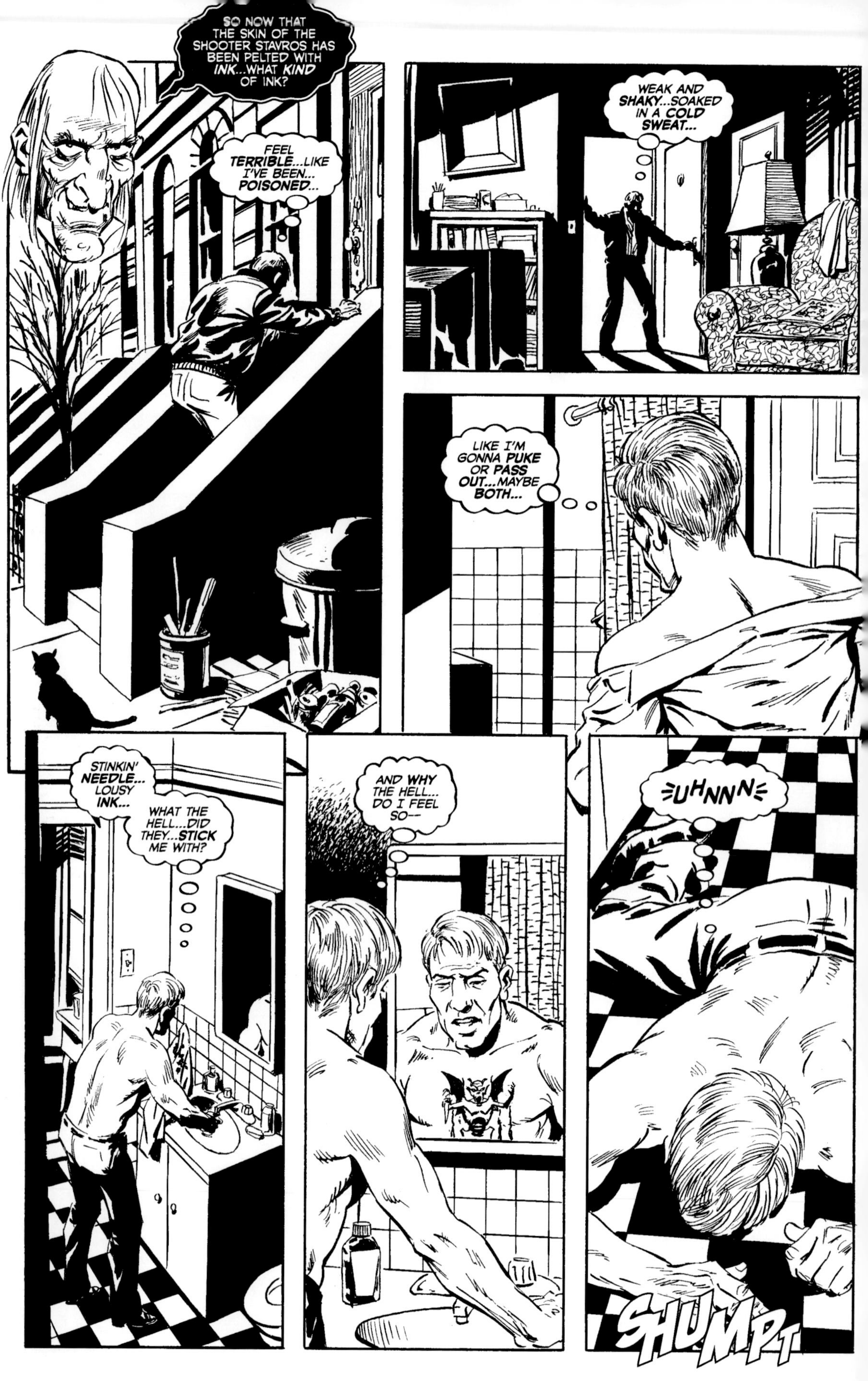
SO NOW THAT THE SKIN OF THE SHOOTER STAVROS HAS BEEN PELTED WITH INK...WHAT KIND OF INK?
FEEL TERRIBLE...LIKE I'VE BEEN... POISONED...
WEAK AND SHAKY...SOAKED IN A COLD SWEAT...
LIKE I'M GONNA PUKE OR PASS OUT...MAYBE BOTH...
STINKIN' NEEDLE... LOUSY INK...
WHAT THE HELL...DID THEY...STICK ME WITH?
AND WHY THE HELL... DO I FEEL SO--
UHNNN
SHUMPT

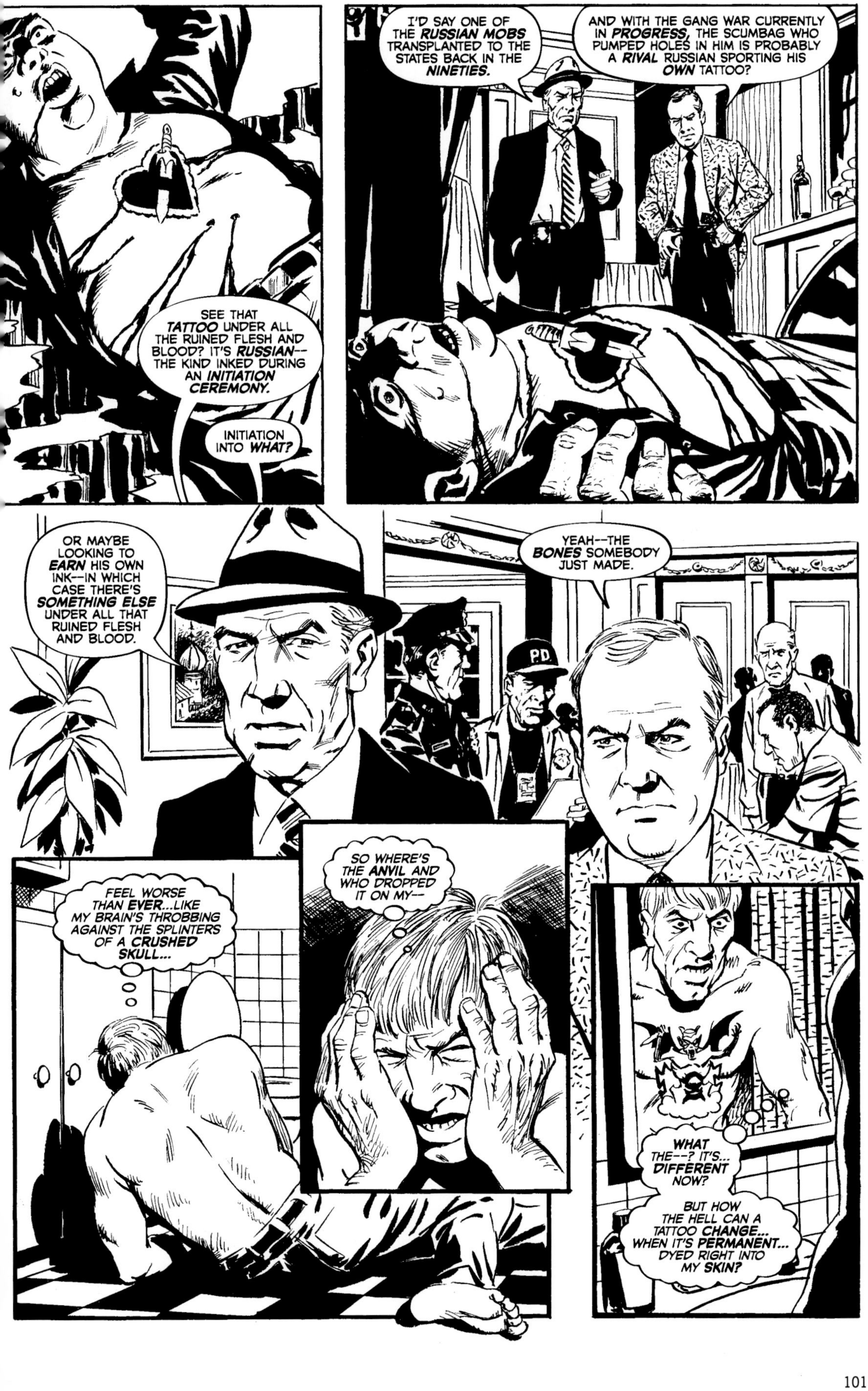
SEE THAT TATTOO UNDER ALL THE RUINED FLESH AND BLOOD? IT'S RUSSIAN-- THE KIND INKED DURING AN INITIATION CEREMONY.
INITIATION INTO WHAT?
I'D SAY ONE OF THE RUSSIAN MOBS TRANSPLANTED TO THE STATES BACK IN THE NINETIES.
AND WITH THE GANG WAR CURRENTLY IN PROGRESS, THE SCUMBAG WHO PUMPED HOLES IN HIM IS PROBABLY A RIVAL RUSSIAN SPORTING HIS OWN TATTOO?
OR MAYBE LOOKING TO EARN HIS OWN INK--IN WHICH CASE THERE'S SOMETHING ELSE UNDER ALL THAT RUINED FLESH AND BLOOD.
YEAH--THE BONES SOMEBODY JUST MADE.
P.D.
FEEL WORSE THAN EVER...LIKE MY BRAIN'S THROBBING AGAINST THE SPLINTERS OF A CRUSHED SKULL...
SO WHERE'S THE ANVIL AND WHO DROPPED IT ON MY--
WHAT THE--? IT'S... DIFFERENT NOW?
BUT HOW THE HELL CAN A TATTOO CHANGE... WHEN IT'S PERMANENT... DYED RIGHT INTO MY SKIN?

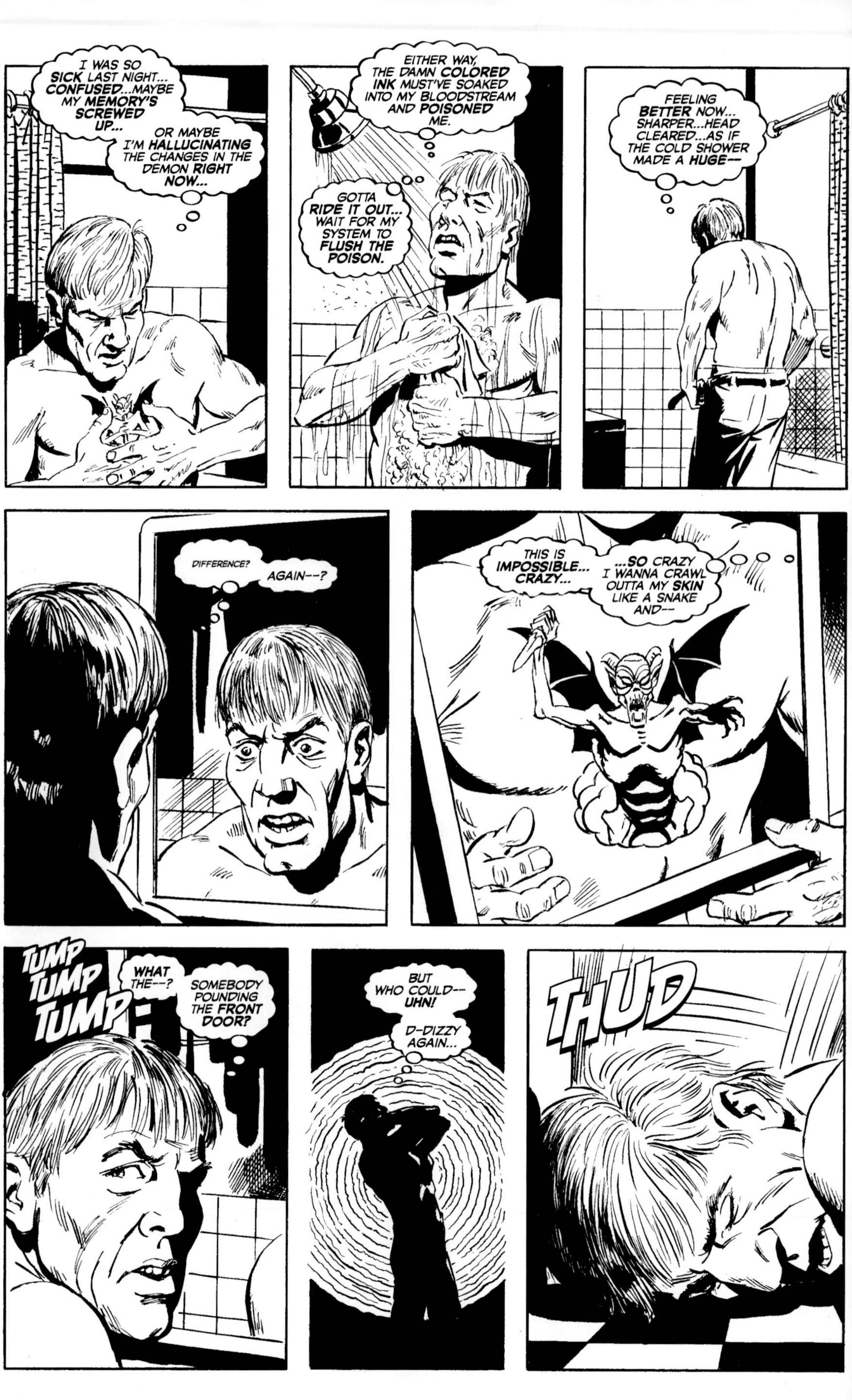
I WAS SO SICK LAST NIGHT... CONFUSED...MAYBE MY MEMORY'S SCREWED UP...
OR MAYBE I'M HALLUCINATING THE CHANGES IN THE DEMON RIGHT NOW...
EITHER WAY, THE DAMN COLORED INK MUST'VE SOAKED INTO MY BLOODSTREAM AND POISONED ME.
GOTTA RIDE IT OUT... WAIT FOR MY SYSTEM TO FLUSH THE POISON.
FEELING BETTER NOW... SHARPER...HEAD CLEARED...AS IF THE COLD SHOWER MADE A HUGE--
DIFFERENCE?
AGAIN--?
THIS IS IMPOSSIBLE... CRAZY...
...SO CRAZY I WANNA CRAWL OUTTA MY SKIN LIKE A SNAKE AND--
TUMP TUMP TUMP
WHAT THE--?
SOMEBODY POUNDING THE FRONT DOOR?
BUT WHO COULD-- UHN!
D-DIZZY AGAIN...
THUD

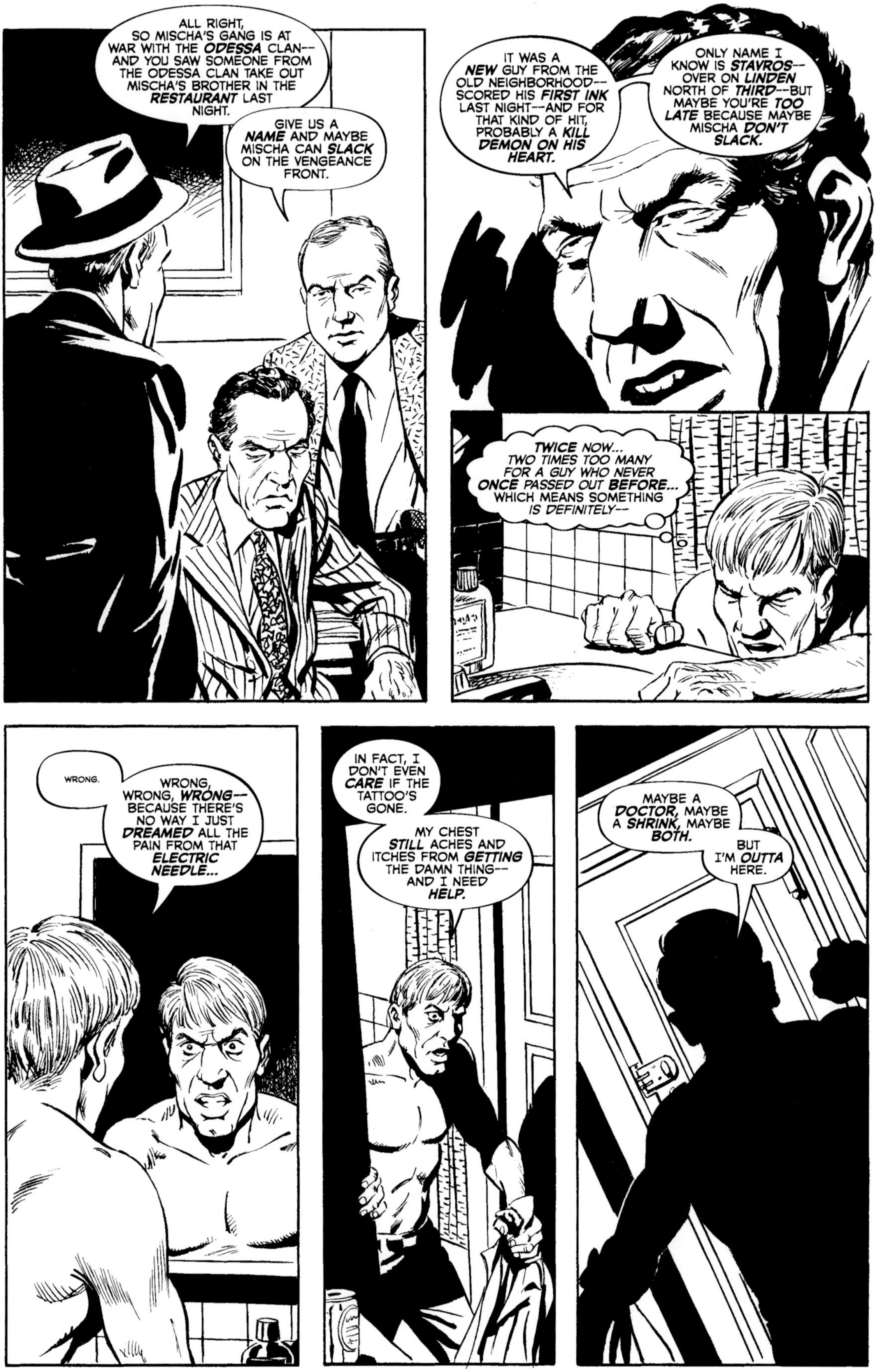
ALL RIGHT, SO MISCHA'S GANG IS AT WAR WITH THE ODESSA CLAN-- AND YOU SAW SOMEONE FROM THE ODESSA CLAN TAKE OUT MISCHA'S BROTHER IN THE RESTAURANT LAST NIGHT.
GIVE US A NAME AND MAYBE MISCHA CAN SLACK ON THE VENGEANCE FRONT.
IT WAS A NEW GUY FROM THE OLD NEIGHBORHOOD-- SCORED HIS FIRST INK LAST NIGHT--AND FOR THAT KIND OF HIT, PROBABLY A KILL DEMON ON HIS HEART.
ONLY NAME I KNOW IS STAVROS-- OVER ON LINDEN NORTH OF THIRD--BUT MAYBE YOU'RE TOO LATE BECAUSE MAYBE MISCHA DON'T SLACK.
TWICE NOW... TWO TIMES TOO MANY FOR A GUY WHO NEVER ONCE PASSED OUT BEFORE... WHICH MEANS SOMETHING IS DEFINITELY--
WRONG.
WRONG, WRONG, WRONG-- BECAUSE THERE'S NO WAY I JUST DREAMED ALL THE PAIN FROM THAT ELECTRIC NEEDLE...
IN FACT, I DON'T EVEN CARE IF THE TATTOO'S GONE.
MY CHEST STILL ACHES AND ITCHES FROM GETTING THE DAMN THING-- AND I NEED HELP.
MAYBE A DOCTOR, MAYBE A SHRINK, MAYBE BOTH.
BUT I'M OUTTA HERE.

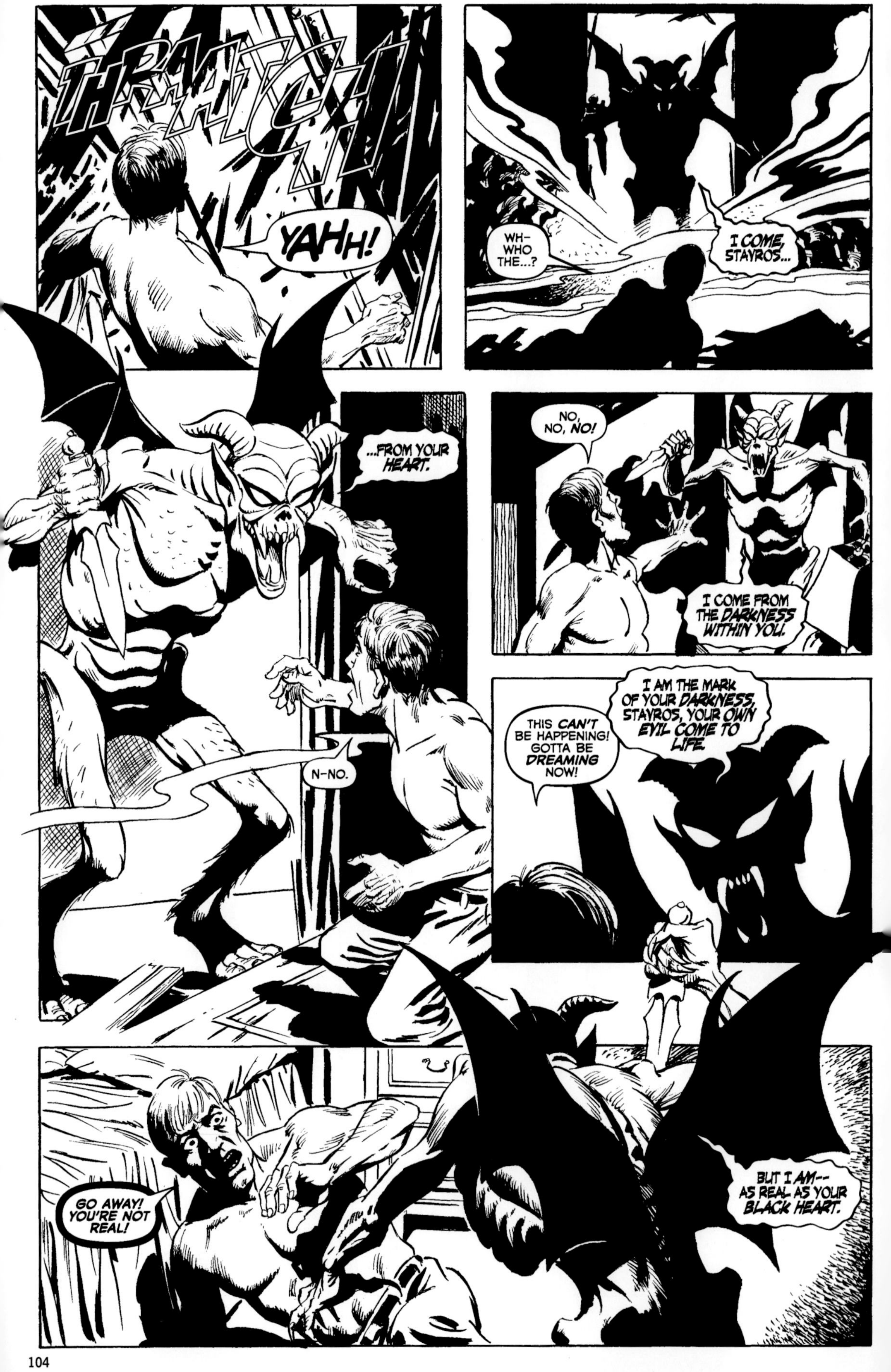
THRAAACCH
YAHH!
WH-WHO THE...?
I COME, STAYROS...
...FROM YOUR HEART.
N-NO.
NO, NO, NO!
I COME FROM THE DARKNESS WITHIN YOU.
THIS CAN'T BE HAPPENING! GOTTA BE DREAMING NOW!
I AM THE MARK OF YOUR DARKNESS, STAYROS, YOUR OWN EVIL COME TO LIFE.
GO AWAY! YOU'RE NOT REAL!
BUT I AM-- AS REAL AS YOUR BLACK HEART.

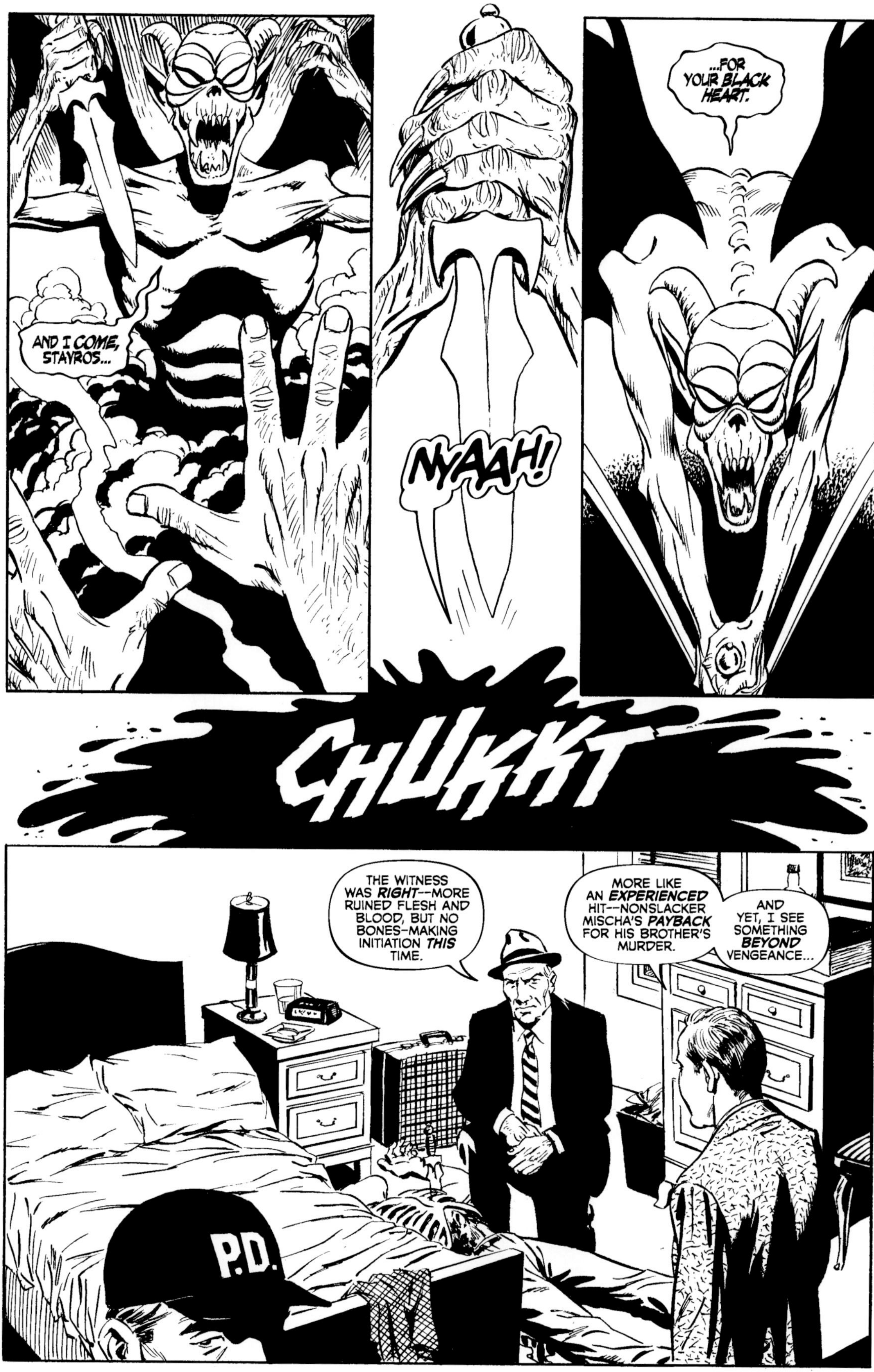

AND I COME, STAYROS...
NYAAH!
...FOR YOUR BLACK HEART.
CHUKKT
THE WITNESS WAS RIGHT--MORE RUINED FLESH AND BLOOD, BUT NO BONES-MAKING INITIATION THIS TIME.
MORE LIKE AN EXPERIENCED HIT--NONSLACKER MISCHA'S PAYBACK FOR HIS BROTHER'S MURDER.
AND YET, I SEE SOMETHING BEYOND VENGEANCE...
P.D.

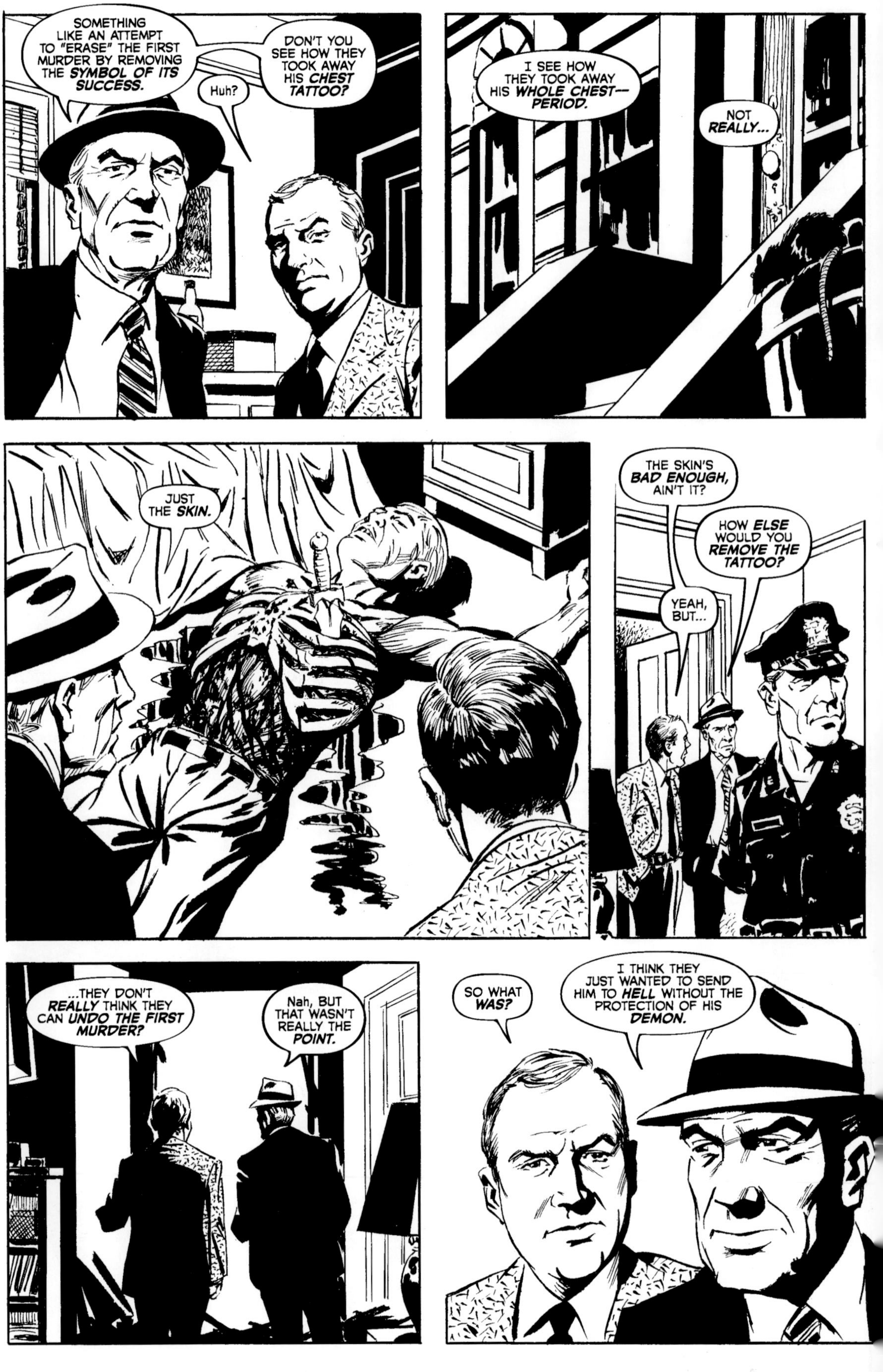
SOMETHING LIKE AN ATTEMPT TO "ERASE" THE FIRST MURDER BY REMOVING THE SYMBOL OF ITS SUCCESS.
Huh?
DON'T YOU SEE HOW THEY TOOK AWAY HIS CHEST TATTOO?
I SEE HOW THEY TOOK AWAY HIS WHOLE CHEST—PERIOD.
NOT REALLY...
JUST THE SKIN.
THE SKIN'S BAD ENOUGH, AIN'T IT?
HOW ELSE WOULD YOU REMOVE THE TATTOO?
YEAH, BUT...
...THEY DON'T REALLY THINK THEY CAN UNDO THE FIRST MURDER?
Nah, BUT THAT WASN'T REALLY THE POINT.
SO WHAT WAS?
I THINK THEY JUST WANTED TO SEND HIM TO HELL WITHOUT THE PROTECTION OF HIS DEMON.

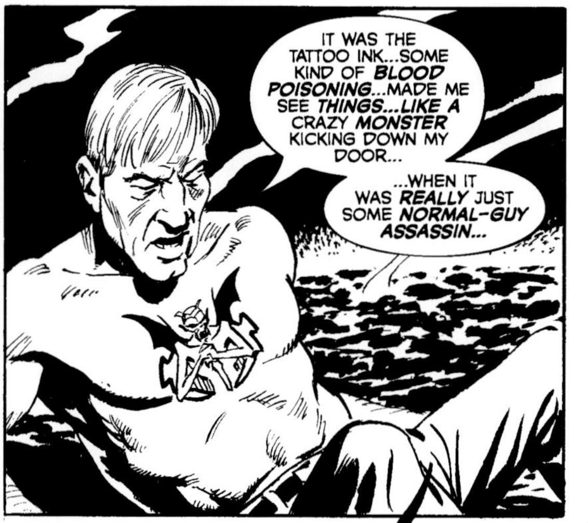
IT WAS THE TATTOO INK...SOME KIND OF BLOOD POISONING...MADE ME SEE THINGS...LIKE A CRAZY MONSTER KICKING DOWN MY DOOR...
...WHEN IT WAS REALLY JUST SOME NORMAL-GUY ASSASSIN...

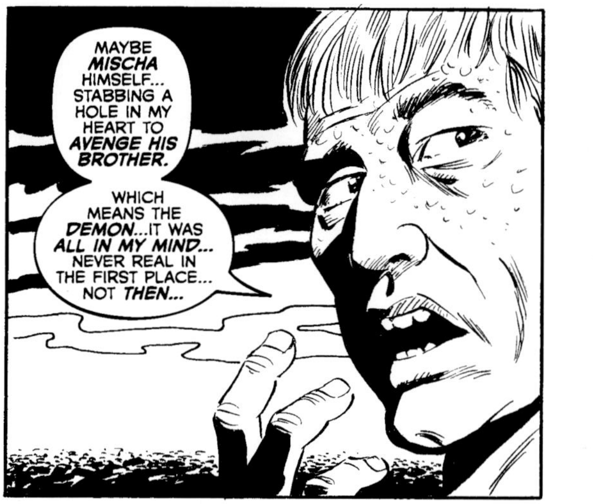
MAYBE MISCHA HIMSELF... STABBING A HOLE IN MY HEART TO AVENGE HIS BROTHER.
WHICH MEANS THE DEMON...IT WAS ALL IN MY MIND... NEVER REAL IN THE FIRST PLACE... NOT THEN...

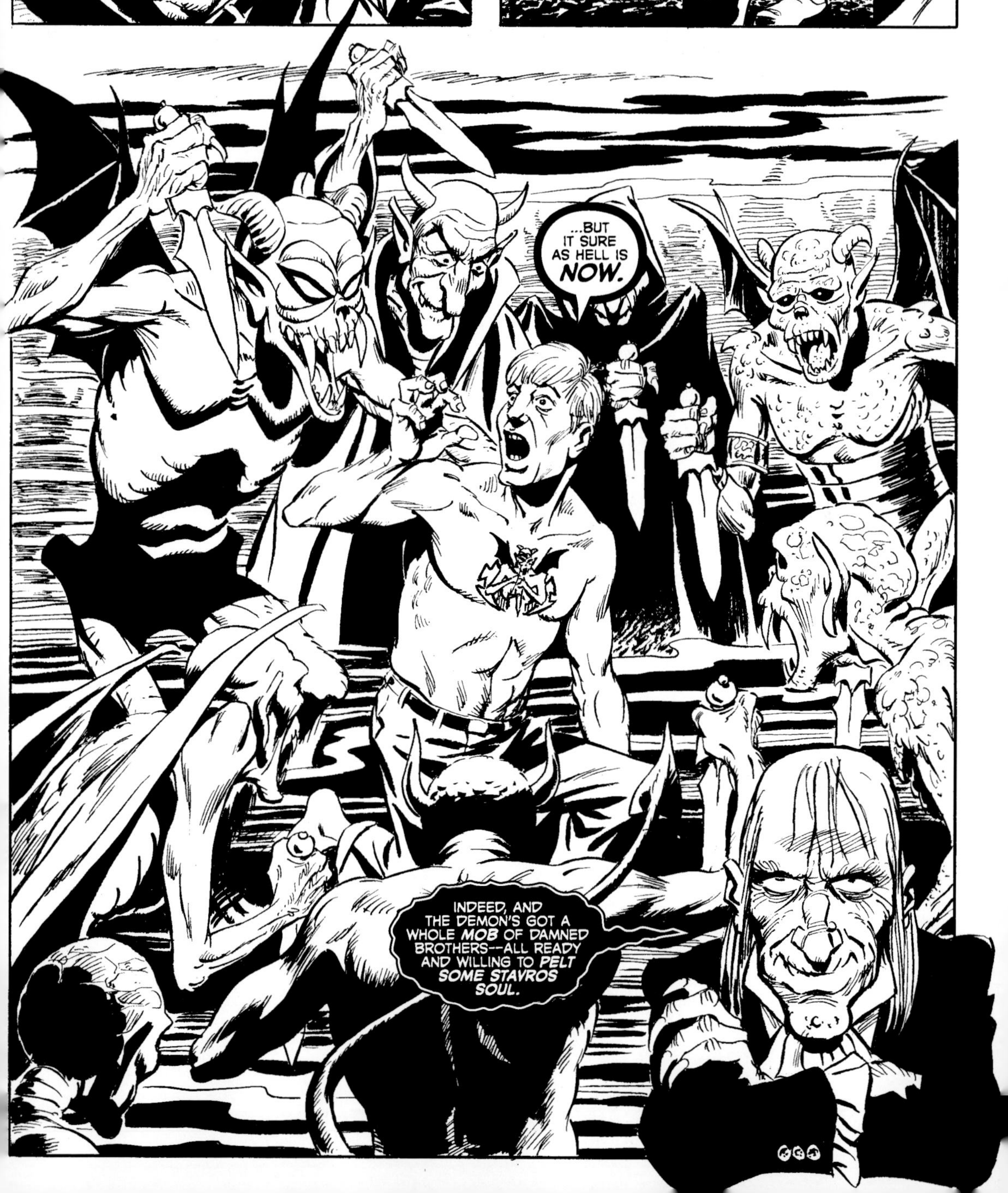
...BUT IT SURE AS HELL IS NOW.
INDEED, AND THE DEMON'S GOT A WHOLE MOB OF DAMNED BROTHERS--ALL READY AND WILLING TO PELT SOME STAVROS SOUL.

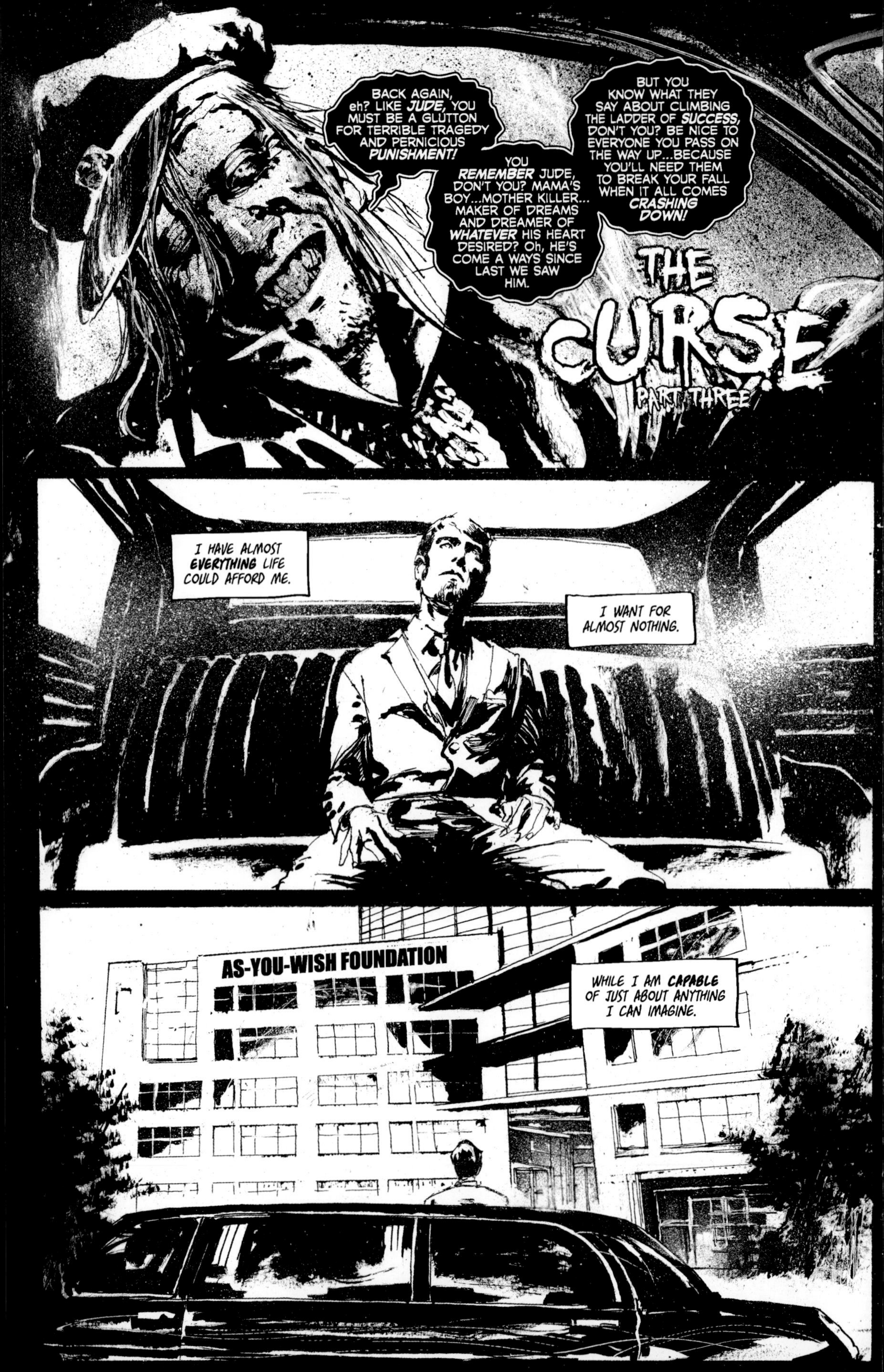
BACK AGAIN, eh? LIKE JUDE, YOU MUST BE A GLUTTON FOR TERRIBLE TRAGEDY AND PERNICIOUS PUNISHMENT!
YOU REMEMBER JUDE, DON'T YOU? MAMA'S BOY...MOTHER KILLER... MAKER OF DREAMS AND DREAMER OF WHATEVER HIS HEART DESIRED? Oh, HE'S COME A WAYS SINCE LAST WE SAW HIM.
BUT YOU KNOW WHAT THEY SAY ABOUT CLIMBING THE LADDER OF SUCCESS, DON'T YOU? BE NICE TO EVERYONE YOU PASS ON THE WAY UP...BECAUSE YOU'LL NEED THEM TO BREAK YOUR FALL WHEN IT ALL COMES CRASHING DOWN!
THE CURSE
PART THREE
I HAVE ALMOST EVERYTHING LIFE COULD AFFORD ME.
I WANT FOR ALMOST NOTHING.
AS-YOU-WISH FOUNDATION
WHILE I AM CAPABLE OF JUST ABOUT ANYTHING I CAN IMAGINE.

 Script by JOE HARRIS / Art by JASON SHAWN ALEXANDER

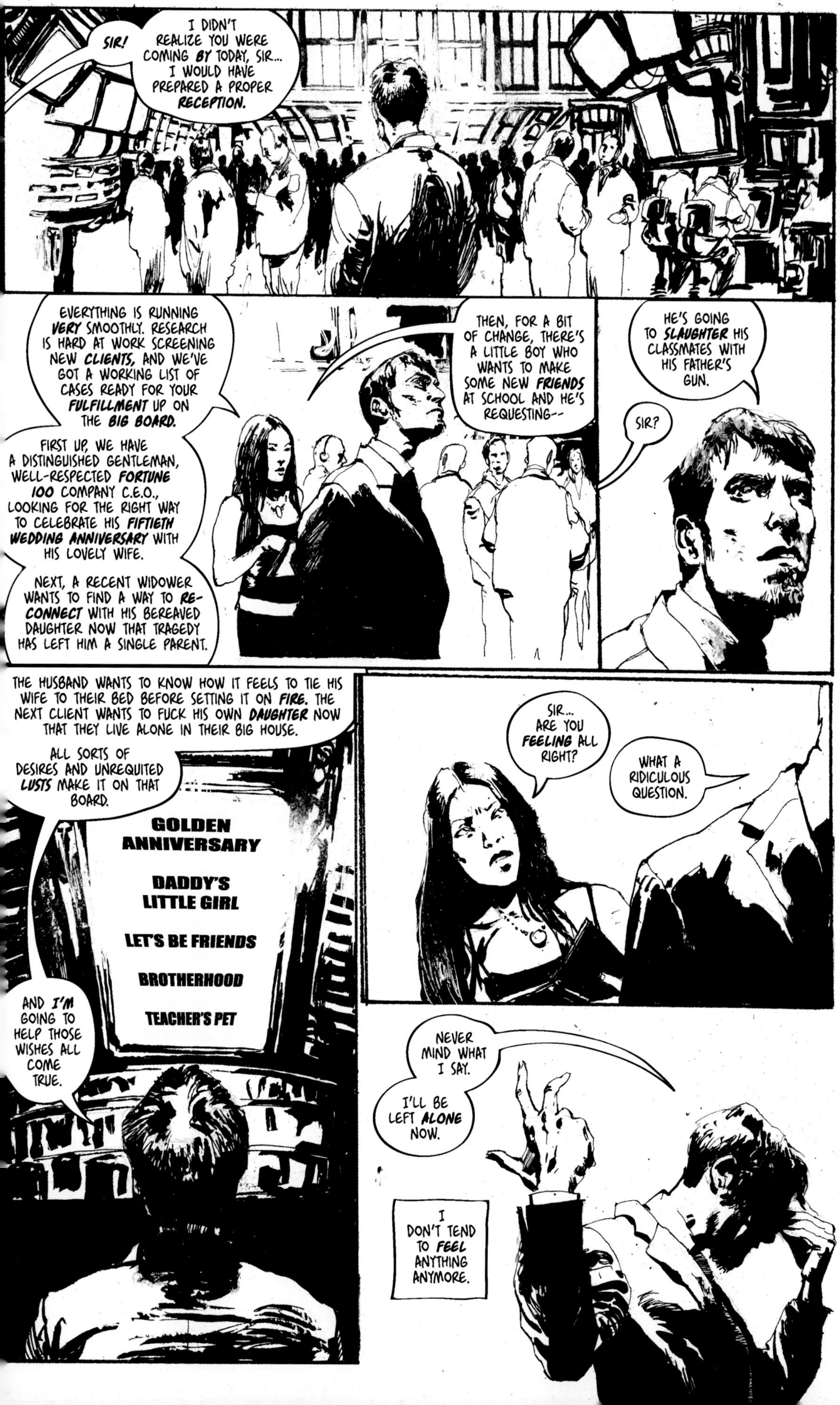
SIR!
I DIDN'T REALIZE YOU WERE COMING BY TODAY, SIR... I WOULD HAVE PREPARED A PROPER RECEPTION.
EVERYTHING IS RUNNING VERY SMOOTHLY. RESEARCH IS HARD AT WORK SCREENING NEW CLIENTS, AND WE'VE GOT A WORKING LIST OF CASES READY FOR YOUR FULFILLMENT UP ON THE BIG BOARD.
FIRST UP, WE HAVE A DISTINGUISHED GENTLEMAN, WELL-RESPECTED FORTUNE 100 COMPANY C.E.O., LOOKING FOR THE RIGHT WAY TO CELEBRATE HIS FIFTIETH WEDDING ANNIVERSARY WITH HIS LOVELY WIFE.
NEXT, A RECENT WIDOWER WANTS TO FIND A WAY TO RE-CONNECT WITH HIS BEREAVED DAUGHTER NOW THAT TRAGEDY HAS LEFT HIM A SINGLE PARENT.
THEN, FOR A BIT OF CHANGE, THERE'S A LITTLE BOY WHO WANTS TO MAKE SOME NEW FRIENDS AT SCHOOL AND HE'S REQUESTING--
HE'S GOING TO SLAUGHTER HIS CLASSMATES WITH HIS FATHER'S GUN.
SIR?
THE HUSBAND WANTS TO KNOW HOW IT FEELS TO TIE HIS WIFE TO THEIR BED BEFORE SETTING IT ON FIRE. THE NEXT CLIENT WANTS TO FUCK HIS OWN DAUGHTER NOW THAT THEY LIVE ALONE IN THEIR BIG HOUSE.
ALL SORTS OF DESIRES AND UNREQUITED LUSTS MAKE IT ON THAT BOARD.
GOLDEN ANNIVERSARY
DADDY'S LITTLE GIRL
LET'S BE FRIENDS
BROTHERHOOD
TEACHER'S PET
AND I'M GOING TO HELP THOSE WISHES ALL COME TRUE.
SIR... ARE YOU FEELING ALL RIGHT?
WHAT A RIDICULOUS QUESTION.
NEVER MIND WHAT I SAY.
I'LL BE LEFT ALONE NOW.
I DON'T TEND TO FEEL ANYTHING ANYMORE.

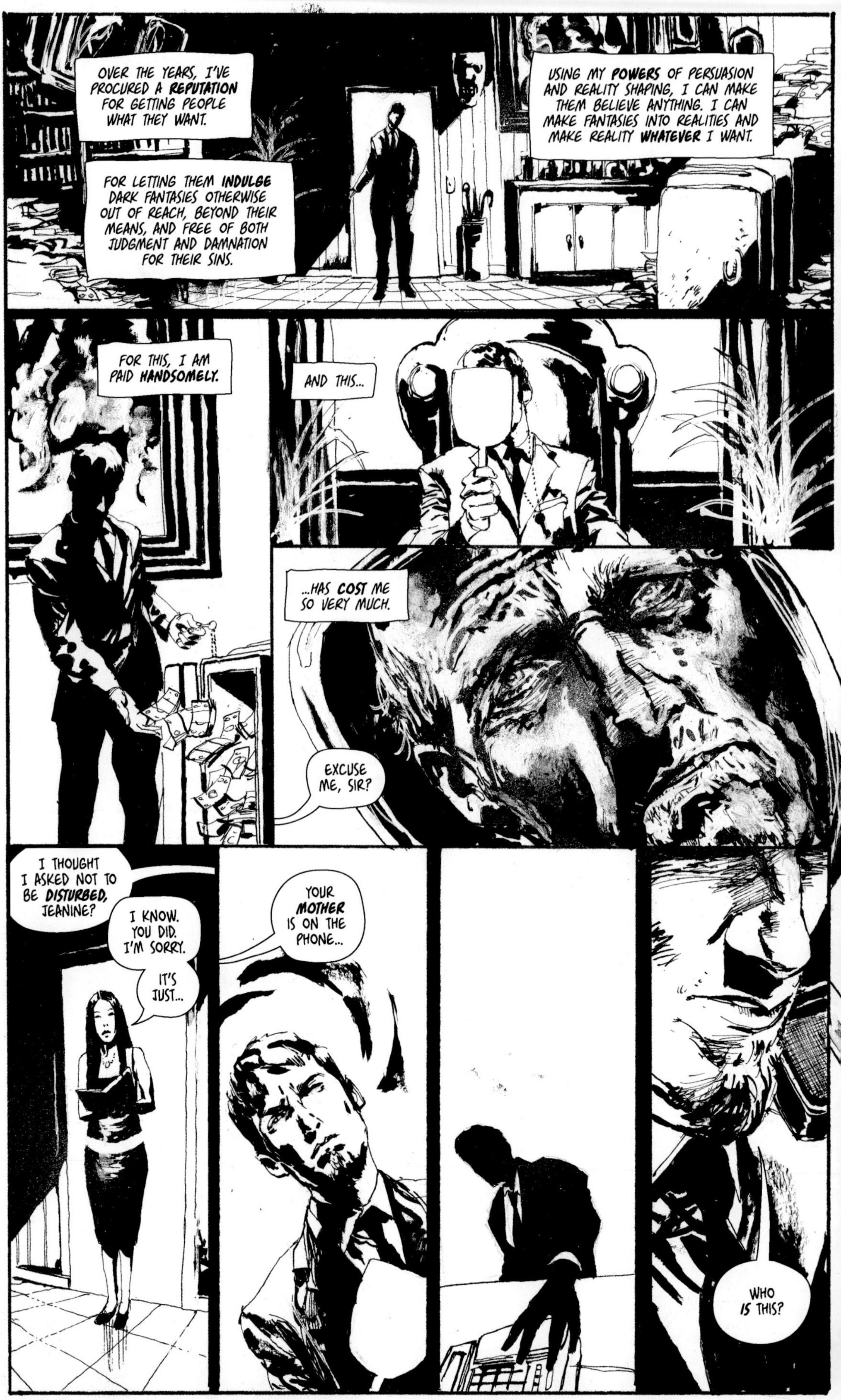
OVER THE YEARS, I'VE PROCURED A **REPUTATION** FOR GETTING PEOPLE WHAT THEY WANT.
FOR LETTING THEM **INDULGE** DARK FANTASIES OTHERWISE OUT OF REACH, BEYOND THEIR MEANS, AND FREE OF BOTH JUDGMENT AND DAMNATION FOR THEIR SINS.
USING MY **POWERS** OF PERSUASION AND REALITY SHAPING, I CAN MAKE THEM BELIEVE ANYTHING. I CAN MAKE FANTASIES INTO REALITIES AND MAKE REALITY **WHATEVER** I WANT.
FOR THIS, I AM PAID **HANDSOMELY.**
AND THIS...
...HAS **COST** ME SO VERY MUCH.
EXCUSE ME, SIR?
I THOUGHT I ASKED NOT TO BE **DISTURBED,** JEANINE?
I KNOW. YOU DID. I'M SORRY.
IT'S JUST...
YOUR **MOTHER** IS ON THE PHONE...
WHO **IS** THIS?

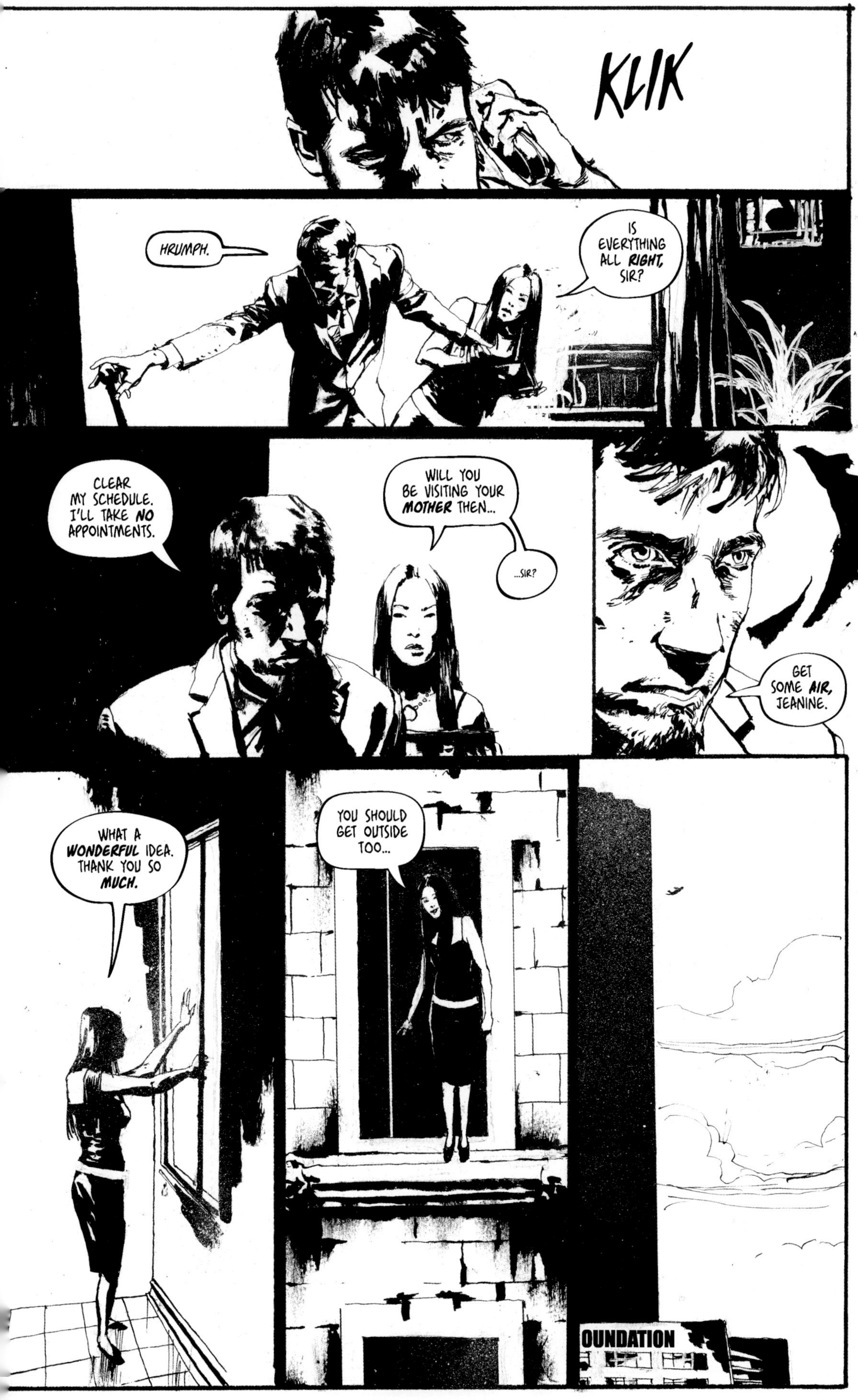
KLIK
HRUMPH.
IS EVERYTHING ALL RIGHT, SIR?
CLEAR MY SCHEDULE. I'LL TAKE NO APPOINTMENTS.
WILL YOU BE VISITING YOUR MOTHER THEN...
...SIR?
GET SOME AIR, JEANINE.
WHAT A WONDERFUL IDEA. THANK YOU SO MUCH.
YOU SHOULD GET OUTSIDE TOO...
OUNDATION

SO LET'S DO THIS THEN.

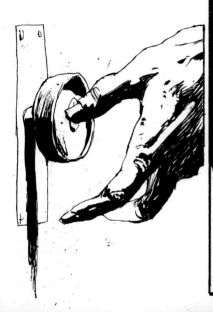

JUDE--!

I TOLD YOU TO MEET ME AT THE *WINDOW*. YOU SAID YOU WAS GONNA COME AROUND *BACK*!

DON'T *MESS* WITH ME. YOU'RE *IN* THIS NOW, MAN.

TOBY.

BUT...I *KILLED* TOBY. AND TOBY HASN'T BEEN ANYWHERE NEAR THE HOUSE SINCE--

NOW LOOK HERE...

FWUMP

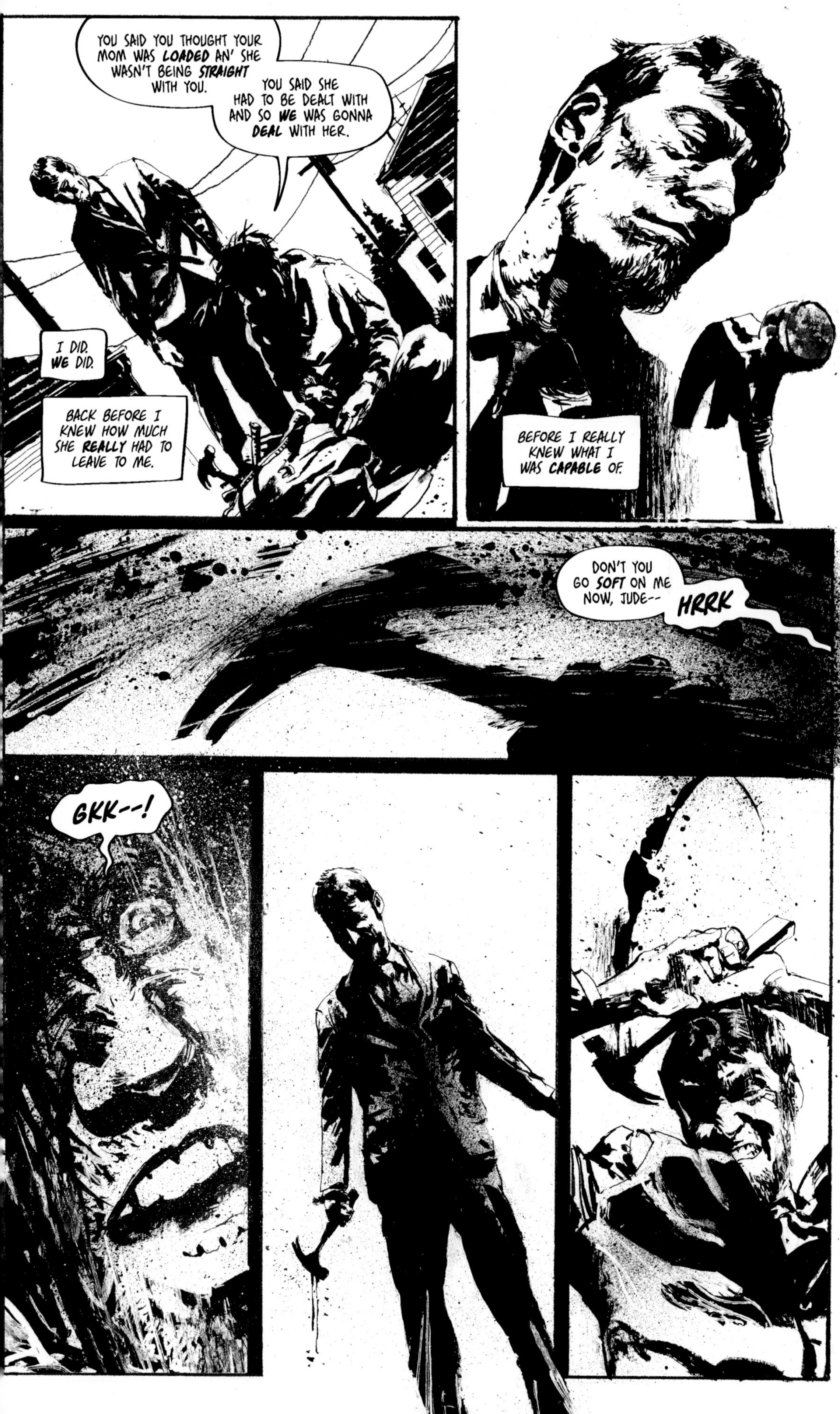
YOU SAID YOU THOUGHT YOUR MOM WAS LOADED AN' SHE WASN'T BEING STRAIGHT WITH YOU.
YOU SAID SHE HAD TO BE DEALT WITH AND SO WE WAS GONNA DEAL WITH HER.
I DID. WE DID.
BACK BEFORE I KNEW HOW MUCH SHE REALLY HAD TO LEAVE TO ME.
BEFORE I REALLY KNEW WHAT I WAS CAPABLE OF.
DON'T YOU GO SOFT ON ME NOW, JUDE--
HRRK
GKK--!

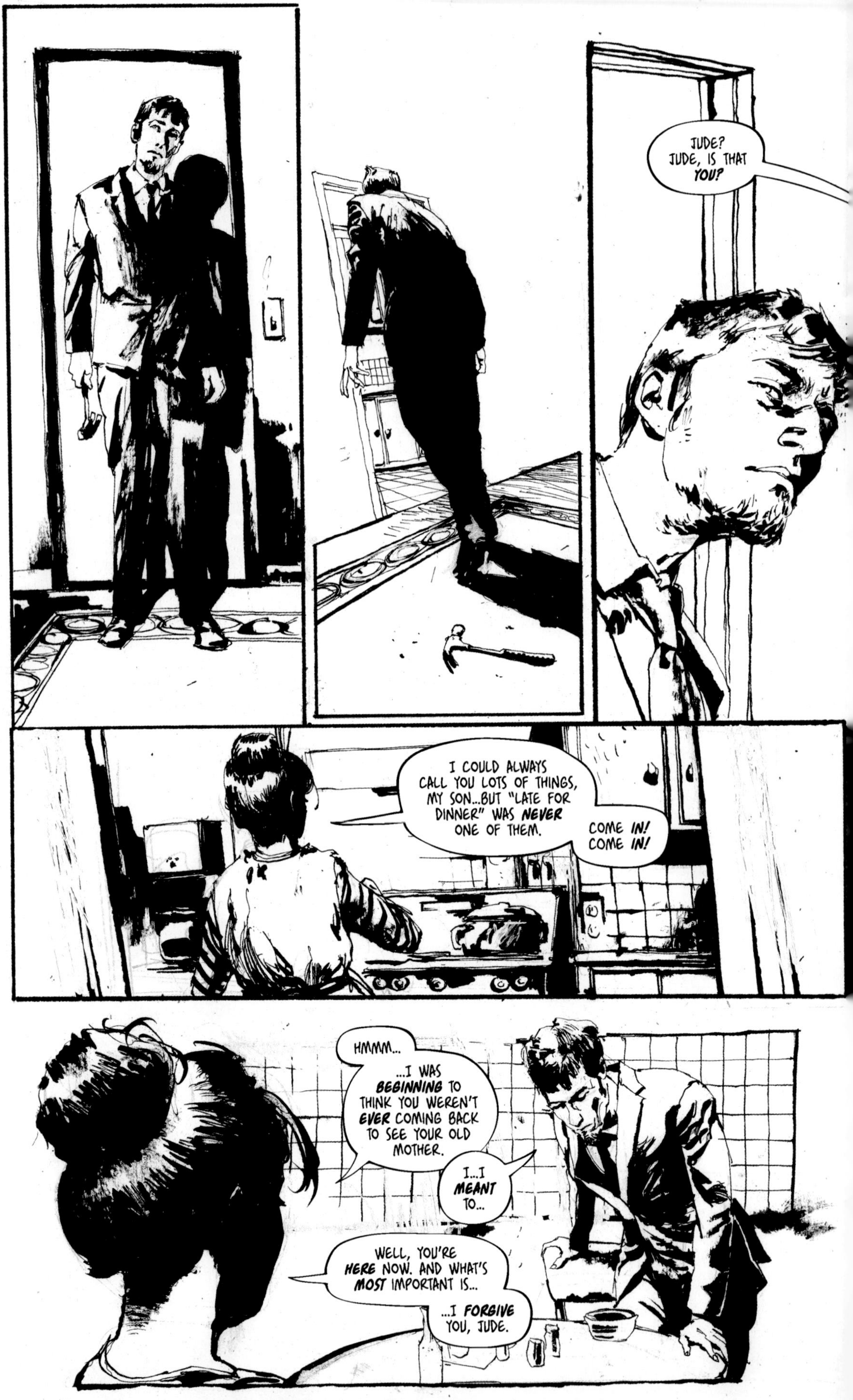
JUDE? JUDE, IS THAT YOU?
I COULD ALWAYS CALL YOU LOTS OF THINGS, MY SON...BUT "LATE FOR DINNER" WAS NEVER ONE OF THEM.
COME IN! COME IN!
HMMM...
...I WAS BEGINNING TO THINK YOU WEREN'T EVER COMING BACK TO SEE YOUR OLD MOTHER.
I...I MEANT TO...
WELL, YOU'RE HERE NOW. AND WHAT'S MOST IMPORTANT IS...
...I FORGIVE YOU, JUDE.

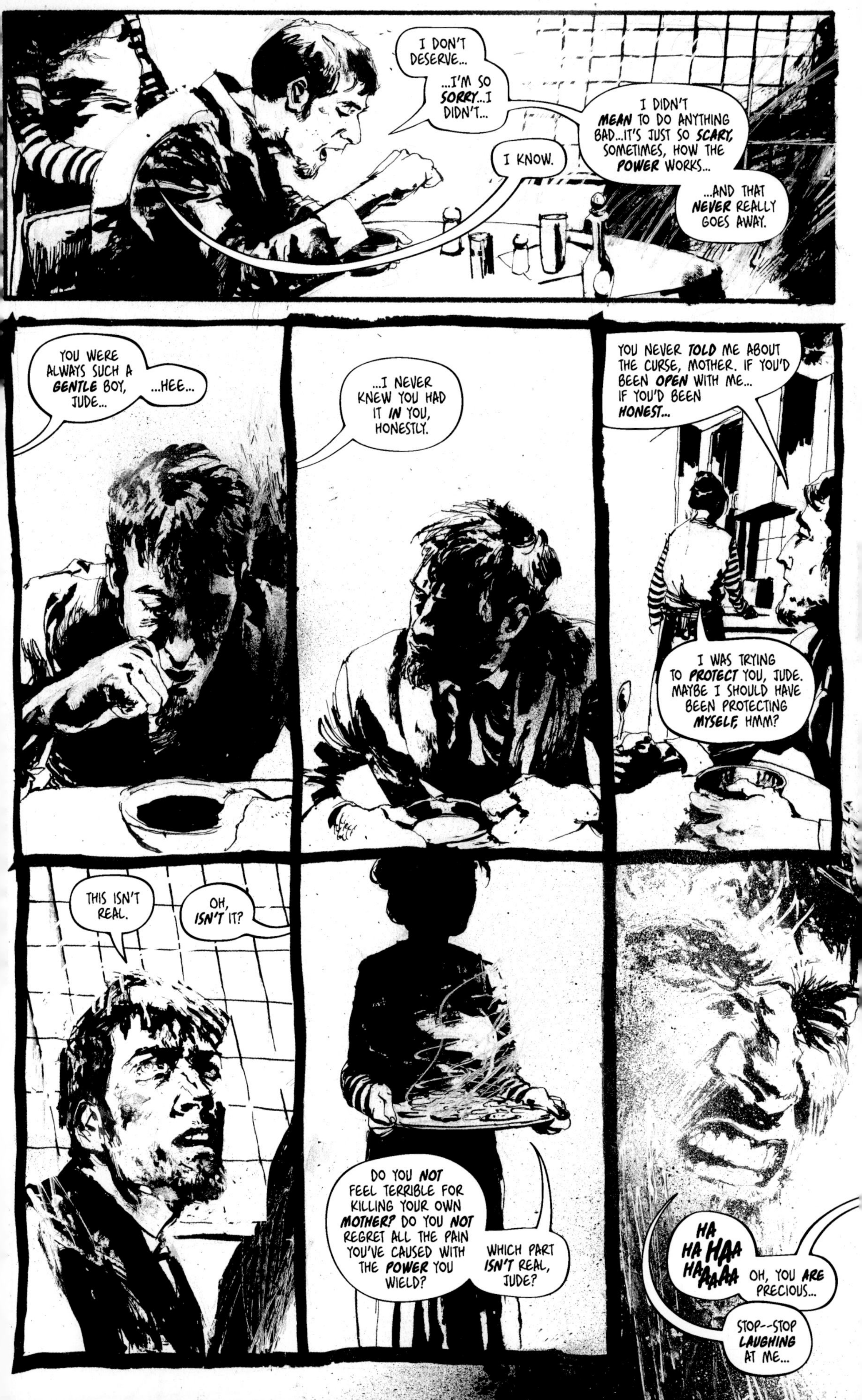
I DON'T DESERVE...
...I'M SO SORRY...I DIDN'T...
I DIDN'T MEAN TO DO ANYTHING BAD...IT'S JUST SO SCARY, SOMETIMES, HOW THE POWER WORKS...
...AND THAT NEVER REALLY GOES AWAY.
I KNOW.
YOU WERE ALWAYS SUCH A GENTLE BOY, JUDE...
...HEE...
...I NEVER KNEW YOU HAD IT IN YOU, HONESTLY.
YOU NEVER TOLD ME ABOUT THE CURSE, MOTHER. IF YOU'D BEEN OPEN WITH ME... IF YOU'D BEEN HONEST...
I WAS TRYING TO PROTECT YOU, JUDE. MAYBE I SHOULD HAVE BEEN PROTECTING MYSELF, HMM?
THIS ISN'T REAL.
OH, ISN'T IT?
DO YOU NOT FEEL TERRIBLE FOR KILLING YOUR OWN MOTHER? DO YOU NOT REGRET ALL THE PAIN YOU'VE CAUSED WITH THE POWER YOU WIELD?
WHICH PART ISN'T REAL, JUDE?
HA HA HAA HAAAAA
OH, YOU ARE PRECIOUS...
STOP--STOP LAUGHING AT ME...

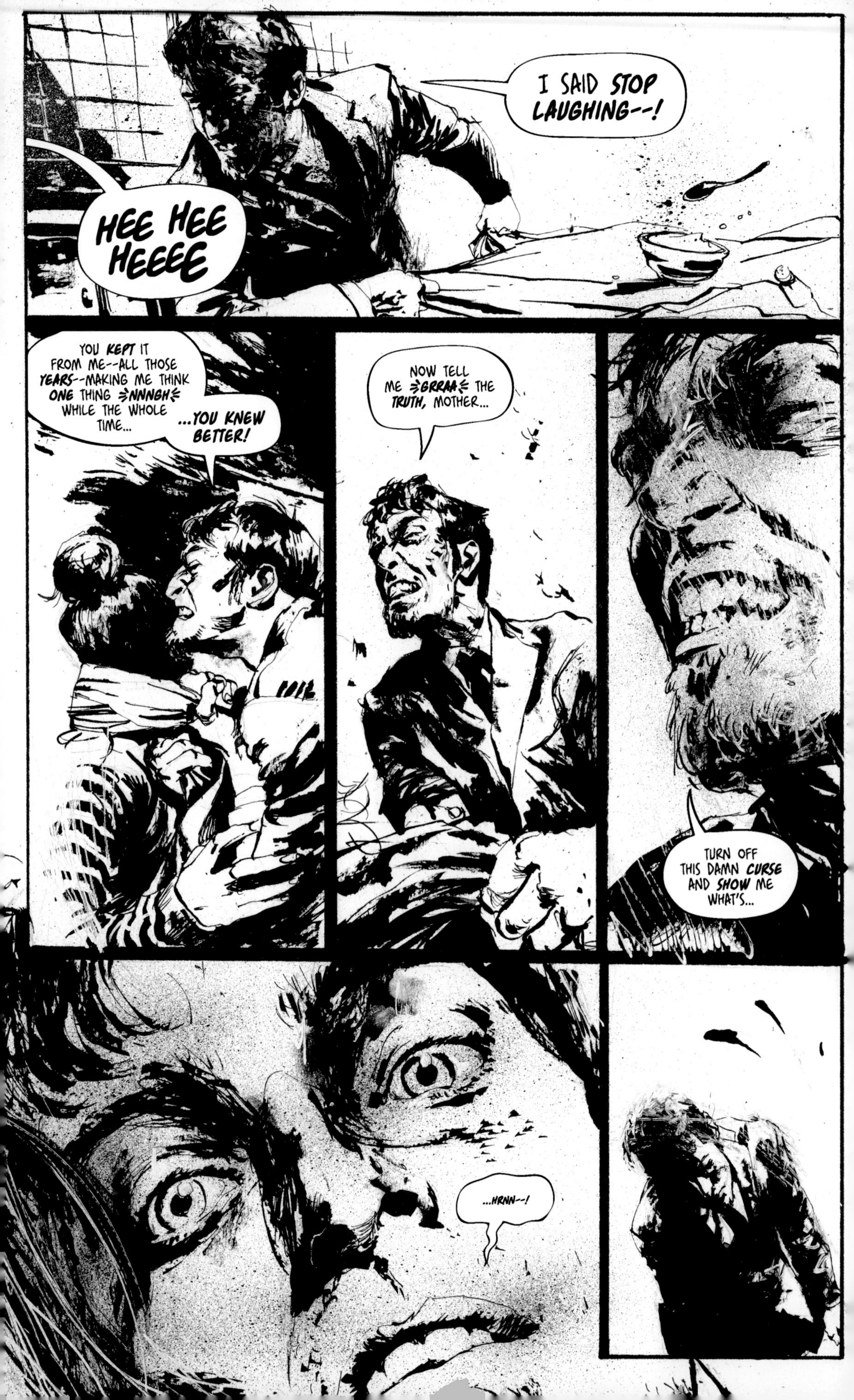
I SAID STOP LAUGHING--!
HEE HEE HEEEE
YOU KEPT IT FROM ME--ALL THOSE YEARS--MAKING ME THINK ONE THING NNNGH WHILE THE WHOLE TIME...
...YOU KNEW BETTER!
NOW TELL ME GRRAA THE TRUTH, MOTHER...
TURN OFF THIS DAMN CURSE AND SHOW ME WHAT'S...
...HRNN--!

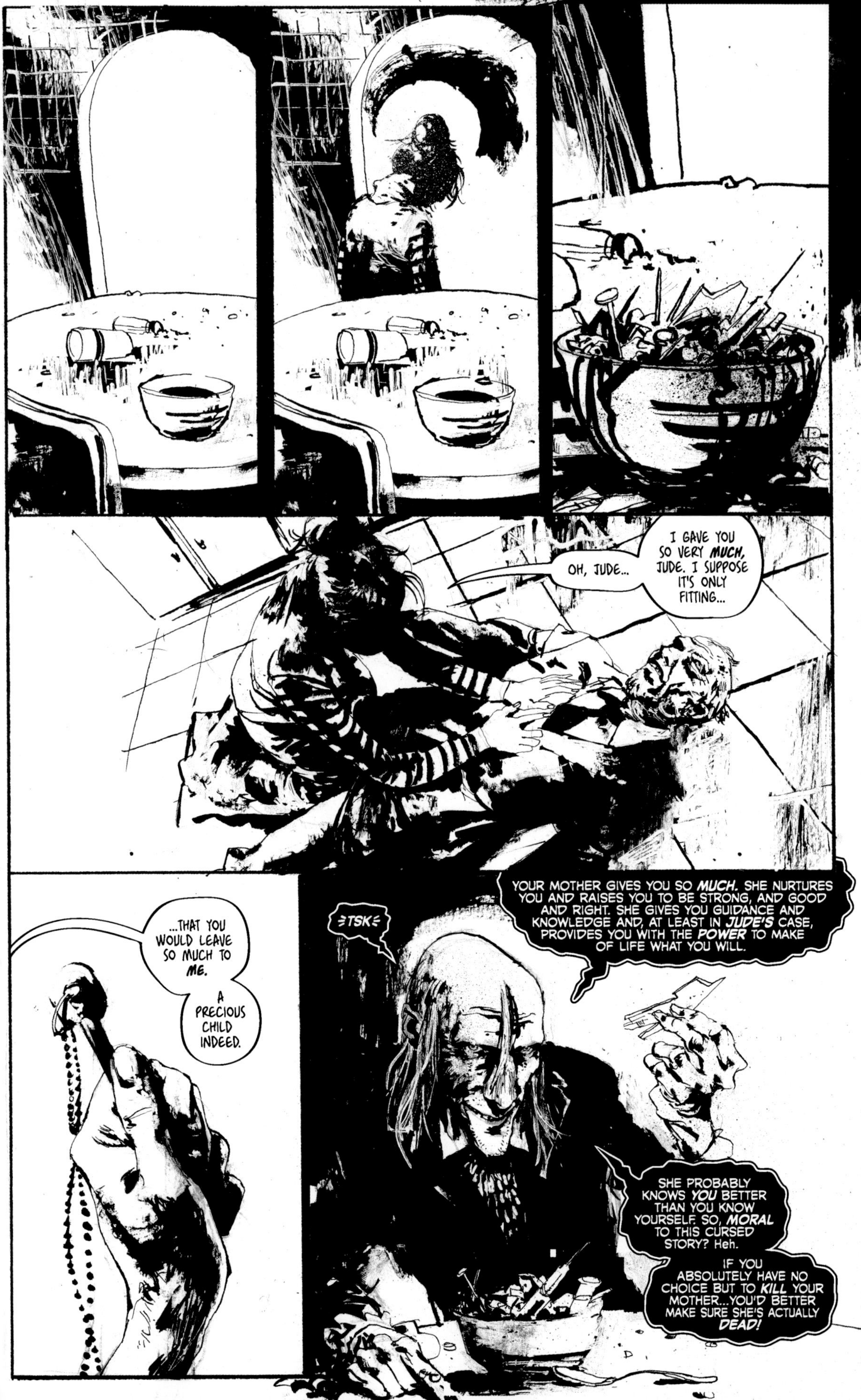
OH, JUDE...
I GAVE YOU SO VERY MUCH, JUDE. I SUPPOSE IT'S ONLY FITTING...
...THAT YOU WOULD LEAVE SO MUCH TO ME.
A PRECIOUS CHILD INDEED.
TSK
YOUR MOTHER GIVES YOU SO MUCH. SHE NURTURES YOU AND RAISES YOU TO BE STRONG, AND GOOD AND RIGHT. SHE GIVES YOU GUIDANCE AND KNOWLEDGE AND, AT LEAST IN JUDE'S CASE, PROVIDES YOU WITH THE POWER TO MAKE OF LIFE WHAT YOU WILL.
SHE PROBABLY KNOWS YOU BETTER THAN YOU KNOW YOURSELF. SO, MORAL TO THIS CURSED STORY? Heh.
IF YOU ABSOLUTELY HAVE NO CHOICE BUT TO KILL YOUR MOTHER...YOU'D BETTER MAKE SURE SHE'S ACTUALLY DEAD!

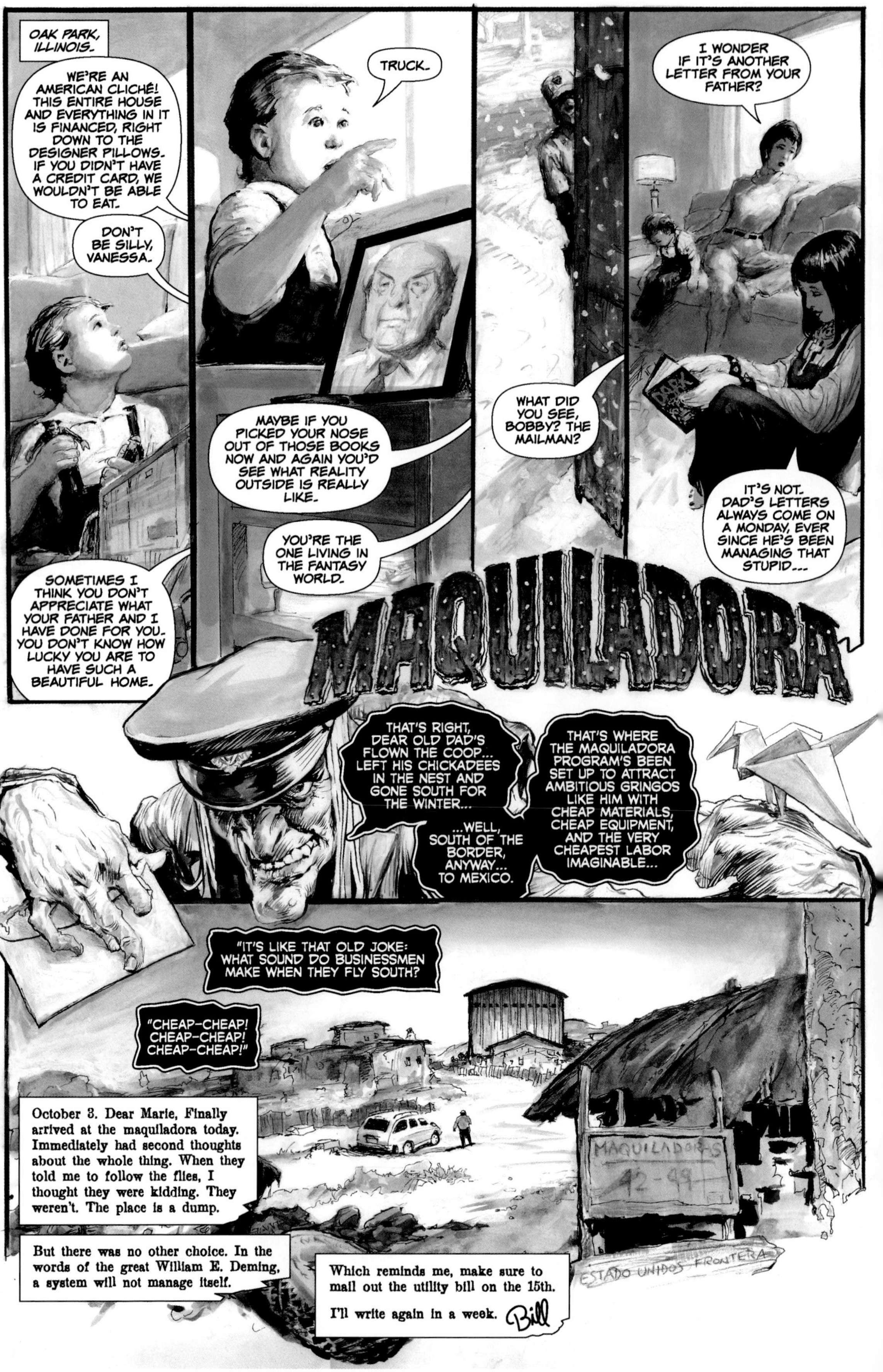

OAK PARK, ILLINOIS.
WE'RE AN AMERICAN CLICHÉ! THIS ENTIRE HOUSE AND EVERYTHING IN IT IS FINANCED, RIGHT DOWN TO THE DESIGNER PILLOWS. IF YOU DIDN'T HAVE A CREDIT CARD, WE WOULDN'T BE ABLE TO EAT.
DON'T BE SILLY, VANESSA.
SOMETIMES I THINK YOU DON'T APPRECIATE WHAT YOUR FATHER AND I HAVE DONE FOR YOU. YOU DON'T KNOW HOW LUCKY YOU ARE TO HAVE SUCH A BEAUTIFUL HOME.
TRUCK.
MAYBE IF YOU PICKED YOUR NOSE OUT OF THOSE BOOKS NOW AND AGAIN YOU'D SEE WHAT REALITY OUTSIDE IS REALLY LIKE.
YOU'RE THE ONE LIVING IN THE FANTASY WORLD.
WHAT DID YOU SEE, BOBBY? THE MAILMAN?
I WONDER IF IT'S ANOTHER LETTER FROM YOUR FATHER?
IT'S NOT. DAD'S LETTERS ALWAYS COME ON A MONDAY, EVER SINCE HE'S BEEN MANAGING THAT STUPID...
MAQUILADORA
THAT'S RIGHT, DEAR OLD DAD'S FLOWN THE COOP... LEFT HIS CHICKADEES IN THE NEST AND GONE SOUTH FOR THE WINTER...
...WELL, SOUTH OF THE BORDER, ANYWAY... TO MEXICO.
THAT'S WHERE THE MAQUILADORA PROGRAM'S BEEN SET UP TO ATTRACT AMBITIOUS GRINGOS LIKE HIM WITH CHEAP MATERIALS, CHEAP EQUIPMENT, AND THE VERY CHEAPEST LABOR IMAGINABLE...
"IT'S LIKE THAT OLD JOKE: WHAT SOUND DO BUSINESSMEN MAKE WHEN THEY FLY SOUTH?
"CHEAP-CHEAP! CHEAP-CHEAP! CHEAP-CHEAP!"
October 3. Dear Marie, Finally arrived at the maquiladora today. Immediately had second thoughts about the whole thing. When they told me to follow the flies, I thought they were kidding. They weren't. The place is a dump.
MAQUILADORAS 42-49
But there was no other choice. In the words of the great William E. Deming, a system will not manage itself.
Which reminds me, make sure to mail out the utility bill on the 15th.
I'll write again in a week. Bill
ESTADO UNIDOS FRONTERA

Story by CODY GOODFELLOW / Script and Art by KEVIN FERRARA

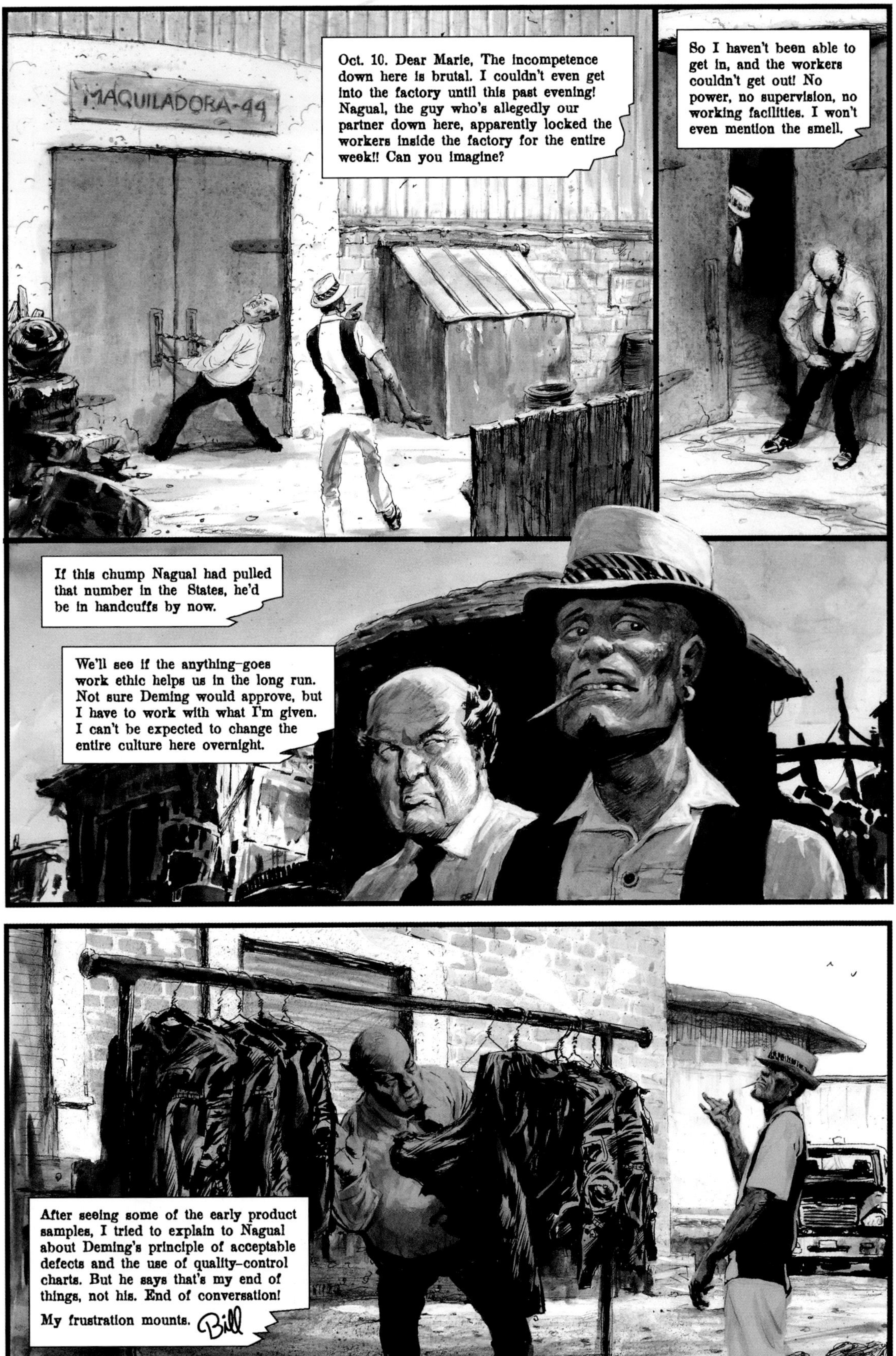

MAQUILADORA-44
Oct. 10. Dear Marie, The incompetence down here is brutal. I couldn't even get into the factory until this past evening! Nagual, the guy who's allegedly our partner down here, apparently locked the workers inside the factory for the entire week!! Can you imagine?
So I haven't been able to get in, and the workers couldn't get out! No power, no supervision, no working facilities. I won't even mention the smell.
If this chump Nagual had pulled that number in the States, he'd be in handcuffs by now.
We'll see if the anything-goes work ethic helps us in the long run. Not sure Deming would approve, but I have to work with what I'm given. I can't be expected to change the entire culture here overnight.
After seeing some of the early product samples, I tried to explain to Nagual about Deming's principle of acceptable defects and the use of quality-control charts. But he says that's my end of things, not his. End of conversation!
My frustration mounts. Bill

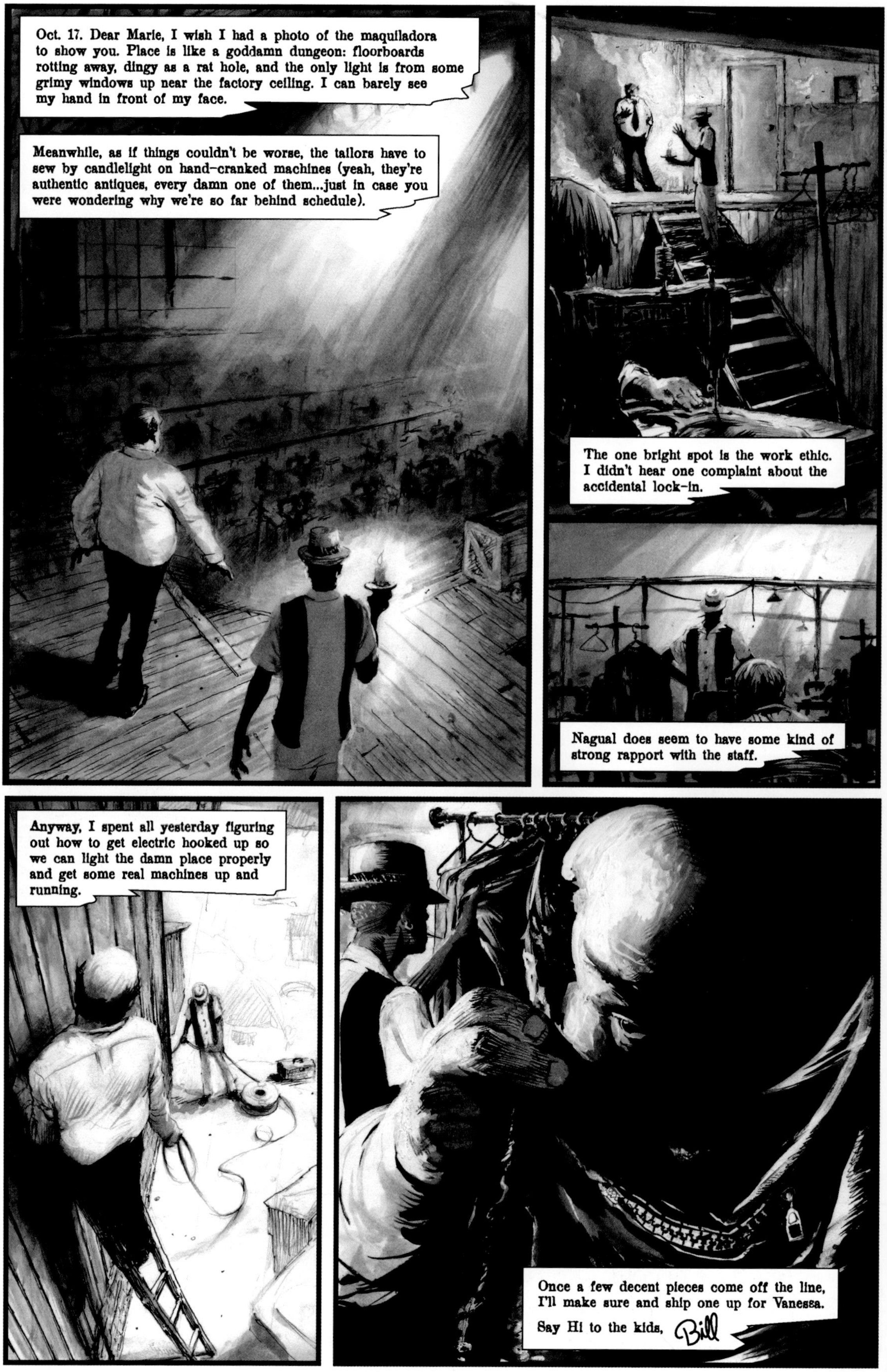

Oct. 17. Dear Marie, I wish I had a photo of the maquiladora to show you. Place is like a goddamn dungeon: floorboards rotting away, dingy as a rat hole, and the only light is from some grimy windows up near the factory ceiling. I can barely see my hand in front of my face.
Meanwhile, as if things couldn't be worse, the tailors have to sew by candlelight on hand-cranked machines (yeah, they're authentic antiques, every damn one of them...just in case you were wondering why we're so far behind schedule).
The one bright spot is the work ethic. I didn't hear one complaint about the accidental lock-in.
Nagual does seem to have some kind of strong rapport with the staff.
Anyway, I spent all yesterday figuring out how to get electric hooked up so we can light the damn place properly and get some real machines up and running.
Once a few decent pieces come off the line, I'll make sure and ship one up for Vanessa.
Say Hi to the kids, Bill

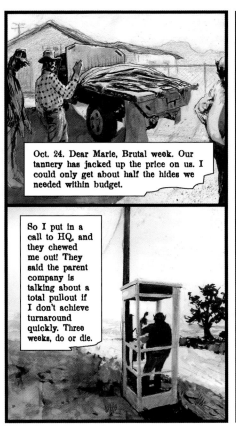

Oct. 24. Dear Marie, Brutal week. Our tannery has jacked up the price on us. I could only get about half the hides we needed within budget.
So I put in a call to HQ, and they chewed me out! They said the parent company is talking about a total pullout if I don't achieve turnaround quickly. Three weeks, do or die.
So when I got back in, I pushed the production issue with Nagual. Result: I finally got my connection to personnel on the floor. But the news there just made things worse...
Turns out we're employing the dregs. THE ABSOLUTE DREGS!
Half of the workers are practically passed out at their machines...I won't even dignify them by calling them grunts. They're unemployable.
No wonder Nagual wanted to keep me off the floor. But like the saying goes, you can't stand outside the system if you want to fix it.
So I told Nagual—either he gets his production numbers up or he hits the bricks. He went out to the floor after that and things picked up. But damn if I know how he did it.
AMERICAN leatha HIDEWEAR
Bit by bit the factory is starting to hum along. But these next few weeks are going to be crucial. Bill

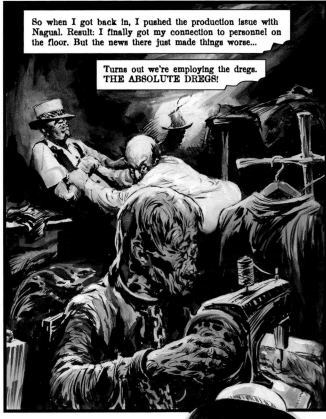

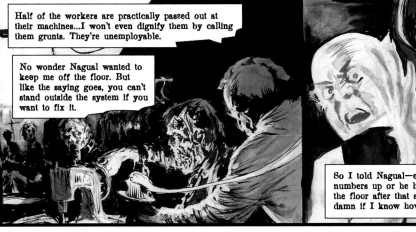

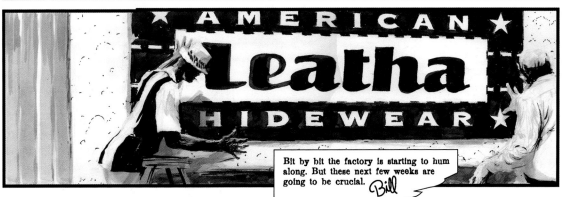

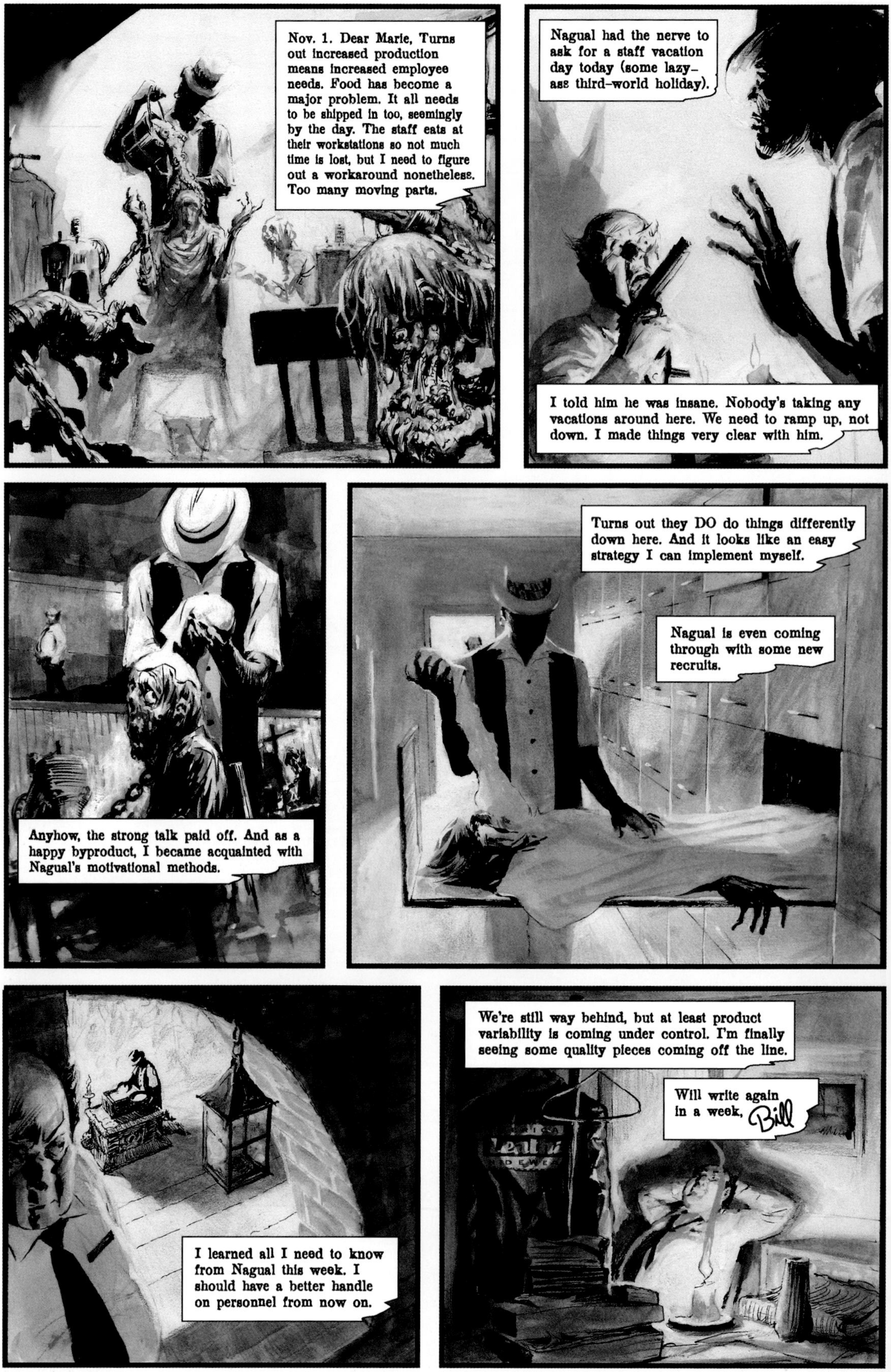
Nov. 1. Dear Marie, Turns out increased production means increased employee needs. Food has become a major problem. It all needs to be shipped in too, seemingly by the day. The staff eats at their workstations so not much time is lost, but I need to figure out a workaround nonetheless. Too many moving parts.
Nagual had the nerve to ask for a staff vacation day today (some lazy-ass third-world holiday).
I told him he was insane. Nobody's taking any vacations around here. We need to ramp up, not down. I made things very clear with him.
Anyhow, the strong talk paid off. And as a happy byproduct, I became acquainted with Nagual's motivational methods.
Turns out they DO do things differently down here. And it looks like an easy strategy I can implement myself.
Nagual is even coming through with some new recruits.
I learned all I need to know from Nagual this week. I should have a better handle on personnel from now on.
We're still way behind, but at least product variability is coming under control. I'm finally seeing some quality pieces coming off the line.
Will write again in a week, Bill

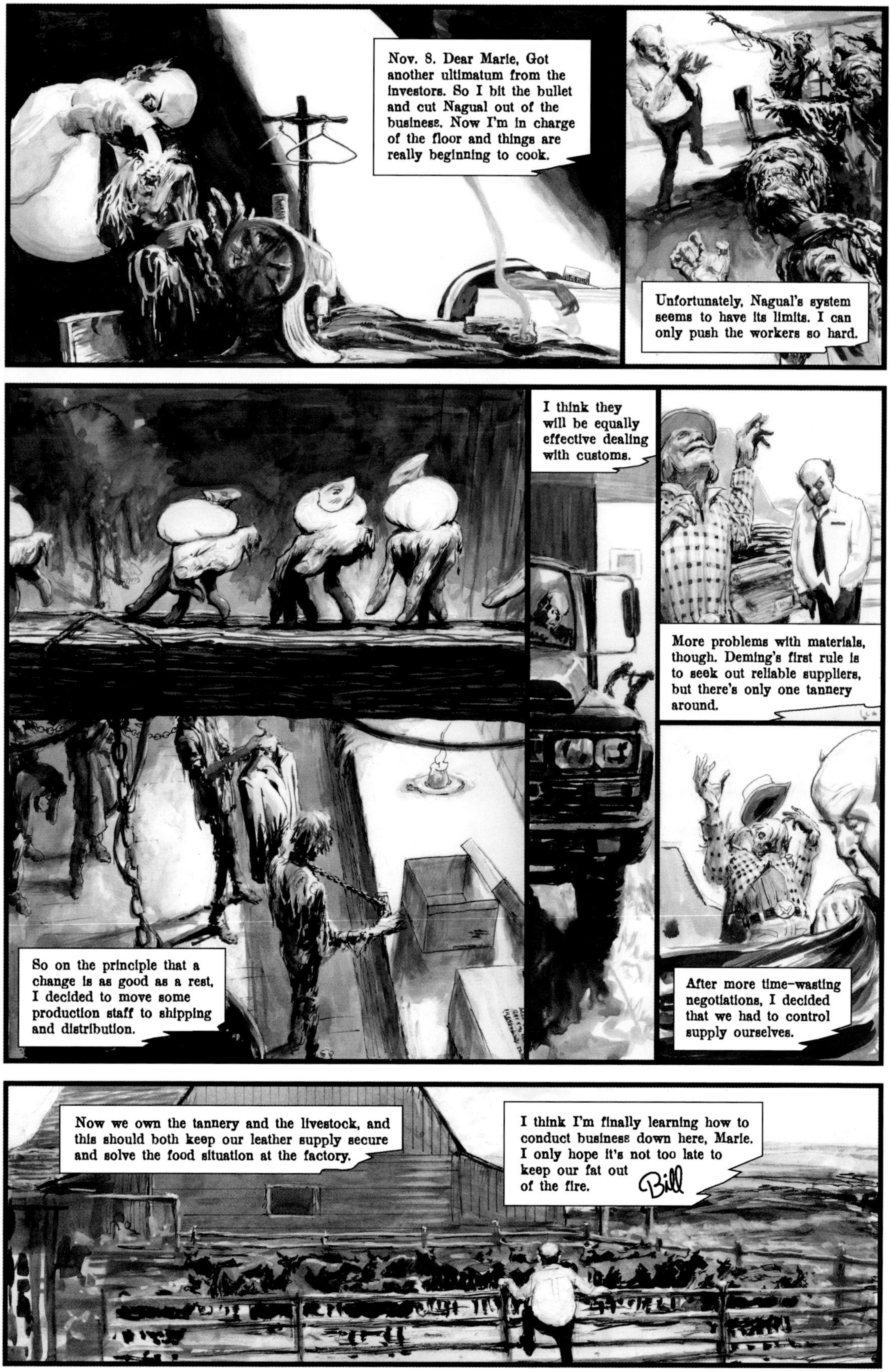
Nov. 8. Dear Marie, Got another ultimatum from the investors. So I bit the bullet and cut Nagual out of the business. Now I'm in charge of the floor and things are really beginning to cook.
Unfortunately, Nagual's system seems to have its limits. I can only push the workers so hard.
So on the principle that a change is as good as a rest, I decided to move some production staff to shipping and distribution.
I think they will be equally effective dealing with customs.
More problems with materials, though. Deming's first rule is to seek out reliable suppliers, but there's only one tannery around.
After more time-wasting negotiations, I decided that we had to control supply ourselves.
Now we own the tannery and the livestock, and this should both keep our leather supply secure and solve the food situation at the factory.
I think I'm finally learning how to conduct business down here, Marie. I only hope it's not too late to keep our fat out of the fire.
Bill

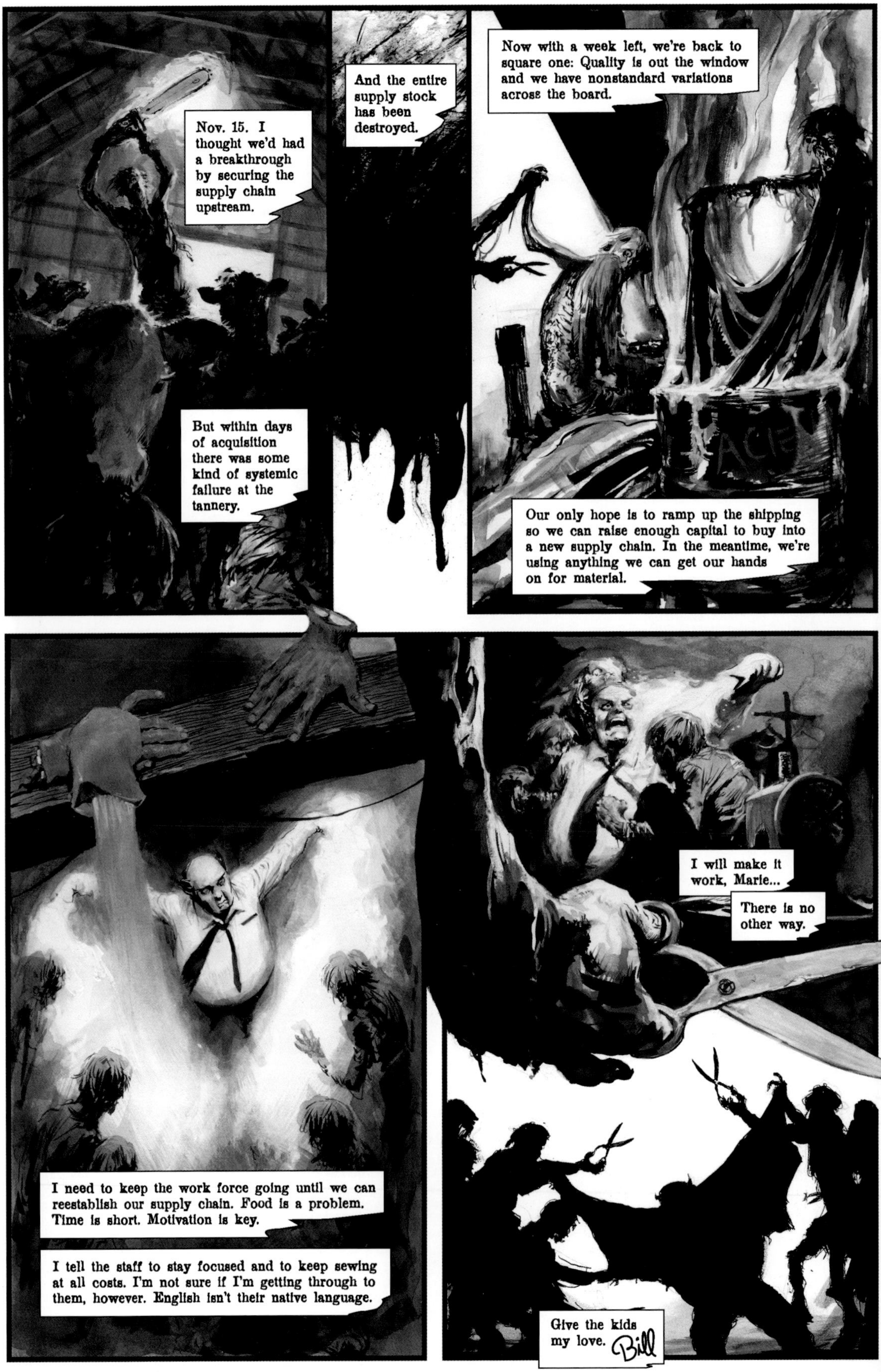
Nov. 15. I thought we'd had a breakthrough by securing the supply chain upstream.
But within days of acquisition there was some kind of systemic failure at the tannery.
And the entire supply stock has been destroyed.
Now with a week left, we're back to square one: Quality is out the window and we have nonstandard variations across the board.
Our only hope is to ramp up the shipping so we can raise enough capital to buy into a new supply chain. In the meantime, we're using anything we can get our hands on for material.
I need to keep the work force going until we can reestablish our supply chain. Food is a problem. Time is short. Motivation is key.
I tell the staff to stay focused and to keep sewing at all costs. I'm not sure if I'm getting through to them, however. English isn't their native language.
I will make it work, Marie...
There is no other way.
Give the kids my love. Bill

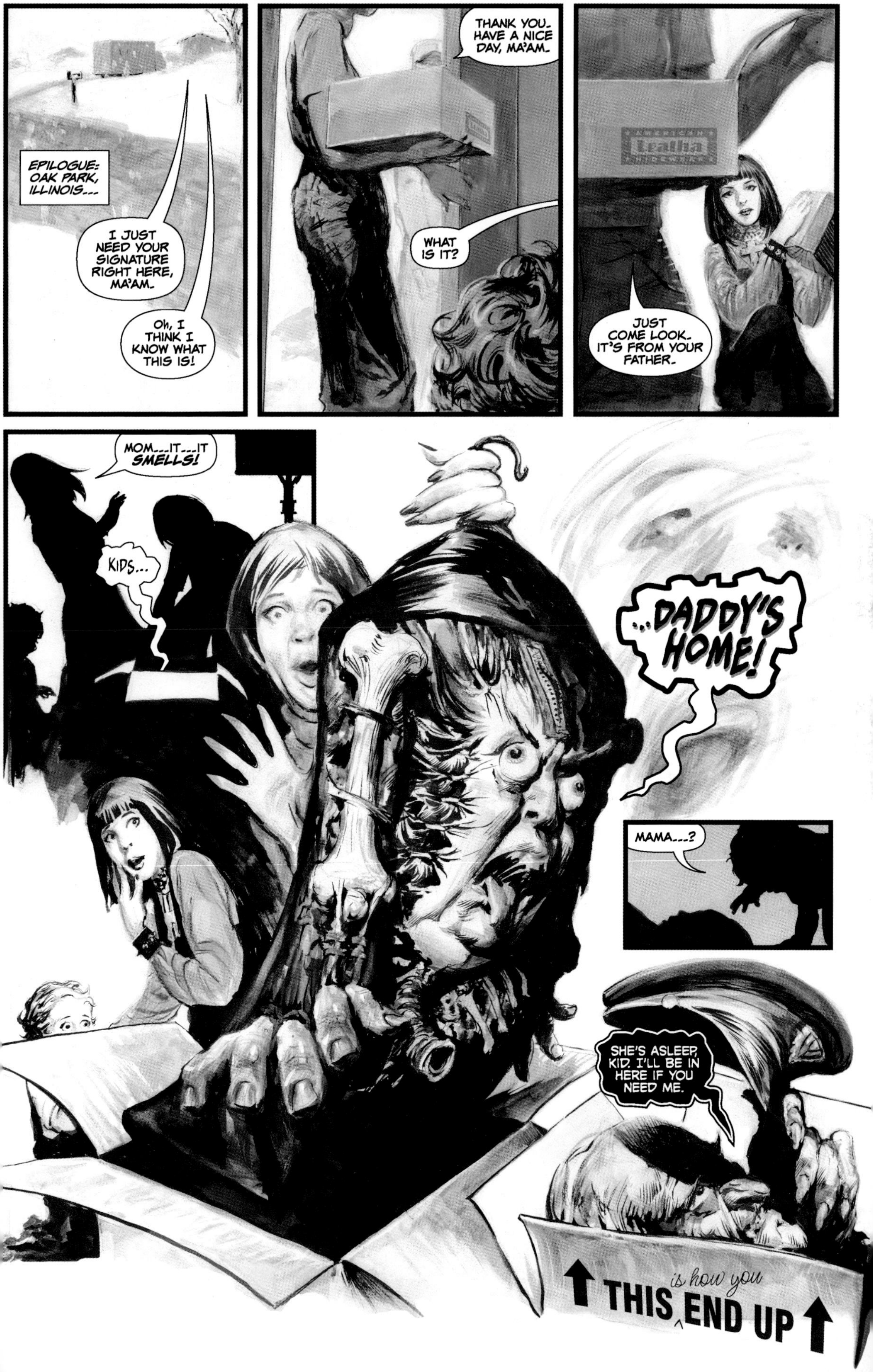
EPILOGUE: OAK PARK, ILLINOIS...
I JUST NEED YOUR SIGNATURE RIGHT HERE, MA'AM.
Oh, I THINK I KNOW WHAT THIS IS!
THANK YOU. HAVE A NICE DAY, MA'AM.
WHAT IS IT?
AMERICAN Leatha HIDEWEAR
JUST COME LOOK. IT'S FROM YOUR FATHER.
MOM...IT...IT SMELLS!
KIDS...
...DADDY'S HOME!
MAMA...?
SHE'S ASLEEP, KID. I'LL BE IN HERE IF YOU NEED ME.
THIS is how you END UP

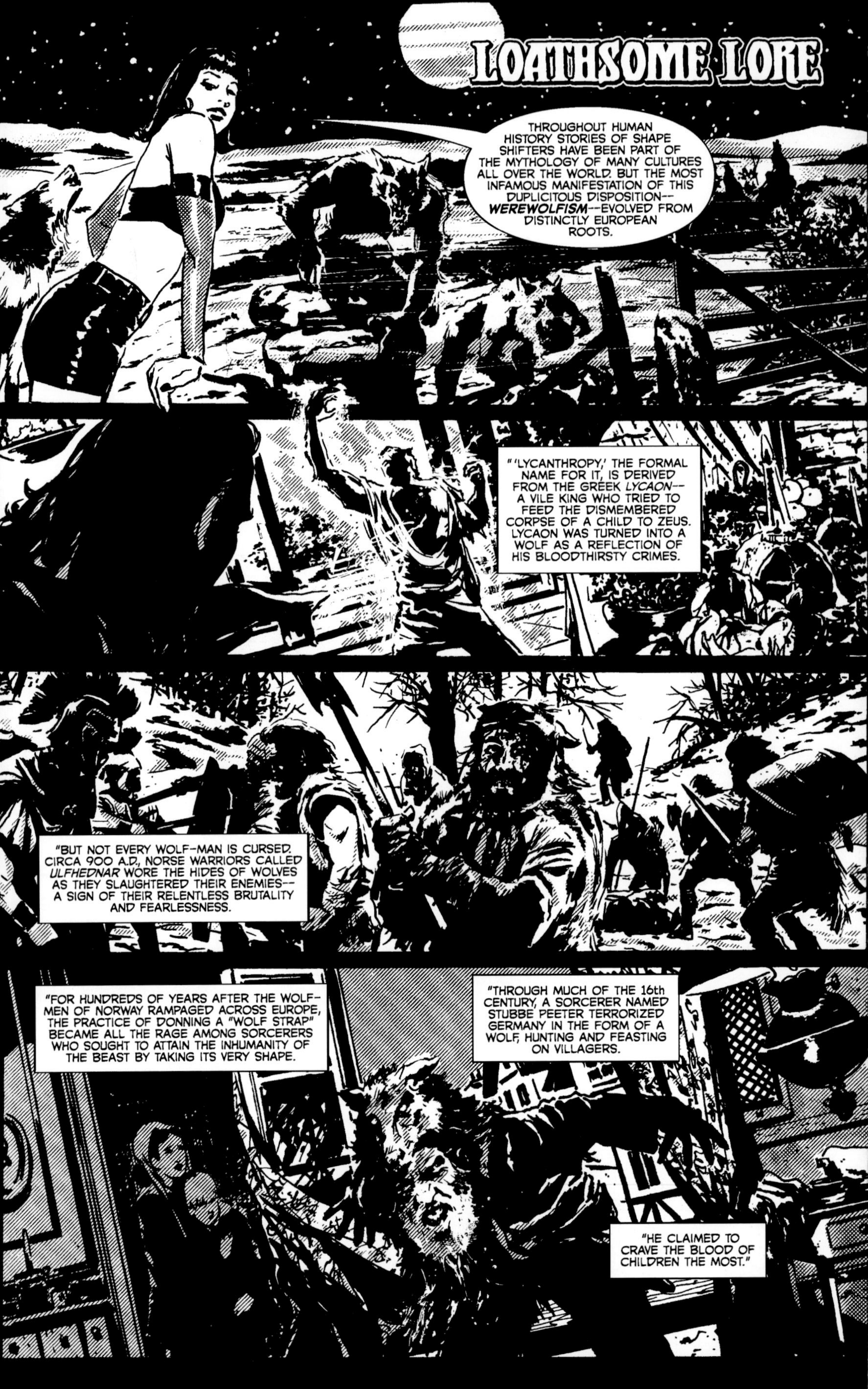
LOATHSOME LORE
THROUGHOUT HUMAN HISTORY STORIES OF SHAPE SHIFTERS HAVE BEEN PART OF THE MYTHOLOGY OF MANY CULTURES ALL OVER THE WORLD. BUT THE MOST INFAMOUS MANIFESTATION OF THIS DUPLICITOUS DISPOSITION-- WEREWOLFISM--EVOLVED FROM DISTINCTLY EUROPEAN ROOTS.
"'LYCANTHROPY,' THE FORMAL NAME FOR IT, IS DERIVED FROM THE GREEK LYCAON-- A VILE KING WHO TRIED TO FEED THE DISMEMBERED CORPSE OF A CHILD TO ZEUS. LYCAON WAS TURNED INTO A WOLF AS A REFLECTION OF HIS BLOODTHIRSTY CRIMES.
"BUT NOT EVERY WOLF-MAN IS CURSED. CIRCA 900 A.D., NORSE WARRIORS CALLED ULFHEDNAR WORE THE HIDES OF WOLVES AS THEY SLAUGHTERED THEIR ENEMIES-- A SIGN OF THEIR RELENTLESS BRUTALITY AND FEARLESSNESS.
"FOR HUNDREDS OF YEARS AFTER THE WOLF-MEN OF NORWAY RAMPAGED ACROSS EUROPE, THE PRACTICE OF DONNING A "WOLF STRAP" BECAME ALL THE RAGE AMONG SORCERERS WHO SOUGHT TO ATTAIN THE INHUMANITY OF THE BEAST BY TAKING ITS VERY SHAPE.
"THROUGH MUCH OF THE 16th CENTURY, A SORCERER NAMED STUBBE PEETER TERRORIZED GERMANY IN THE FORM OF A WOLF, HUNTING AND FEASTING ON VILLAGERS.
"HE CLAIMED TO CRAVE THE BLOOD OF CHILDREN THE MOST."

Script by BRAUN, GORE, and HAFFNER / Art by GREG SCOTT

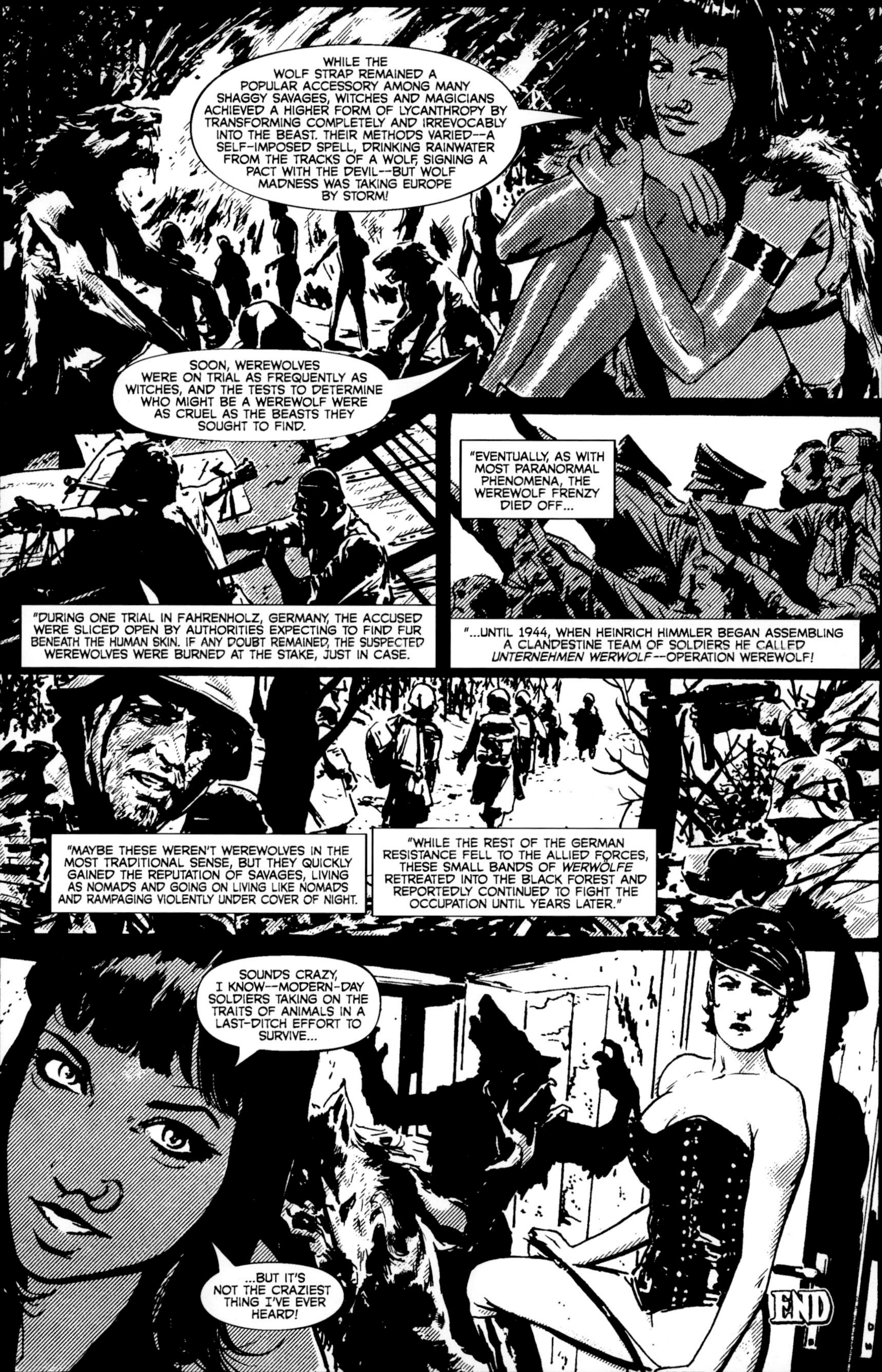
WHILE THE WOLF STRAP REMAINED A POPULAR ACCESSORY AMONG MANY SHAGGY SAVAGES, WITCHES AND MAGICIANS ACHIEVED A HIGHER FORM OF LYCANTHROPY BY TRANSFORMING COMPLETELY AND IRREVOCABLY INTO THE BEAST. THEIR METHODS VARIED--A SELF-IMPOSED SPELL, DRINKING RAINWATER FROM THE TRACKS OF A WOLF, SIGNING A PACT WITH THE DEVIL--BUT WOLF MADNESS WAS TAKING EUROPE BY STORM!
SOON, WEREWOLVES WERE ON TRIAL AS FREQUENTLY AS WITCHES, AND THE TESTS TO DETERMINE WHO MIGHT BE A WEREWOLF WERE AS CRUEL AS THE BEASTS THEY SOUGHT TO FIND.
"DURING ONE TRIAL IN FAHRENHOLZ, GERMANY, THE ACCUSED WERE SLICED OPEN BY AUTHORITIES EXPECTING TO FIND FUR BENEATH THE HUMAN SKIN. IF ANY DOUBT REMAINED, THE SUSPECTED WEREWOLVES WERE BURNED AT THE STAKE, JUST IN CASE.
"EVENTUALLY, AS WITH MOST PARANORMAL PHENOMENA, THE WEREWOLF FRENZY DIED OFF...
"...UNTIL 1944, WHEN HEINRICH HIMMLER BEGAN ASSEMBLING A CLANDESTINE TEAM OF SOLDIERS HE CALLED *UNTERNEHMEN WERWOLF*--OPERATION WEREWOLF!
"MAYBE THESE WEREN'T WEREWOLVES IN THE MOST TRADITIONAL SENSE, BUT THEY QUICKLY GAINED THE REPUTATION OF SAVAGES, LIVING AS NOMADS AND GOING ON LIVING LIKE NOMADS AND RAMPAGING VIOLENTLY UNDER COVER OF NIGHT.
"WHILE THE REST OF THE GERMAN RESISTANCE FELL TO THE ALLIED FORCES, THESE SMALL BANDS OF *WERWÖLFE* RETREATED INTO THE BLACK FOREST AND REPORTEDLY CONTINUED TO FIGHT THE OCCUPATION UNTIL YEARS LATER."
SOUNDS CRAZY, I KNOW--MODERN-DAY SOLDIERS TAKING ON THE TRAITS OF ANIMALS IN A LAST-DITCH EFFORT TO SURVIVE...
...BUT IT'S NOT THE CRAZIEST THING I'VE EVER HEARD!
END

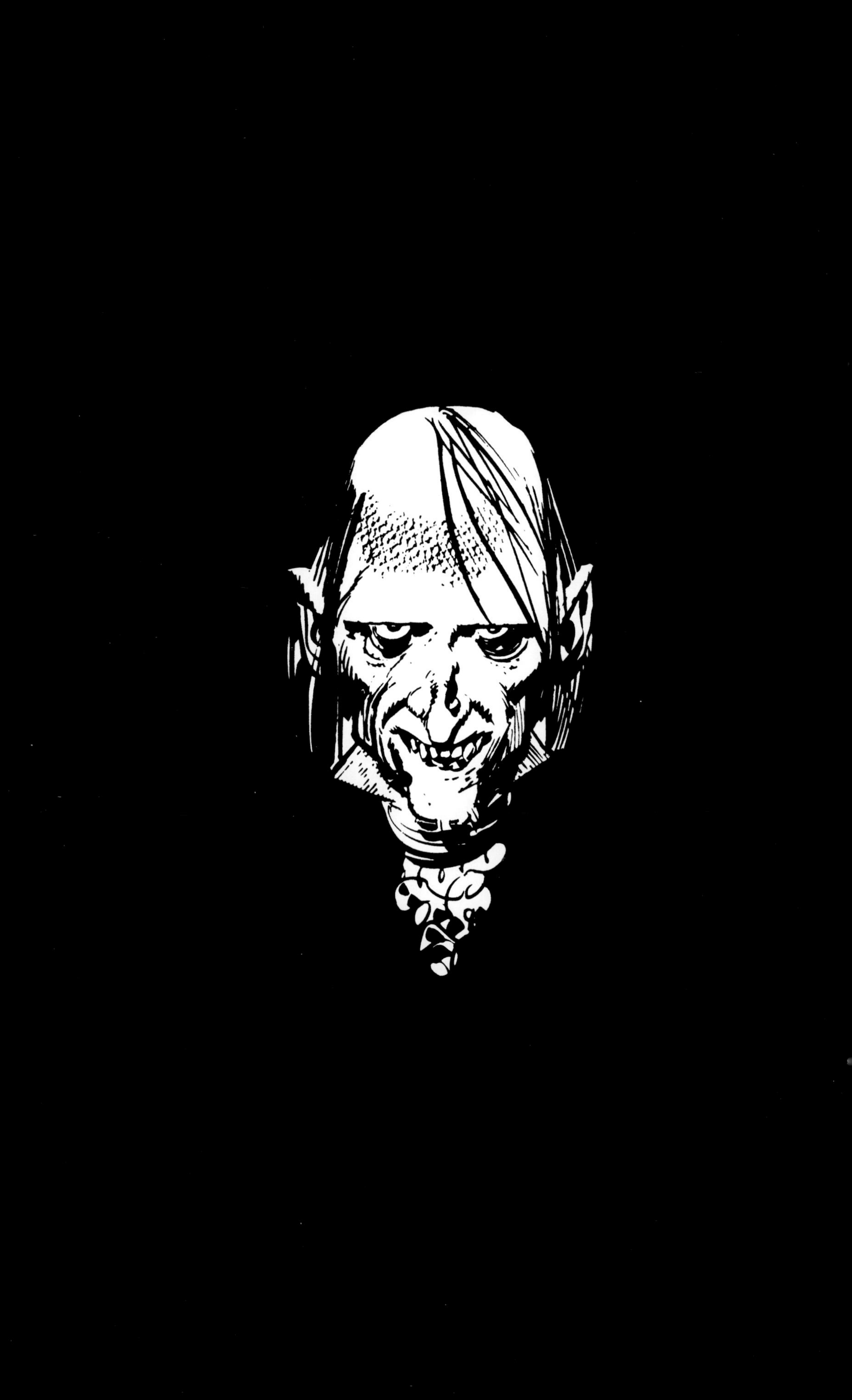

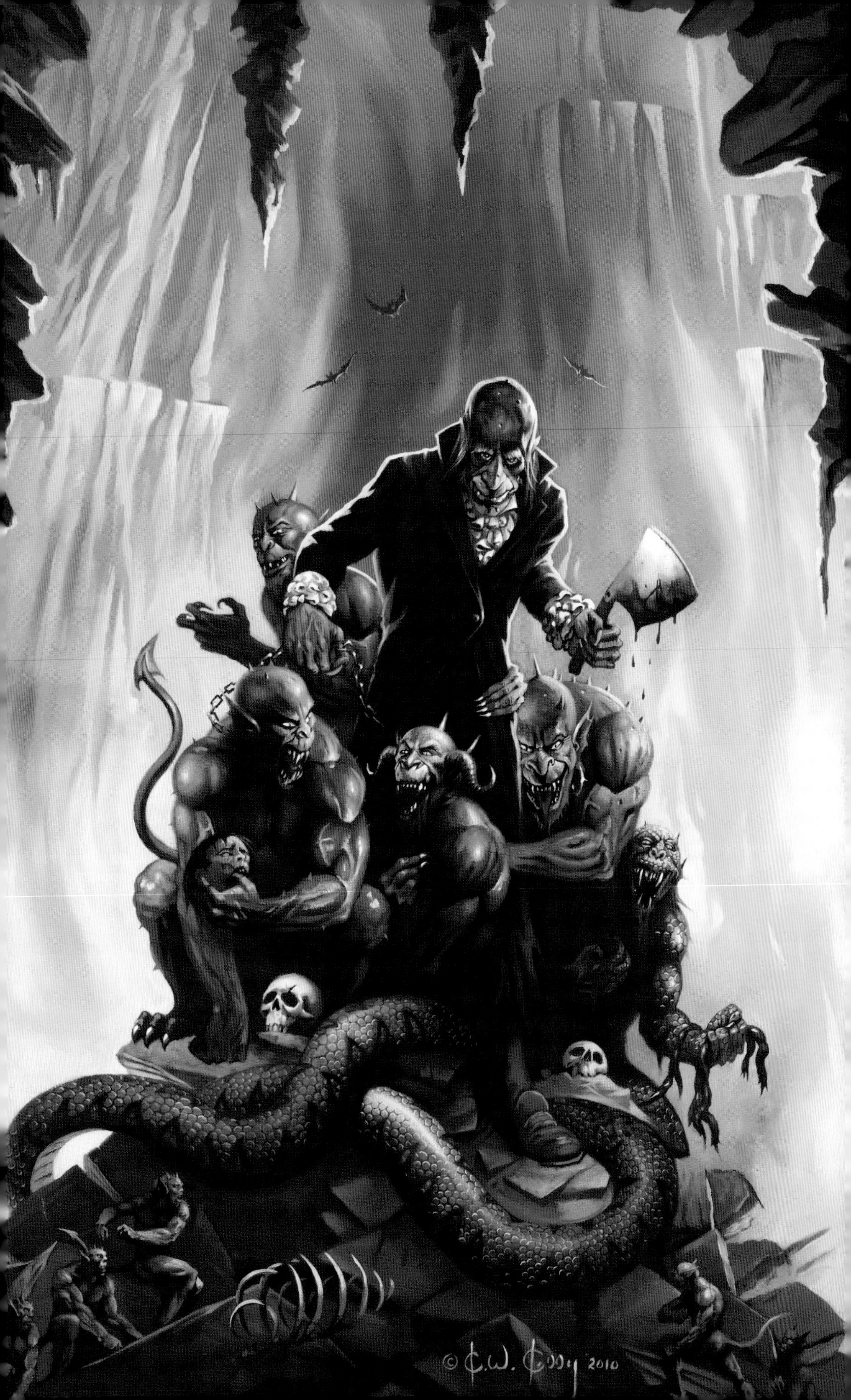
© C.W. Cody 2010

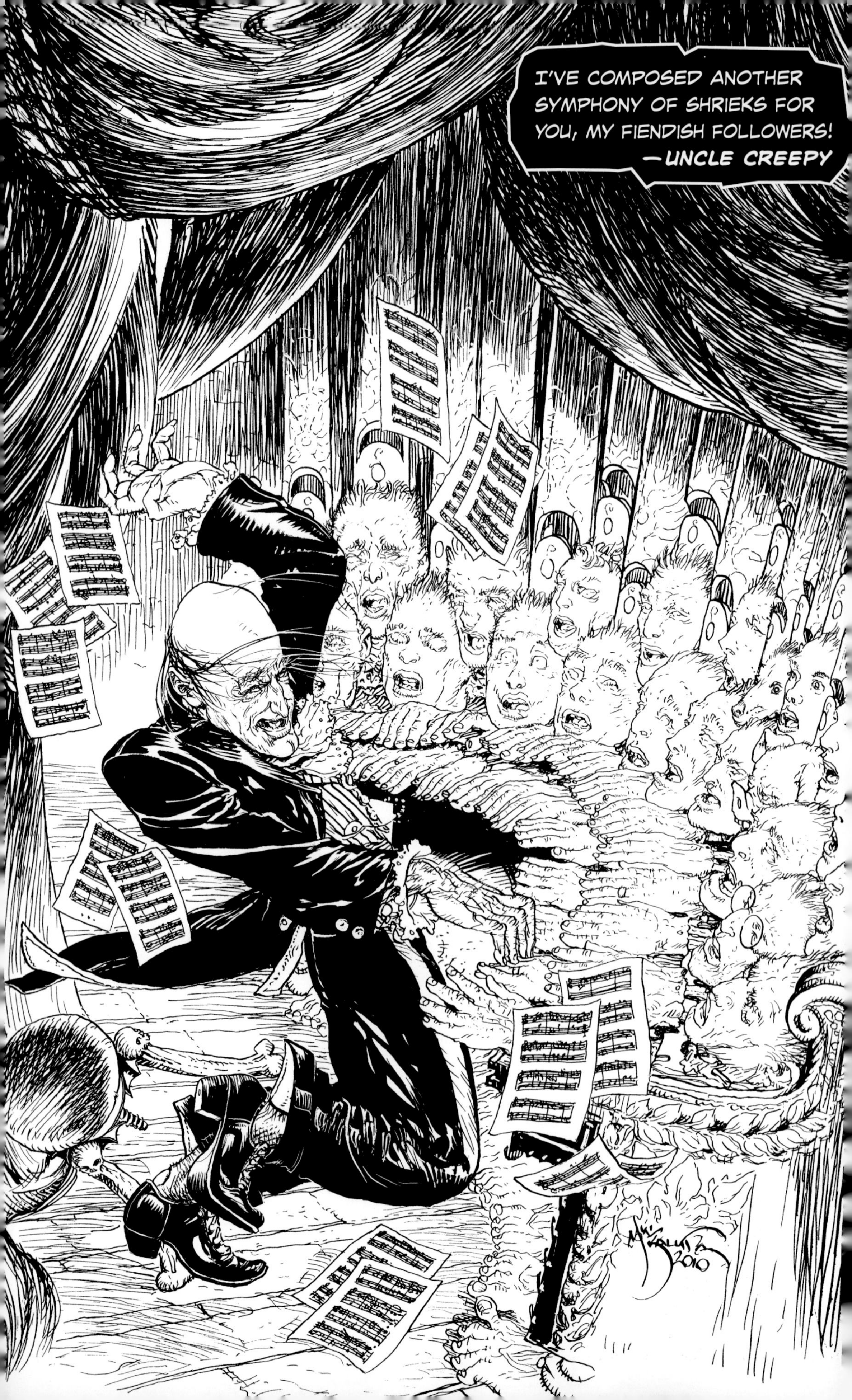
I'VE COMPOSED ANOTHER SYMPHONY OF SHRIEKS FOR YOU, MY FIENDISH FOLLOWERS!
—UNCLE CREEPY

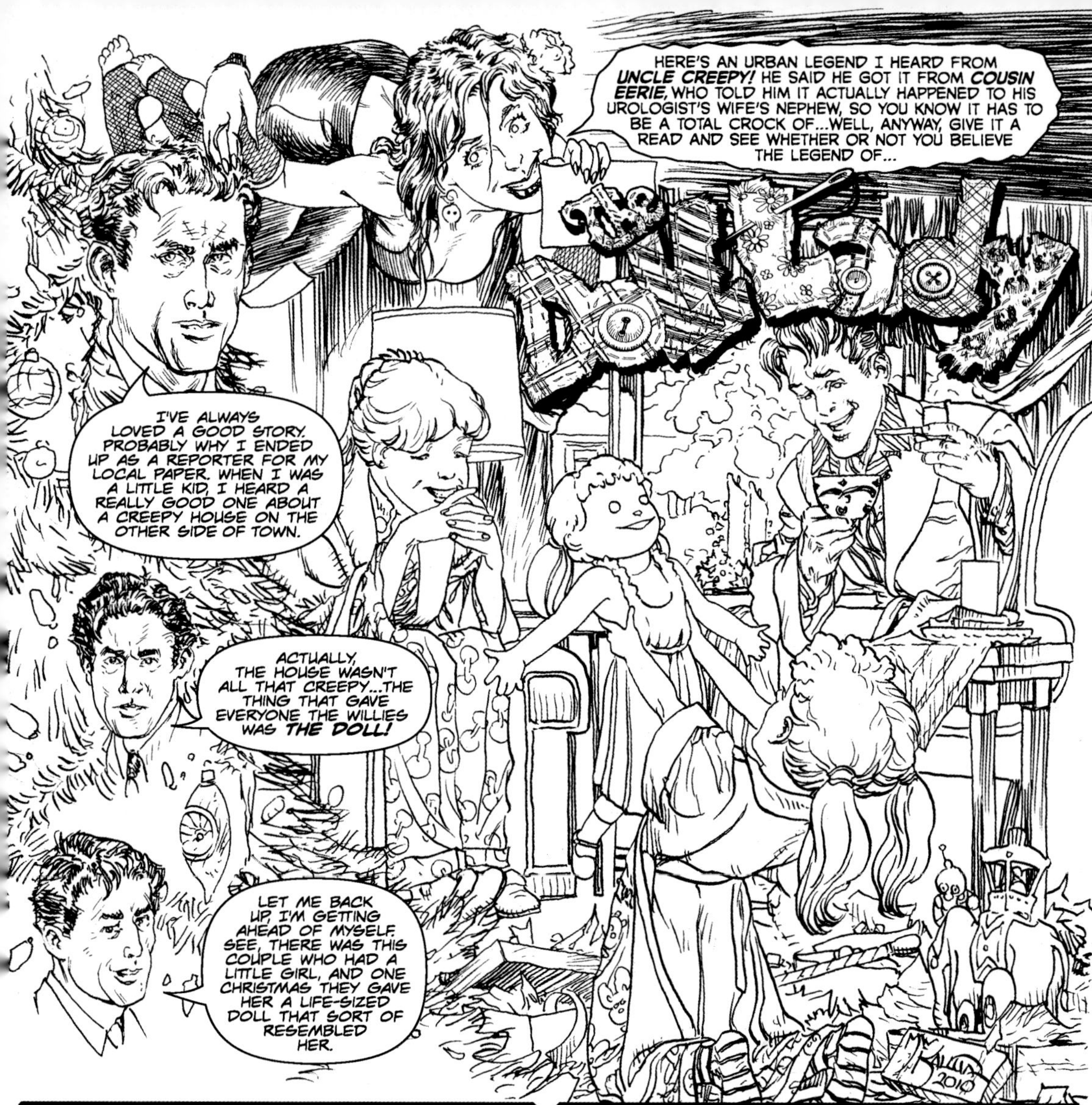
HERE'S AN URBAN LEGEND I HEARD FROM UNCLE CREEPY! HE SAID HE GOT IT FROM COUSIN EERIE, WHO TOLD HIM IT ACTUALLY HAPPENED TO HIS UROLOGIST'S WIFE'S NEPHEW, SO YOU KNOW IT HAS TO BE A TOTAL CROCK OF...WELL, ANYWAY, GIVE IT A READ AND SEE WHETHER OR NOT YOU BELIEVE THE LEGEND OF...
THE DOLL
I'VE ALWAYS LOVED A GOOD STORY. PROBABLY WHY I ENDED UP AS A REPORTER FOR MY LOCAL PAPER. WHEN I WAS A LITTLE KID, I HEARD A REALLY GOOD ONE ABOUT A CREEPY HOUSE ON THE OTHER SIDE OF TOWN.
ACTUALLY, THE HOUSE WASN'T ALL THAT CREEPY...THE THING THAT GAVE EVERYONE THE WILLIES WAS THE DOLL!
LET ME BACK UP, I'M GETTING AHEAD OF MYSELF. SEE, THERE WAS THIS COUPLE WHO HAD A LITTLE GIRL, AND ONE CHRISTMAS THEY GAVE HER A LIFE-SIZED DOLL THAT SORT OF RESEMBLED HER.

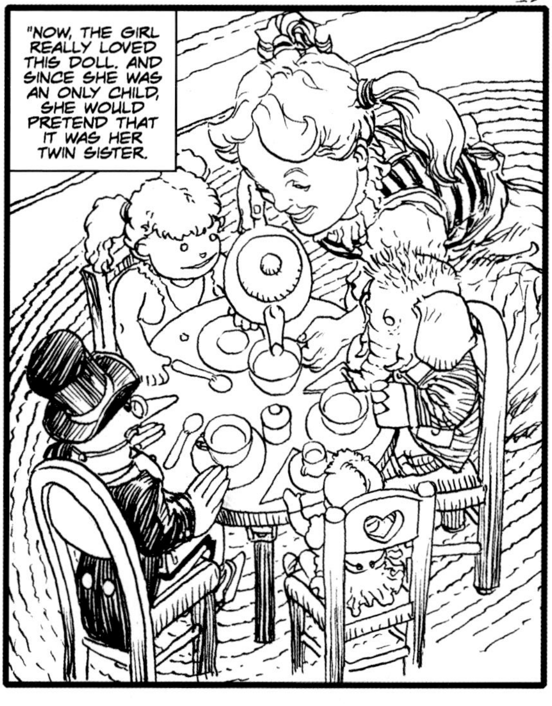
"NOW, THE GIRL REALLY LOVED THIS DOLL. AND SINCE SHE WAS AN ONLY CHILD, SHE WOULD PRETEND THAT IT WAS HER TWIN SISTER.

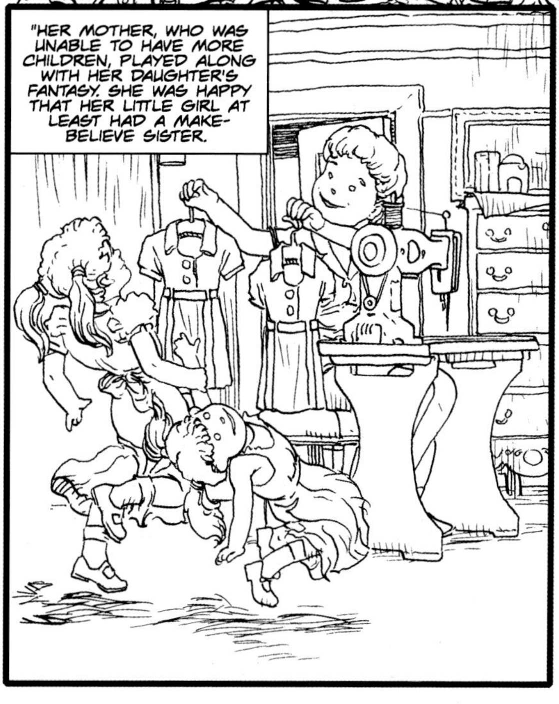
"HER MOTHER, WHO WAS UNABLE TO HAVE MORE CHILDREN, PLAYED ALONG WITH HER DAUGHTER'S FANTASY. SHE WAS HAPPY THAT HER LITTLE GIRL AT LEAST HAD A MAKE-BELIEVE SISTER.

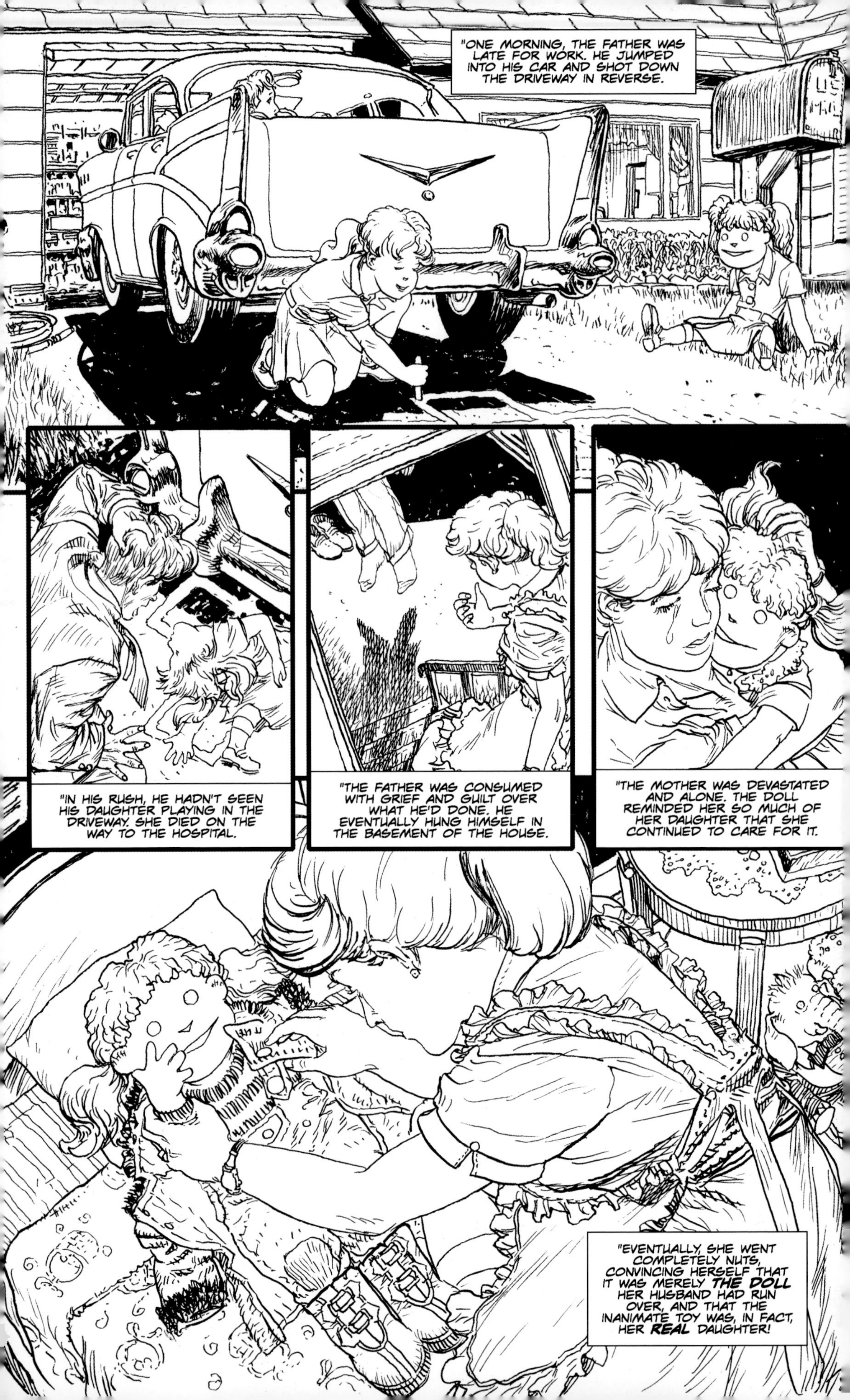
"ONE MORNING, THE FATHER WAS LATE FOR WORK. HE JUMPED INTO HIS CAR AND SHOT DOWN THE DRIVEWAY IN REVERSE.
"IN HIS RUSH, HE HADN'T SEEN HIS DAUGHTER PLAYING IN THE DRIVEWAY. SHE DIED ON THE WAY TO THE HOSPITAL.
"THE FATHER WAS CONSUMED WITH GRIEF AND GUILT OVER WHAT HE'D DONE. HE EVENTUALLY HUNG HIMSELF IN THE BASEMENT OF THE HOUSE.
"THE MOTHER WAS DEVASTATED AND ALONE. THE DOLL REMINDED HER SO MUCH OF HER DAUGHTER THAT SHE CONTINUED TO CARE FOR IT.
"EVENTUALLY, SHE WENT COMPLETELY NUTS, CONVINCING HERSELF THAT IT WAS MERELY **THE DOLL** HER HUSBAND HAD RUN OVER, AND THAT THE INANIMATE TOY WAS, IN FACT, HER **REAL** DAUGHTER!

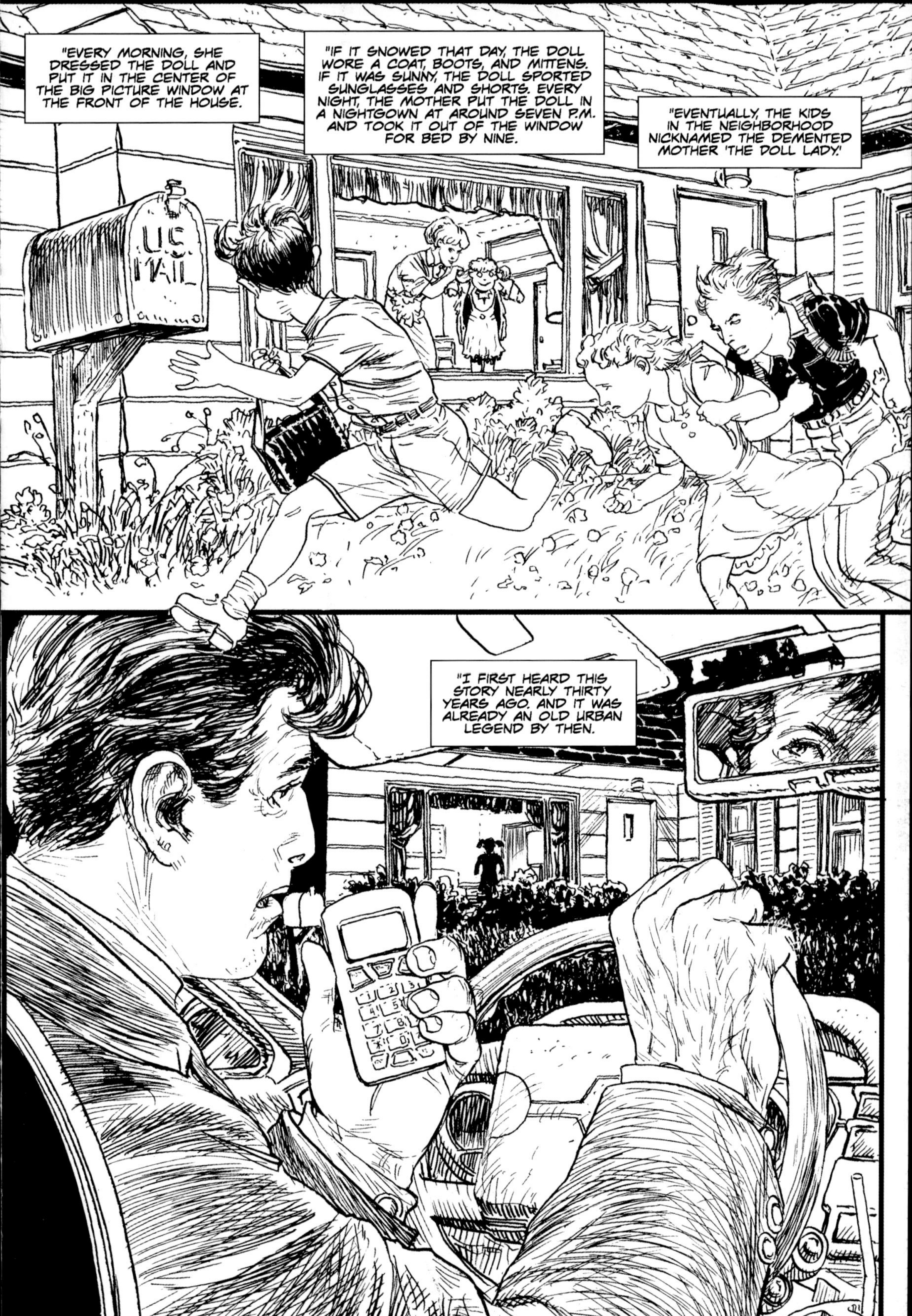
"EVERY MORNING, SHE DRESSED THE DOLL AND PUT IT IN THE CENTER OF THE BIG PICTURE WINDOW AT THE FRONT OF THE HOUSE.
"IF IT SNOWED THAT DAY, THE DOLL WORE A COAT, BOOTS, AND MITTENS. IF IT WAS SUNNY, THE DOLL SPORTED SUNGLASSES AND SHORTS. EVERY NIGHT, THE MOTHER PUT THE DOLL IN A NIGHTGOWN AT AROUND SEVEN P.M. AND TOOK IT OUT OF THE WINDOW FOR BED BY NINE.
"EVENTUALLY, THE KIDS IN THE NEIGHBORHOOD NICKNAMED THE DEMENTED MOTHER 'THE DOLL LADY.'
U.S. MAIL
"I FIRST HEARD THIS STORY NEARLY THIRTY YEARS AGO. AND IT WAS ALREADY AN OLD URBAN LEGEND BY THEN.

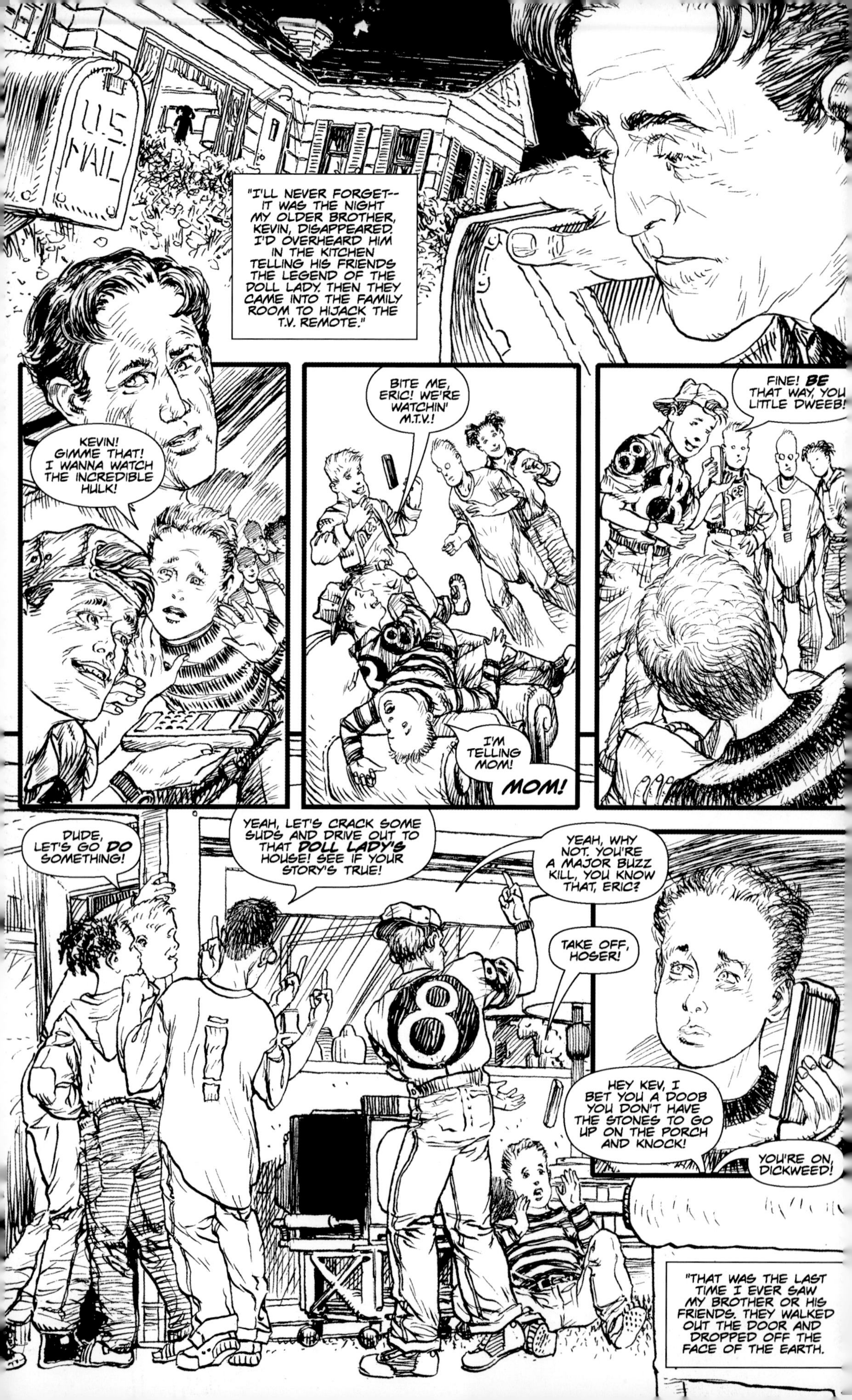
"I'LL NEVER FORGET-- IT WAS THE NIGHT MY OLDER BROTHER, KEVIN, DISAPPEARED. I'D OVERHEARD HIM IN THE KITCHEN TELLING HIS FRIENDS THE LEGEND OF THE DOLL LADY. THEN THEY CAME INTO THE FAMILY ROOM TO HIJACK THE T.V. REMOTE."
U.S. MAIL
KEVIN! GIMME THAT! I WANNA WATCH THE INCREDIBLE HULK!
BITE ME, ERIC! WE'RE WATCHIN' M.T.V.!
I'M TELLING MOM!
MOM!
FINE! BE THAT WAY, YOU LITTLE DWEEB!
DUDE, LET'S GO DO SOMETHING!
YEAH, LET'S CRACK SOME SUDS AND DRIVE OUT TO THAT DOLL LADY'S HOUSE! SEE IF YOUR STORY'S TRUE!
YEAH, WHY NOT. YOU'RE A MAJOR BUZZ KILL, YOU KNOW THAT, ERIC?
TAKE OFF, HOSER!
HEY KEV, I BET YOU A DOOB YOU DON'T HAVE THE STONES TO GO UP ON THE PORCH AND KNOCK!
YOU'RE ON, DICKWEED!
"THAT WAS THE LAST TIME I EVER SAW MY BROTHER OR HIS FRIENDS. THEY WALKED OUT THE DOOR AND DROPPED OFF THE FACE OF THE EARTH.

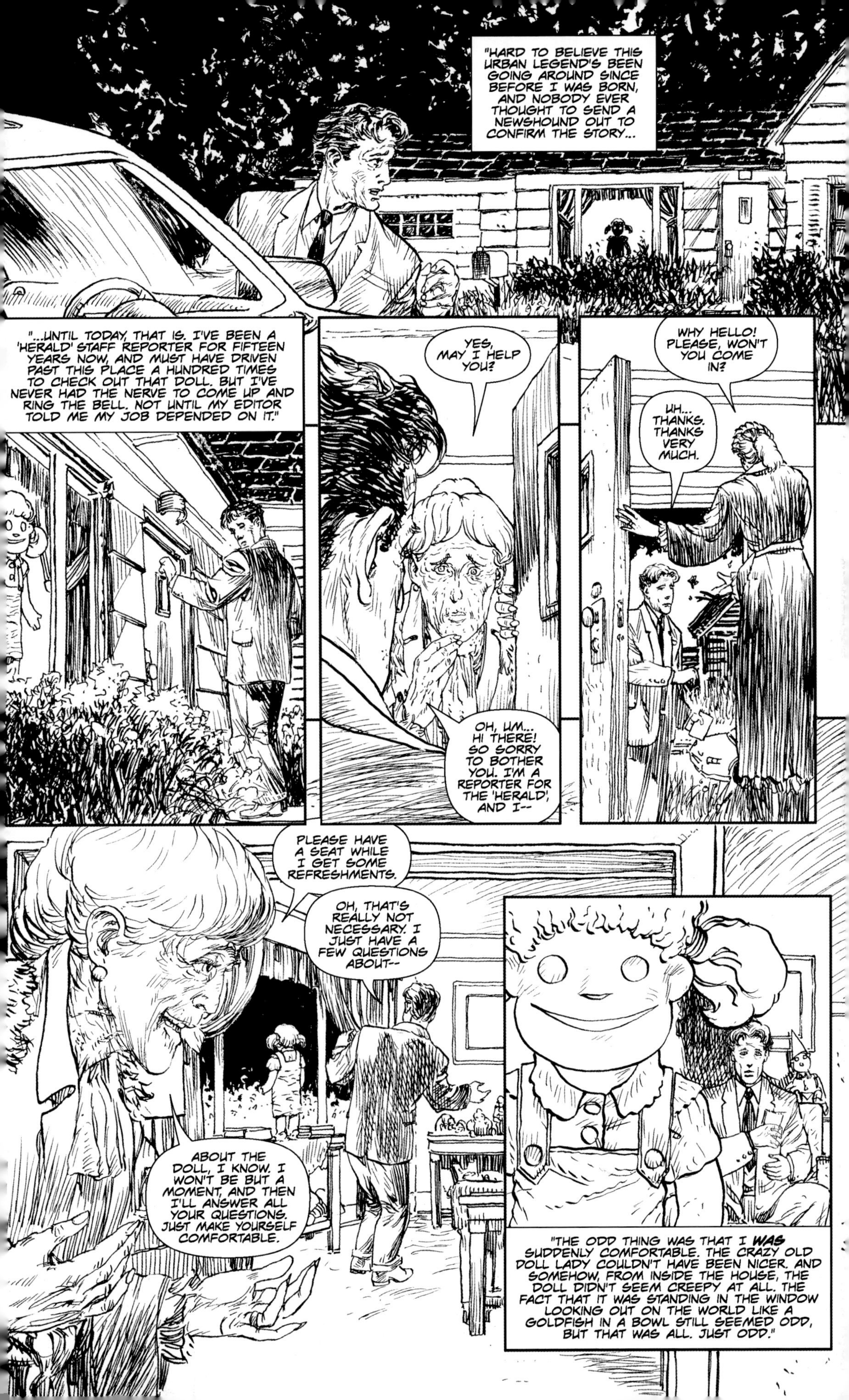
"HARD TO BELIEVE THIS URBAN LEGEND'S BEEN GOING AROUND SINCE BEFORE I WAS BORN, AND NOBODY EVER THOUGHT TO SEND A NEWSHOUND OUT TO CONFIRM THE STORY...
"...UNTIL TODAY, THAT IS. I'VE BEEN A 'HERALD' STAFF REPORTER FOR FIFTEEN YEARS NOW, AND MUST HAVE DRIVEN PAST THIS PLACE A HUNDRED TIMES TO CHECK OUT THAT DOLL. BUT I'VE NEVER HAD THE NERVE TO COME UP AND RING THE BELL. NOT UNTIL MY EDITOR TOLD ME MY JOB DEPENDED ON IT."
YES, MAY I HELP YOU?
OH, UM... HI THERE! SO SORRY TO BOTHER YOU. I'M A REPORTER FOR THE 'HERALD', AND I--
WHY HELLO! PLEASE, WON'T YOU COME IN?
UH... THANKS. THANKS VERY MUCH.
PLEASE HAVE A SEAT WHILE I GET SOME REFRESHMENTS.
OH, THAT'S REALLY NOT NECESSARY. I JUST HAVE A FEW QUESTIONS ABOUT--
ABOUT THE DOLL, I KNOW. I WON'T BE BUT A MOMENT, AND THEN I'LL ANSWER ALL YOUR QUESTIONS. JUST MAKE YOURSELF COMFORTABLE.
"THE ODD THING WAS THAT I WAS SUDDENLY COMFORTABLE. THE CRAZY OLD DOLL LADY COULDN'T HAVE BEEN NICER. AND SOMEHOW, FROM INSIDE THE HOUSE, THE DOLL DIDN'T SEEM CREEPY AT ALL. THE FACT THAT IT WAS STANDING IN THE WINDOW LOOKING OUT ON THE WORLD LIKE A GOLDFISH IN A BOWL STILL SEEMED ODD, BUT THAT WAS ALL. JUST ODD."

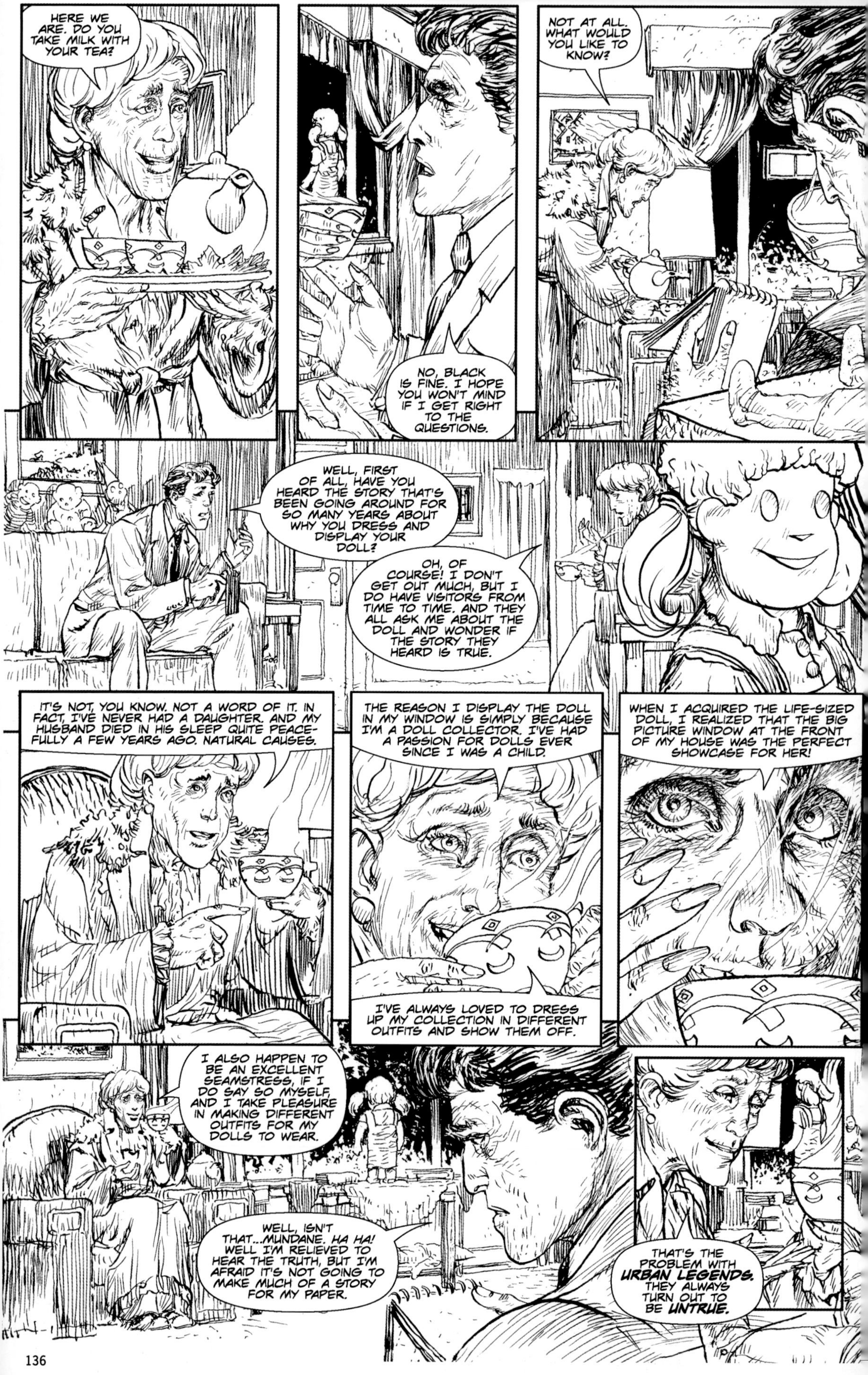
HERE WE ARE. DO YOU TAKE MILK WITH YOUR TEA?
NO, BLACK IS FINE. I HOPE YOU WON'T MIND IF I GET RIGHT TO THE QUESTIONS.
NOT AT ALL. WHAT WOULD YOU LIKE TO KNOW?
WELL, FIRST OF ALL, HAVE YOU HEARD THE STORY THAT'S BEEN GOING AROUND FOR SO MANY YEARS ABOUT WHY YOU DRESS AND DISPLAY YOUR DOLL?
OH, OF COURSE! I DON'T GET OUT MUCH, BUT I DO HAVE VISITORS FROM TIME TO TIME. AND THEY ALL ASK ME ABOUT THE DOLL AND WONDER IF THE STORY THEY HEARD IS TRUE.
IT'S NOT, YOU KNOW. NOT A WORD OF IT. IN FACT, I'VE NEVER HAD A DAUGHTER. AND MY HUSBAND DIED IN HIS SLEEP QUITE PEACEFULLY A FEW YEARS AGO. NATURAL CAUSES.
THE REASON I DISPLAY THE DOLL IN MY WINDOW IS SIMPLY BECAUSE I'M A DOLL COLLECTOR. I'VE HAD A PASSION FOR DOLLS EVER SINCE I WAS A CHILD.
I'VE ALWAYS LOVED TO DRESS UP MY COLLECTION IN DIFFERENT OUTFITS AND SHOW THEM OFF.
WHEN I ACQUIRED THE LIFE-SIZED DOLL, I REALIZED THAT THE BIG PICTURE WINDOW AT THE FRONT OF MY HOUSE WAS THE PERFECT SHOWCASE FOR HER!
I ALSO HAPPEN TO BE AN EXCELLENT SEAMSTRESS, IF I DO SAY SO MYSELF, AND I TAKE PLEASURE IN MAKING DIFFERENT OUTFITS FOR MY DOLLS TO WEAR.
WELL, ISN'T THAT...MUNDANE. HA HA! WELL I'M RELIEVED TO HEAR THE TRUTH, BUT I'M AFRAID IT'S NOT GOING TO MAKE MUCH OF A STORY FOR MY PAPER.
THAT'S THE PROBLEM WITH URBAN LEGENDS. THEY ALWAYS TURN OUT TO BE UNTRUE.

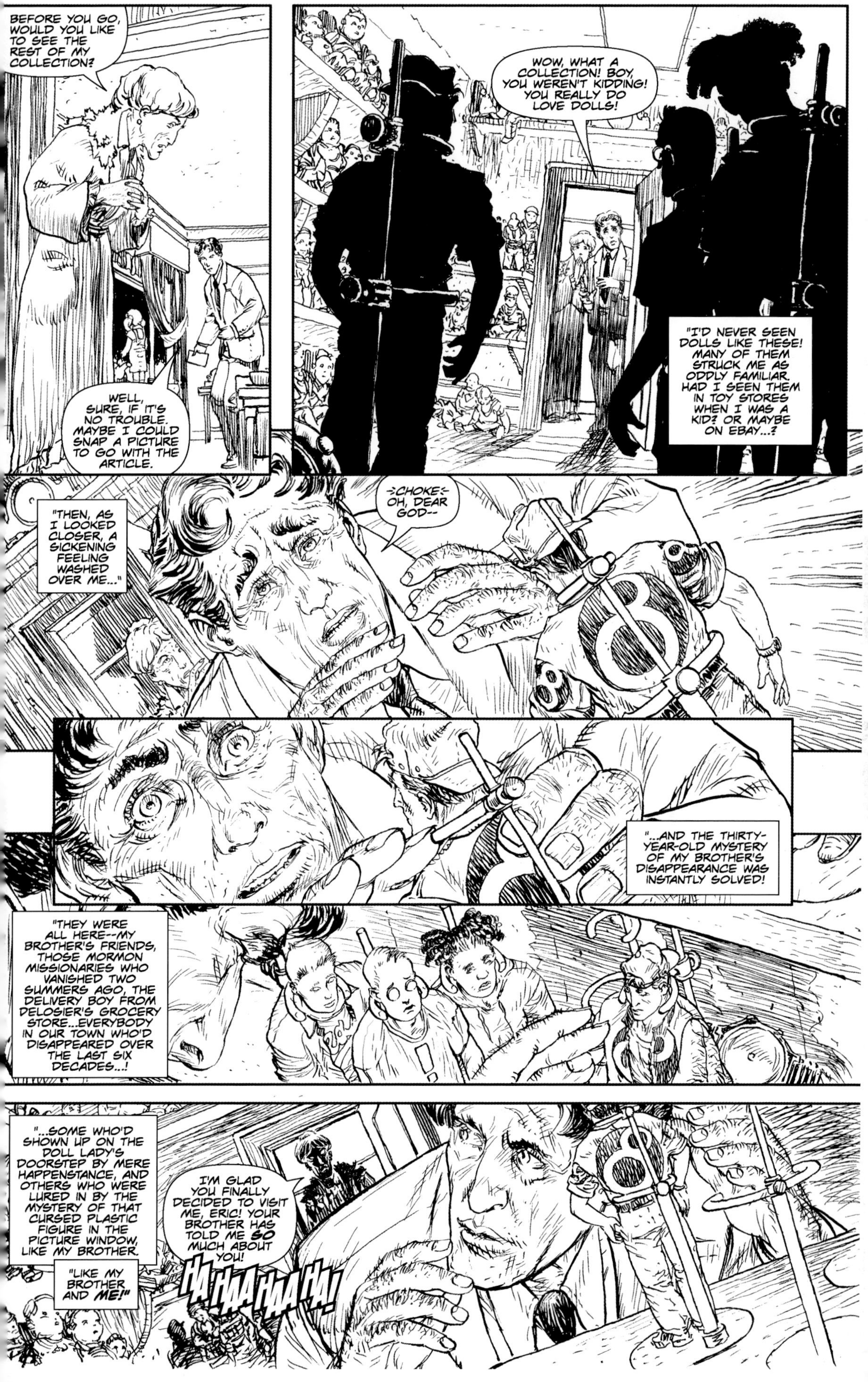
BEFORE YOU GO, WOULD YOU LIKE TO SEE THE REST OF MY COLLECTION?
WELL, SURE, IF IT'S NO TROUBLE. MAYBE I COULD SNAP A PICTURE TO GO WITH THE ARTICLE.
WOW, WHAT A COLLECTION! BOY, YOU WEREN'T KIDDING! YOU REALLY DO LOVE DOLLS!
"I'D NEVER SEEN DOLLS LIKE THESE! MANY OF THEM STRUCK ME AS ODDLY FAMILIAR. HAD I SEEN THEM IN TOY STORES WHEN I WAS A KID? OR MAYBE ON EBAY...?
"THEN, AS I LOOKED CLOSER, A SICKENING FEELING WASHED OVER ME..."
-CHOKE- OH, DEAR GOD--
"...AND THE THIRTY-YEAR-OLD MYSTERY OF MY BROTHER'S DISAPPEARANCE WAS INSTANTLY SOLVED!
"THEY WERE ALL HERE--MY BROTHER'S FRIENDS, THOSE MORMON MISSIONARIES WHO VANISHED TWO SUMMERS AGO, THE DELIVERY BOY FROM DELOSIER'S GROCERY STORE...EVERYBODY IN OUR TOWN WHO'D DISAPPEARED OVER THE LAST SIX DECADES...!
"...SOME WHO'D SHOWN UP ON THE DOLL LADY'S DOORSTEP BY MERE HAPPENSTANCE, AND OTHERS WHO WERE LURED IN BY THE MYSTERY OF THAT CURSED PLASTIC FIGURE IN THE PICTURE WINDOW, LIKE MY BROTHER.
"LIKE MY BROTHER AND **ME!**"
I'M GLAD YOU FINALLY DECIDED TO VISIT ME, ERIC! YOUR BROTHER HAS TOLD ME **SO** MUCH ABOUT YOU!
HA HAA HAA HA!

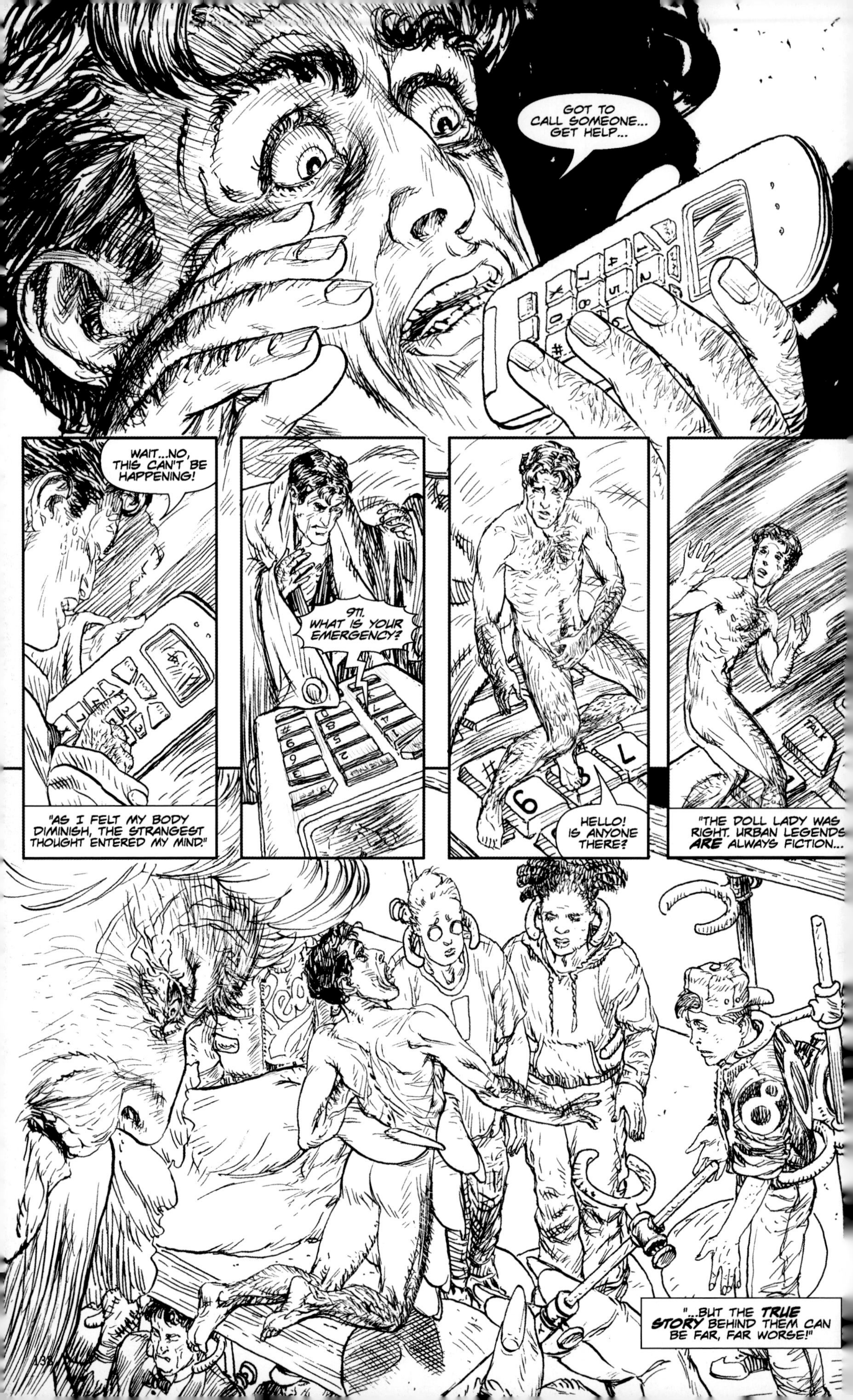
GOT TO CALL SOMEONE... GET HELP...
WAIT...NO, THIS CAN'T BE HAPPENING!
"AS I FELT MY BODY DIMINISH, THE STRANGEST THOUGHT ENTERED MY MIND."
911. WHAT IS YOUR EMERGENCY?
HELLO! IS ANYONE THERE?
TALK
"THE DOLL LADY WAS RIGHT. URBAN LEGENDS **ARE** ALWAYS FICTION...
"...BUT THE **TRUE STORY** BEHIND THEM CAN BE FAR, FAR WORSE!"

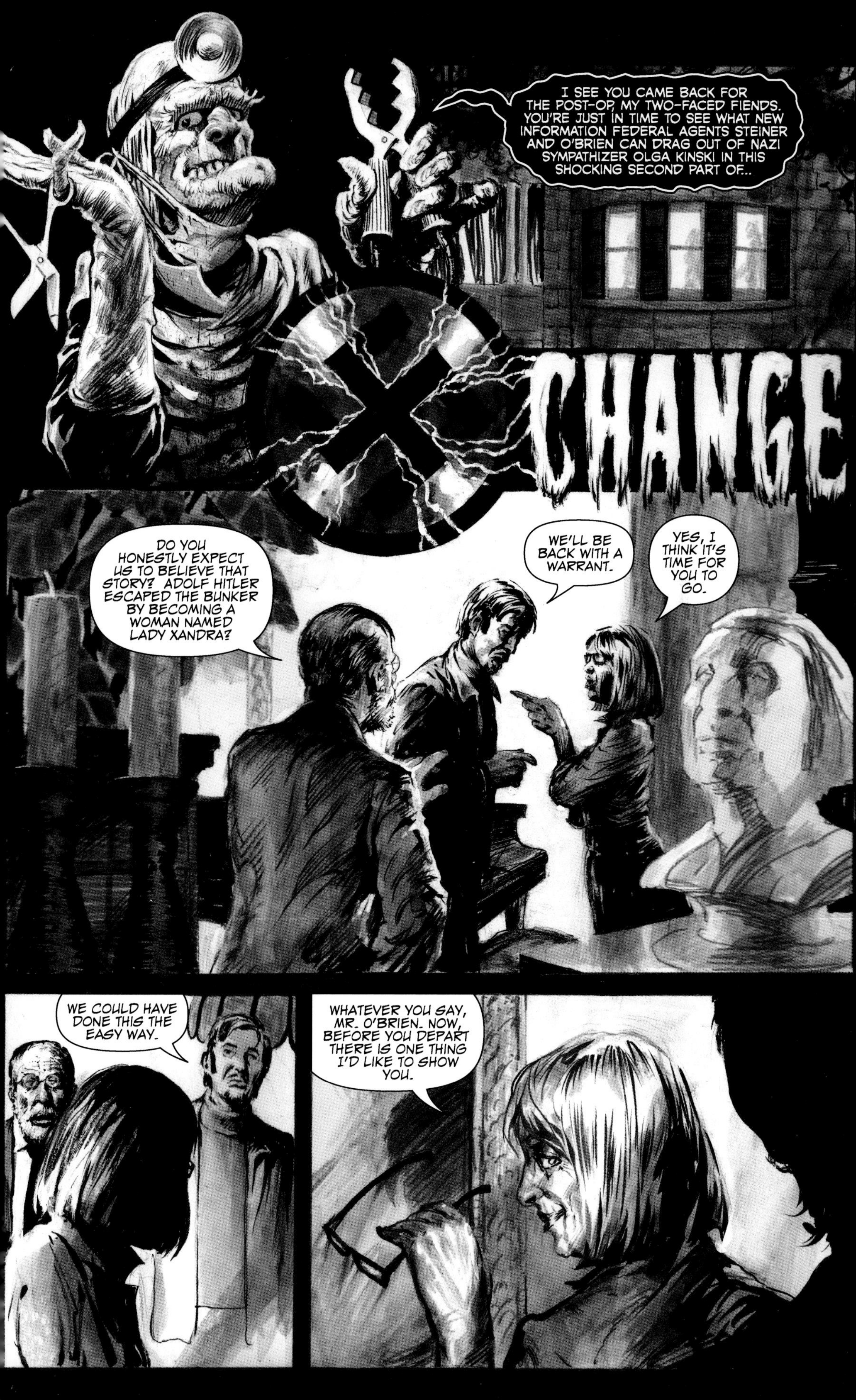
I SEE YOU CAME BACK FOR THE POST-OP, MY TWO-FACED FIENDS. YOU'RE JUST IN TIME TO SEE WHAT NEW INFORMATION FEDERAL AGENTS STEINER AND O'BRIEN CAN DRAG OUT OF NAZI SYMPATHIZER OLGA KINSKI IN THIS SHOCKING SECOND PART OF...
X-CHANGE
DO YOU HONESTLY EXPECT US TO BELIEVE THAT STORY? ADOLF HITLER ESCAPED THE BUNKER BY BECOMING A WOMAN NAMED LADY XANDRA?
WE'LL BE BACK WITH A WARRANT.
YES, I THINK IT'S TIME FOR YOU TO GO.
WE COULD HAVE DONE THIS THE EASY WAY.
WHATEVER YOU SAY, MR. O'BRIEN. NOW, BEFORE YOU DEPART THERE IS ONE THING I'D LIKE TO SHOW YOU.

Story by CRAIG HAFFNER AND DAN BRAUN / Script by DAN BRAUN / Art by KEVIN FERRARA

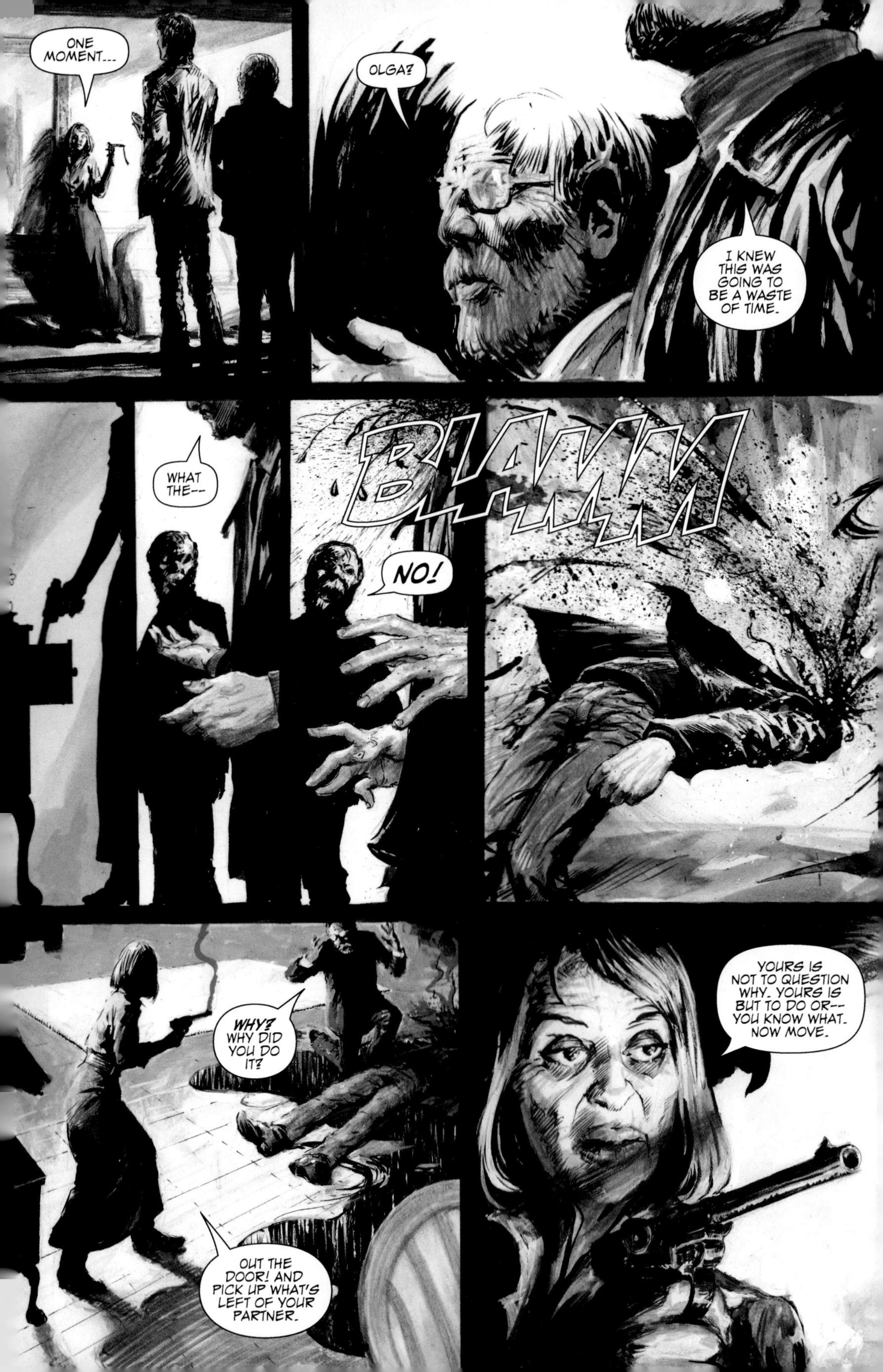
ONE MOMENT...
OLGA?
I KNEW THIS WAS GOING TO BE A WASTE OF TIME.
WHAT THE--
BLAMM
NO!
WHY? WHY DID YOU DO IT?
OUT THE DOOR! AND PICK UP WHAT'S LEFT OF YOUR PARTNER.
YOURS IS NOT TO QUESTION WHY. YOURS IS BUT TO DO OR-- YOU KNOW WHAT. NOW MOVE.

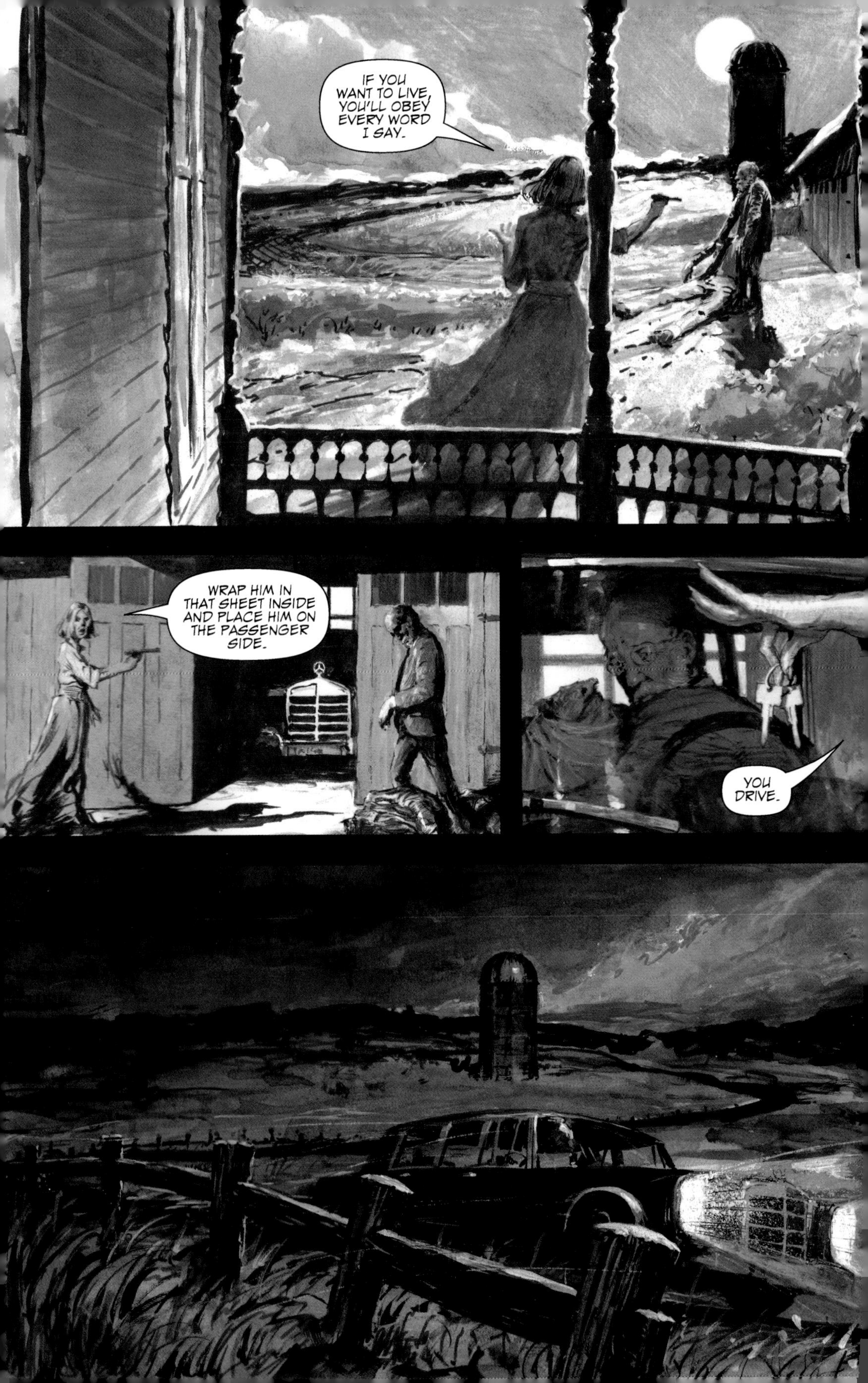
IF YOU WANT TO LIVE, YOU'LL OBEY EVERY WORD I SAY.
WRAP HIM IN THAT SHEET INSIDE AND PLACE HIM ON THE PASSENGER SIDE.
YOU DRIVE.

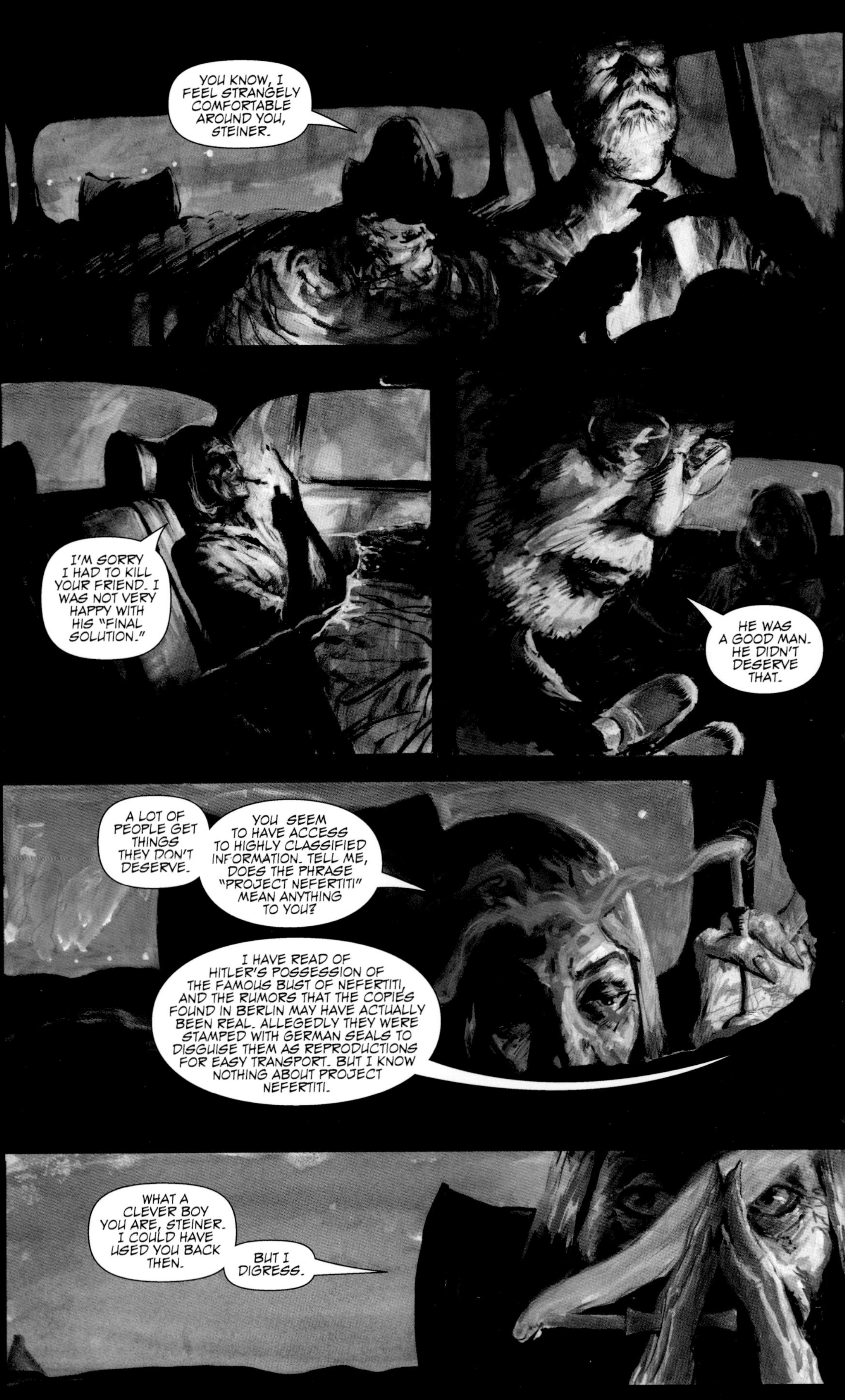
YOU KNOW, I FEEL STRANGELY COMFORTABLE AROUND YOU, STEINER.
I'M SORRY I HAD TO KILL YOUR FRIEND. I WAS NOT VERY HAPPY WITH HIS "FINAL SOLUTION."
HE WAS A GOOD MAN. HE DIDN'T DESERVE THAT.
A LOT OF PEOPLE GET THINGS THEY DON'T DESERVE.
YOU SEEM TO HAVE ACCESS TO HIGHLY CLASSIFIED INFORMATION. TELL ME, DOES THE PHRASE "PROJECT NEFERTITI" MEAN ANYTHING TO YOU?
I HAVE READ OF HITLER'S POSSESSION OF THE FAMOUS BUST OF NEFERTITI, AND THE RUMORS THAT THE COPIES FOUND IN BERLIN MAY HAVE ACTUALLY BEEN REAL. ALLEGEDLY THEY WERE STAMPED WITH GERMAN SEALS TO DISGUISE THEM AS REPRODUCTIONS FOR EASY TRANSPORT. BUT I KNOW NOTHING ABOUT PROJECT NEFERTITI.
WHAT A CLEVER BOY YOU ARE, STEINER. I COULD HAVE USED YOU BACK THEN.
BUT I DIGRESS.

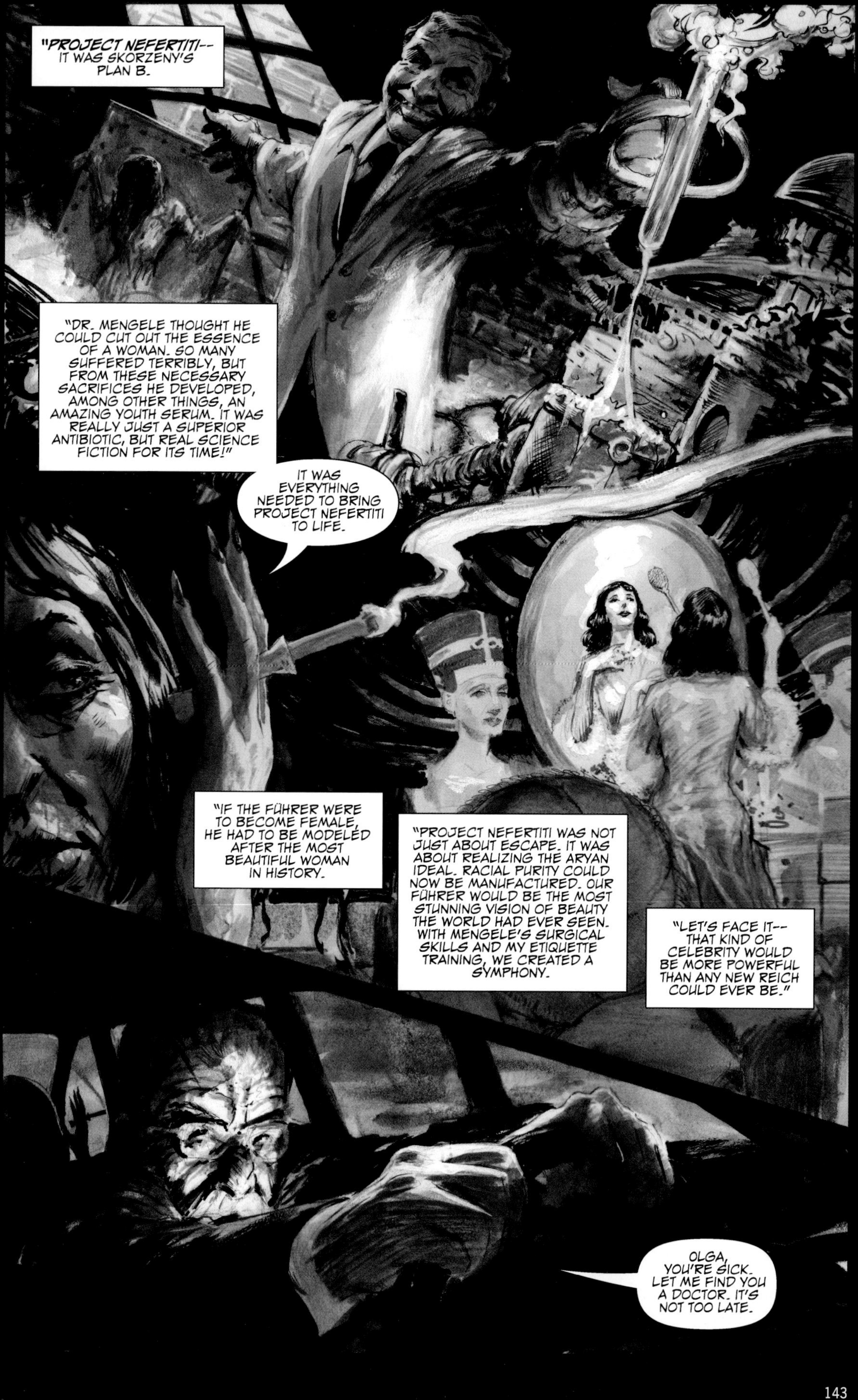
"PROJECT NEFERTITI-- IT WAS SKORZENY'S PLAN B.
"DR. MENGELE THOUGHT HE COULD CUT OUT THE ESSENCE OF A WOMAN. SO MANY SUFFERED TERRIBLY, BUT FROM THESE NECESSARY SACRIFICES HE DEVELOPED, AMONG OTHER THINGS, AN AMAZING YOUTH SERUM. IT WAS REALLY JUST A SUPERIOR ANTIBIOTIC, BUT REAL SCIENCE FICTION FOR ITS TIME!"
IT WAS EVERYTHING NEEDED TO BRING PROJECT NEFERTITI TO LIFE.
"IF THE FÜHRER WERE TO BECOME FEMALE, HE HAD TO BE MODELED AFTER THE MOST BEAUTIFUL WOMAN IN HISTORY.
"PROJECT NEFERTITI WAS NOT JUST ABOUT ESCAPE. IT WAS ABOUT REALIZING THE ARYAN IDEAL. RACIAL PURITY COULD NOW BE MANUFACTURED. OUR FÜHRER WOULD BE THE MOST STUNNING VISION OF BEAUTY THE WORLD HAD EVER SEEN. WITH MENGELE'S SURGICAL SKILLS AND MY ETIQUETTE TRAINING, WE CREATED A SYMPHONY.
"LET'S FACE IT-- THAT KIND OF CELEBRITY WOULD BE MORE POWERFUL THAN ANY NEW REICH COULD EVER BE."
OLGA, YOU'RE SICK. LET ME FIND YOU A DOCTOR. IT'S NOT TOO LATE.

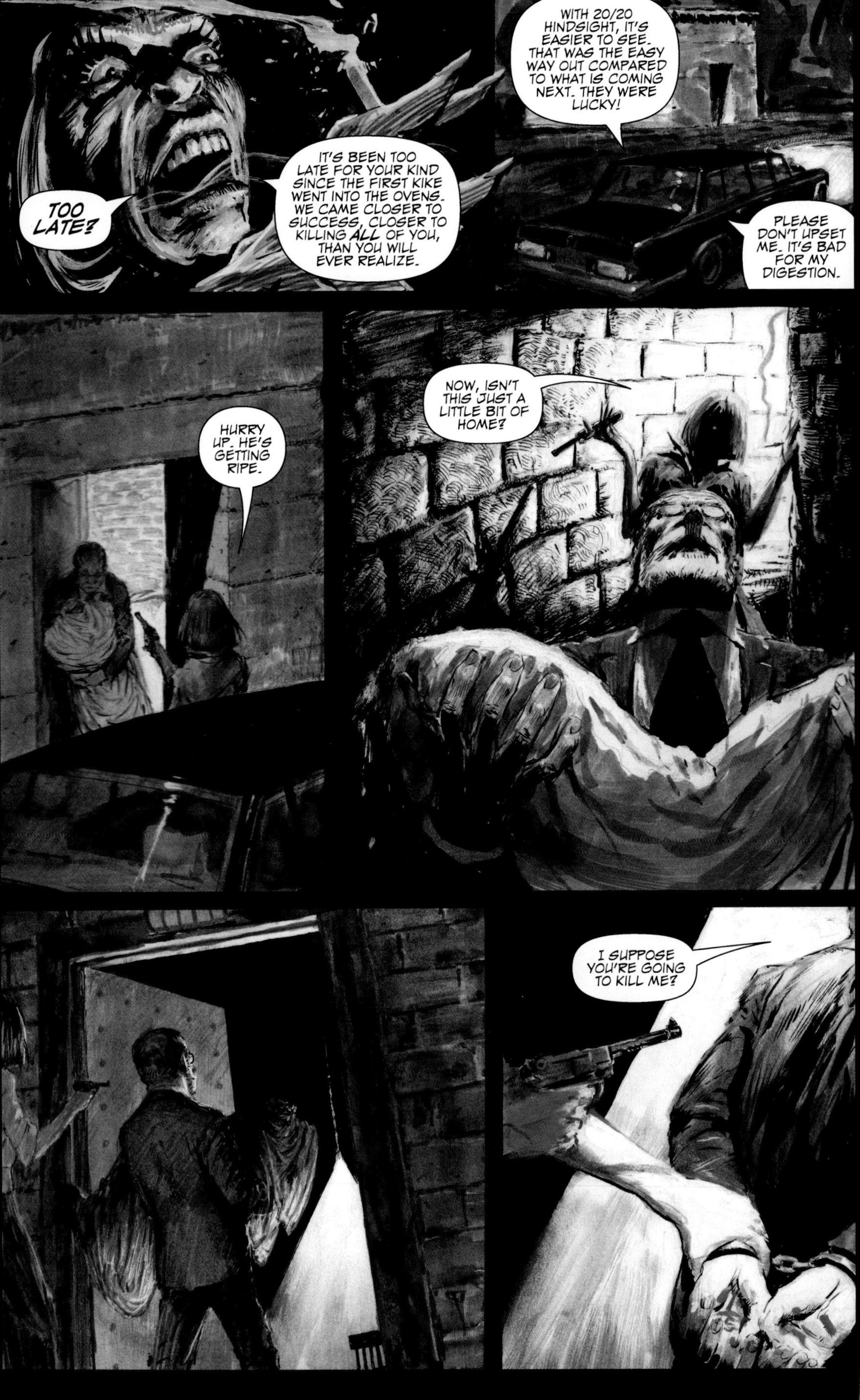
TOO LATE?
IT'S BEEN TOO LATE FOR YOUR KIND SINCE THE FIRST KIKE WENT INTO THE OVENS. WE CAME CLOSER TO SUCCESS, CLOSER TO KILLING *ALL* OF YOU, THAN YOU WILL EVER REALIZE.
WITH 20/20 HINDSIGHT, IT'S EASIER TO SEE. THAT WAS THE EASY WAY OUT COMPARED TO WHAT IS COMING NEXT. THEY WERE LUCKY!
PLEASE DON'T UPSET ME. IT'S BAD FOR MY DIGESTION.
HURRY UP. HE'S GETTING RIPE.
NOW, ISN'T THIS JUST A LITTLE BIT OF HOME?
I SUPPOSE YOU'RE GOING TO KILL ME?

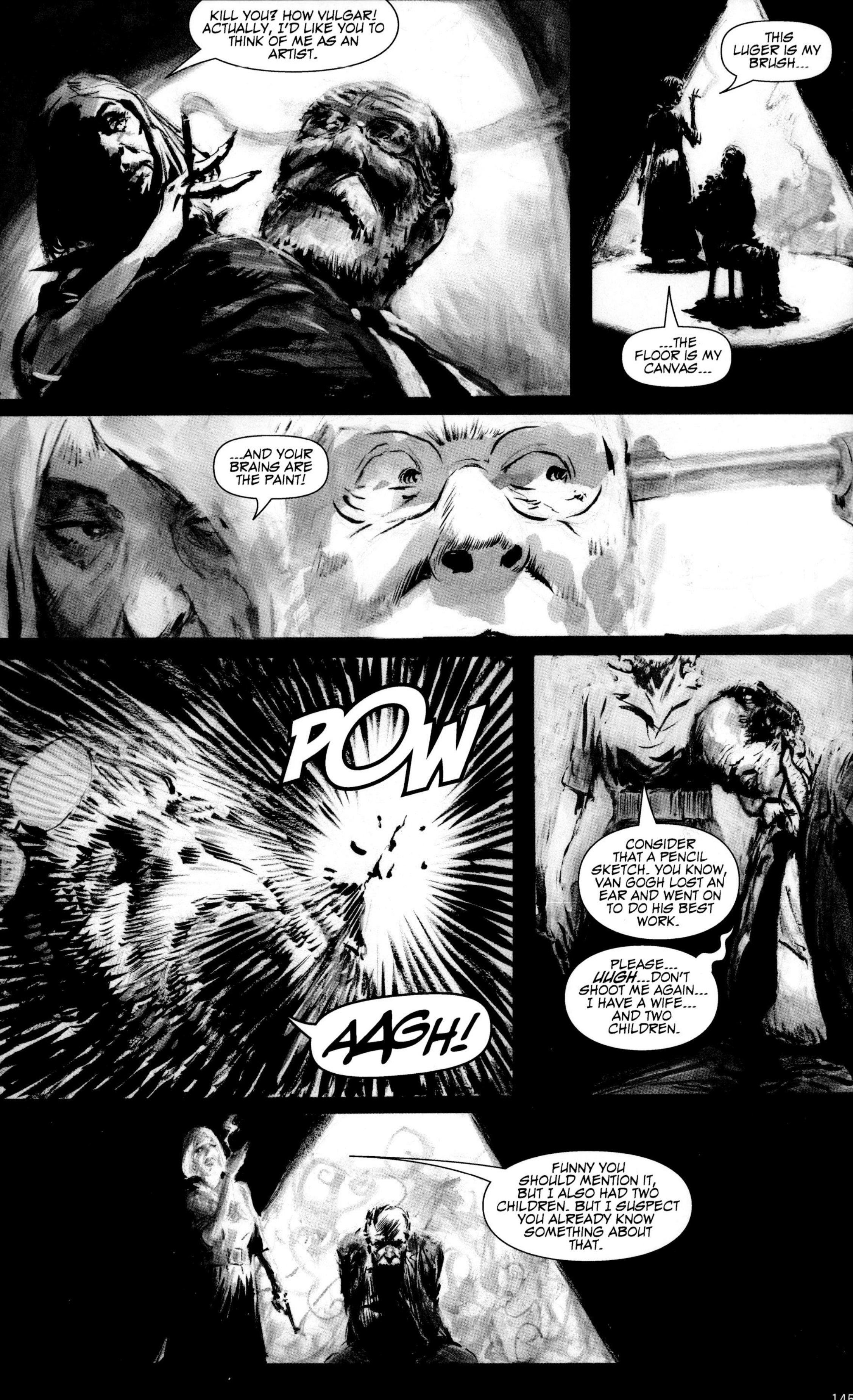
KILL YOU? HOW VULGAR! ACTUALLY, I'D LIKE YOU TO THINK OF ME AS AN ARTIST.
THIS LUGER IS MY BRUSH...
...THE FLOOR IS MY CANVAS...
...AND YOUR BRAINS ARE THE PAINT!
POW
AAGH!
CONSIDER THAT A PENCIL SKETCH. YOU KNOW, VAN GOGH LOST AN EAR AND WENT ON TO DO HIS BEST WORK.
PLEASE... UUGH...DON'T SHOOT ME AGAIN... I HAVE A WIFE... AND TWO CHILDREN.
FUNNY YOU SHOULD MENTION IT, BUT I ALSO HAD TWO CHILDREN. BUT I SUSPECT YOU ALREADY KNOW SOMETHING ABOUT THAT.

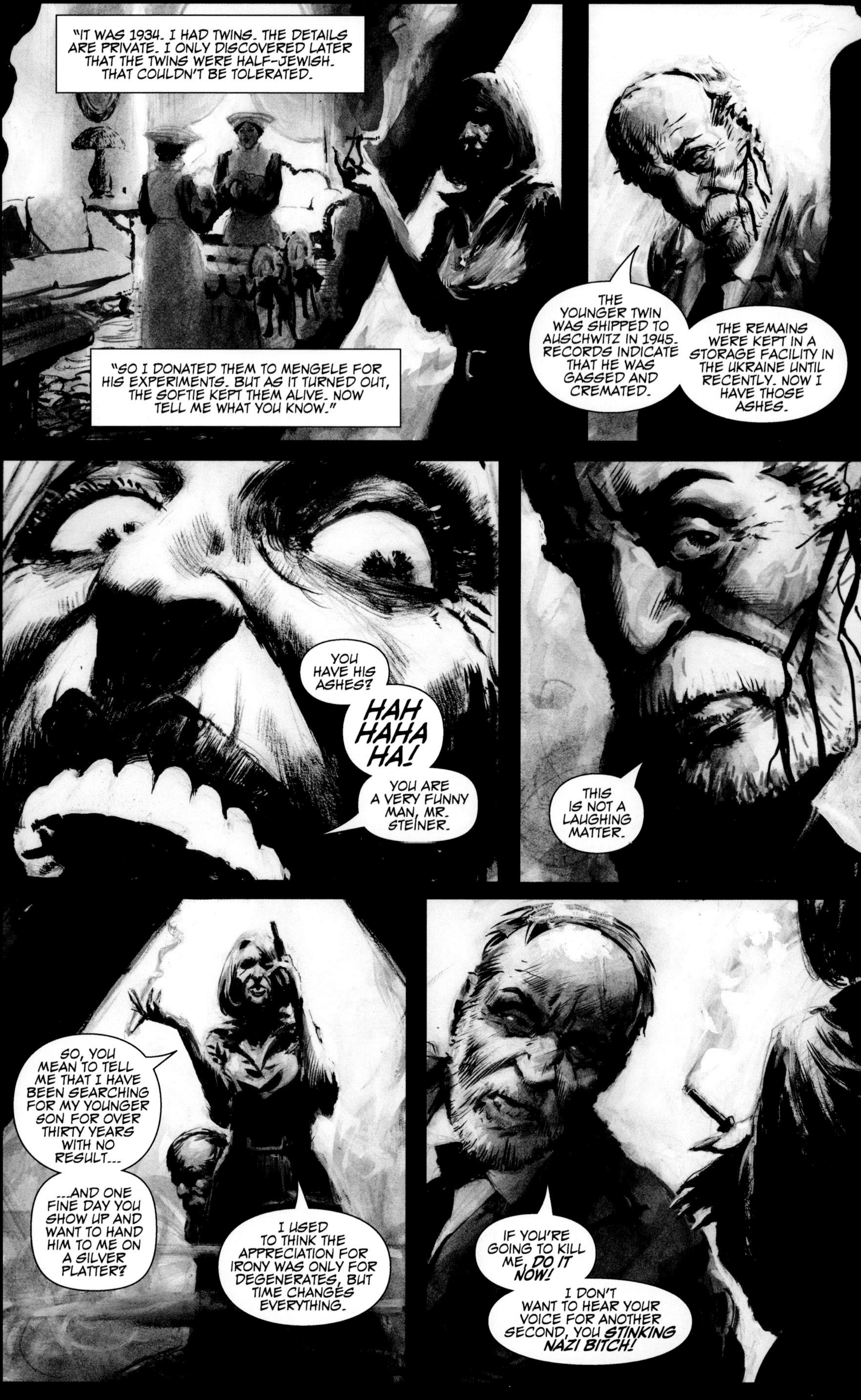
"IT WAS 1934. I HAD TWINS. THE DETAILS ARE PRIVATE. I ONLY DISCOVERED LATER THAT THE TWINS WERE HALF-JEWISH. THAT COULDN'T BE TOLERATED.
"SO I DONATED THEM TO MENGELE FOR HIS EXPERIMENTS. BUT AS IT TURNED OUT, THE SOFTIE KEPT THEM ALIVE. NOW TELL ME WHAT YOU KNOW."
THE YOUNGER TWIN WAS SHIPPED TO AUSCHWITZ IN 1945. RECORDS INDICATE THAT HE WAS GASSED AND CREMATED.
THE REMAINS WERE KEPT IN A STORAGE FACILITY IN THE UKRAINE UNTIL RECENTLY. NOW I HAVE THOSE ASHES.
YOU HAVE HIS ASHES?
HAH HAHA HA!
YOU ARE A VERY FUNNY MAN, MR. STEINER.
THIS IS NOT A LAUGHING MATTER.
SO, YOU MEAN TO TELL ME THAT I HAVE BEEN SEARCHING FOR MY YOUNGER SON FOR OVER THIRTY YEARS WITH NO RESULT...
...AND ONE FINE DAY YOU SHOW UP AND WANT TO HAND HIM TO ME ON A SILVER PLATTER?
I USED TO THINK THE APPRECIATION FOR IRONY WAS ONLY FOR DEGENERATES, BUT TIME CHANGES EVERYTHING.
IF YOU'RE GOING TO KILL ME, DO IT NOW!
I DON'T WANT TO HEAR YOUR VOICE FOR ANOTHER SECOND, YOU STINKING NAZI BITCH!

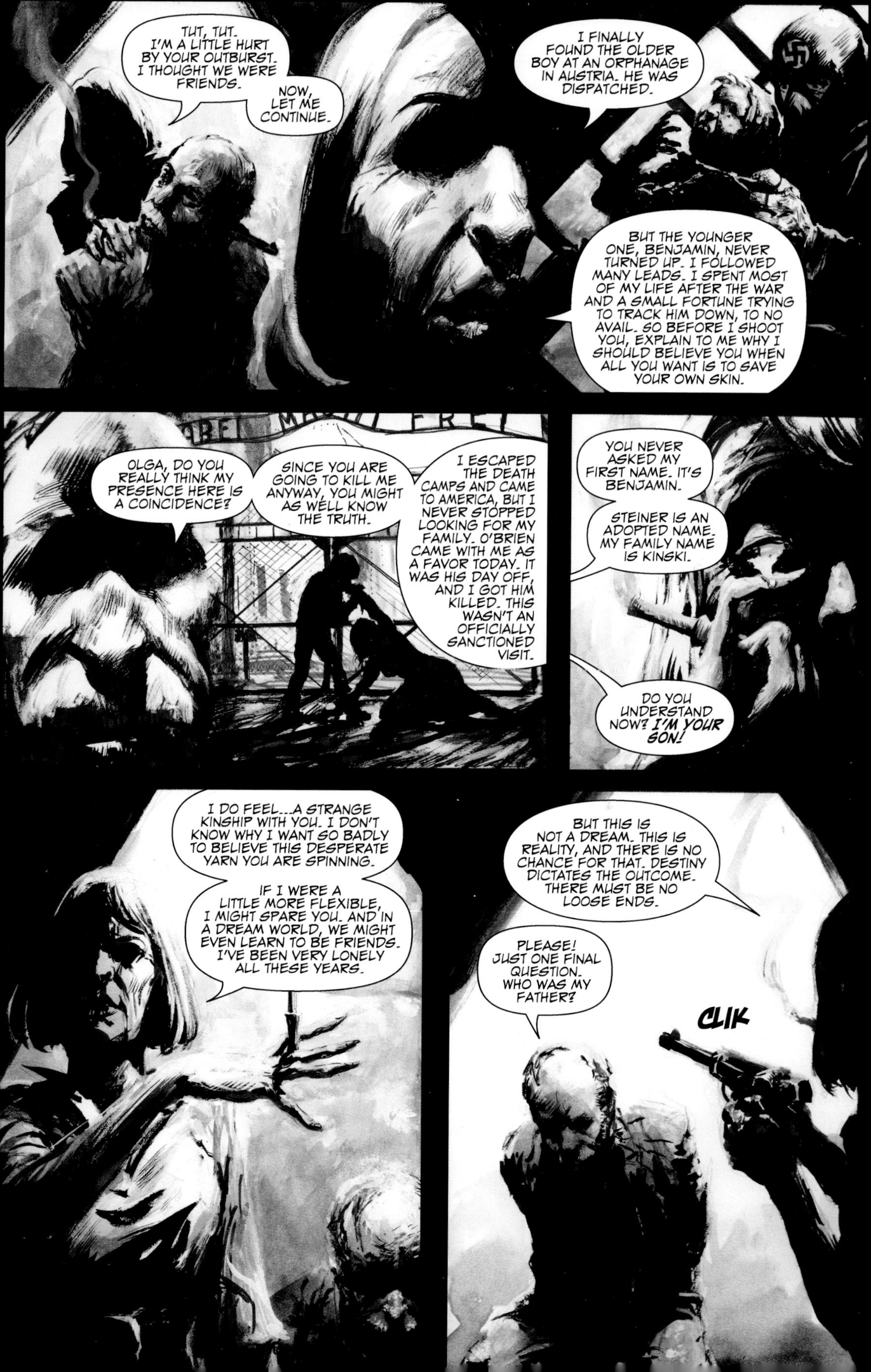
TUT, TUT. I'M A LITTLE HURT BY YOUR OUTBURST. I THOUGHT WE WERE FRIENDS.
NOW, LET ME CONTINUE.
I FINALLY FOUND THE OLDER BOY AT AN ORPHANAGE IN AUSTRIA. HE WAS DISPATCHED.
BUT THE YOUNGER ONE, BENJAMIN, NEVER TURNED UP. I FOLLOWED MANY LEADS. I SPENT MOST OF MY LIFE AFTER THE WAR AND A SMALL FORTUNE TRYING TO TRACK HIM DOWN, TO NO AVAIL. SO BEFORE I SHOOT YOU, EXPLAIN TO ME WHY I SHOULD BELIEVE YOU WHEN ALL YOU WANT IS TO SAVE YOUR OWN SKIN.
OLGA, DO YOU REALLY THINK MY PRESENCE HERE IS A COINCIDENCE?
SINCE YOU ARE GOING TO KILL ME ANYWAY, YOU MIGHT AS WELL KNOW THE TRUTH.
I ESCAPED THE DEATH CAMPS AND CAME TO AMERICA, BUT I NEVER STOPPED LOOKING FOR MY FAMILY. O'BRIEN CAME WITH ME AS A FAVOR TODAY. IT WAS HIS DAY OFF, AND I GOT HIM KILLED. THIS WASN'T AN OFFICIALLY SANCTIONED VISIT.
YOU NEVER ASKED MY FIRST NAME. IT'S BENJAMIN.
STEINER IS AN ADOPTED NAME. MY FAMILY NAME IS KINSKI.
DO YOU UNDERSTAND NOW? I'M YOUR SON!
I DO FEEL...A STRANGE KINSHIP WITH YOU. I DON'T KNOW WHY I WANT SO BADLY TO BELIEVE THIS DESPERATE YARN YOU ARE SPINNING.
IF I WERE A LITTLE MORE FLEXIBLE, I MIGHT SPARE YOU. AND IN A DREAM WORLD, WE MIGHT EVEN LEARN TO BE FRIENDS. I'VE BEEN VERY LONELY ALL THESE YEARS.
BUT THIS IS NOT A DREAM. THIS IS REALITY, AND THERE IS NO CHANCE FOR THAT. DESTINY DICTATES THE OUTCOME. THERE MUST BE NO LOOSE ENDS.
PLEASE! JUST ONE FINAL QUESTION. WHO WAS MY FATHER?
CLIK

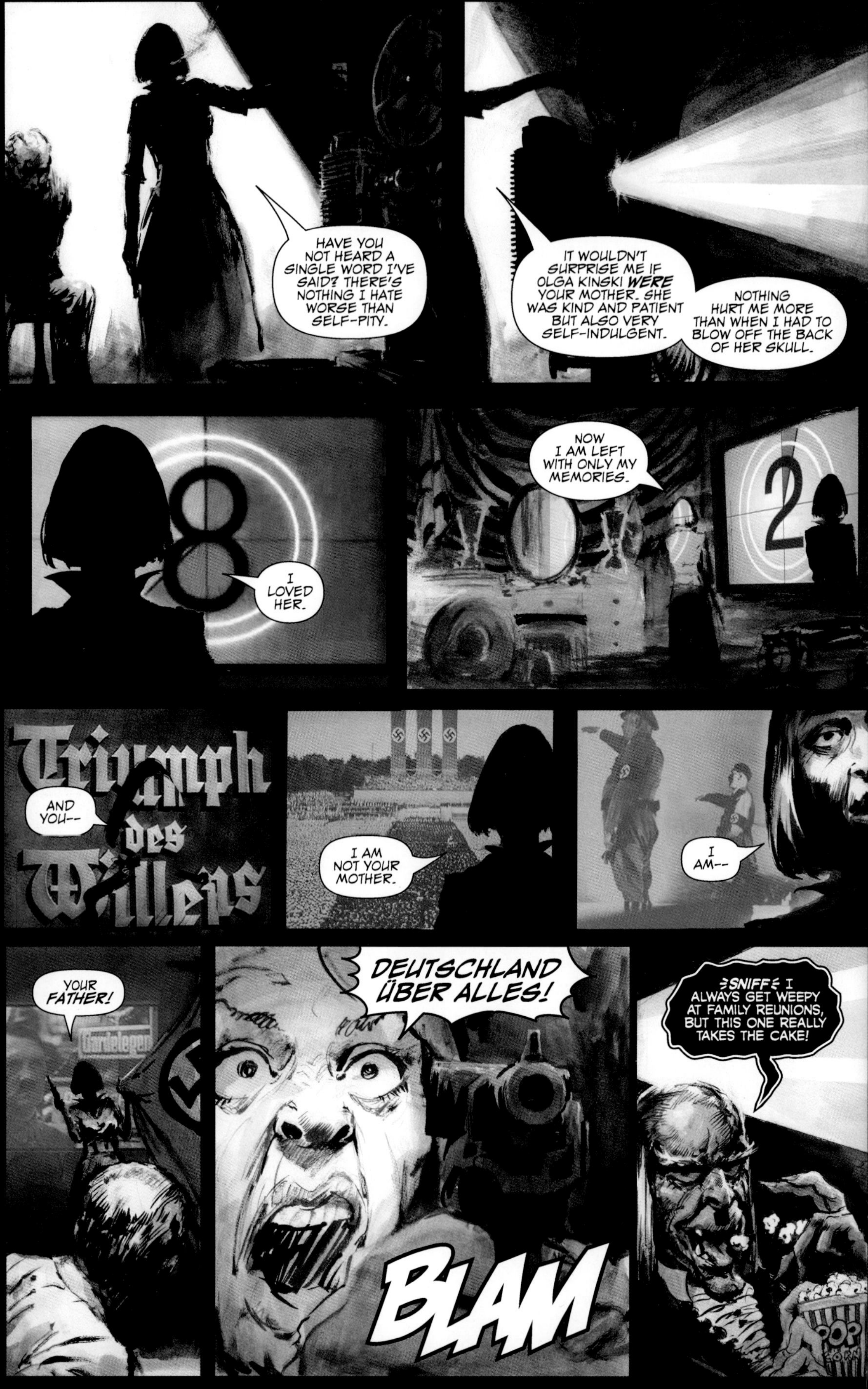
HAVE YOU NOT HEARD A SINGLE WORD I'VE SAID? THERE'S NOTHING I HATE WORSE THAN SELF-PITY.
IT WOULDN'T SURPRISE ME IF OLGA KINSKI WERE YOUR MOTHER. SHE WAS KIND AND PATIENT BUT ALSO VERY SELF-INDULGENT.
NOTHING HURT ME MORE THAN WHEN I HAD TO BLOW OFF THE BACK OF HER SKULL.
8
I LOVED HER.
NOW I AM LEFT WITH ONLY MY MEMORIES.
2
Triumph des Willens
AND YOU--
I AM NOT YOUR MOTHER.
I AM--
YOUR FATHER!
Gardelegen
DEUTSCHLAND ÜBER ALLES!
BLAM
SNIFF I ALWAYS GET WEEPY AT FAMILY REUNIONS, BUT THIS ONE REALLY TAKES THE CAKE!
POP CORN

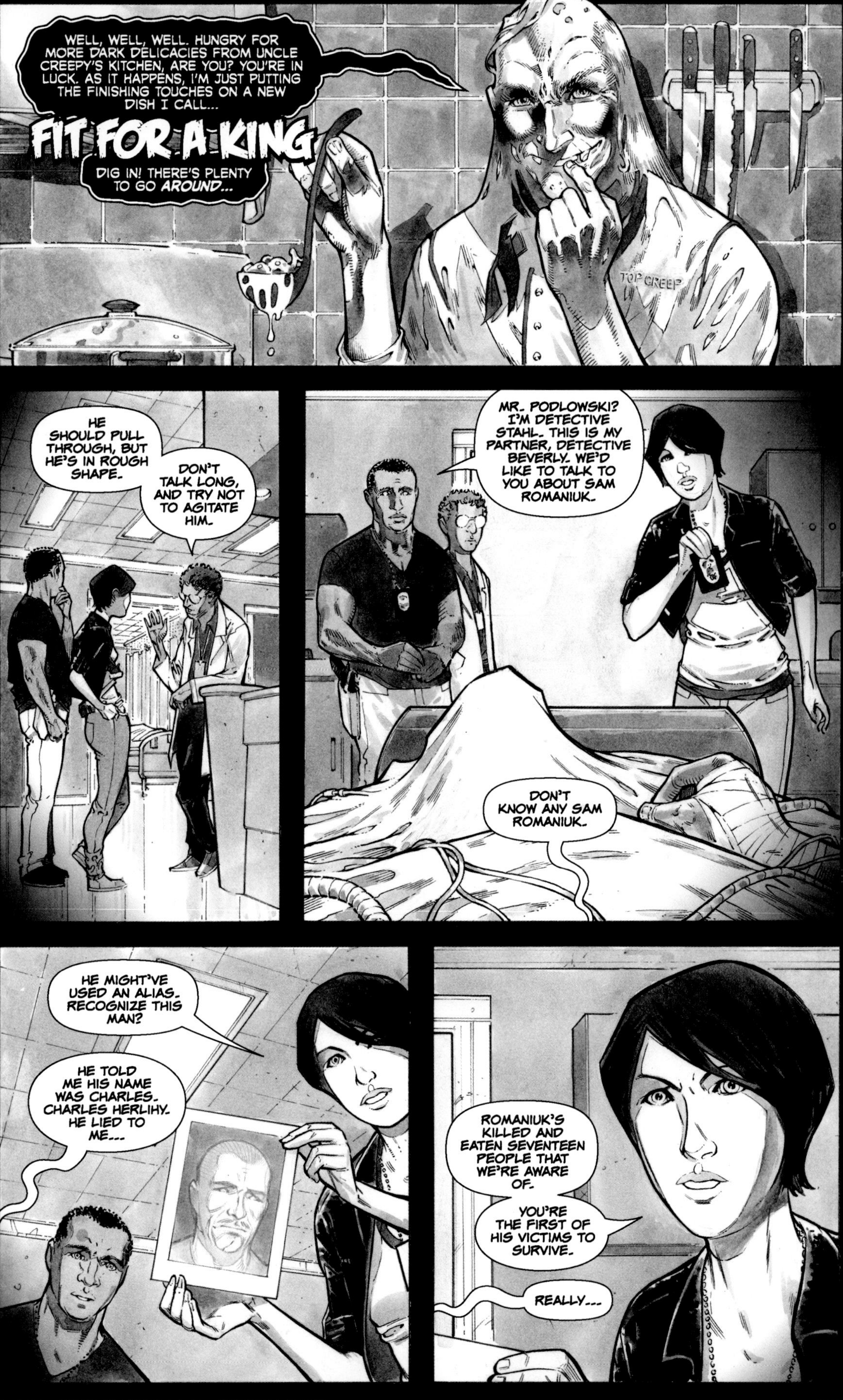
WELL, WELL, WELL. HUNGRY FOR MORE DARK DELICACIES FROM UNCLE CREEPY'S KITCHEN, ARE YOU? YOU'RE IN LUCK. AS IT HAPPENS, I'M JUST PUTTING THE FINISHING TOUCHES ON A NEW DISH I CALL...
FIT FOR A KING
DIG IN! THERE'S PLENTY TO GO *AROUND...*
TOP CREEP
HE SHOULD PULL THROUGH, BUT HE'S IN ROUGH SHAPE.
DON'T TALK LONG, AND TRY NOT TO AGITATE HIM.
MR. PODLOWSKI? I'M DETECTIVE STAHL. THIS IS MY PARTNER, DETECTIVE BEVERLY. WE'D LIKE TO TALK TO YOU ABOUT SAM ROMANIUK.
DON'T KNOW ANY SAM ROMANIUK.
HE MIGHT'VE USED AN ALIAS. RECOGNIZE THIS MAN?
HE TOLD ME HIS NAME WAS CHARLES. CHARLES HERLIHY. HE LIED TO ME...
ROMANIUK'S KILLED AND EATEN SEVENTEEN PEOPLE THAT WE'RE AWARE OF.
YOU'RE THE FIRST OF HIS VICTIMS TO SURVIVE.
REALLY...

Script by ANDREW FOLEY / Art by RAHSAN EKEDAL

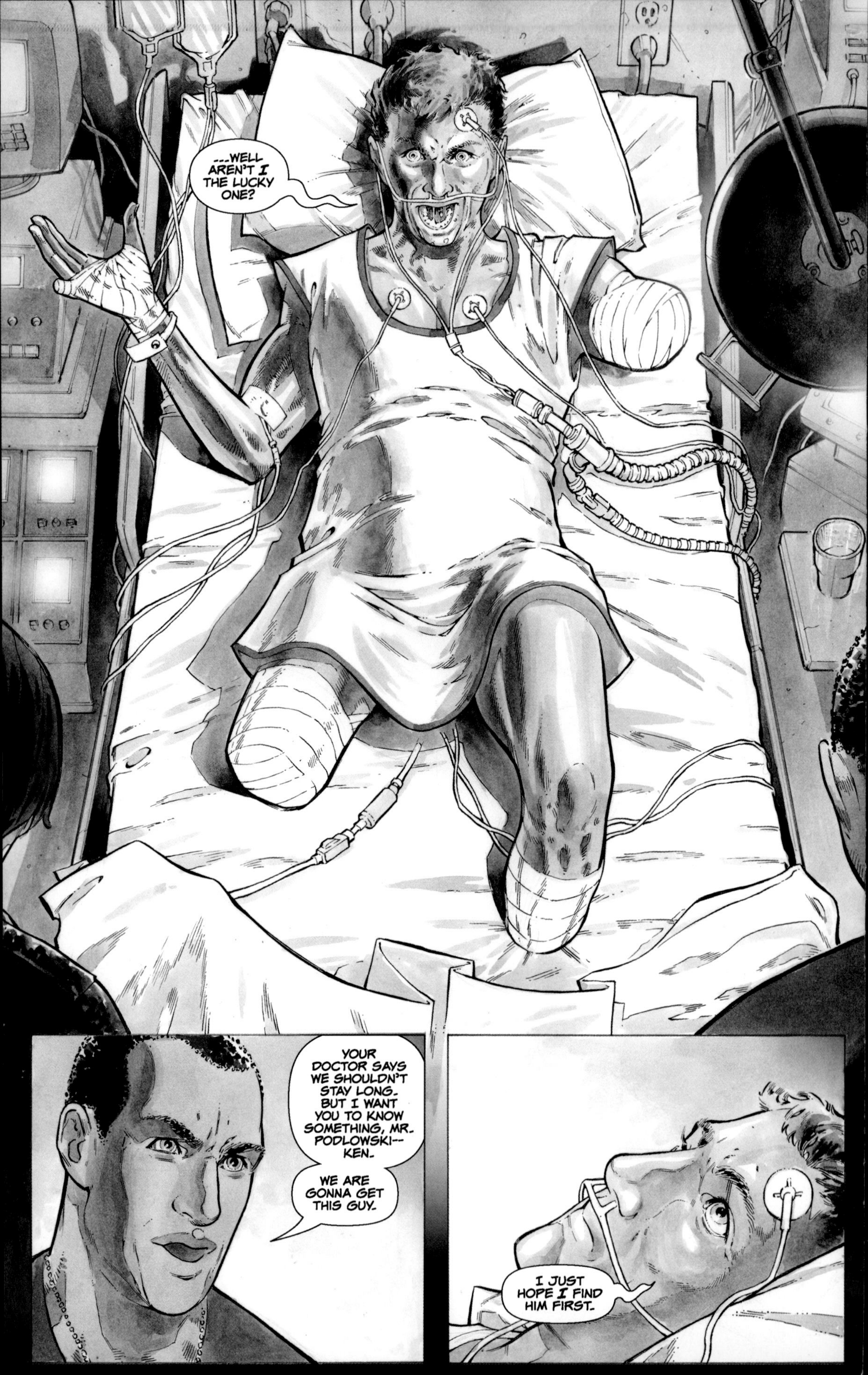
---WELL AREN'T I THE LUCKY ONE?
YOUR DOCTOR SAYS WE SHOULDN'T STAY LONG. BUT I WANT YOU TO KNOW SOMETHING, MR. PODLOWSKI-- KEN.
WE ARE GONNA GET THIS GUY.
I JUST HOPE I FIND HIM FIRST.

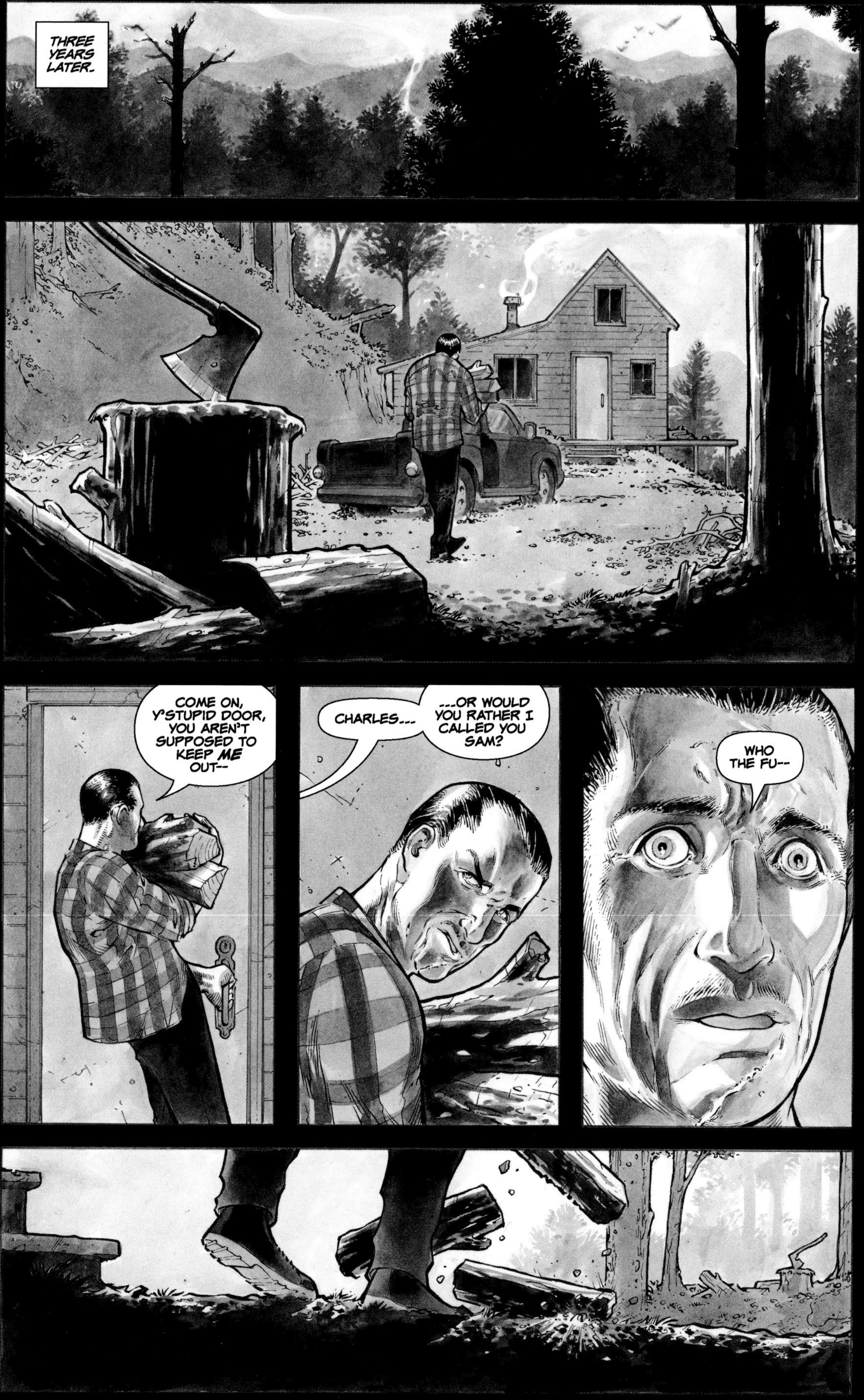
THREE YEARS LATER.
COME ON, Y'STUPID DOOR, YOU AREN'T SUPPOSED TO KEEP *ME* OUT--
CHARLES...
...OR WOULD YOU RATHER I CALLED YOU SAM?
WHO THE FU--

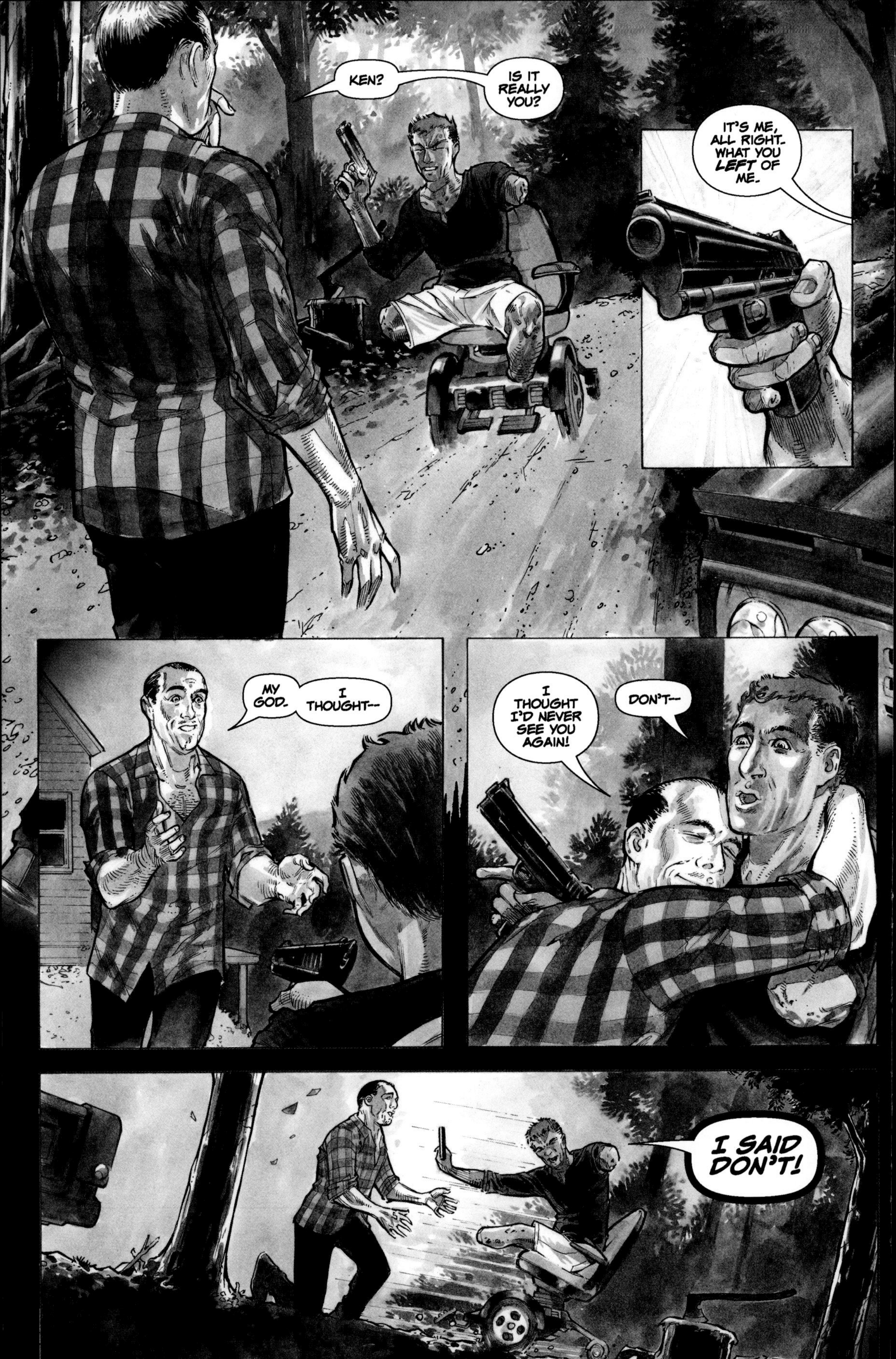
KEN?
IS IT REALLY YOU?
IT'S ME, ALL RIGHT. WHAT YOU LEFT OF ME.
MY GOD.
I THOUGHT--
I THOUGHT I'D NEVER SEE YOU AGAIN!
DON'T--
I SAID DON'T!

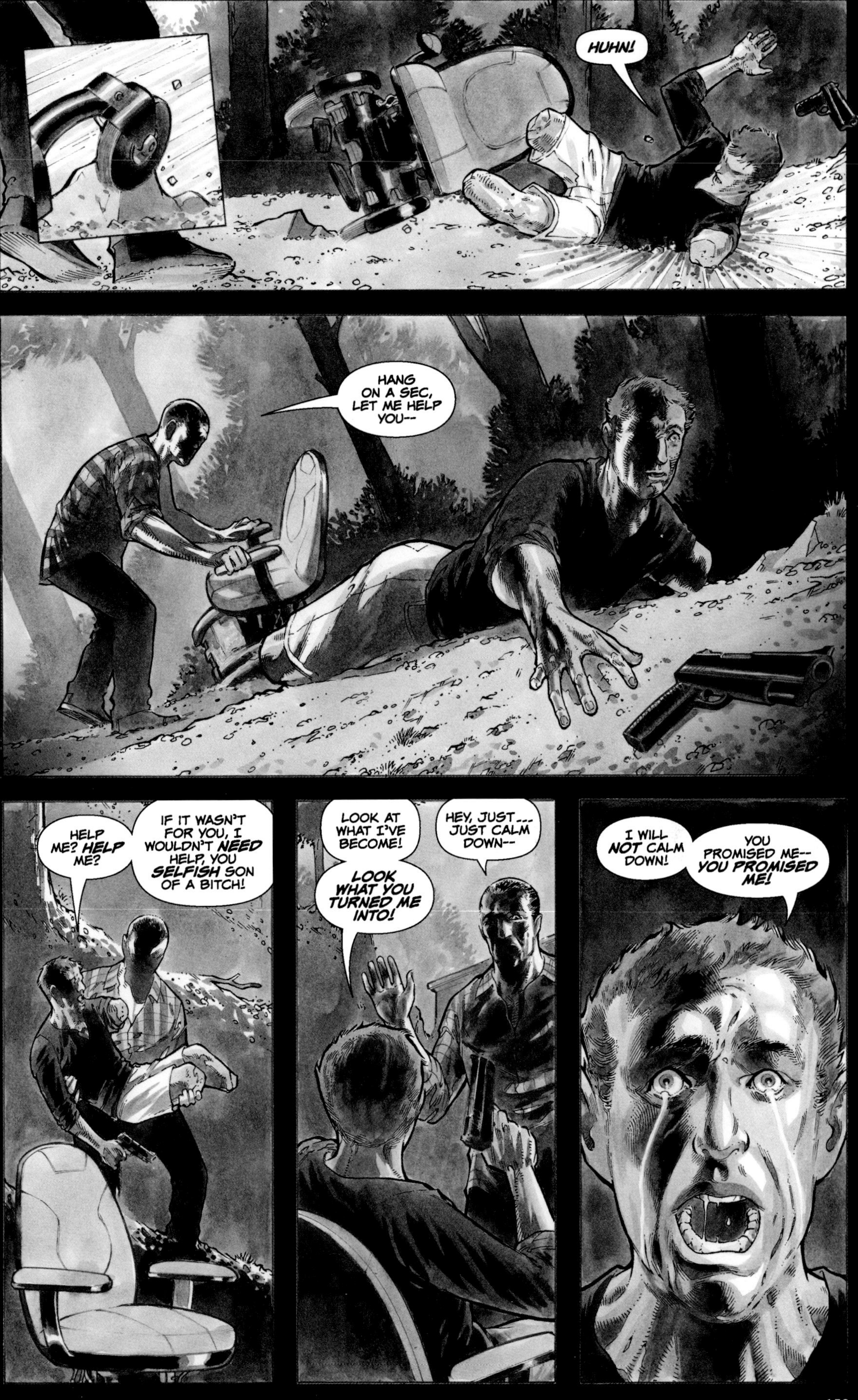
HUHN!
HANG ON A SEC, LET ME HELP YOU--
HELP ME? HELP ME?
IF IT WASN'T FOR YOU, I WOULDN'T NEED HELP, YOU SELFISH SON OF A BITCH!
LOOK AT WHAT I'VE BECOME!
LOOK WHAT YOU TURNED ME INTO!
HEY, JUST... JUST CALM DOWN--
I WILL NOT CALM DOWN!
YOU PROMISED ME-- YOU PROMISED ME!

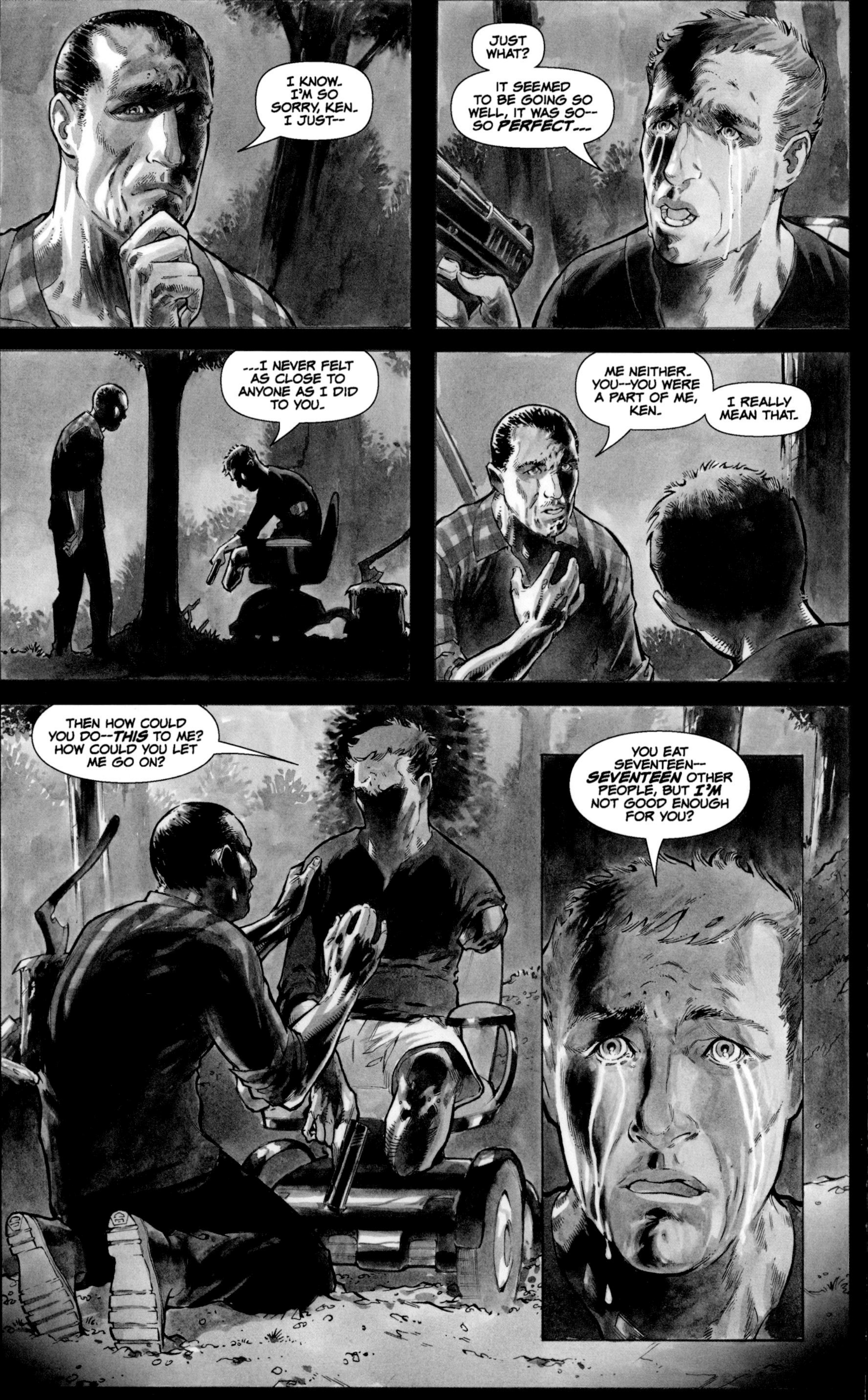
I KNOW. I'M SO SORRY, KEN. I JUST--
JUST WHAT?
IT SEEMED TO BE GOING SO WELL, IT WAS SO-- SO PERFECT---
---I NEVER FELT AS CLOSE TO ANYONE AS I DID TO YOU.
ME NEITHER. YOU--YOU WERE A PART OF ME, KEN.
I REALLY MEAN THAT.
THEN HOW COULD YOU DO--THIS TO ME? HOW COULD YOU LET ME GO ON?
YOU EAT SEVENTEEN-- SEVENTEEN OTHER PEOPLE, BUT I'M NOT GOOD ENOUGH FOR YOU?

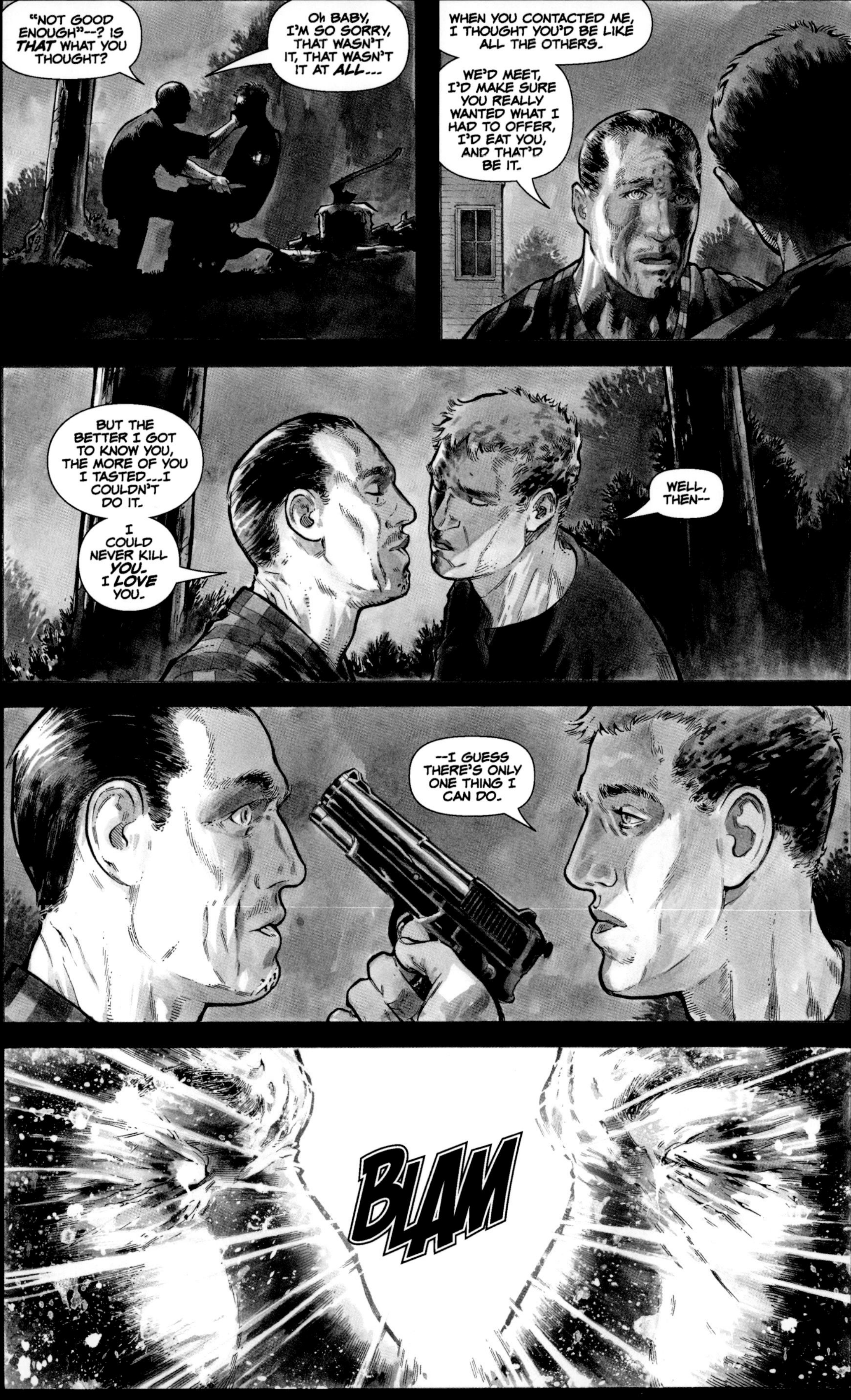
"NOT GOOD ENOUGH"--? IS THAT WHAT YOU THOUGHT?
Oh BABY, I'M SO SORRY, THAT WASN'T IT, THAT WASN'T IT AT ALL...
WHEN YOU CONTACTED ME, I THOUGHT YOU'D BE LIKE ALL THE OTHERS.
WE'D MEET, I'D MAKE SURE YOU REALLY WANTED WHAT I HAD TO OFFER, I'D EAT YOU, AND THAT'D BE IT.
BUT THE BETTER I GOT TO KNOW YOU, THE MORE OF YOU I TASTED...I COULDN'T DO IT.
I COULD NEVER KILL YOU. I LOVE YOU.
WELL, THEN--
--I GUESS THERE'S ONLY ONE THING I CAN DO.
BLAM

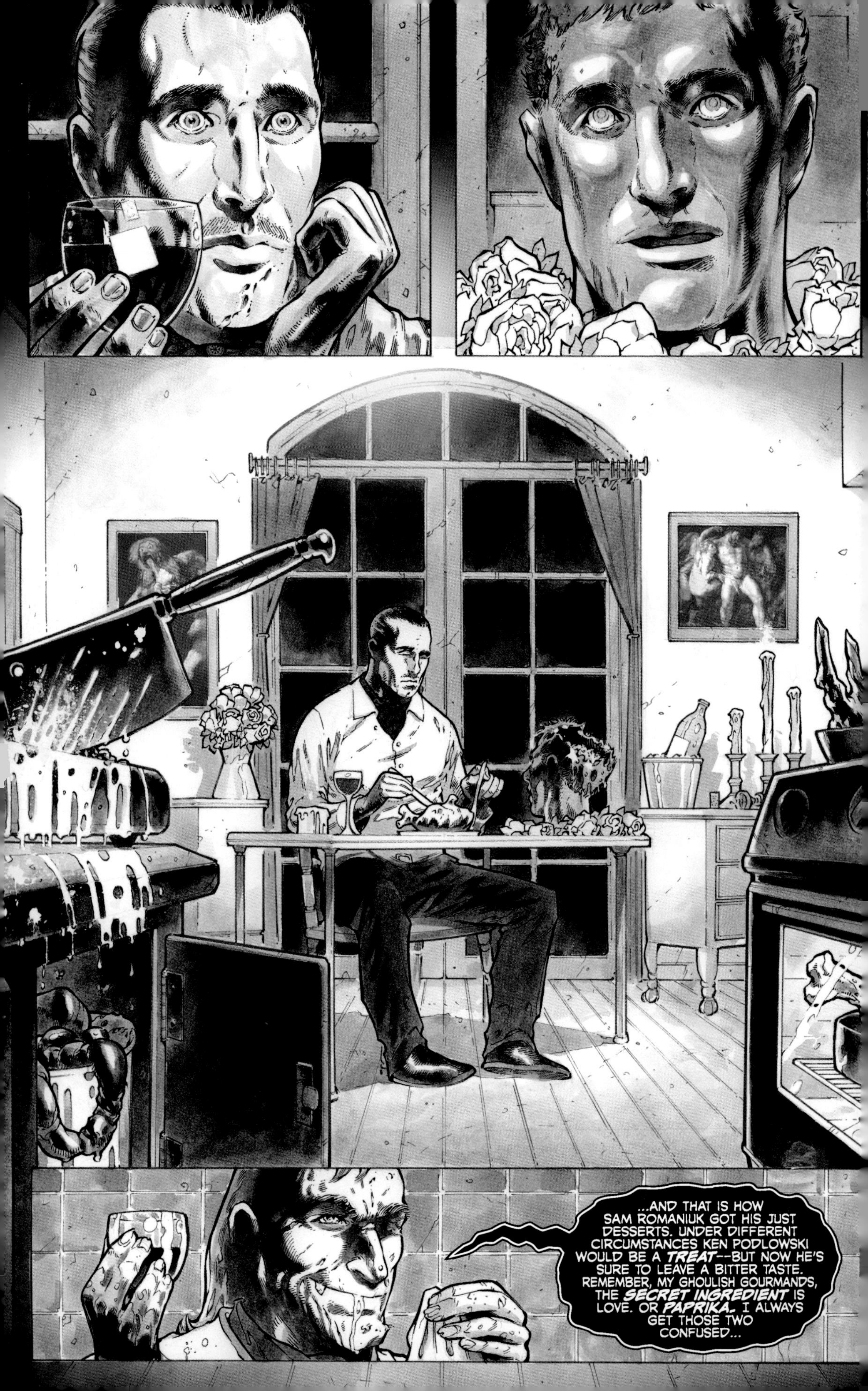
...AND THAT IS HOW SAM ROMANIUK GOT HIS JUST DESSERTS. UNDER DIFFERENT CIRCUMSTANCES KEN PODLOWSKI WOULD BE A *TREAT*--BUT NOW HE'S SURE TO LEAVE A BITTER TASTE. REMEMBER, MY GHOULISH GOURMANDS, THE *SECRET INGREDIENT* IS LOVE. OR *PAPRIKA.* I ALWAYS GET THOSE TWO CONFUSED...

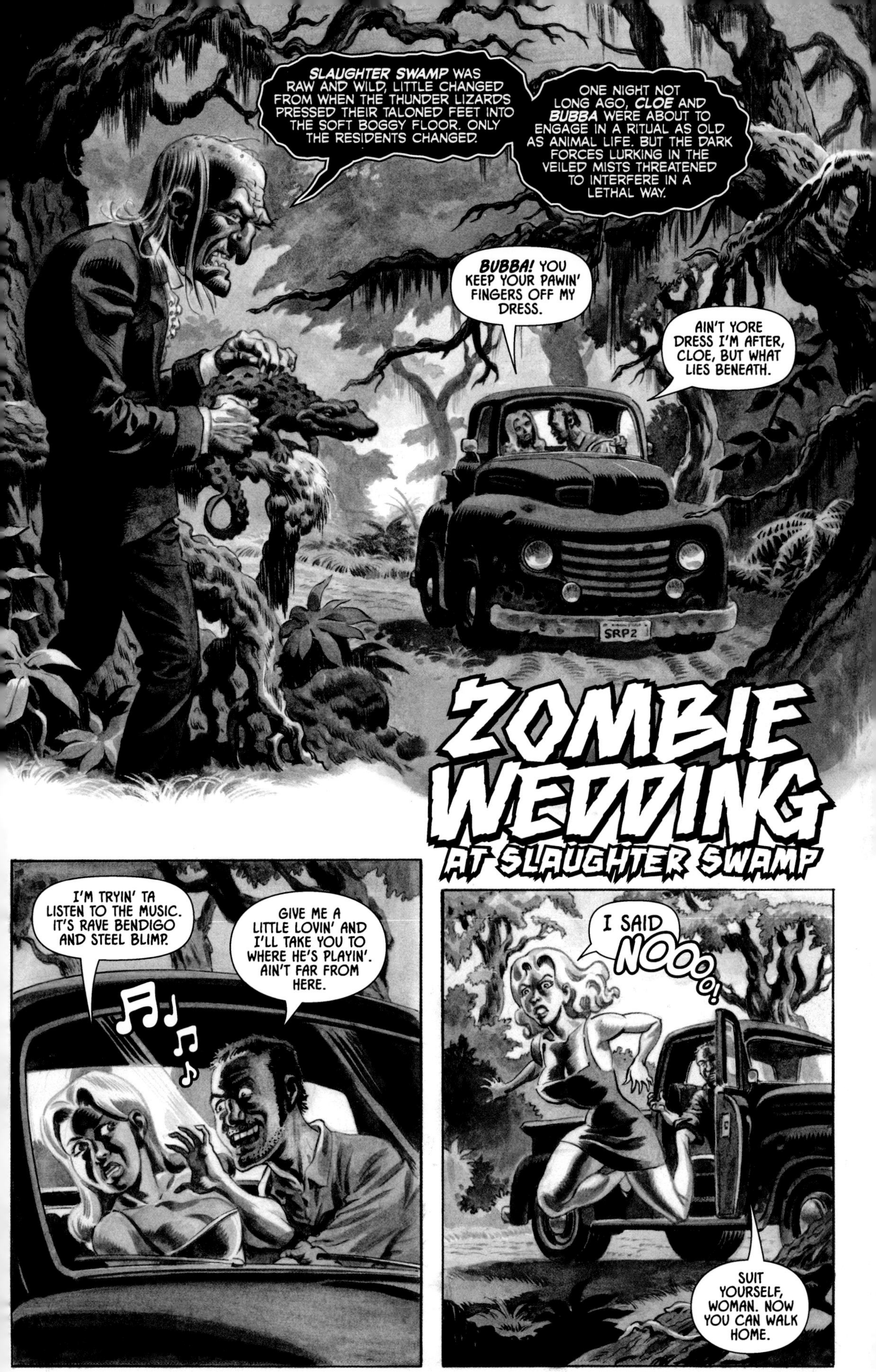
SLAUGHTER SWAMP WAS RAW AND WILD, LITTLE CHANGED FROM WHEN THE THUNDER LIZARDS PRESSED THEIR TALONED FEET INTO THE SOFT BOGGY FLOOR. ONLY THE RESIDENTS CHANGED.
ONE NIGHT NOT LONG AGO, CLOE AND BUBBA WERE ABOUT TO ENGAGE IN A RITUAL AS OLD AS ANIMAL LIFE. BUT THE DARK FORCES LURKING IN THE VEILED MISTS THREATENED TO INTERFERE IN A LETHAL WAY.
BUBBA! YOU KEEP YOUR PAWIN' FINGERS OFF MY DRESS.
AIN'T YORE DRESS I'M AFTER, CLOE, BUT WHAT LIES BENEATH.
SRP2
ZOMBIE WEDDING AT SLAUGHTER SWAMP
I'M TRYIN' TA LISTEN TO THE MUSIC. IT'S RAVE BENDIGO AND STEEL BLIMP.
GIVE ME A LITTLE LOVIN' AND I'LL TAKE YOU TO WHERE HE'S PLAYIN'. AIN'T FAR FROM HERE.
I SAID NOooo!
SUIT YOURSELF, WOMAN. NOW YOU CAN WALK HOME.

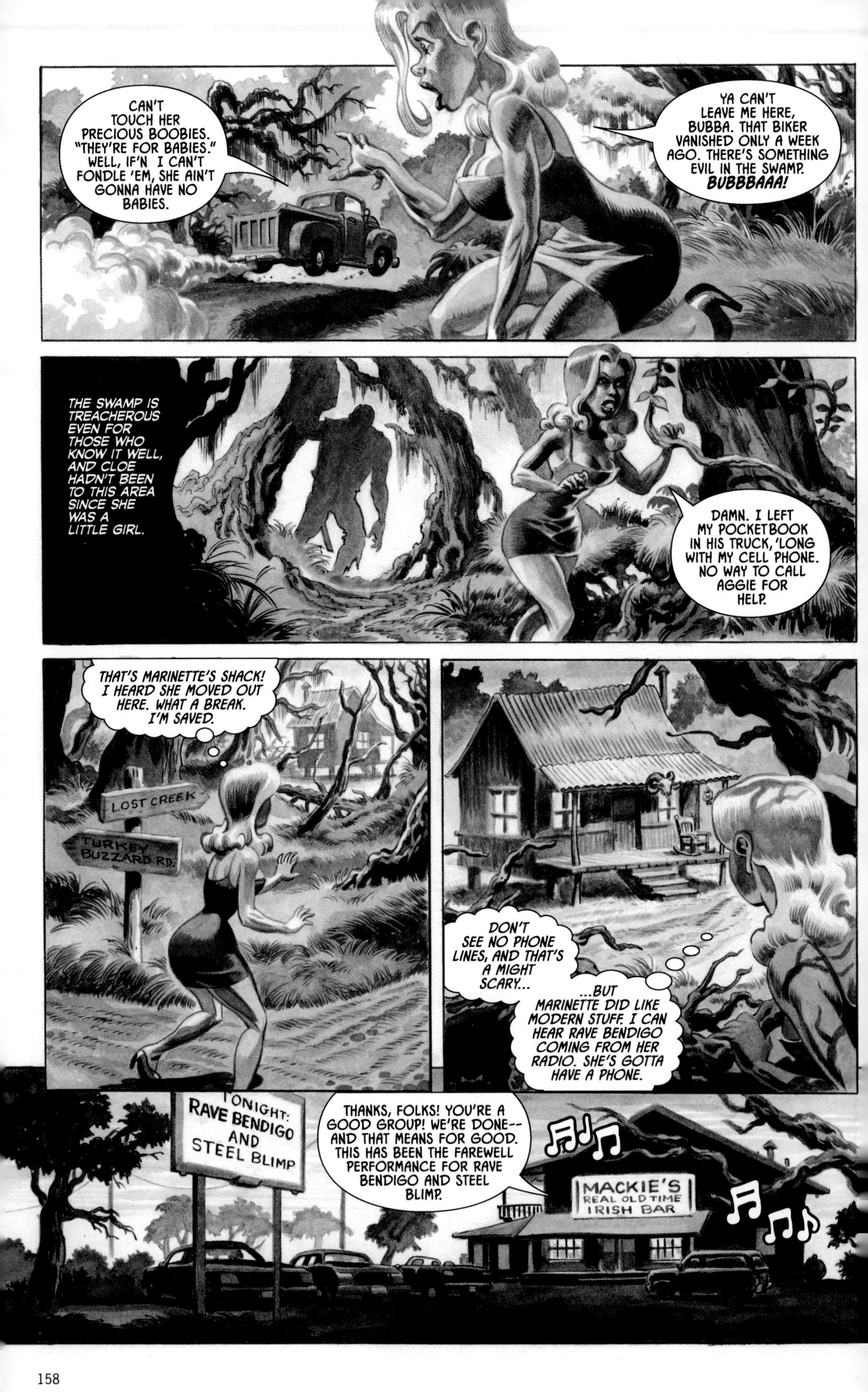
CAN'T TOUCH HER PRECIOUS BOOBIES. "THEY'RE FOR BABIES." WELL, IF'N I CAN'T FONDLE 'EM, SHE AIN'T GONNA HAVE NO BABIES.
YA CAN'T LEAVE ME HERE, BUBBA. THAT BIKER VANISHED ONLY A WEEK AGO. THERE'S SOMETHING EVIL IN THE SWAMP. BUBBBAAA!
THE SWAMP IS TREACHEROUS EVEN FOR THOSE WHO KNOW IT WELL, AND CLOE HADN'T BEEN TO THIS AREA SINCE SHE WAS A LITTLE GIRL.
DAMN. I LEFT MY POCKETBOOK IN HIS TRUCK, 'LONG WITH MY CELL PHONE. NO WAY TO CALL AGGIE FOR HELP.
THAT'S MARINETTE'S SHACK! I HEARD SHE MOVED OUT HERE. WHAT A BREAK. I'M SAVED.
LOST CREEK
TURKEY BUZZARD RD.
DON'T SEE NO PHONE LINES, AND THAT'S A MIGHT SCARY...
...BUT MARINETTE DID LIKE MODERN STUFF. I CAN HEAR RAVE BENDIGO COMING FROM HER RADIO. SHE'S GOTTA HAVE A PHONE.
TONIGHT: RAVE BENDIGO AND STEEL BLIMP
THANKS, FOLKS! YOU'RE A GOOD GROUP! WE'RE DONE-- AND THAT MEANS FOR GOOD. THIS HAS BEEN THE FAREWELL PERFORMANCE FOR RAVE BENDIGO AND STEEL BLIMP.
MACKIE'S REAL OLD TIME IRISH BAR

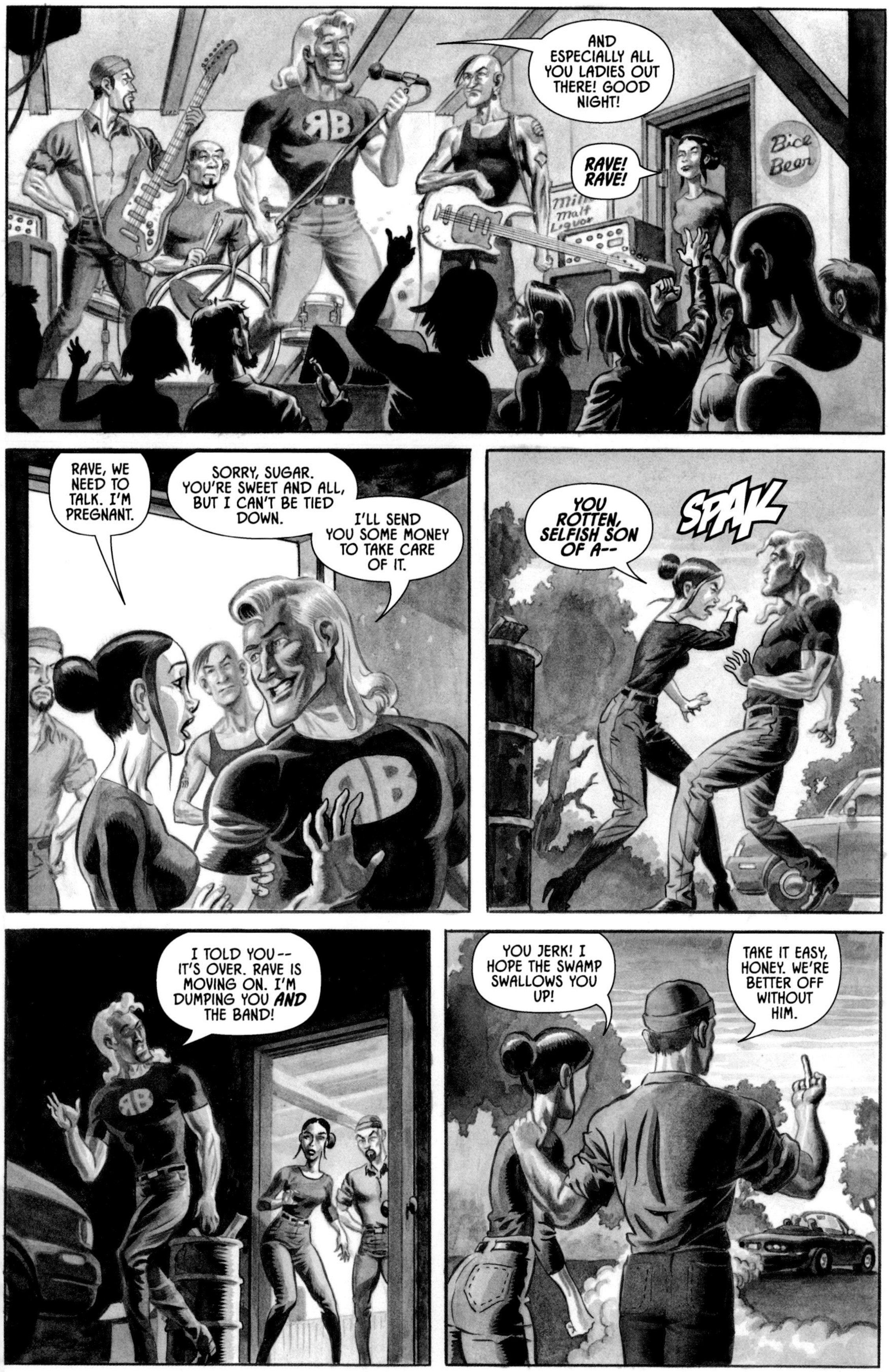
AND ESPECIALLY ALL YOU LADIES OUT THERE! GOOD NIGHT!
RAVE! RAVE!
Bice Beer
Milw Malt Liquor
RAVE, WE NEED TO TALK. I'M PREGNANT.
SORRY, SUGAR. YOU'RE SWEET AND ALL, BUT I CAN'T BE TIED DOWN.
I'LL SEND YOU SOME MONEY TO TAKE CARE OF IT.
YOU ROTTEN, SELFISH SON OF A--
SPAK
I TOLD YOU-- IT'S OVER. RAVE IS MOVING ON. I'M DUMPING YOU AND THE BAND!
YOU JERK! I HOPE THE SWAMP SWALLOWS YOU UP!
TAKE IT EASY, HONEY. WE'RE BETTER OFF WITHOUT HIM.

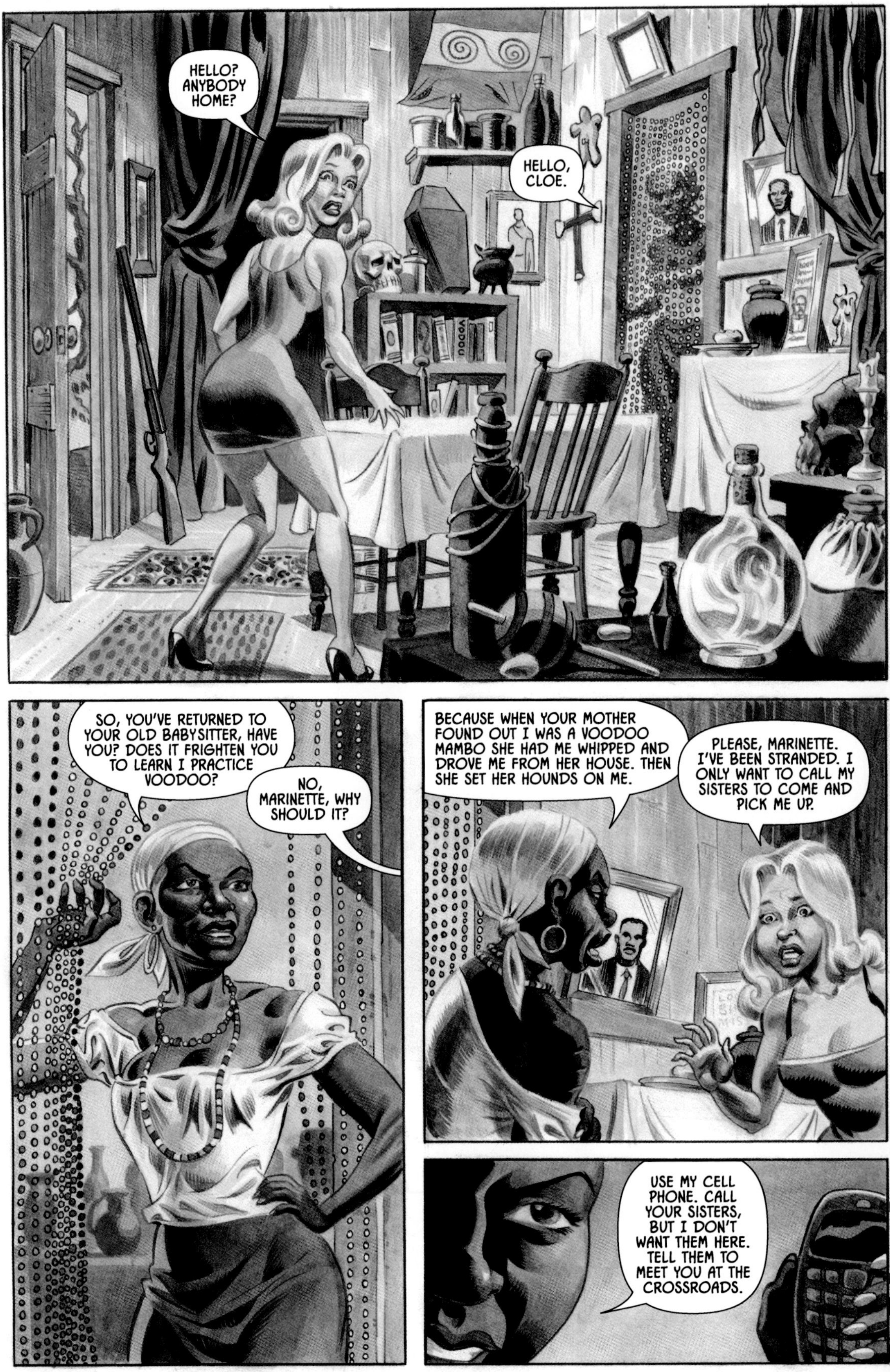
HELLO? ANYBODY HOME?
HELLO, CLOE.
VODOU
SO, YOU'VE RETURNED TO YOUR OLD BABYSITTER, HAVE YOU? DOES IT FRIGHTEN YOU TO LEARN I PRACTICE VOODOO?
NO, MARINETTE, WHY SHOULD IT?
BECAUSE WHEN YOUR MOTHER FOUND OUT I WAS A VOODOO MAMBO SHE HAD ME WHIPPED AND DROVE ME FROM HER HOUSE. THEN SHE SET HER HOUNDS ON ME.
PLEASE, MARINETTE. I'VE BEEN STRANDED. I ONLY WANT TO CALL MY SISTERS TO COME AND PICK ME UP.
USE MY CELL PHONE. CALL YOUR SISTERS, BUT I DON'T WANT THEM HERE. TELL THEM TO MEET YOU AT THE CROSSROADS.

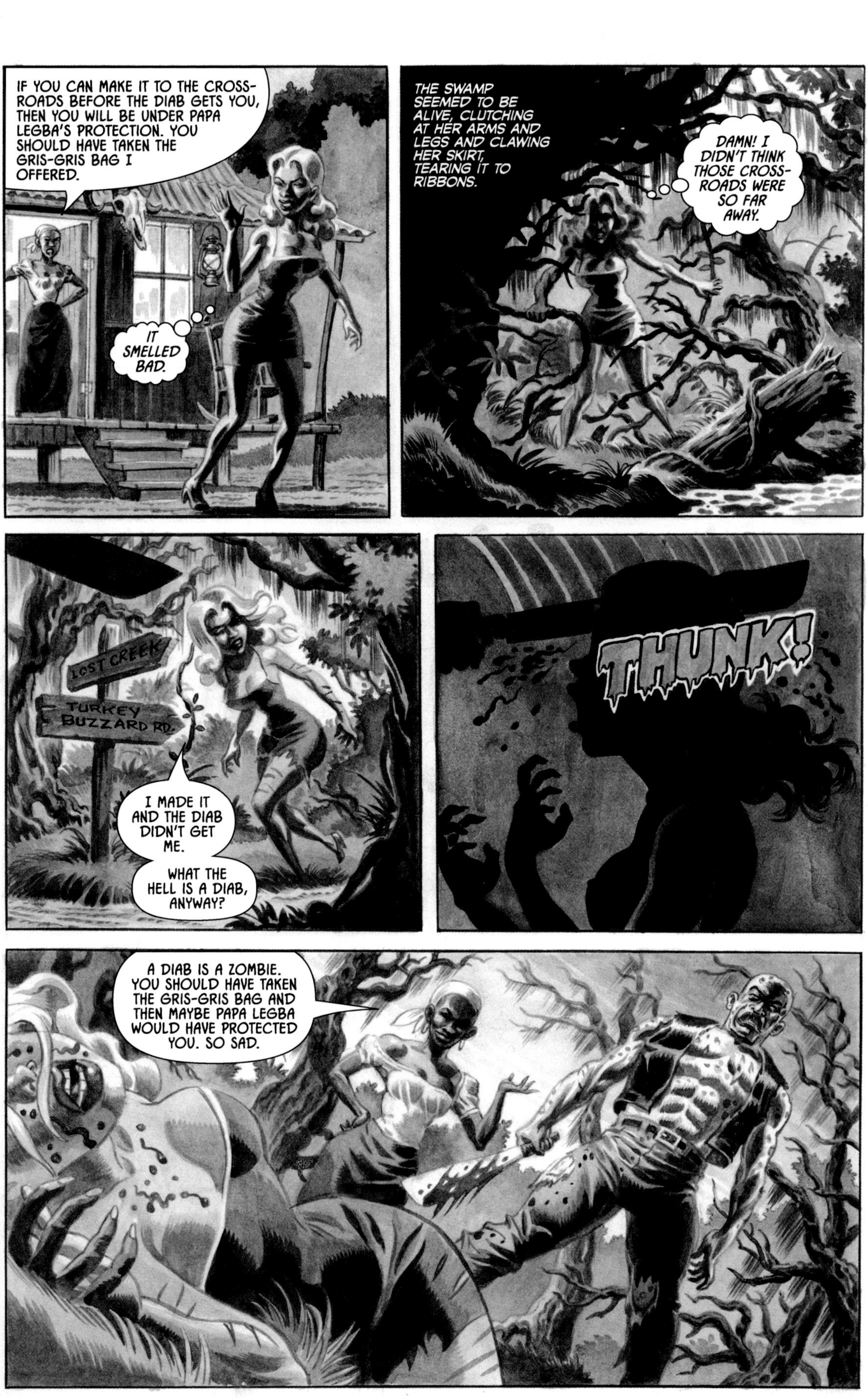
IF YOU CAN MAKE IT TO THE CROSS-ROADS BEFORE THE DIAB GETS YOU, THEN YOU WILL BE UNDER PAPA LEGBA'S PROTECTION. YOU SHOULD HAVE TAKEN THE GRIS-GRIS BAG I OFFERED.
IT SMELLED BAD.
THE SWAMP SEEMED TO BE ALIVE, CLUTCHING AT HER ARMS AND LEGS AND CLAWING HER SKIRT, TEARING IT TO RIBBONS.
DAMN! I DIDN'T THINK THOSE CROSS-ROADS WERE SO FAR AWAY.
LOST CREEK
TURKEY BUZZARD RD.
I MADE IT AND THE DIAB DIDN'T GET ME.
WHAT THE HELL IS A DIAB, ANYWAY?
THUNK!
A DIAB IS A ZOMBIE. YOU SHOULD HAVE TAKEN THE GRIS-GRIS BAG AND THEN MAYBE PAPA LEGBA WOULD HAVE PROTECTED YOU. SO SAD.

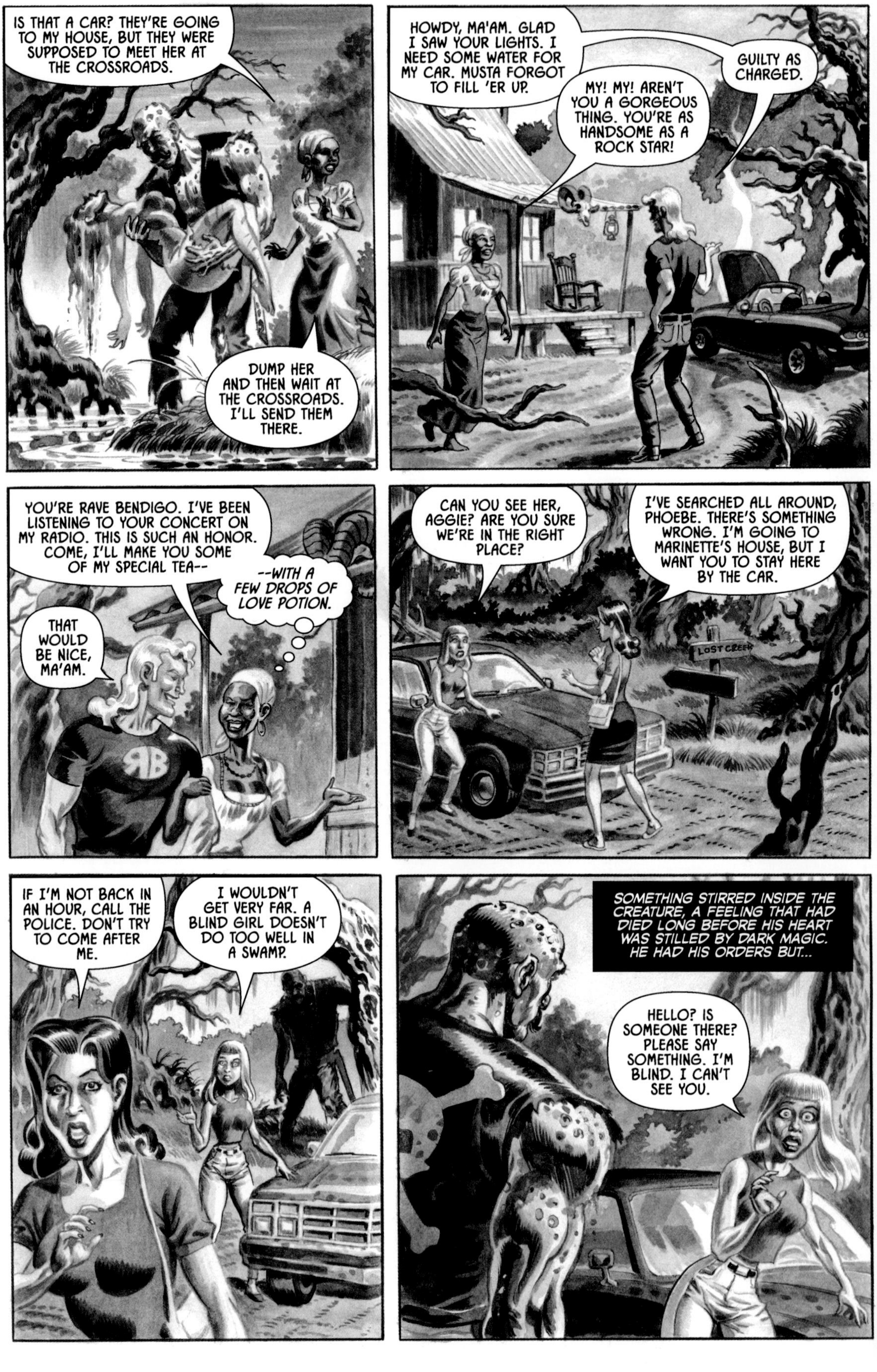
IS THAT A CAR? THEY'RE GOING TO MY HOUSE, BUT THEY WERE SUPPOSED TO MEET HER AT THE CROSSROADS.
DUMP HER AND THEN WAIT AT THE CROSSROADS. I'LL SEND THEM THERE.
HOWDY, MA'AM. GLAD I SAW YOUR LIGHTS. I NEED SOME WATER FOR MY CAR. MUSTA FORGOT TO FILL 'ER UP.
MY! MY! AREN'T YOU A GORGEOUS THING. YOU'RE AS HANDSOME AS A ROCK STAR!
GUILTY AS CHARGED.
YOU'RE RAVE BENDIGO. I'VE BEEN LISTENING TO YOUR CONCERT ON MY RADIO. THIS IS SUCH AN HONOR. COME, I'LL MAKE YOU SOME OF MY SPECIAL TEA--
--WITH A FEW DROPS OF LOVE POTION.
THAT WOULD BE NICE, MA'AM.
CAN YOU SEE HER, AGGIE? ARE YOU SURE WE'RE IN THE RIGHT PLACE?
I'VE SEARCHED ALL AROUND, PHOEBE. THERE'S SOMETHING WRONG. I'M GOING TO MARINETTE'S HOUSE, BUT I WANT YOU TO STAY HERE BY THE CAR.
LOST CREEK
IF I'M NOT BACK IN AN HOUR, CALL THE POLICE. DON'T TRY TO COME AFTER ME.
I WOULDN'T GET VERY FAR. A BLIND GIRL DOESN'T DO TOO WELL IN A SWAMP.
SOMETHING STIRRED INSIDE THE CREATURE, A FEELING THAT HAD DIED LONG BEFORE HIS HEART WAS STILLED BY DARK MAGIC. HE HAD HIS ORDERS BUT...
HELLO? IS SOMEONE THERE? PLEASE SAY SOMETHING. I'M BLIND. I CAN'T SEE YOU.

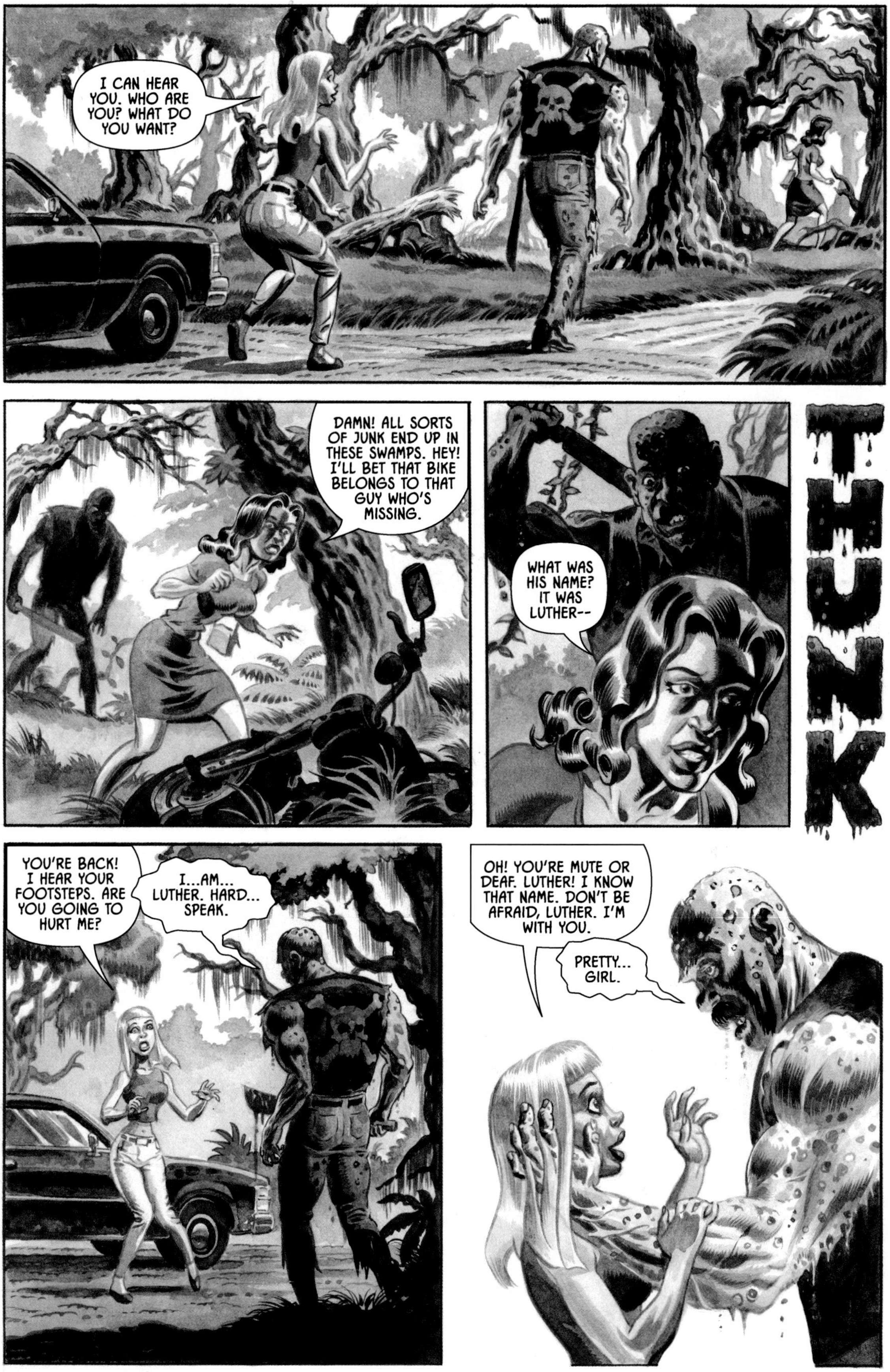
I CAN HEAR YOU. WHO ARE YOU? WHAT DO YOU WANT?
DAMN! ALL SORTS OF JUNK END UP IN THESE SWAMPS. HEY! I'LL BET THAT BIKE BELONGS TO THAT GUY WHO'S MISSING.
WHAT WAS HIS NAME? IT WAS LUTHER--
THUNK
YOU'RE BACK! I HEAR YOUR FOOTSTEPS. ARE YOU GOING TO HURT ME?
I...AM... LUTHER. HARD... SPEAK.
OH! YOU'RE MUTE OR DEAF. LUTHER! I KNOW THAT NAME. DON'T BE AFRAID, LUTHER. I'M WITH YOU.
PRETTY... GIRL.

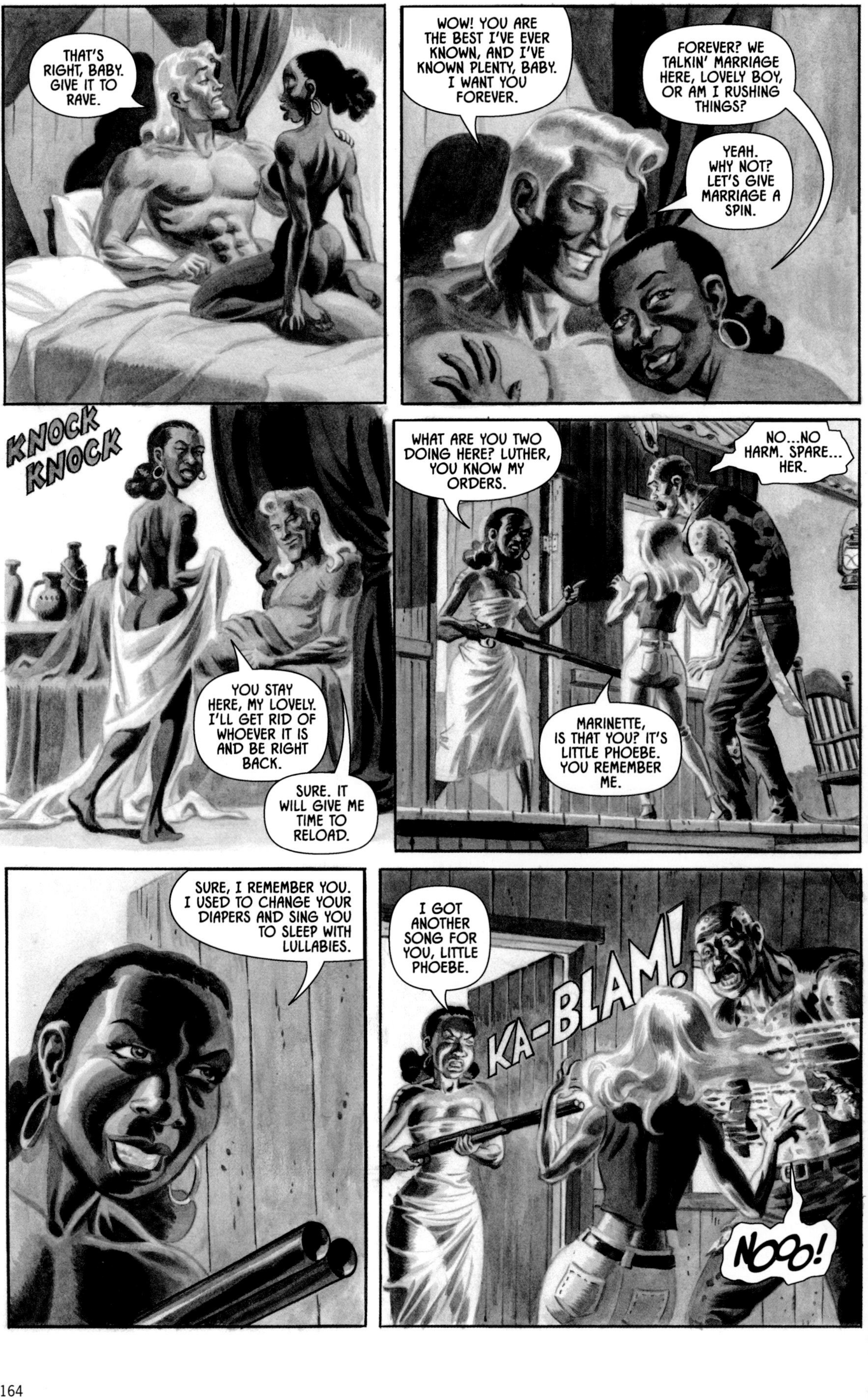
THAT'S RIGHT, BABY. GIVE IT TO RAVE.
WOW! YOU ARE THE BEST I'VE EVER KNOWN, AND I'VE KNOWN PLENTY, BABY. I WANT YOU FOREVER.
FOREVER? WE TALKIN' MARRIAGE HERE, LOVELY BOY, OR AM I RUSHING THINGS?
YEAH. WHY NOT? LET'S GIVE MARRIAGE A SPIN.
KNOCK KNOCK
YOU STAY HERE, MY LOVELY. I'LL GET RID OF WHOEVER IT IS AND BE RIGHT BACK.
SURE. IT WILL GIVE ME TIME TO RELOAD.
WHAT ARE YOU TWO DOING HERE? LUTHER, YOU KNOW MY ORDERS.
NO...NO HARM. SPARE... HER.
MARINETTE, IS THAT YOU? IT'S LITTLE PHOEBE. YOU REMEMBER ME.
SURE, I REMEMBER YOU. I USED TO CHANGE YOUR DIAPERS AND SING YOU TO SLEEP WITH LULLABIES.
I GOT ANOTHER SONG FOR YOU, LITTLE PHOEBE.
KA-BLAM!
NOOO!

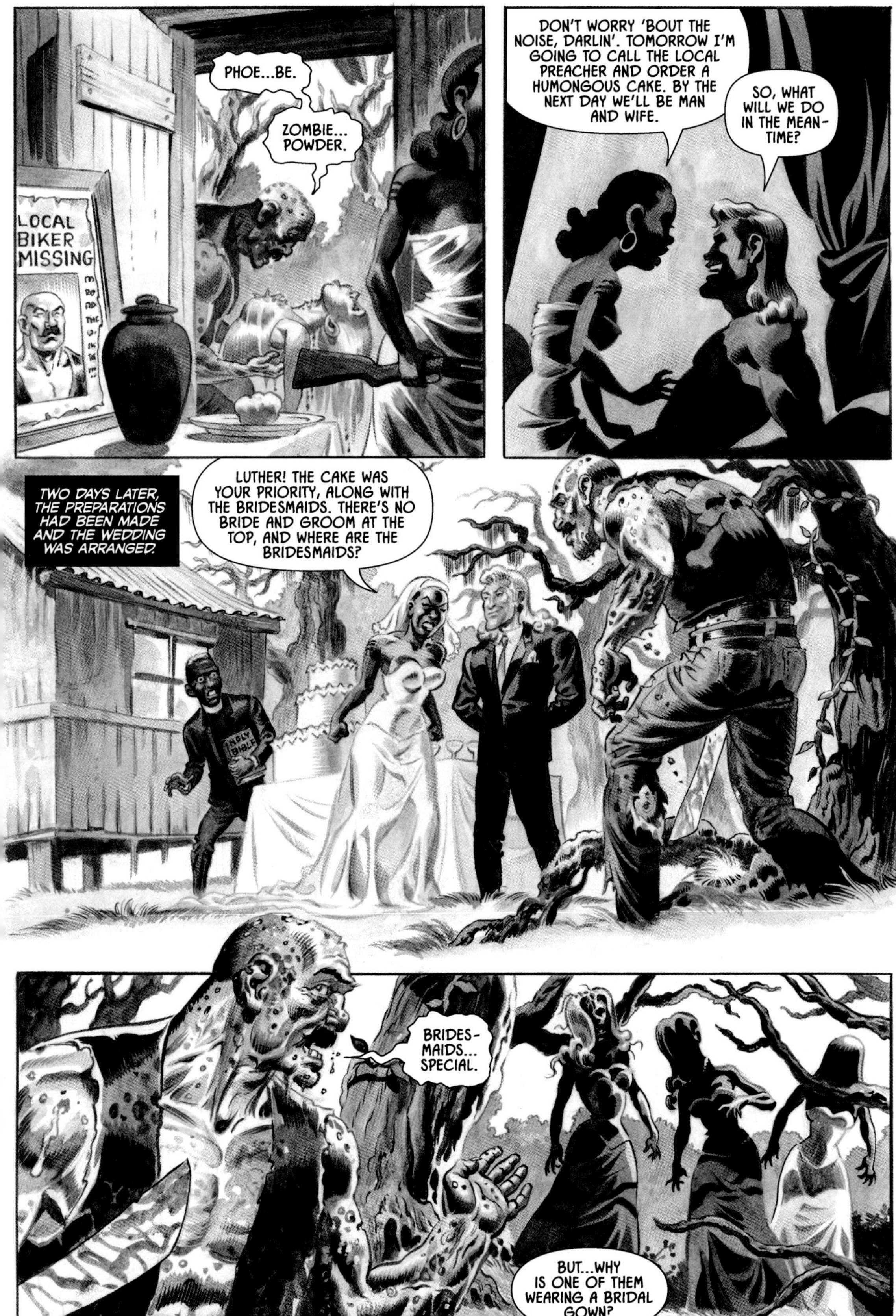
PHOE...BE.
ZOMBIE... POWDER.
LOCAL BIKER MISSING
DON'T WORRY 'BOUT THE NOISE, DARLIN'. TOMORROW I'M GOING TO CALL THE LOCAL PREACHER AND ORDER A HUMONGOUS CAKE. BY THE NEXT DAY WE'LL BE MAN AND WIFE.
SO, WHAT WILL WE DO IN THE MEAN-TIME?
TWO DAYS LATER, THE PREPARATIONS HAD BEEN MADE AND THE WEDDING WAS ARRANGED.
LUTHER! THE CAKE WAS YOUR PRIORITY, ALONG WITH THE BRIDESMAIDS. THERE'S NO BRIDE AND GROOM AT THE TOP, AND WHERE ARE THE BRIDESMAIDS?
HOLY BIBLE
BRIDES-MAIDS... SPECIAL.
BUT...WHY IS ONE OF THEM WEARING A BRIDAL GOWN?

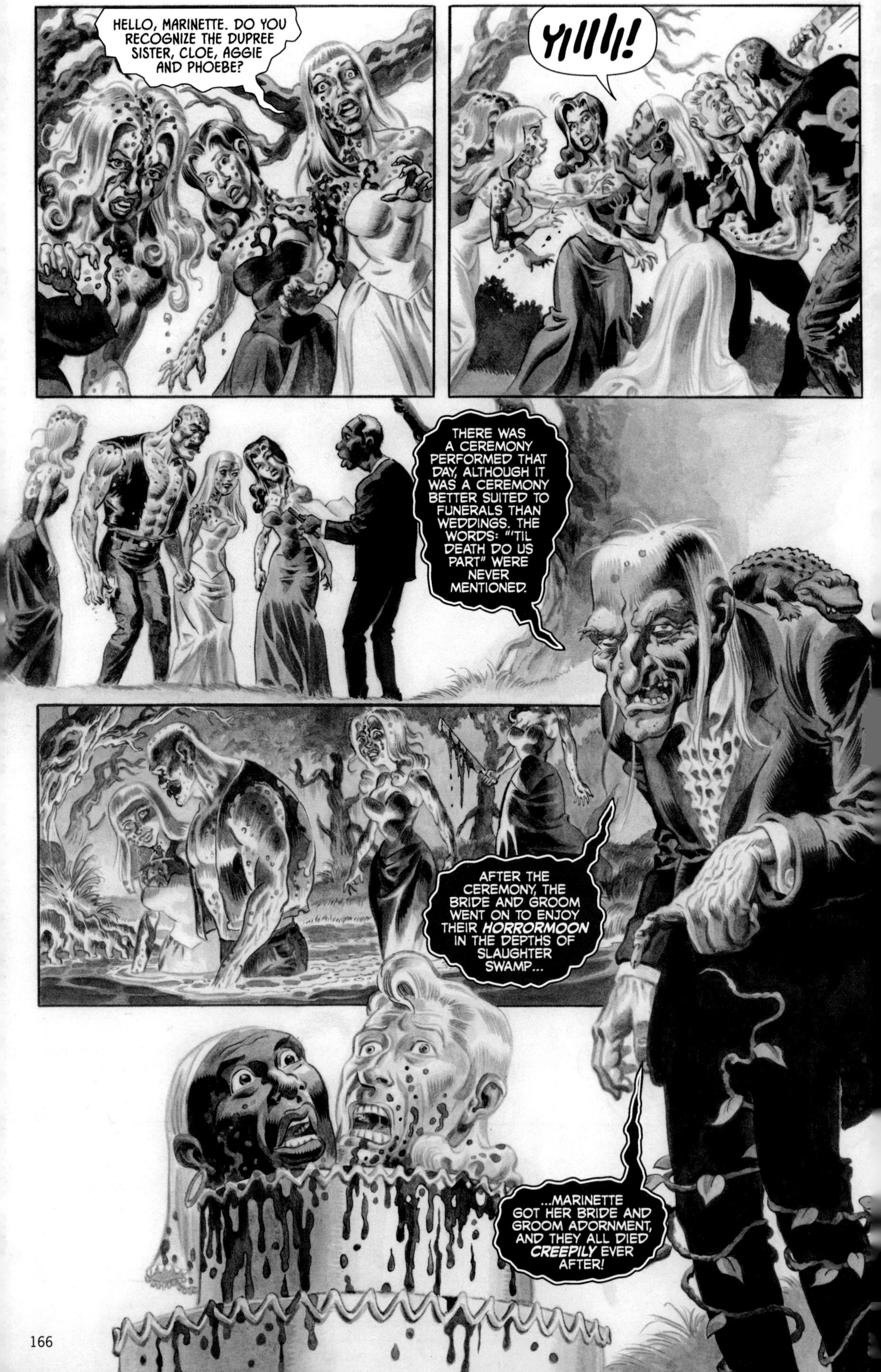
HELLO, MARINETTE. DO YOU RECOGNIZE THE DUPREE SISTER, CLOE, AGGIE AND PHOEBE?
YIIIII!
THERE WAS A CEREMONY PERFORMED THAT DAY, ALTHOUGH IT WAS A CEREMONY BETTER SUITED TO FUNERALS THAN WEDDINGS. THE WORDS: "'TIL DEATH DO US PART" WERE NEVER MENTIONED.
AFTER THE CEREMONY, THE BRIDE AND GROOM WENT ON TO ENJOY THEIR ***HORRORMOON*** IN THE DEPTHS OF SLAUGHTER SWAMP...
...MARINETTE GOT HER BRIDE AND GROOM ADORNMENT, AND THEY ALL DIED ***CREEPILY*** EVER AFTER!

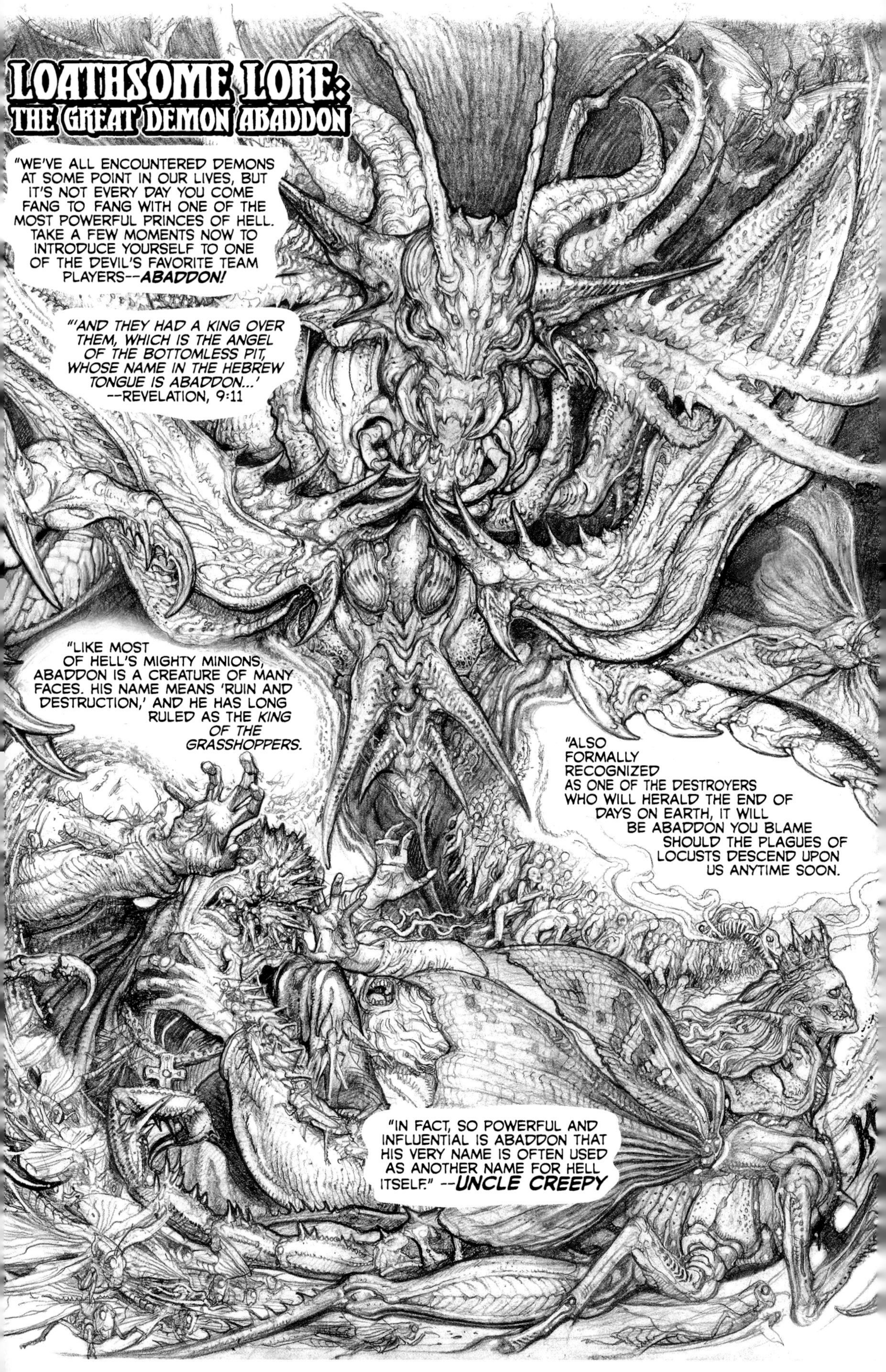
LOATHSOME LORE:
THE GREAT DEMON ABADDON
"WE'VE ALL ENCOUNTERED DEMONS AT SOME POINT IN OUR LIVES, BUT IT'S NOT EVERY DAY YOU COME FANG TO FANG WITH ONE OF THE MOST POWERFUL PRINCES OF HELL. TAKE A FEW MOMENTS NOW TO INTRODUCE YOURSELF TO ONE OF THE DEVIL'S FAVORITE TEAM PLAYERS--ABADDON!
"'AND THEY HAD A KING OVER THEM, WHICH IS THE ANGEL OF THE BOTTOMLESS PIT, WHOSE NAME IN THE HEBREW TONGUE IS ABADDON...' --REVELATION, 9:11
"LIKE MOST OF HELL'S MIGHTY MINIONS, ABADDON IS A CREATURE OF MANY FACES. HIS NAME MEANS 'RUIN AND DESTRUCTION,' AND HE HAS LONG RULED AS THE KING OF THE GRASSHOPPERS.
"ALSO FORMALLY RECOGNIZED AS ONE OF THE DESTROYERS WHO WILL HERALD THE END OF DAYS ON EARTH, IT WILL BE ABADDON YOU BLAME SHOULD THE PLAGUES OF LOCUSTS DESCEND UPON US ANYTIME SOON.
"IN FACT, SO POWERFUL AND INFLUENTIAL IS ABADDON THAT HIS VERY NAME IS OFTEN USED AS ANOTHER NAME FOR HELL ITSELF." --UNCLE CREEPY

Script by SHAWNA GORE / Art by PAUL KOMODA

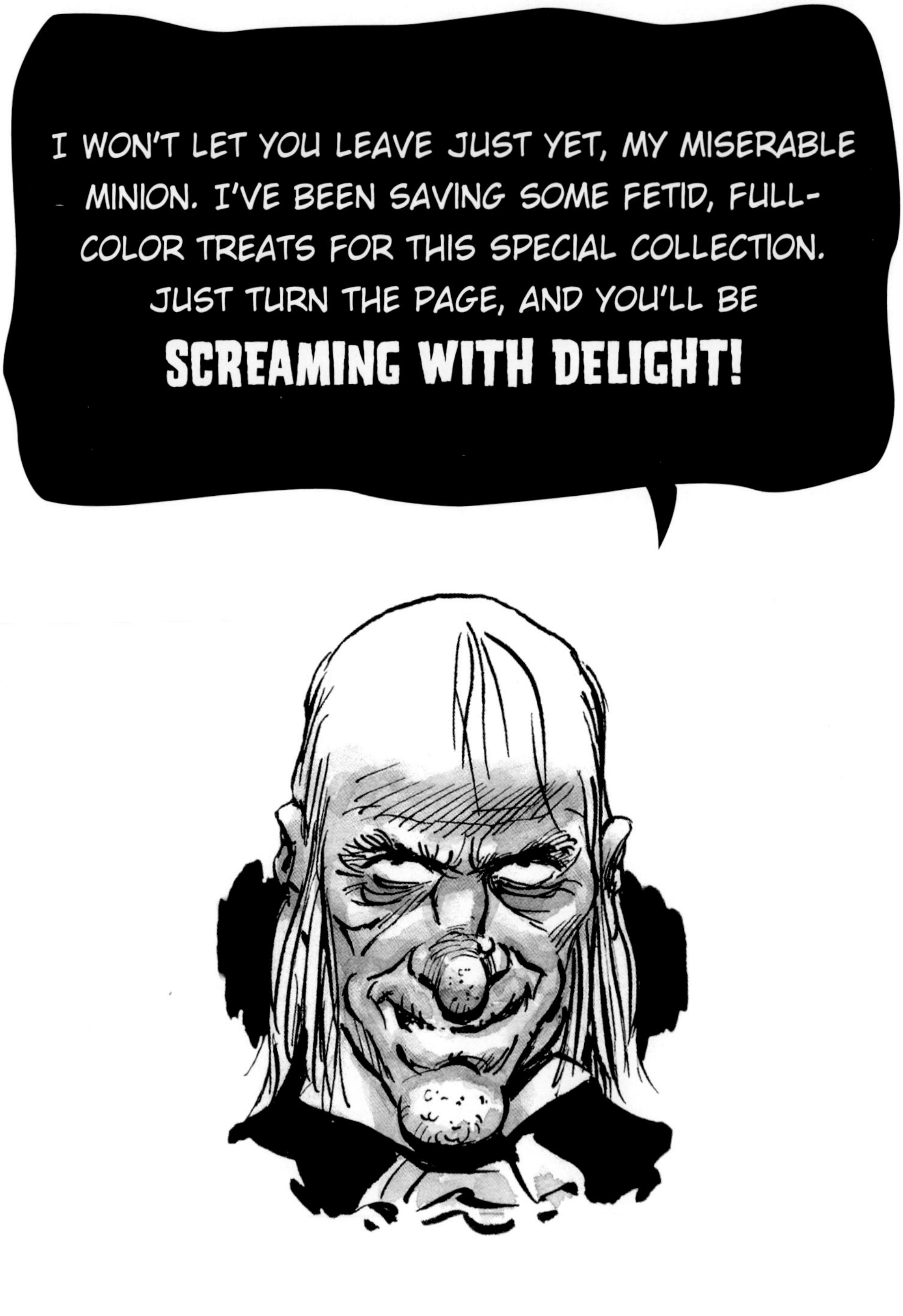
I WON'T LET YOU LEAVE JUST YET, MY MISERABLE MINION. I'VE BEEN SAVING SOME FETID, FULL-COLOR TREATS FOR THIS SPECIAL COLLECTION. JUST TURN THE PAGE, AND YOU'LL BE SCREAMING WITH DELIGHT!

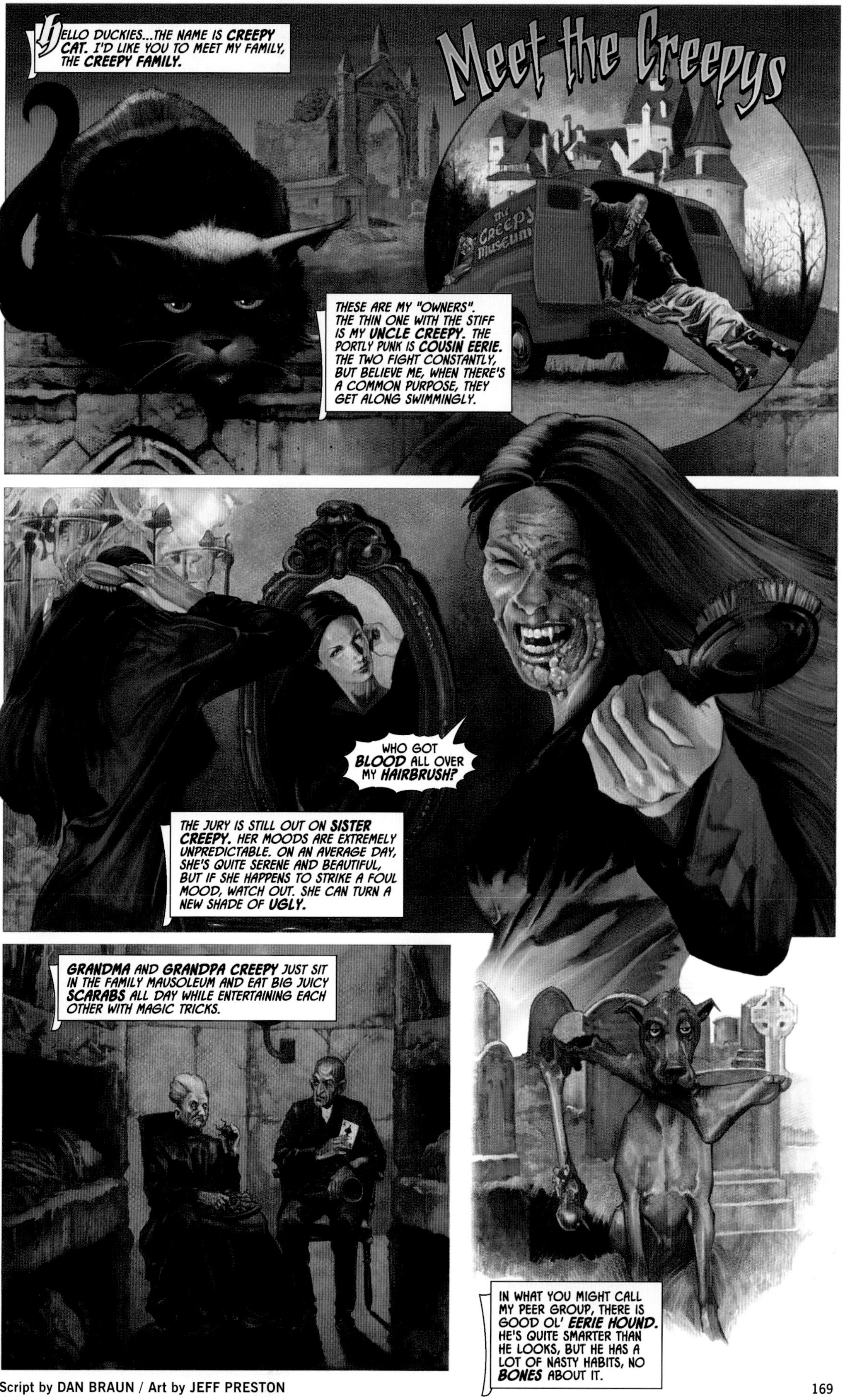
Meet the Creepys
HELLO DUCKIES...THE NAME IS CREEPY CAT. I'D LIKE YOU TO MEET MY FAMILY, THE CREEPY FAMILY.
the Creepy Museum
THESE ARE MY "OWNERS". THE THIN ONE WITH THE STIFF IS MY UNCLE CREEPY. THE PORTLY PUNK IS COUSIN EERIE. THE TWO FIGHT CONSTANTLY, BUT BELIEVE ME, WHEN THERE'S A COMMON PURPOSE, THEY GET ALONG SWIMMINGLY.
WHO GOT BLOOD ALL OVER MY HAIRBRUSH?
THE JURY IS STILL OUT ON SISTER CREEPY. HER MOODS ARE EXTREMELY UNPREDICTABLE. ON AN AVERAGE DAY, SHE'S QUITE SERENE AND BEAUTIFUL, BUT IF SHE HAPPENS TO STRIKE A FOUL MOOD, WATCH OUT. SHE CAN TURN A NEW SHADE OF UGLY.
GRANDMA AND GRANDPA CREEPY JUST SIT IN THE FAMILY MAUSOLEUM AND EAT BIG JUICY SCARABS ALL DAY WHILE ENTERTAINING EACH OTHER WITH MAGIC TRICKS.
IN WHAT YOU MIGHT CALL MY PEER GROUP, THERE IS GOOD OL' EERIE HOUND. HE'S QUITE SMARTER THAN HE LOOKS, BUT HE HAS A LOT OF NASTY HABITS, NO BONES ABOUT IT.

Script by DAN BRAUN / Art by JEFF PRESTON

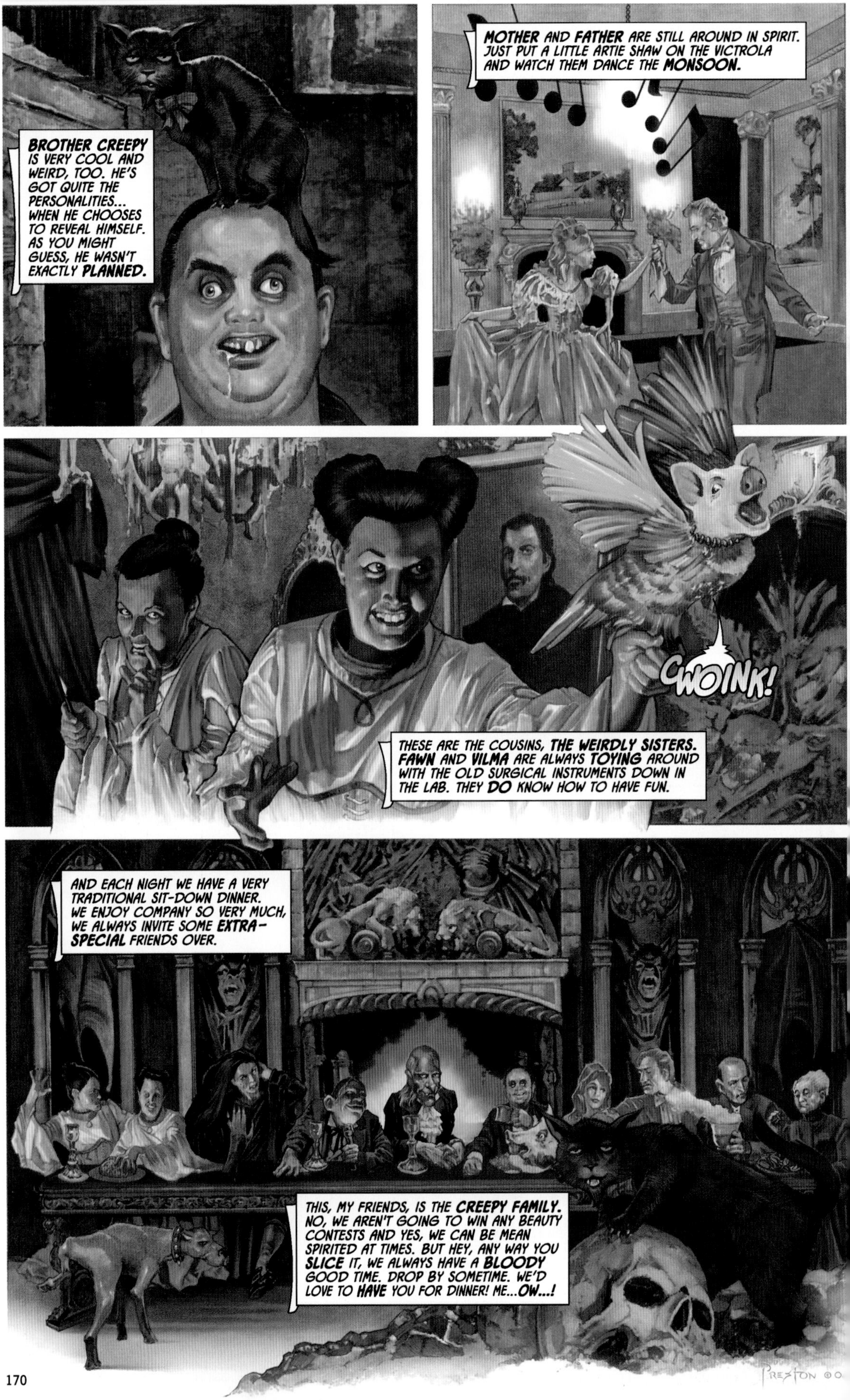
BROTHER CREEPY IS VERY COOL AND WEIRD, TOO. HE'S GOT QUITE THE PERSONALITIES... WHEN HE CHOOSES TO REVEAL HIMSELF. AS YOU MIGHT GUESS, HE WASN'T EXACTLY PLANNED.
MOTHER AND FATHER ARE STILL AROUND IN SPIRIT. JUST PUT A LITTLE ARTIE SHAW ON THE VICTROLA AND WATCH THEM DANCE THE MONSOON.
CWOINK!
THESE ARE THE COUSINS, THE WEIRDLY SISTERS. FAWN AND VILMA ARE ALWAYS TOYING AROUND WITH THE OLD SURGICAL INSTRUMENTS DOWN IN THE LAB. THEY DO KNOW HOW TO HAVE FUN.
AND EACH NIGHT WE HAVE A VERY TRADITIONAL SIT-DOWN DINNER. WE ENJOY COMPANY SO VERY MUCH, WE ALWAYS INVITE SOME EXTRA-SPECIAL FRIENDS OVER.
THIS, MY FRIENDS, IS THE CREEPY FAMILY. NO, WE AREN'T GOING TO WIN ANY BEAUTY CONTESTS AND YES, WE CAN BE MEAN SPIRITED AT TIMES. BUT HEY, ANY WAY YOU SLICE IT, WE ALWAYS HAVE A BLOODY GOOD TIME. DROP BY SOMETIME. WE'D LOVE TO HAVE YOU FOR DINNER! ME...OW...!
PRESTON 00

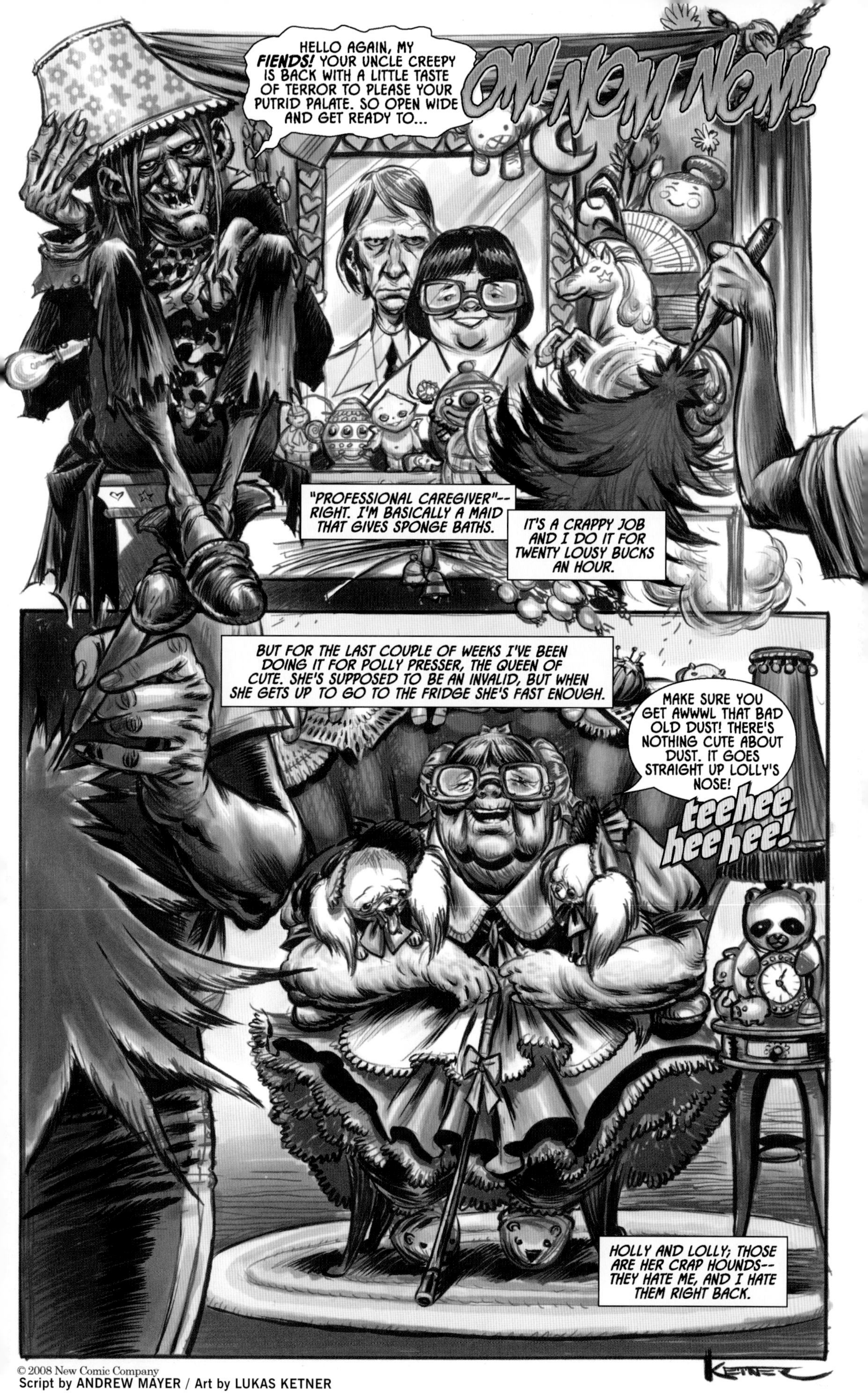
HELLO AGAIN, MY FIENDS! YOUR UNCLE CREEPY IS BACK WITH A LITTLE TASTE OF TERROR TO PLEASE YOUR PUTRID PALATE. SO OPEN WIDE AND GET READY TO...
OM NOM NOM!
"PROFESSIONAL CAREGIVER"-- RIGHT. I'M BASICALLY A MAID THAT GIVES SPONGE BATHS.
IT'S A CRAPPY JOB AND I DO IT FOR TWENTY LOUSY BUCKS AN HOUR.
BUT FOR THE LAST COUPLE OF WEEKS I'VE BEEN DOING IT FOR POLLY PRESSER, THE QUEEN OF CUTE. SHE'S SUPPOSED TO BE AN INVALID, BUT WHEN SHE GETS UP TO GO TO THE FRIDGE SHE'S FAST ENOUGH.
MAKE SURE YOU GET AWWWL THAT BAD OLD DUST! THERE'S NOTHING CUTE ABOUT DUST. IT GOES STRAIGHT UP LOLLY'S NOSE!
teehee heehee!
HOLLY AND LOLLY; THOSE ARE HER CRAP HOUNDS-- THEY HATE ME, AND I HATE THEM RIGHT BACK.
KETNER

Script by ANDREW MAYER / Art by LUKAS KETNER

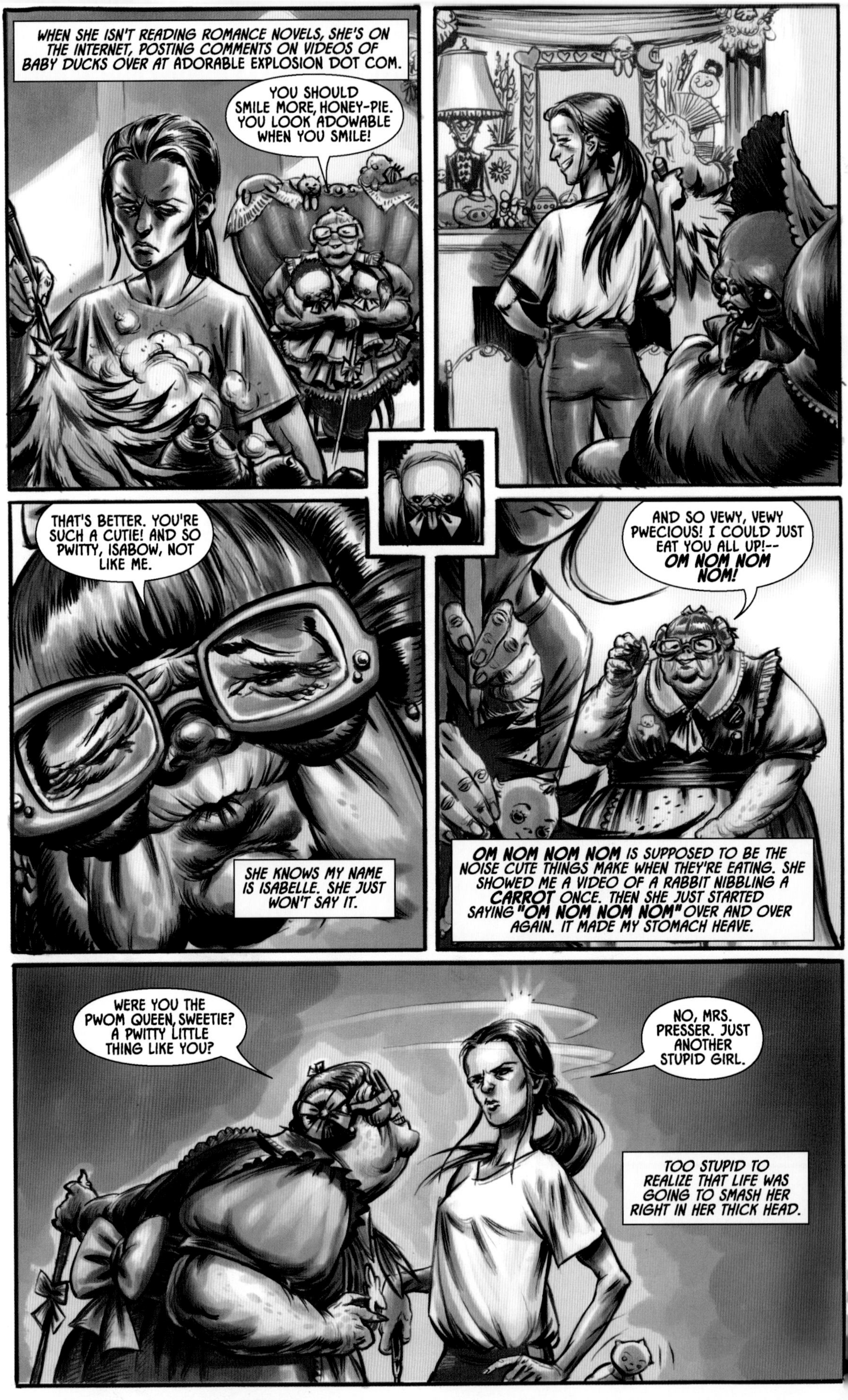
WHEN SHE ISN'T READING ROMANCE NOVELS, SHE'S ON THE INTERNET, POSTING COMMENTS ON VIDEOS OF BABY DUCKS OVER AT ADORABLE EXPLOSION DOT COM.
YOU SHOULD SMILE MORE, HONEY-PIE. YOU LOOK ADOWABLE WHEN YOU SMILE!
THAT'S BETTER. YOU'RE SUCH A CUTIE! AND SO PWITTY, ISABOW, NOT LIKE ME.
SHE KNOWS MY NAME IS ISABELLE. SHE JUST WON'T SAY IT.
AND SO VEWY, VEWY PWECIOUS! I COULD JUST EAT YOU ALL UP!-- OM NOM NOM NOM!
OM NOM NOM NOM IS SUPPOSED TO BE THE NOISE CUTE THINGS MAKE WHEN THEY'RE EATING. SHE SHOWED ME A VIDEO OF A RABBIT NIBBLING A CARROT ONCE. THEN SHE JUST STARTED SAYING "OM NOM NOM NOM" OVER AND OVER AGAIN. IT MADE MY STOMACH HEAVE.
WERE YOU THE PWOM QUEEN, SWEETIE? A PWITTY LITTLE THING LIKE YOU?
NO, MRS. PRESSER. JUST ANOTHER STUPID GIRL.
TOO STUPID TO REALIZE THAT LIFE WAS GOING TO SMASH HER RIGHT IN HER THICK HEAD.

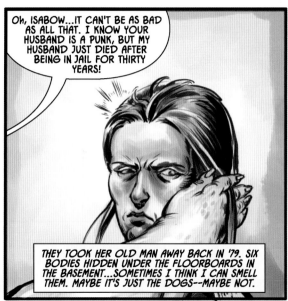

OH, ISABOW...IT CAN'T BE AS BAD AS ALL THAT. I KNOW YOUR HUSBAND IS A PUNK, BUT MY HUSBAND JUST DIED AFTER BEING IN JAIL FOR THIRTY YEARS!

THEY TOOK HER OLD MAN AWAY BACK IN '79. SIX BODIES HIDDEN UNDER THE FLOORBOARDS IN THE BASEMENT...SOMETIMES I THINK I CAN SMELL THEM. MAYBE IT'S JUST THE DOGS--MAYBE NOT.

LIFE IS TOO SHORT TO BE SO SAD, ISN'T IT, ISABOW? YOU JUST HAVE TO HOLD ON TO THE THINGS THAT ARE NEAR AND DEAR TO YOU. THE PWITTY THINGS FADE SO FAST... ALL THE THINGS YOU WUV...

I'VE GOT TO GET BACK TO WORK, MRS. PRESSER...

OF COURSE YOU DO, SWEETIE. BUT WEMEMBER, NO MATTER WHAT PEOPLE TELL YOU, IT'S YOUR LITTLE TWEASURES THAT MATTER MOST.

WHAT DO YOU MEAN? ALL THESE THINGS?

OH, NO, NO, NO...I WUV MY WITTLE PEOPLES VEWY, VEWY MUCH, BUT I'M TALKING ABOUT REAL TWEASURES--

I KNEW THE OLD BAG HAD TO HAVE SOMETHING VALUABLE HIDDEN AWAY SOMEWHERE. HOW ELSE COULD SHE AFFORD ALL THE CRAP SHE BUYS?

THE PWECIOUS THINGS YOU HAVE TO KEEP HIDDEN FROM THE WORLD SO THE BAD PEOPLE CAN'T STEAL THEM AWAY FROM YOU.

THE THINGS YOU KEEP IN YOUR TWEASURE CHEST... teehee heehee!

"THERE'S A TREASURE CHEST IN HER BASEMENT?"

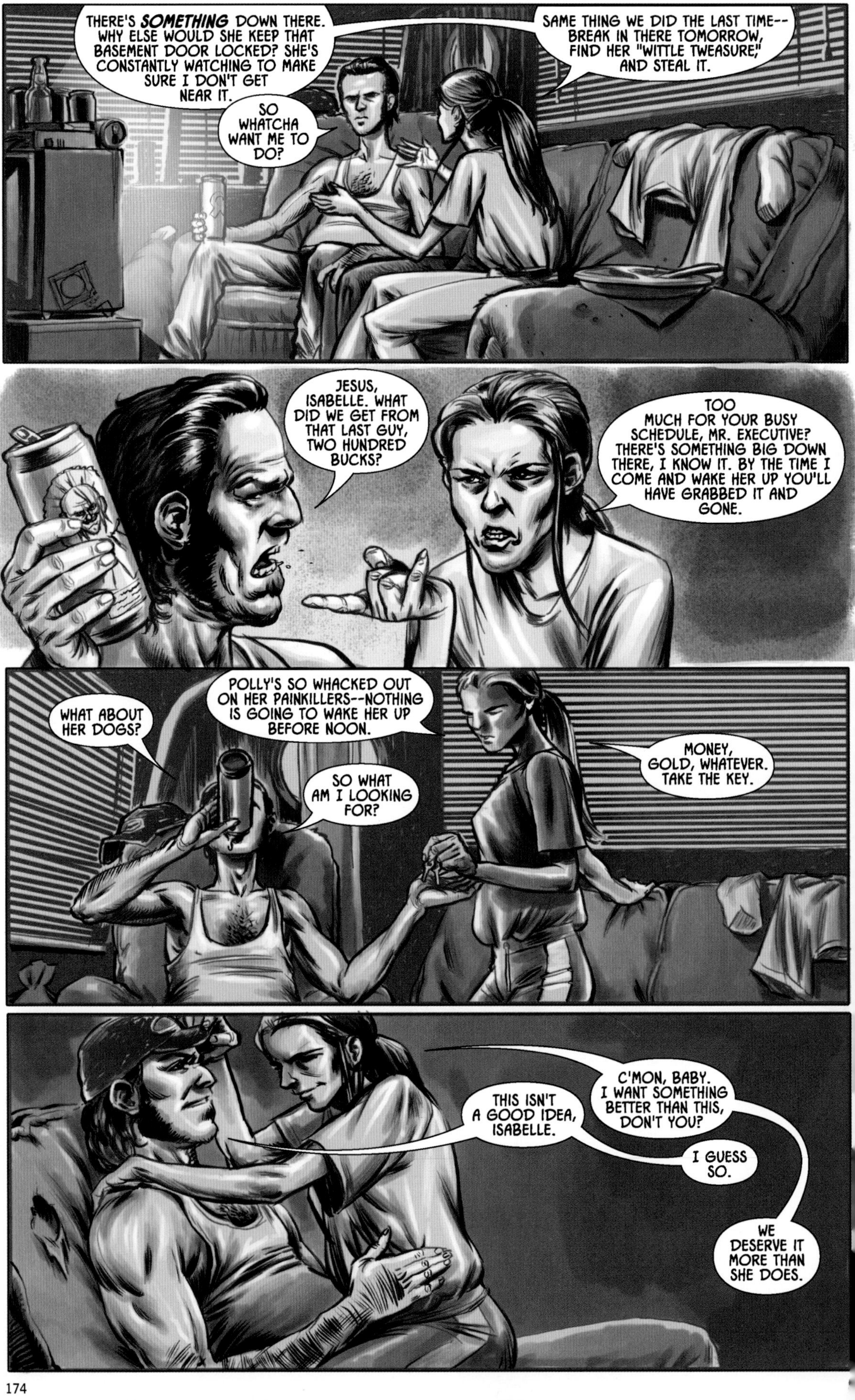
THERE'S SOMETHING DOWN THERE. WHY ELSE WOULD SHE KEEP THAT BASEMENT DOOR LOCKED? SHE'S CONSTANTLY WATCHING TO MAKE SURE I DON'T GET NEAR IT.
SO WHATCHA WANT ME TO DO?
SAME THING WE DID THE LAST TIME-- BREAK IN THERE TOMORROW, FIND HER "WITTLE TWEASURE," AND STEAL IT.
JESUS, ISABELLE. WHAT DID WE GET FROM THAT LAST GUY, TWO HUNDRED BUCKS?
TOO MUCH FOR YOUR BUSY SCHEDULE, MR. EXECUTIVE? THERE'S SOMETHING BIG DOWN THERE, I KNOW IT. BY THE TIME I COME AND WAKE HER UP YOU'LL HAVE GRABBED IT AND GONE.
WHAT ABOUT HER DOGS?
POLLY'S SO WHACKED OUT ON HER PAINKILLERS--NOTHING IS GOING TO WAKE HER UP BEFORE NOON.
SO WHAT AM I LOOKING FOR?
MONEY, GOLD, WHATEVER. TAKE THE KEY.
THIS ISN'T A GOOD IDEA, ISABELLE.
C'MON, BABY. I WANT SOMETHING BETTER THAN THIS, DON'T YOU?
I GUESS SO.
WE DESERVE IT MORE THAN SHE DOES.

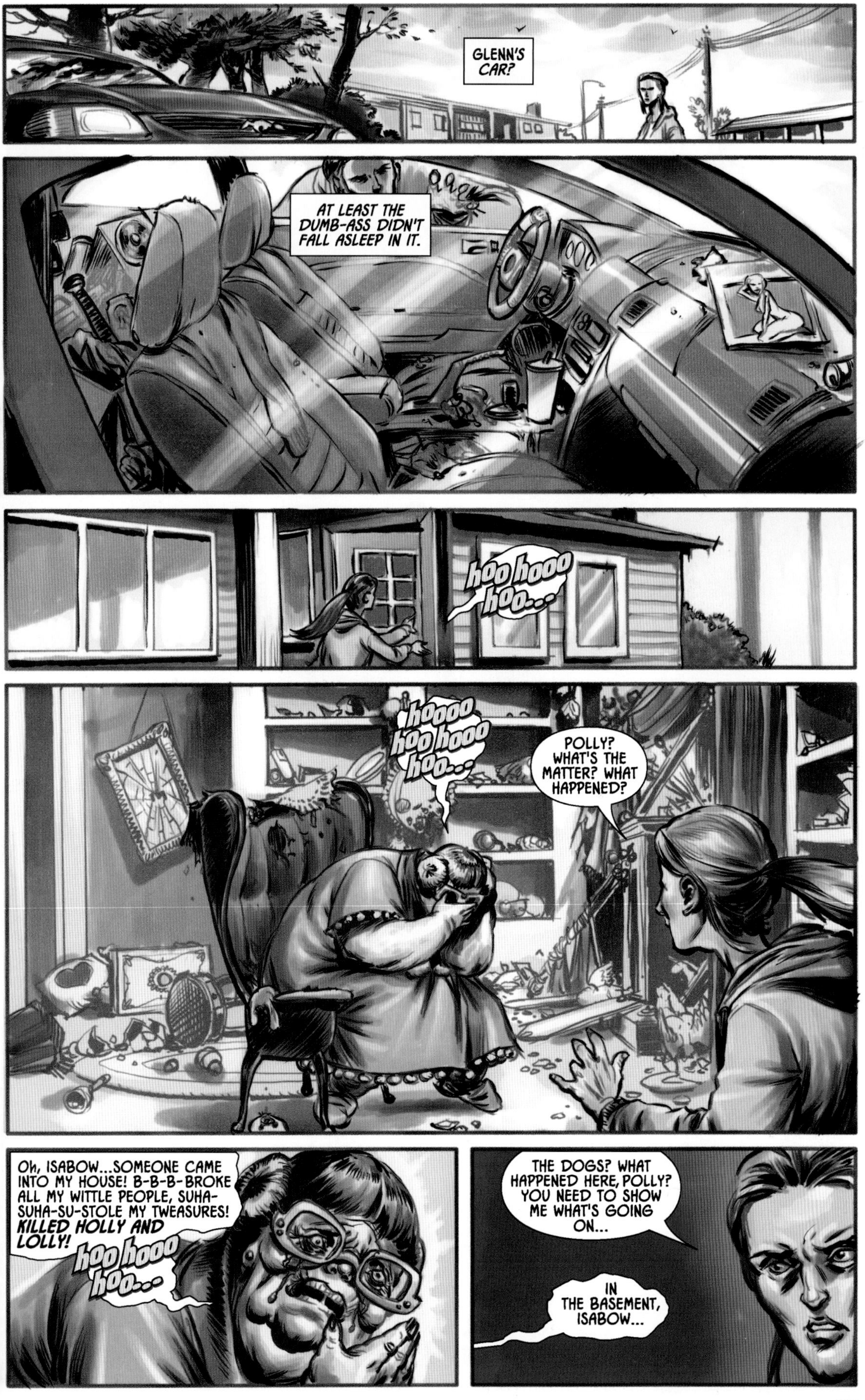
GLENN'S CAR?
AT LEAST THE DUMB-ASS DIDN'T FALL ASLEEP IN IT.
hoo hooo hoo...
hoooo hoo hooo hoo...
POLLY? WHAT'S THE MATTER? WHAT HAPPENED?
Oh, ISABOW...SOMEONE CAME INTO MY HOUSE! B-B-B-BROKE ALL MY WITTLE PEOPLE, SUHA-SUHA-SU-STOLE MY TWEASURES! KILLED HOLLY AND LOLLY!
hoo hooo hoo...
THE DOGS? WHAT HAPPENED HERE, POLLY? YOU NEED TO SHOW ME WHAT'S GOING ON...
IN THE BASEMENT, ISABOW...

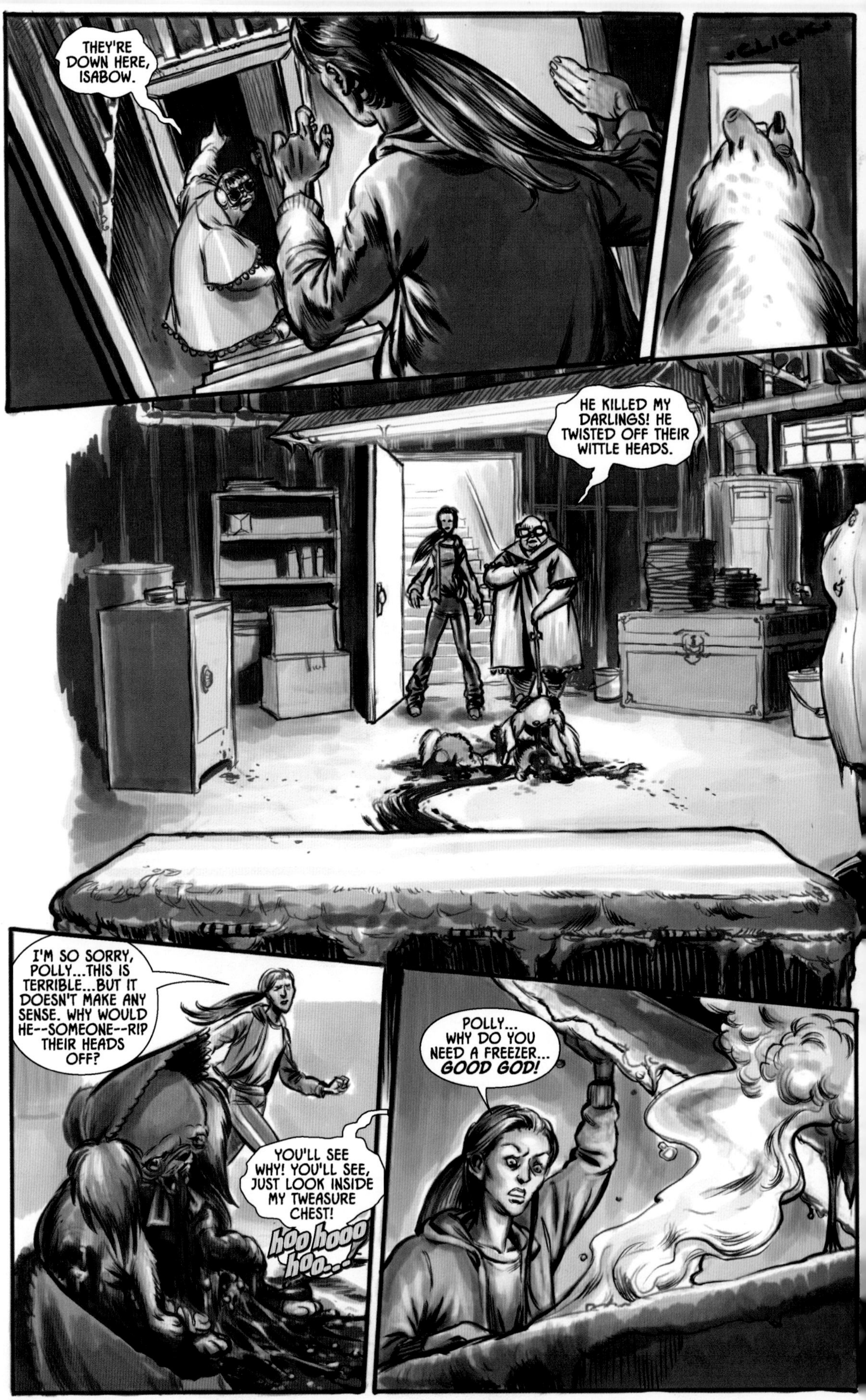
THEY'RE DOWN HERE, ISABOW.
CLICK
HE KILLED MY DARLINGS! HE TWISTED OFF THEIR WITTLE HEADS.
I'M SO SORRY, POLLY...THIS IS TERRIBLE...BUT IT DOESN'T MAKE ANY SENSE. WHY WOULD HE--SOMEONE--RIP THEIR HEADS OFF?
YOU'LL SEE WHY! YOU'LL SEE, JUST LOOK INSIDE MY TWEASURE CHEST!
hoo hooo hoo...!
POLLY... WHY DO YOU NEED A FREEZER... ***GOOD GOD!***

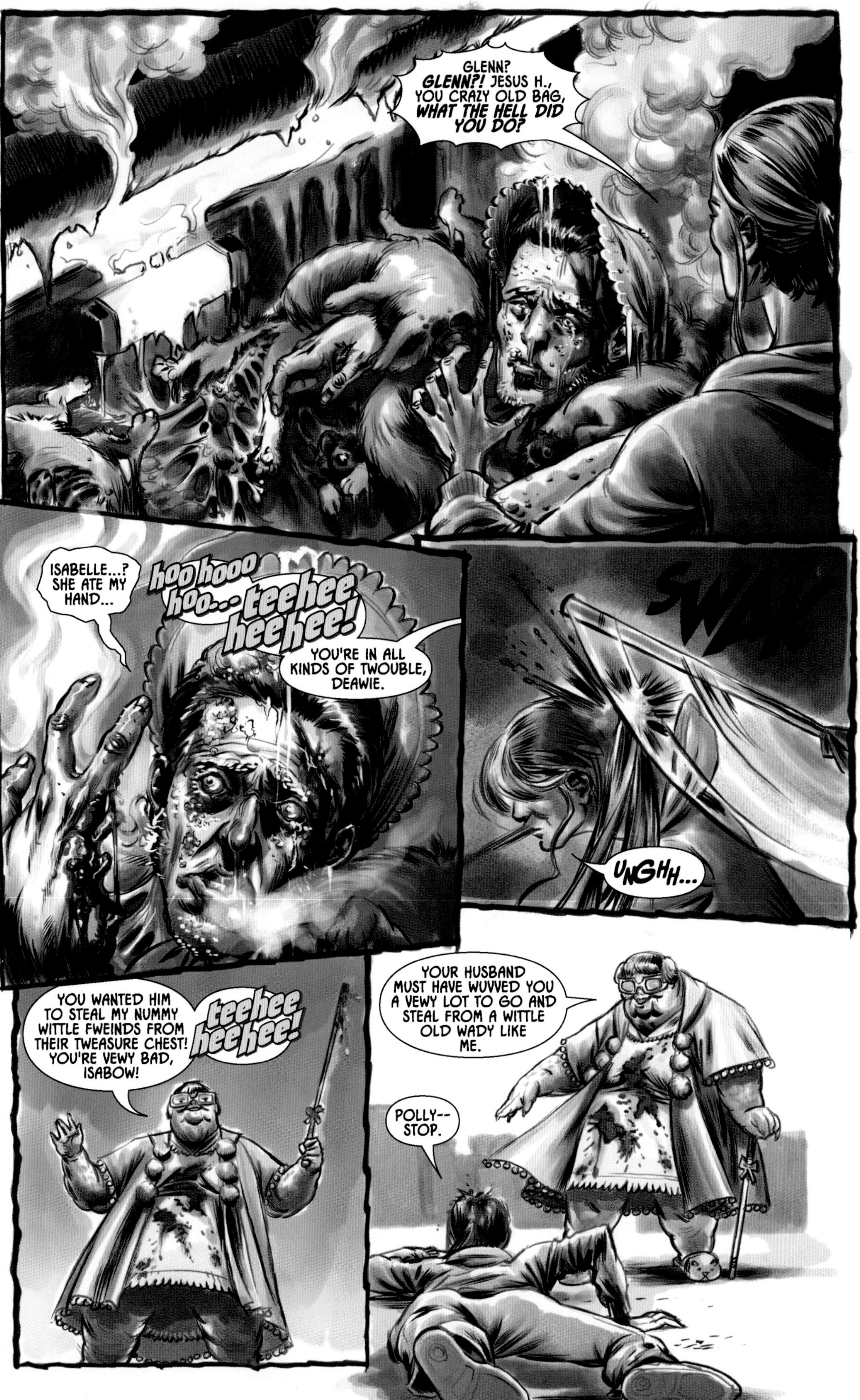

GLENN? GLENN?! JESUS H., YOU CRAZY OLD BAG, WHAT THE HELL DID YOU DO?
ISABELLE...? SHE ATE MY HAND...
hoo hooo hoo... teehee heehee!
YOU'RE IN ALL KINDS OF TWOUBLE, DEAWIE.
UNGHH...
YOU WANTED HIM TO STEAL MY NUMMY WITTLE FWEINDS FROM THEIR TWEASURE CHEST! YOU'RE VEWY BAD, ISABOW!
teehee heehee!
YOUR HUSBAND MUST HAVE WUVVED YOU A VEWY LOT TO GO AND STEAL FROM A WITTLE OLD WADY LIKE ME.
POLLY-- STOP.

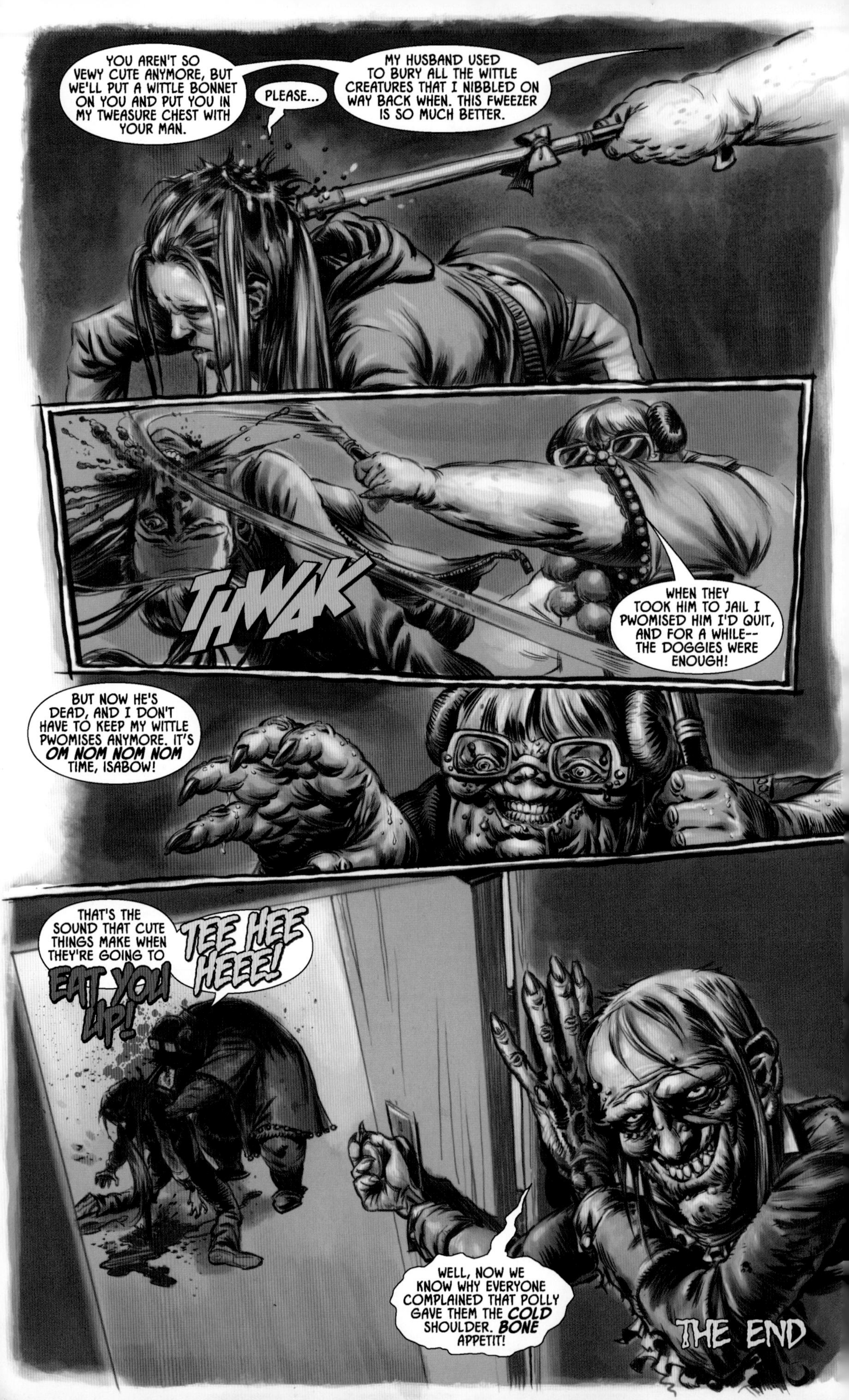
YOU AREN'T SO VEWY CUTE ANYMORE, BUT WE'LL PUT A WITTLE BONNET ON YOU AND PUT YOU IN MY TWEASURE CHEST WITH YOUR MAN.
PLEASE...
MY HUSBAND USED TO BURY ALL THE WITTLE CREATURES THAT I NIBBLED ON WAY BACK WHEN. THIS FWEEZER IS SO MUCH BETTER.
THWAK
WHEN THEY TOOK HIM TO JAIL I PWOMISED HIM I'D QUIT, AND FOR A WHILE-- THE DOGGIES WERE ENOUGH!
BUT NOW HE'S DEAD, AND I DON'T HAVE TO KEEP MY WITTLE PWOMISES ANYMORE. IT'S *OM NOM NOM NOM* TIME, ISABOW!
THAT'S THE SOUND THAT CUTE THINGS MAKE WHEN THEY'RE GOING TO
EAT YOU UP!
TEE HEE HEEE!
WELL, NOW WE KNOW WHY EVERYONE COMPLAINED THAT POLLY GAVE THEM THE *COLD* SHOULDER. *BONE* APPETIT!
THE END

NOW BEFORE I LET YOU CRAWL AWAY,

I HAVE A FINAL CREEPY TREAT IN STORE FOR YOU. ONE OF THE GRAVEST JOYS I'VE EXPERIENCED IN RESURRECTING MY CLASSIC *CREEPY* MAGAZINE HAS BEEN RECONNECTING WITH SOME OF MY FAVORITE ARTISTS FROM THE BAD OLD DAYS, INCLUDING *GENE COLAN, BERNIE WRIGHTSON, ANGELO TORRES, MICHAEL KALUTA,* AND *KEN KELLY.* EACH OF THESE FREAKISHLY TALENTED FIENDS HAS CONTRIBUTED NEW MANIACAL MATERIAL TO THIS CRUSTY COLLECTION, AND I'M NOT LETTING THEM OFF THE MEAT HOOKS UNTIL THEY SWEAR THEY'LL DO MORE. BUT INSTEAD OF LEAVING YOU HANGING WHILE I DECIDE WHAT TERRIBLE TREATS I'LL PUT TOGETHER FOR YOU IN THE NEXT ROUND OF NEW *CREEPY* COMICS, LET'S REVISIT THESE GRUESOMELY GREGARIOUS INNARDVIEWS I CONDUCTED WITH *ANGELO TORRES* AND *KEN KELLY.*

THAT'S RIGHT, MY FIENDS. I'VE GOT TWO MORE PAGES OF TERROR FOR YOU—IF YOU CAN TAKE IT!
—*UNCLE CREEPY*

ANGELO TORRES

THE CLASSIC *CREEPY* ARTIST RETURNS!

ANGELO TORRES has always been one of the sharpest implements in my ghoulbox, and I'm pleased I was able to dig him up and get some more morbid work from this master of light and shadow. Let's see what else your Uncle Creepy can extract from the brain of this living legend!

UNCLE CREEPY: Aaah, yes. "Atrocious" Angelo Torres! You always were one of the best in my dungeon of draw-ers. The last time I saw you was 1971 or thereabouts. Tell me what you've been up to since we last met.

ANGELO TORRES: Yes, Uncle Creepy, I've been very busy since we last worked together. During those many years I've been called on to draw a wide variety of subjects, ranging from superheroes to the Civil War. I must confess, however, that a good part of that time was spent working with a most unusual gang of idiots at a place called *MAD*.

UC: *MAD*, you say? Sounds like my kind of place. Now, one of the reasons I came after you again is because you seem to have a knack for capturing perfectly scary atmosphere and settings. Where do you find your inspiration for such wretched scenery? Do you live in a dungeon yourself, or do you just have good reference material?

AT: The dungeon has been a great help, even though the bulk of the credit has to go to the hours spent watching those great black-and-white horror movies made in the thirties.

UC: Looking back at your early years on *Creepy*, can you recall which of the stories you worked on that you enjoyed the most?

AT: I really enjoyed working on "Pursuit of the Vampire," it being the first story I ever did for you. There were others, but "Ogre's Castle" was great fun to do because of the subject matter.

UC: Speaking of those early years, you worked alongside some of the other greats of the industry—artists like Wallace Wood, Reed Crandall, Roy Krenkel, and Al Williamson. Do you have a favorite artist among that group of guys? Anyone whose work was a particular influence on you?

AT: I loved them all. It was a privilege to work alongside the best people in the business. I would say my biggest influence had to be Al Williamson, whom I had worked with on a variety of projects, and who was also a close friend. But what an incredible array of talent you put together.

UC: I am good, aren't I? Now, you've spent a long time drawing nightmares for other people. If you could work on the project of your dreams, what would it be? Historical? A war story? The Wild West?

AT: It would probably be something historical involving some armed conflict. Having worked on World War II and Civil War projects, it would be fun to do something with lots of pageantry and color and great costumes. Something like the Crusades comes to mind, although you would probably prefer I do the Black Plague.

UC: It's nice that after all these years, you still know me so well, Angelo. Just one more question to bring our little interview to a close: What scares Angelo Torres? Giant bugs? Werewolves? Ghostly visitors from the beyond? The cable bill?

AT: What scares me? Many things. Short deadlines, ink spills, the Met bullpen. But nothing comes close to those nightmares I had growing up, fleeing in terror with the Frankenstein monster or the Mummy on my tail.

KEN KELLY

THE BEAST WITH THE BRUSH!

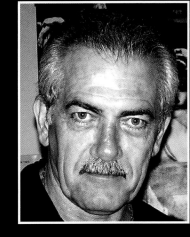

I'm so happy I could scare up another monsterpiece from master painter and heavy-metal enthusiast **KEN KELLY** for the cover of *Creepy* #4. You're probably wondering what the devil this old hack has been up to since you last saw his weird work gracing glorious old *Creepy* covers from yesteryear. I was too, so I cornered him and asked!

UNCLE CREEPY: Crusty Ken Kelly! You escaped from my dungeon so long ago; I've always wondered what became of you. What have you been up to since the last time I got my claws on your terrible talents?

KEN KELLY: It has been a long time, hasn't it? It took a very strange happening to free me from your imprisonment, and it was a little-known heavy-metal band that gave me the keys to escape your tyrannical hold. Strange name too: KISS. Who would have thought these nuts dressed up in heels and heavy face makeup would have the clout to wrench me away, but it worked. Then it was on to my heavy-metal home, Manowar, where I have shined for decades.

UC: Since you're such a favorite of many of our longtime fans, can you tell us a little bit about how you work? Do you paint from photographs, or do your icky images just appear out of the nebulous slime of your mind?

KK: Oh, I'm impressed that you're curious, knowing what a self-centered (CENSORED) you are, but all right, I'll share it with you. The nebulous slime of my mind still holds many treasures, and yes, they just pop up as if I were watching a movie in my head. Have to be careful while driving, because these thoughts can happen anywhere. As soon as you start to describe your concept to me, my mind throws up pictures. All I have to do is transfer them to paper, and bingo, the painting has begun. Now all the drawing and painting talents come to play to express the emotions of that concept on a canvas.

UC: Besides your dear old Uncle Creepy, whom else have you enjoyed working with in your long career? Any editors you really clicked with? How about other artists or painters? Is there anyone whose work you just flat-out admire?

KK: The list of other artists I admire would be too long for your magazine. But the most admired of all would be Frank Frazetta, whom I put in the category of the old masters now in another place: Rockwell, Rembrandt, Michelangelo, and the like. Editors and publishers. Now, that list is rather small, but includes your own servant, Shawna Gore, who was most helpful with my Dark Horse assignment and guided and directed me as only a professional could. Another champion in that field would be the now-departed Mr. D. Wollheim, publisher of DAW Books.

UC: Now, if someone were interested in giving you a real, bloodcurdling scare, what would I . . . erm, I mean, what would this person need to do to achieve that? How about a shark in your bathtub? Send the IRS knocking? What scares Ken Kelly?

KK: What an evil insect you are, Uncle, trying to get me to reveal a weakness that could allow slime like you to reimprison my sorry (CENSORED) again. But I guess I would have to say there are two experiences that leave me wanting. One is bridges—I just don't enjoy being off the ground that far while seemingly entombed in an automobile. The other is that I'm a bit claustrophobic; don't appreciate seriously enclosed places, MRI machines, and the like. Now don't go taking advantage—I'll be watching.

UC: When you look back at your past work for *Creepy* and *Eerie*, do you have a favorite cover image? Is there any one piece you did for the original series that still makes your skin crawl?

KK: I find it tremendously satisfying to know that a cover I was forced to do while in your imprisonment was the key to my freedom. That cover was *Creepy* #72. The KISS management people saw that magazine on a newsstand in Manhattan while they were searching for an artist to illustrate their KISS *Destroyer* cover. It was a struggle, but they freed me from your evil clutches, and for that I am eternally grateful. Another cover I concocted especially for you was *Creepy* #84. If the gods of the underworld were with me, that grenade would have ended your reign a long time ago. It seems you have feline tendencies with multiple lives. I fear I may meet you again along life's path. Oh, woe is me.

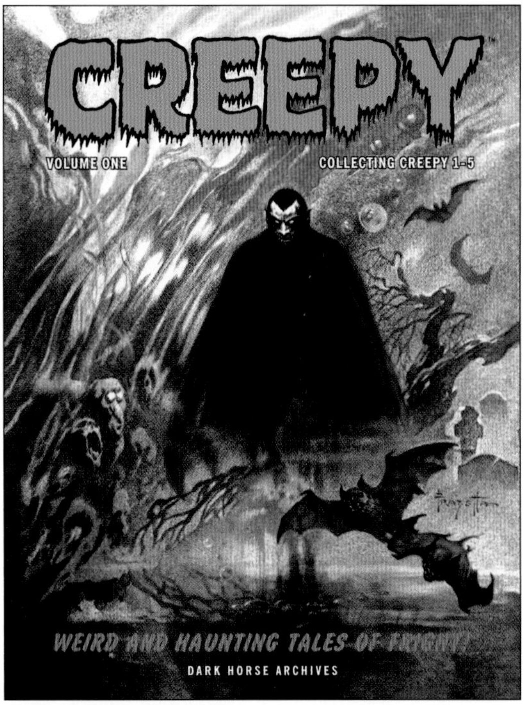
CREEPY
VOLUME ONE
COLLECTING CREEPY 1-5
WEIRD AND HAUNTING TALES OF FRIGHT!
DARK HORSE ARCHIVES

Volume 1 ISBN 978-1-59307-973-4

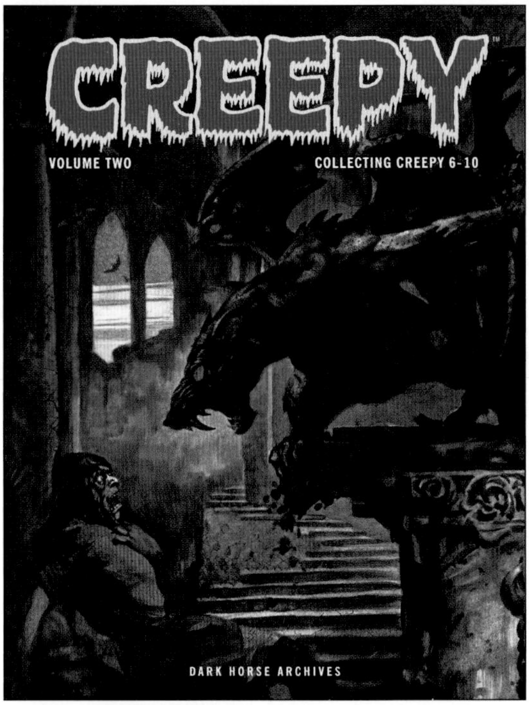
CREEPY
VOLUME TWO
COLLECTING CREEPY 6-10
DARK HORSE ARCHIVES

Volume 2 ISBN 978-1-59582-168-3

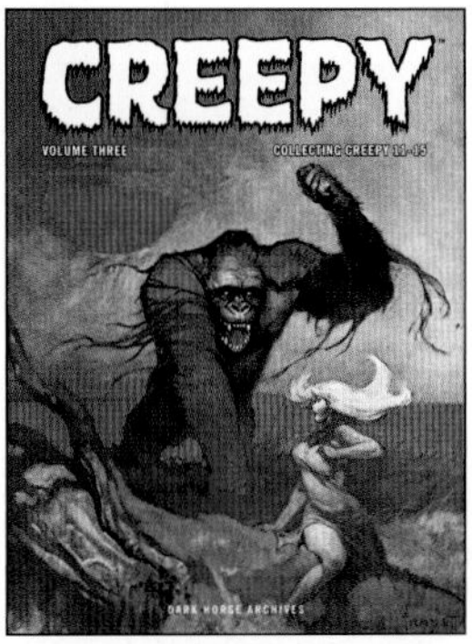
CREEPY
VOLUME THREE

Volume 3 ISBN 978-1-59582-259-8

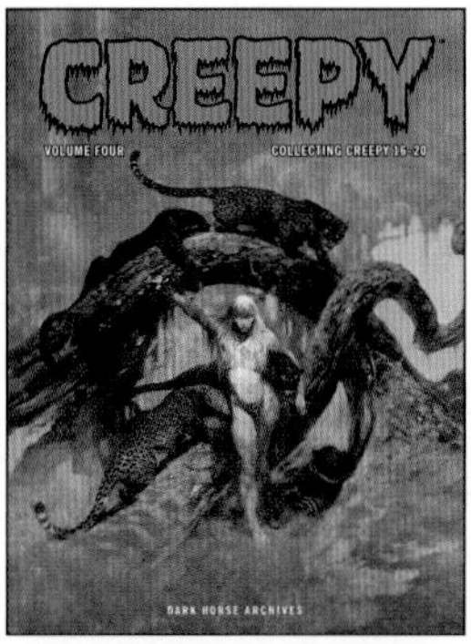
CREEPY
VOLUME FOUR
COLLECTING CREEPY 16-20

Volume 4 ISBN 978-1-59582-308-3

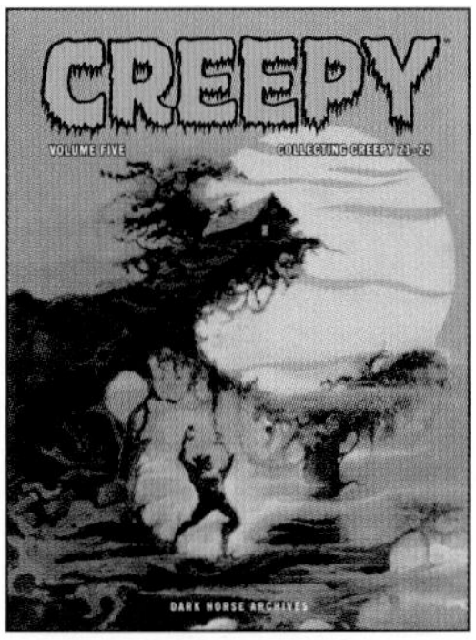
CREEPY
VOLUME FIVE

Volume 5 ISBN 978-1-59582-353-3

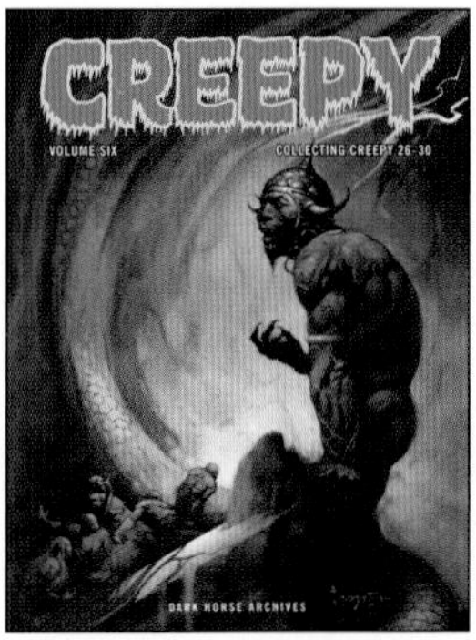
CREEPY
VOLUME SIX
COLLECTING CREEPY 26-30

Volume 6 ISBN 978-1-59582-354-0

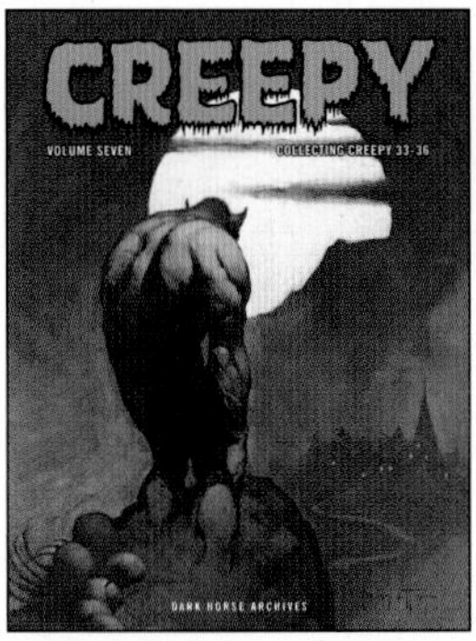
CREEPY
VOLUME SEVEN

Volume 7 ISBN 978-1-59582-516-2

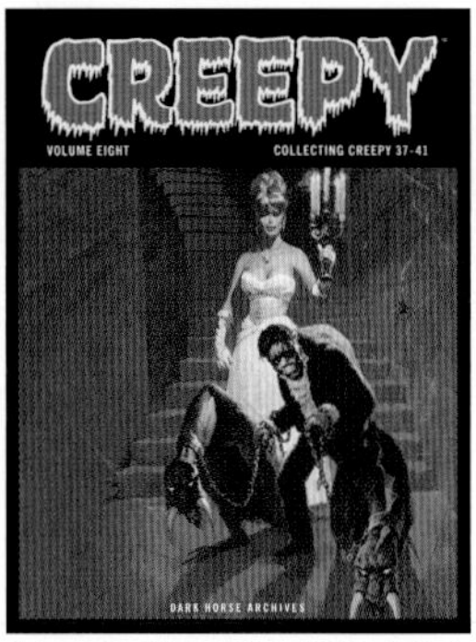
CREEPY
VOLUME EIGHT
COLLECTING CREEPY 37-41

Volume 8 ISBN 978-1-59582-568-1

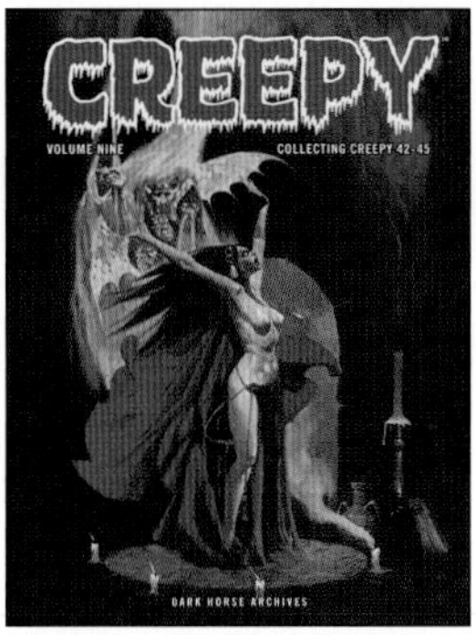
CREEPY
VOLUME NINE

Volume 9 ISBN 978-1-59582-693-0

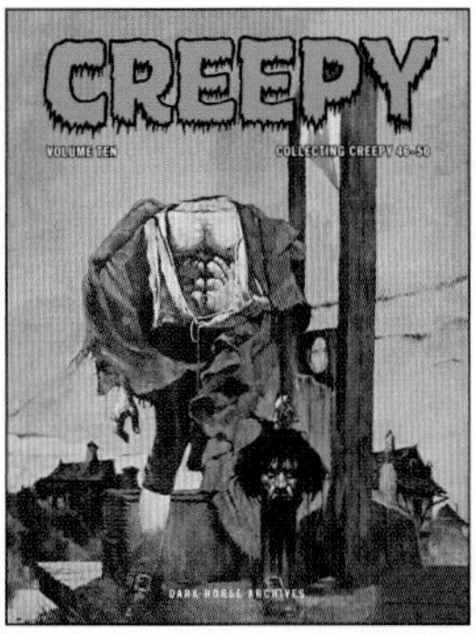
CREEPY
VOLUME TEN

Volume 10 ISBN 978-1-59582-719-7

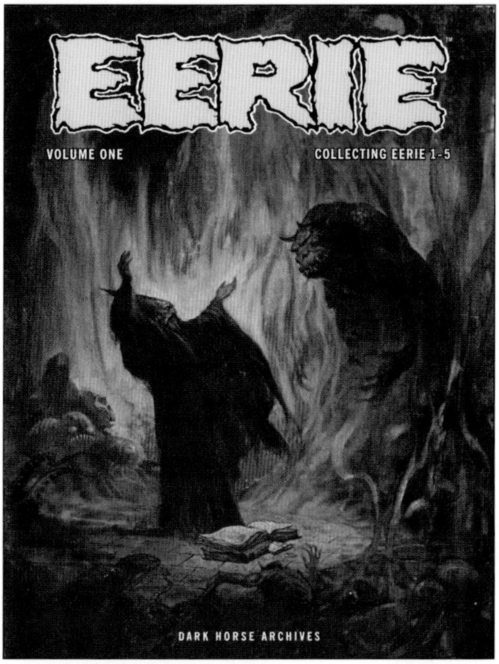
EERIE
VOLUME ONE
COLLECTING EERIE 1-5
DARK HORSE ARCHIVES

Volume 1 ISBN 978-1-59582-245-1

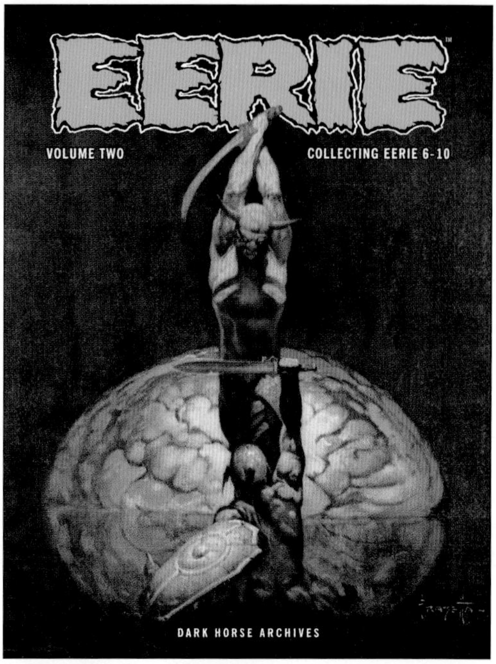
EERIE
VOLUME TWO
COLLECTING EERIE 6-10
DARK HORSE ARCHIVES

Volume 2 ISBN 978-1-59582-315-1

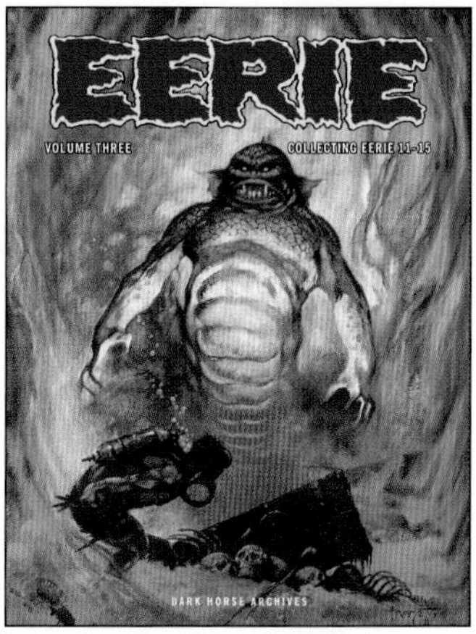
EERIE
VOLUME THREE
COLLECTING EERIE 11-15
DARK HORSE ARCHIVES

Volume 3 ISBN 978-1-59582-369-4

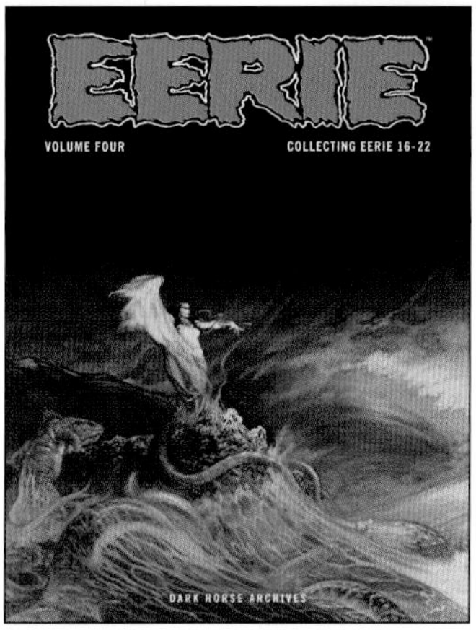
EERIE
VOLUME FOUR
COLLECTING EERIE 16-22
DARK HORSE ARCHIVES

Volume 4 ISBN 978-1-59582-429-5

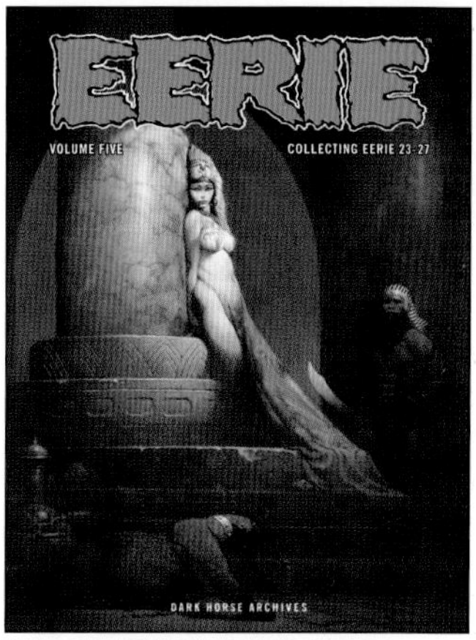
EERIE
VOLUME FIVE
COLLECTING EERIE 23-27
DARK HORSE ARCHIVES

Volume 5 ISBN 978-1-59582-525-4

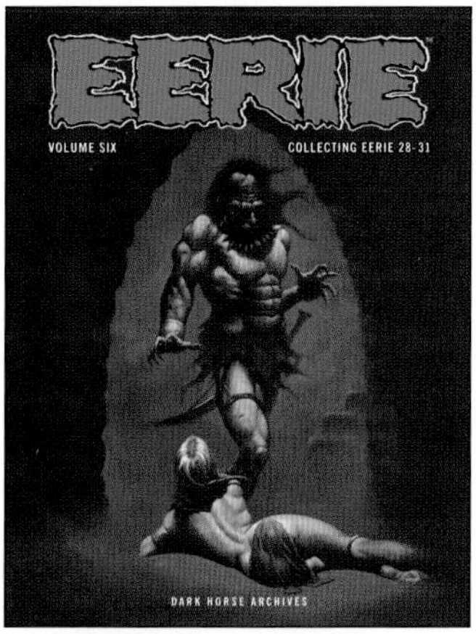
EERIE
VOLUME SIX
COLLECTING EERIE 28-31
DARK HORSE ARCHIVES

Volume 6 ISBN 978-1-59582-569-8

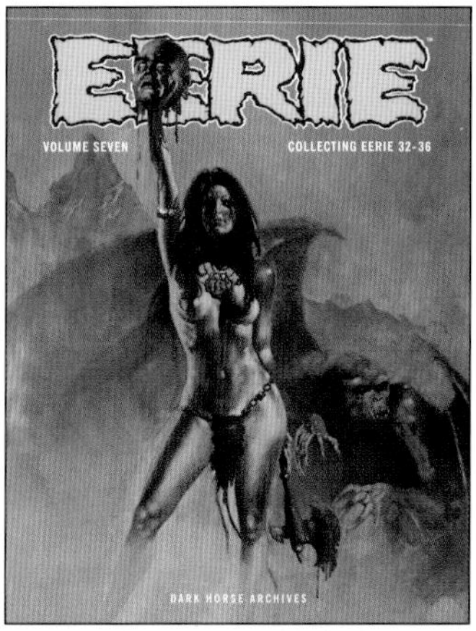
EERIE
VOLUME SEVEN
COLLECTING EERIE 32-36
DARK HORSE ARCHIVES

Volume 7 ISBN 978-1-59582-703-6

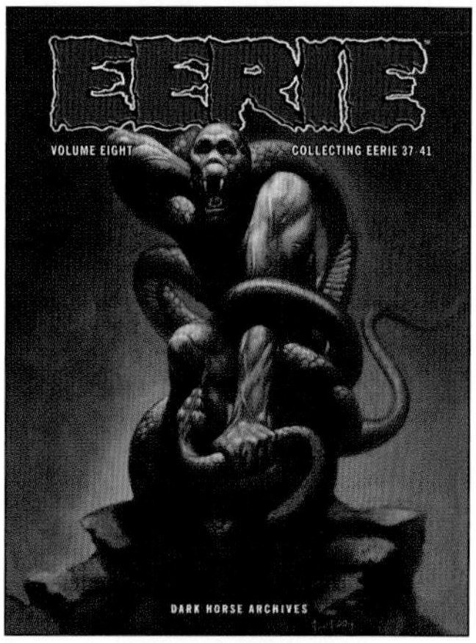
EERIE
VOLUME EIGHT
COLLECTING EERIE 37-41
DARK HORSE ARCHIVES

Volume 8 ISBN 978-1-59582-760-9

GET THEM NOW!

CREEPY ARCHIVES AND EERIE ARCHIVES

$49.99 EACH

Dark Horse Comics

Mike Richardson
President and Publisher

Neil Hankerson
Executive Vice President

Tom Weddle
Chief Financial Officer

Randy Stradley
Vice President of Publishing

Michael Martens
Vice President of Book Trade Sales

Anita Nelson
Vice President of Business Affairs

Micha Hershman
Vice President of Marketing

David Scroggy
Vice President of Product Development

Dale LaFountain
Vice President of Information Technology

Darlene Vogel
Senior Director of Print, Design, and Production

Ken Lizzi
General Counsel

Davey Estrada
Editorial Director

Scott Allie
Senior Managing Editor

Chris Warner
Senior Books Editor

Diana Schutz
Executive Editor

Cary Grazzini
Director of Print and Development

Lia Ribacchi
Art Director

Cara Niece
Director of Scheduling

New Comic Company

Dan Braun **Josh Braun** **Rick Brookwell** **Craig Haffner**